UNION of WORDS

UNION *of* WORDS

A History of Presidential Eloquence

WAYNE FIELDS

THE FREE PRESS

NEW YORK   LONDON   TORONTO   SYDNEY   TOKYO   SINGAPORE

THE FREE PRESS
A Division of Simon & Schuster Inc.
1230 Avenue of the Americas
New York, NY 10020

THE FREE PRESS and colophon are trademarks
of Simon & Schuster, Inc.

Designed by Carla Bolte

Manufactured in the United States of America

10 9 8 7 6 5 4 3 2 1

Library of Congress Cataloging-in-Publication Data

Fields, Wayne.
    Union of words : a history of presidential eloquence / Wayne
Fields.
        p.   cm.
    Includes bibliographical references and index.
    ISBN 0-684-82285-7
    1. Presidents—United States—History.   2. Presidents—United
States—Messages—History.   3. Political oratory—United States—
History.   4. Rhetoric—Political aspects—United States—History.
I. Title.
JK518.F54   1996   95-40877
973'.092'2—dc20   CIP

ISBN 0-684-82285-7

For

ROBERT E. STREETER

JARVIS THURSTON

ROBERT H. SALISBURY

You and I ought not to die, before We have explained ourselves to each other.

—John Adams to Thomas Jefferson, July 15, 1813

I have thus stated my opinion on a point on which we differ, not with a view to controversy, for we are both too old to change opinions which are the result of a long life of inquiry and reflection; but on the suggestion of a former letter of yours, that we ought not to die before we have explained ourselves to each other. We acted in perfect harmony thro' a long and perilous contest for our liberty and independence. A constitution has been acquired which, tho neither of us think perfect, yet both consider as competent to render our fellow-citizens the happiest and the securest on whom the sun has ever shone. If we do not think exactly alike as to its imperfections, it matters little to our country which, after devoting to it long lives of disinterested labor, we have delivered over to our successors in life, who will be able to take care of it, and of themselves.

—Thomas Jefferson to John Adams, October 28, 1813

CONTENTS

Chapter One

The One and the Many

An Introduction

> For, I say, the true nationality of the States, the genuine union,
> when we come to a mortal crisis, is . . . after all, neither the
> written law, nor (as is generally supposed) either self-interest, or
> common pecuniary or material objects—but the fervid and
> tremendous IDEA, melting everything else with resistless heat,
> and solving all lesser and definite distinctions in vast, indefinite,
> spiritual, emotional power.
>
> —Walt Whitman, *Democratic Vistas* (1871)

In 1836, after years of discussion about the best way to memorialize America's first president, a winner was declared in the competition for a Washington National Monument. The architect Robert Mills took the prize with plans for a great stone obelisk surrounded by a 100-foot-high colonnaded base bearing the seals of the states in an elaborate sculptured frieze. Despite the contest committee's enthusiasm, some objected to the proposal, most significantly the celebrated sculptor Horatio Greenough, whose own 20-ton marble statue of Washington as Jupiter delivering the law, at the time still on display in the Capitol, had been widely ridiculed as inappropriate.[1]

What most offended Greenough in Mills's original design was the architect's "intermarriage" of an Egyptian obelisk with the Doric columns at the base. "I do not think," Greenough argued, "it is in the power of art to effect such an amalgamation without corrupting and destroying the special beauties and characters of the two elements." The Greek structure from which the Egyptian monument was to rise consisted, the sculptor observed, "of organized parts assembled for a common object," but the obelisk, "simple even to monotony, may be defined as a gigantic expression of unity." It was the blatant conjunction of singularity with multiplicity that offended Greenough's aesthetic sensibility, and in retrospect Mills's original design does strike a discordant note, especially when compared with the powerful simplicity of the finished monument.

Eventually the base was rejected in favor of the simple shaft, and on July 4, 1848, the cornerstone was finally laid, witnessed by a distinguished gathering that included a young congressman named Lincoln and a chained American eagle.[2] Lincoln, fresh from the West, had attended few such auspicious ceremonies, but the eagle was more experienced; among other notable events, a quarter-century earlier it had witnessed the celebrated return to American shores of Lafayette, the French hero of the American Revolution.

Construction halted in the mid-1850s, its progress impeded by growing national division and unrest, and the monolith, only one-third constructed, remained topless until work was resumed in 1880. What started with President Polk's blessing was begun again under Hayes and completed during Chester Alan Arthur's presidency. The simple silhouette of the finished monument looks more like Greenough's corrected version than Mills's plan, but the interior stones, those visible only to stair-climbers, still bear the carvings the Doric columns were designed to carry. Gifts from different groups and governments, including the American states and territories, the blocks are each labeled with a proud assertion of the donor's identity, followed as often as not by a statement praising the collective whole. Typical is Indiana's grand pronouncement: "Knows No North, No South, Nothing But The Union."

The function of an obelisk, Greenough declared, is to say "but one word, but it speaks it loud. If I understand its voice, it says, 'Here!' It says no more."[3] The fact that the structure dominating the present-day capital skyline is the solitary presidential obelisk uncluttered by a Doric base suggests how correctly Greenough understood George Washington's unifying significance and how deeply runs the American longing for oneness. That the monolith, under its marble skin, testifies to the pride of jealous states demonstrates the central paradox of America's national life—a union of states, a *plura* that is, as the great seal proclaims, also *unum*—a paradox that George Washington tried throughout his presidential career to tip to the side of singularity.[4]

A literal translation of the motto on the national seal, "*E Pluribus Unum,*" suggests that the many are *becoming* one ("pluribus" is in the Latin ablative case, so the meaning would roughly be "*out of* many one"), that multiplicity is actively moving toward singularity. Read this way, the statement describes an ongoing process rather than a completed action, one by which "plura" never wholly becomes "unum."

The national seal represents tension as much as or more than resolution, a tension inherent in the very underpinnings of American government. The Declaration of Independence, first and foremost, asserts each individual's right to liberty, and in its opening line it speaks not of union but of divorce.[5] The preamble to the United States Constitution, by contrast, emphasizes the communal, the promise of being one. The first of those commitments, the matter of personal protection, is served by suspicion, by an eye to the subtle inroads the state can make into the lives of its citizens and the ways in which the whole can take precedence over the particular. The second, union, is served by love. The unfurled banner on the seal that asserts our double commitment is firmly grasped in the beak of America's eagle with *pluribus* to the right wing side and *unum* to the left. Whether by chance or through wishful thinking, the talons on the side of the many hold an olive branch while the clutch of arrows remain wholly in the grip of *unum*, implying that only united are we to take up arms, while in our internal relations we are always to be agents of peace.

The duality at the core of American identity is not, however, a simple opposition that pits one revered document against another. Both the Declaration and the Constitution contain a similar double-mindedness and are to a remarkable degree—intentionally or not—collaborative in developing the theme of being both one and many. Thomas Jefferson added to the list of inalienable rights in his Declaration, after the properly enlightened and predictable "life" and "liberty," a peculiar third term, "the pursuit of happiness." This broad category was most likely to be understood—then as now—as "property," the word that in other political documents of the period regularly follows "life" and "liberty." But the very fact that Jefferson and his independence-minded colleagues chose the abstract over the concrete, the ideal over the material, suggests a more ambitious aspiration than mere possessions. Having affirmed the right of *self*-possession and then claiming the liberty that would allow individuals to manage their lives for themselves, the founders acknowledged a longing they could identify only as a still unrealized contentment. What exactly they thought most worth pursuing with their new liberty, they could not or would not directly say. But what the Declaration leaves vague and uncertain the Constitution renders more precisely when it introduces in its preamble an extraordinary new ambition for government: the political conception of "a more perfect union."[6] This is more than a pleasant turn of phrase and proved to be—despite the objections of confederationalists and nullifiers—the central preoccupation of presidents from Washington through Lincoln, the former insisting that the greater patriotism was due the nation rather than the individual states, and the latter arguing that our mutual relationship is even more fundamental than that of marriage, since it does not allow the possibility of physical separation or divorce.

Above all else, our documents suggest we long to be whole, but on the condition that, in that wholeness, we do not lose our individual selves. Without denying the Declaration's commitment to individual rights, the executive office found its unique work in service to that whole, the larger community of the Constitution's "more perfect union," not as a means to an end but as itself an end. Consequently, given the balancing presence of a Congress chosen by districts and states, American politics revolves around our double devotion to being independent *and* being together, and the greatest domestic crises that this government has faced have grown from the inevitable tension generated by those two contrary aspirations.

THE WITCHES' CAULDRON AND THE POLAR STAR

Henry Adams—great-grandson of John and grandson of John Quincy—spent a lifetime as an uneasy student of America, a subject he illuminated in his nine-volume history of the Jefferson and Madison administrations (1889–91), his novels *Democracy* (1880) and *Esther* (1884), and his autobiography, *The Education of Henry Adams* (1907). Much of his astute commentary on our life and character grew from the profound way in which—despite his insistence to the contrary—he exemplified his countrymen. Graduating from college at the outbreak of the Civil War, Adams came to maturity at a time when the lingering question of whether Americans were to be one or many was being pressed toward an ultimate resolution. Born into a United States that identified itself in the plural ("the United States *are* . . ."), he lived into an age when the singular carried the day.

It is telling that Adams, a descendant of presidents, chose as his first subject of sustained study not the chief executive but the legislature. In an essay describing the 1869 congressional session (one dominated not only by a single party but by one wing of that party), he directed his countrymen's attention to the bewildering "crash and war of jealous and hostile interests" that rages behind the doors of Congress, the arena in which multiplicity gets its constitutional due:

> Within the walls of two rooms are forced together in close contact the jealousies of thirty-five million people,—between individuals, between cliques, between industries, between parties, between branches of the Government, between sections of the country, between the nation and its neighbors. As years pass on, the noise and the confusion, the vehemence of this scramble for power or for plunder, the shouting of reckless adventurers, of wearied partisans, and of red-hot zealots in new issues,—the boiling and bubbling of this witches' cauldron, into which we have thrown eye of newt and toe of frog and all the venomous ingredients of corruption, and from which is expected to issue the future and more perfect republic,—in short, the conflict and riot of interests, grow more and more overwhelming.[7]

Adams's fascination with American politics, like that of all our most instructive political commentators, was inevitably rooted in the amusement provided by wildly divergent interests contending for influence. He found that tumult, the reckless and vulgar machinations of self-interest, both exciting and frightening. The fear of democracy, still widespread in eighteenth-century Europe but as old as Plato's writings, was precisely the fear of such disorder and the dissolution it seemed to threaten, and many in pre-Civil War America doubted the possibility of containing so much diversity in a single republic. For enthusiastic democrats, however—at least when things were going their way—Adams's "witches' cal-dron" testified to the vigor of a pluralistic society, evidence of a healthy political community in which all interests could be robustly expressed. Yet for them, as for Adams, health depended upon some larger continuity that could contain the sprawl of the many, a transcending *unum* to provide a coherence for the *plura*.

This is where the presidency enters our national story. If Congress embodies the many which Americans so zealously champion on the one hand, then the president embodies the *one* that the many must also, corporately, affirm—either as reality or as aspiration. The sides, of course, are hopelessly uneven, so the one must find its balancing weight in something other than numbers.

The Constitutional debates of 1787 included prolonged discussion over whether the executive office itself should be single or plural, whether there should be one or several executive officers. George Mason of Virginia urged a sort of trinitarian presidency, one influenced by geography rather than theology. He suggested:

> If the Executive is vested in three persons, one chosen from the Northern, one from the Middle, and one from the Southern States, will it not contribute to quiet the minds of the people, and convince them that there will be proper attention paid to their respective concerns? Will not three men so chosen bring with them, into office, a more perfect and extensive knowledge of the real interests of this great Union?[8]

Mason's strategy was to make the executive branch into yet another representation of American differences, but the Pennsylvanian James Wilson argued that the idea of "three heads" would lead only to animosity and strife and would "poison" the entire system. The debate, fueled by a suspicion of monarchs and powerful governments, hinged upon whether the presidency stands for the one or, itself multiplied, the many. The fact that the convention, chaired by George Washington, eventually affirmed the former suggests—despite the delegates' fear of centralized authority and their awareness of how profoundly at odds were the interests of their constituencies—the powerful hold that the idea of a shared community and a common purpose had from the start on those deciding the balance between the "united" and the "states."[9]

For Henry Adams, as for nearly all of his countrymen, the model of the unifying presidency was Washington, the political "polar star" who "stands alone" in American history, the one presence—incredibly, given all their personal differences—who did not disappoint even the Adamses, a family much given to disappointment.[10] Washington's appeal was neither intellectual (he hardly ranked as high in this regard as Jefferson or the Adamses themselves) nor that of personal charm; it lay rather in his own apparent singularity, what others saw as an internal consistency and reliability. He defined the presidency for his countrymen because he seemed himself, somehow, to be one thing, and the reverence with which he was regarded provided part of the weight union required if it was to hold its own against the hosts of special interest.

Elected not by popular vote but through an even clumsier version of the Electoral College, Washington was the unanimous choice of electors and the public. As commander of the motley troops, mostly drawn from local militias, that became America's revolutionary army, he had defied conventional wisdom and prevailed over one of the world's great military powers. At war's end he was tangible evidence of the states' common identity, the symbol of their capacity for—if not their commitment to— union. When he came to the presidency he brought that earlier trust with him. Upon retirement, he left it as a fundamental responsibility of the executive office.

The lesson Washington applied from his military experience to civilian leadership concerned the fraternal bonds that he believed to be as essential to his nation's future success as to his army's past accomplishment. He strongly expressed that opinion in his 1783 farewell to his officers, calling upon them to help build this common feeling, and he made the presidency the chief instrument of union, responsible to the nation as a whole rather than to the individual states. At a moment when, the revolution concluded, many of his countrymen agreed with Thomas Jefferson that the need for centralized government had ended and that it was now time to "separate and return to our respective states," Washington's commitment to a larger patriotism was leading him in the opposite direction. From an army at war he had learned the importance not only of authority but of affection, and in peace he conceived of the presidential work as encouraging love no less than exercising power.[11]

IF HE RIGHTLY INTERPRET

"There is," Woodrow Wilson declared more than a century later, "but one national voice in the country and that is the voice of the President."[12] Wilson, who as a professor of American history had long studied the office before occupying it, based much of his understanding on the examples of Washington and Lincoln—the first embodying the Union through his unique service, and the second, whose own election became the occasion for disunion, by preserving it, even when its inherent divisions had destroyed any semblance of wholeness. The wellspring of their leadership, Wilson maintained, was the ability to give form and meaning to American community. They managed that largely through words, and on those occasions requiring more direct intervention (putting down the Whiskey Rebellion in 1794 or blockading Southern ports in 1861), public support had to be won through rhetorical rationalization that presented those necessarily divisive actions as essential to the ultimate well-being of Union. Wilson understood the presidency's double obligation to create and represent the whole, to speak a public mind that, in a sense, it has invented from the multitude of interests and views that flourish in so pluralist a society. "If he rightly interpret the national thought and boldly insist upon it," Wilson asserted, "he is irresistible; and the country never feels the zest of action so much as when its President is of such insight and calibre. Its instinct is for unified action, and it craves a single leader."[13] Supporting this claim are not only the formal utterances of Washington and Lincoln that Wilson had most in mind but also, in the twentieth century, the national speaking tours with which a crusading Theodore Roosevelt energized his countrymen and the radio "chats" of Franklin Roosevelt that buoyed the country during depression and war. But Wilson was recognizing more than a pragmatic instrument by which a leader can inspire his countrymen to action; he was observing as well a hunger in the audience to be led in this way. So convinced are Americans—despite an often asserted suspicion of all things rhetorical—of the importance of eloquence to the presidency that a single speech delivered at the 1984 Democratic party's nominating convention kept New York governor Mario Cuomo's peculiar noncandidacy alive for two subsequent campaigns.

Two fictions are crucial to American public life. The first is that of a unified audience, a constituency more one than many, and the second is the presidential persona. The latter, more than just the character of a single person, is a construct, built around a particular individual, of an entire administration, and the "national voice" is more accurately a synthesis or collaboration.[14] Both the rhetorical audience and the speaker are artful creations, the result of painstaking efforts to reconcile divergent interests in the one case and a great many individuals in the other. From the beginning, American presidents have administered policies generated by advisers and Cabinet members and have spoken words composed by a wide variety of hands. Washington's finest rhetorical moments were often scripted by James Madison or Alexander Hamilton; President Monroe's most famous address was largely crafted by his Secretary of State, John Quincy Adams; and Andrew Jackson's first inaugural included important contributions from his Vice President, John C. Calhoun.[15] Wilson spoke of this collaborative aspect of the office in a 1914 speech to the National Press Club: "I am diligently trying to collect all the brains that are borrowable in order that I may not make more blunders than it is inevitable that a man should make who has great limitations of knowledge and capacity." Later in the same address he commented, "I can hardly refrain every now and again from tipping the public the wink, as much as to say, 'It is only "me" inside this thing. I know perfectly well that I will have to get out presently. I know that then I will look just my own proper size, and that for the time being the proportions are somewhat refracted and misrepresented to the eye by the large thing I am inside of, from which I am tipping you this wink.' "[16]

BY REASON AND PERSUASION

The eloquence Americans hope for in their executive is ill defined and reflects a long-standing uncertainty about what kind of public discourse can be trusted. To define rhetoric simply as the art of speaking well, the usual explanation, is to beg the important questions of measurement and purpose. Socrates in his attacks on the Sophists (the rhetoric teachers of his day) condemned the art as selfish, concerned only with influencing opinion regardless of the truth of a matter, an art that used emotions and prejudice to push reason aside.[17] Aristotle, while conceding the frequent abuses of speech in courts and political assemblies, tried to describe a rhetoric whose purpose was to persuade on rational grounds, a discourse that contributed to public understanding. From that perspective the means as well as the end matter, because in the long run the way in which an audience is persuaded greatly influences the depth of its convictions. For that reason Aristotle's orator builds compelling arguments, and his primary skill is understanding the nature of that process.

Aristotle's rhetoric builds on three elements: "audience," "speaker," and the "speech." With each comes a related form of proof, a particular influence on persuasion. While the goal of the "speech" is above all to present a logical argument, each audience also comes with its own particular psychological state and its own emotional connections to the issues being discussed. It cannot be persuaded unless those "feelings" are appropriately addressed. So, as well, does the character of the speaker influence persuasion, especially through the persona that emerges indirectly in the "speech." Thus, besides the logical center of the case, the orator must also recognize that audiences are influenced by the emotional baggage they bring to an issue and their attitudes toward the speaker. Those three components of every rhetorical occasion greatly overlap—the way a speaker argues, for instance, is a crucial part of self-characterization, and logical arguments justify particular emotional responses—but Aristotle's distinctions suggest key questions to be asked in any consideration of speeches: Who is speaking? To whom is the speech addressed? and What, all things considered, is being said?

Without denying the inevitable power of emotion and charisma, the forces that control and corrupt public discourse in the Platonic dialogues, Aristotle defined a rhetoric in which they served a logical argument. But such an approach to deliberative decision-making requires more than just a trained speaker; it demands a rhetorical culture in which the audience is also rhetorically sophisticated and understands and judges the specific appeals offered by advocates conducting policy debate. By placing logic, rational proof, at the center instead of accentuating the personal and emotional appeals favored by the Sophists of Plato's dialogues, Aristotle emphasized audience and community rather than a single articulate and willful individual. The discourse he describes demands a rational audience as well as a reasoning speaker, a public that can think as well as feel.

It was precisely such a rhetorical culture that America's founders struggled to create. Thomas Jefferson, borrowing heavily from the writings of John Locke (a former teacher of rhetoric), made it an objective of his own paradigm for republican higher education, the University of Virginia; he advocated "a republican nation, whose citizens" would be "led by reason and persuasion, and not by force," one in which "the art of reasoning becomes of first importance."[18] Similarly Benjamin Franklin, in his *Autobiography*, praises rhetorical culture almost as effusively as he celebrates himself as an exemplary rhetorical citizen, allying it with scientific advancement as well as political enlightenment, the twin forces of human progress. In this context it is telling that the gesture of reconciliation from the Federalist John Adams to Jefferson, the Democratic-Republican who, in 1800, had prevented his reelection, after years of estrangement, was the newly published lectures Adams's son John Quincy had delivered as Harvard's first Boylston Professor of Rhetoric.

Jefferson and the Adamses, in their attention to rhetorical culture, were primarily interested in the deliberations of legislative bodies, not in the presidency and its unique oratorical challenge. Inherent in that office is a particular president's personality and history, the office itself with all that has previously defined it, and the unique historical moment. The first obviously corresponds to Aristotle's speaker, and the third, with its emphasis on the particularities of an occasion, to audience. The second is the argument that in every age and with every president defines the work of the executive office. That argument is union, and where rhetorical eloquence in all circumstances can be measured by the extent to which the disparate entities of speaker, argument, and audience are brought into a mutually affirming harmony, presidential eloquence must similarly coalesce the America of the moment, an executive's own person, and the presidential office. Sometimes it may come with all the poetic power of the Gettysburg Address, and in another context it may be achieved through the plain speaking of a Harry Truman. But in every instance success depends on the capacity of presidents to draw together what had previously seemed disparate elements, effectively conjoining themselves, their office, and the issue. In that endeavor they especially need a way to match their own idiosyncrasy with the time in which they serve, to become themselves a part of their eloquence. Franklin Roosevelt's spirit, for example, unflagging in the face of disease and disability, could exemplify a nation unbroken by depression and war. Reagan's self-deprecating humor at the time of grave personal injury—inflicted by a would-be assassin—greatly served a people who had been deeply wounded by earlier assassinations and by the decade of conflict that attended those deaths.

Every presidential campaign, either for the nomination or for the office itself, amounts to a sort of choreographed courtship in which the political matchmakers (in the days of smoke-filled rooms bosses like Mark Hannah of Ohio; at present the spin doctors and image-makers like James Carville and Mary Matalin) do their work, arguing their claims for a natural conjunction of identities between the wooer and the wooed. In presenting a would-be president as the product of a log cabin or as a drinker of hard cider, a rail-splitter or a war hero, a political outsider or an experienced public servant, the campaign managers characterize both their candidates and the country that they hope will embrace them. In each instance the desired effect is some kind of national self-recognition, if not of who we are in fact, then of who we'd like to be. Americans saw in FDR's confidence less a reflection of their own psychological condition than one they longed for. They discerned in Reagan's upbeat homilies on the national spirit a faith they envied more than shared.

Despite Chester Arthur's declaration, "I may be President of the United States, but my private life is nobody's damned business,"[19] the lives of those would-be presidents do matter both to a curious public and to an administration trying to match the country's character with that of its leader.

A great part of our fascination with presidential history is the scope of its dramatic possibilities, the amazing range of interpretations the role can tolerate, and the considerable body of contradictions it indulges. Filled at one time or another by failed haberdashers and victorious generals, college professors and Hollywood actors, Southern tailors and Northern engineers, the office is as amenable to comedy as to tragedy, to love stories and betrayals, to sophisticated drawing room dialogue and broad farce. The presidency over time has become larger and more complex than any one of its players, having acquired a portion of its identity from each who has won the part. No one person ever fully fills the role; the office includes all its occupants in its encompassing nature. So too is its eloquence cumulative, enriched by all the echoes and divergences that can be observed in the larger body of presidential utterance, giving the oratorical efforts of its least distinguished occupants an unexpected poignance.

ROMAN SENATORS AND RING-TAILED ROARERS

Even as it embodies the fundamental characteristics of rhetoric, presidential speechmaking is necessarily different from that heard elsewhere in America. Except for Lincoln's addresses, the most admired oratory of the nation's first hundred years came not from the executive branch but from churches, lecture halls, and most especially from Congress, where great orators honed their skills in verbal combat. Speakers at national anniversaries and celebrations were more typically drawn from those environs than from the White House. Published sermons by William Ellery Channing and Henry Ward Beecher, for example, sold well, as did those "preached" in more secular surroundings by Ralph Waldo Emerson. Abolitionists like William Lloyd Garrison and Frederick Douglass, too, were celebrated for their eloquence as well as their convictions. But between the time of its creation until the Civil War, the Senate produced the foremost orators of the age. That was appropriate, given the general assumption that the best of republican oratory had been spoken in ancient Rome, and the most Roman of America's political institutions was the Senate. John C. Calhoun, one of the great triumvirate of Senators who defined the conflicts and forged the compromises that dominated national politics from the 1820s to the 1850s, was eulogized by his principle antagonist among that threesome with the epitaph, "We saw before us a senator of Rome, when Rome survived."[20]

Those words better described the speaker, Daniel Webster, than the subject. It was Webster, the orator most frequently called the "American Cicero," who delivered in 1830 the reply to nullifiers that his countrymen cited for more than thirty years as the most sublime of the Union's verbal defenses. In addition to his contributions to formative congressional battles, he helped shape America's popular history through addresses at Bunker Hill and Plymouth Rock, and he provided the double eulogy following the amazing coincidental deaths of Adams and Jefferson on the nation's fiftieth birthday. Like Henry Clay, the third member of the trio, Webster coveted the presidency, and like Clay, whom Lincoln thought the most eloquent of the three, he was repeatedly and pointedly denied that office. The missed oratorical opportunities did not go unnoted by his own eulogists. One, apparently grieving the lost speeches as much as the deceased statesman, declared, "What a feast, with what a glow of patriot pride would every American have perused his inaugural address. What annual messages would have illustrated the policy, and enriched the literature of this country."

Webster's mourners recognized the unique importance of the presidency as an oratorical office, even if they did not contemplate why the nation's foremost orators so rarely occupied it. But for all their eloquence, Webster, Clay, and Calhoun were sectional champions, and as such they were unable to claim an office that transcended the very fragmentation they represented. In those moments when they laid their regional causes aside in an effort to preserve the fragile ties of Union, they became identified as "compromisers," a title that contaminated even the nobler purposes that compromise might serve.

There is as well a difference of style that distinguishes congressional from presidential eloquence. In a system in which the House of Representatives (then the only federal legislative body chosen by popular election) was assumed to be the rowdiest governmental institution, while the aristocratic Senate was expected to be more refined and more learned (its members chosen by state legislatures until passage of the Seventeenth Amendment), an appropriate executive discourse would necessarily differ from that practiced in either legislative body. The "half horse, half alligator" speeches attributed to Representative Davy Crockett (and other "ring-tailed roarers" who delivered frontier opinions in the popular press) in almanacs and other popular literature, while they hardly reflected the typical tone and style of the House, suggested the clamor of both an empowered people and their regionalized and sometimes vulgar tongues.[21] By contrast, senatorial grandiloquence, with its susceptibility to affectation and pomposity, became a common subject of parody. It was the excesses of this oratory that the nineteenth-century comedian Artemus Ward was describing when he declared:

The prevailin weakness in most public men is to SLOP OVER! . . . They get filled up and slop. They Rush Things. They travel too much on the high presher principle. They get on to the fust popular hobbyhoss whitch trots along, not carin a sent whether the beest is even goin, clear sited and sound or spavined, blind, and bawky. Of course they git throwed eventooaly, if not sooner![22]

Frequently the parodies of the nation's most pretentious public speaking took the form of mock Fourth of July orations of the sort another literary comedian, John Phoenix (the stage name used by George H. Derby), offered his audience. One such speech concluded:

For on this day the great American eagle flaps her wings, and soars aloft, until it makes your eyes sore to look at her, and looking down on her myriads of free and enlightened children, with flaming eye, she screams, "*E Pluribus Unum*," which may be freely interpreted, "Aint I some?" and myriads of freemen answer back with joyous shout: "You *are* punkins!"[23]

Though far removed from the great Senate oratory of Daniel Webster, Phoenix's lampoon comes uncomfortably close to the bombast of the second participant in the famous Webster–Hayne debates:

Fellow Citizens!

   Our country at this moment exhibits one of the most interesting spectacles the world has ever seen. A spectacle, so august, so splendid, so sublime, that it must be grateful to the sight of God and Man. Millions of freemen now crowd the temples of the Most High, and offer the incense of gratitude on his holy altars. Ten thousand voices now chant "A nation's Choral hymn for tyranny O'erthrown."[24]

Of necessity the executive voice must strike a delicate balance between the elevated senatorial style and the trivializing populism of Crockett. It must have a distinct personality, and yet if it is to represent all the people, its idiosyncrasy must be contained. Its speaker must manage to be both apart and included, must be at once particular *and* universal, challenges that do not necessarily confront congressmen or senators.

   Based in their Enlightenment beliefs, the nation's founders assumed that reason had a "language" that allowed men of good will and intellectual integrity to pursue matters of controversy. That language, described by such philosophers as John Locke, was derived from science and dedicated above all else to precision and clarity. It avoided the pretensions of class and so provided a democratic middle ground between a senatorial high style and the low-style caricatures of popular assemblies. It was this model that Washington and Jefferson and Madison favored in their own rhetoric.

While not all American presidents have sounded like John Locke or even like one another, their audience from the start was the "people" in a way that has not usually been the case for legislators. Presidents speak at once *for* the people and *to* the people, and that peculiar conjunction is what sets their rhetorical challenge apart from that of other political leaders; they struggle to unify speaker and audience. Presidential eloquence attempts to synthesize apparently disparate elements into a single whole, and wholeness is always, directly or indirectly, the message presidents have to deliver.

DESIRE AND SEDUCTION

The primary complication in fulfilling the rhetorical office comes from a deep suspicion that, no matter how dependent this democracy is upon political discourse, Americans bring to rhetoric, the apprehension that all such talk is inevitably deceitful. That fear has changed little since Plato voiced it, and no matter how thorough Aristotle's redeeming work, the old doubts have never gone away. Nor should they. When Cicero, the Roman senator who served as America's most famed oratorical model, the favorite alike of Calvin Coolidge and Daniel Webster, extolled the speaker's art, he began by imagining a time before social organization, when humans lived, individually, in fear of the superior physical prowess of other individuals. Unable on their own to secure their property and lives against the dangers of brute force, they formed communities to protect themselves against the whims of stronger neighbors. The longing for security, the possibility of community, Cicero insisted, had to be articulated by an orator before it could be expressed in laws and social contracts. "To me, at least," he wrote, "it does not seem possible that a mute and voiceless wisdom could have turned men suddenly from their habits and introduced them to different patterns of life."[25] For Cicero the world—always in danger of being controlled by brute strength—can be harnessed and composed only by words. Because rhetoric offers this salvation, it is to be honored among us.

There is in this simple myth-making a suggestion as to why we might both revere *and* condemn orators. On one hand, they offer collective hope in the face of individual despair, but in doing so they remind us of our own inadequacy and our need for one another. We condemn the orator because in articulating our vulnerability he gains an advantage that can be exploited at our expense. Thus we fear that we have succeeded in taking power from the brute only to hand it to the seducer, and this is somehow even more humiliating. When we tremble before physical power, we are threatened by that which does not know us, is uninterested in who we are or what we desire, but the seducer knows us as well as if not better than we know ourselves, and he makes it his business to learn our secret aspirations and most guarded terrors. Cicero's orator is a savior, one who creates a community and delivers us from our divided weakness; but the orator of our nightmares entraps us, calls us together to serve his ends, then holds us in thrall spiritually as well as physically. The insult of this dark vision is that the seducer professes to love us, then abuses our trust and degrades us. "For the one point in which we have our greatest advantage over the brute creation," Cicero wrote elsewhere, "is that we hold converse with one another, and can reproduce our thought in words." But some, like Cicero, do this better than the rest of us, and that, too, can be a fearful advantage.

The deepest suspicions of rhetoric grow from our fear of human passions, from the apprehension that reason can be overwhelmed by emotions, that our "higher" nature can be defeated by a "lower" one. Though this doubt is most often expressed in regard to others, to some "mob" of which we are not a part, it is a powerful and persistent view precisely because it is reinforced by self-knowledge, by the awareness of the "mob" each of us contains. There is terrifying historical evidence to support our fears, especially in the century of Hitler's Germany and—on a smaller scale but closer to home—of demagogues like Huey Long and Joseph McCarthy, who well understood how fear and prejudice could unseat reason in a democracy. Implicit in our doubts about rhetoric are doubts about our capacity to rule ourselves and about the viability of democratic institutions, not because of corrupt leaders but because of a flawed citizenry.

Thus the irony: The art most essential to union-building and presidential obligation is, as well, that which makes us vulnerable to the charlatan and the quack. In the mouths of false teachers it spreads lies and misinformation, from false prophets it corrupts the spirit and endangers the soul, and spoken by perverse politicians it threatens liberty and even life. That is especially true for the message Washington insisted presidents were charged above all to deliver, that of affection. Desiring love, we are fearful of seduction by those who feign intimacy for their own advantage. Since the vocabularies of love and seduction are identical, our suspicions are often justified. That is why we bring, simultaneously, such high expectation and such persistent wariness to the presidential message of the mutual affection upon which our union depends. Yet, if suspicion alone serves as our guide, our lives and our politics will be driven by despair, an intolerable condition in a democracy whose central premise must be hope.

The founders shared our suspicions and built checks into every aspect of the governing process. But the near-miraculous success of their constitutional convention greatly encouraged them. Benjamin Franklin, at eighty-two the nation's elder statesman, told his fellow convention delegates as they prepared to sign the Constitution that "when you assemble a number of men to have the advantage of their joint wisdom, you inevitably assemble with those men, all their prejudices, their passions, their errors of opinion, their local interests, and their selfish views." But having acknowledged all those weaknesses, he continued:

> It therefore astonishes me . . . to find this system approaching so near to
> perfection as it does; and I think it will astonish our enemies, who are
> waiting with confidence to hear our councils are confounded like those of
> the Builders of Babel; and that our States are on the point of separation,
> only to meet hereafter for the purpose of cutting one another's throats.[26]

That America had not yet proven to be Babel—the emblem of language's limitation—and that their convention had not been "confounded" by the alien tongues of interest and prejudice argued for the possibility of a government that could survive through reasoned deliberation.

But the system the delegates were erecting relied on more than legislative debates to protect the country's well-being. They also appointed a referee, creating even before the Union's existence an executive to represent the Union, to be its advocate as he presided over a government driven by lesser interests. A few months before the constitutional convention convened, Washington—anticipating Franklin's benediction—had written of his hope that a "federal government" would "be considered with . . . calm and deliberate attention," that "prejudices, unreasonable jealousies, and local interests" would yield to a truly national perspective. So he began defining the presidency even before it had been invented.[27]

The founders saw their work as a great experiment, one whose outcome was uncertain, in part because the instruments upon which it depended—including civil discourse—were uncertain, and it required, they recognized, both confidence and suspicion, affection and wariness. They were most absorbed in the mechanics of a legislative process, the negotiation among representatives of different and particular interests, and of national laws and policies, but the ambitiousness of their political creation, their very emphasis on legislating bodies, gave heightened significance to the presidential office and made it central to national survival. They recognized their own, and ultimately the nation's, profound commitment to contradictory ideals. We are as committed to multiplicity as we are to unity, as jealous of separateness as we are devoted to reconciliation. The president, constitutionally and in the national psyche, represents the longing to be whole, but in serving that charge, the president must acknowledge the resistence ingrained in Americans, recognize it not as a vice but as an equally important virtue.

Union, like the eloquence through which it is represented and to some extent achieved, is also a thing we are sometimes inclined to distrust. Fearful that the appeal to a common identity or a common cause might conceal important differences, might repress or exploit our interests and principles, we are tempted to withdraw into the particulars of our own circumstances and affiliations, regarding those smaller loyalties as a protection against the crushing power of larger and impersonal powers. Thus the rhetorical presidency[28] has emerged with the specific challenge of helping Americans maintain a delicate balance between our instinctive move toward the many and our desire to become one. Our chief executives are called not to overwhelm either with the other but to interpret national life in ways that affirm both with the loss of neither. Ironically, they manage this through personalizing the government whose impersonality we fear, by giving a sense of the particular to the general.

A TRUST ABOVE ALL OTHERS

Among the many paradoxes contained in our conception of the presidency is the fact that those who attain it—with the notable exception of Washington—do so by prevailing in divisive and often vitriolic national contests. They enter primaries as the representatives of factions within their party, distinguished by previous experience, region, or ideology and emphasizing their differences from other candidates. Successful in this part of the process, at their national convention they must minimize the very distinctions they had previously worked so hard to establish and must emphasize instead their common ground with their defeated opponents. The process then begins once more, this time in the struggle between Democrats and Republicans. In the heat of a campaign, political ideologies can seem irreconcilable, as the differences dividing parties are pushed to extremes. Once elected, the new president must again argue for what is shared rather than for that which sets apart, playing down differences that a few weeks earlier had been accentuated.

While such near-contradictory behavior might seem to threaten the office it seeks—and sometimes it does, when an especially bitter campaign continues to divide Americans after the Inauguration—it also provides a useful test of a candidate's capacity to manage the tension central to our politics, a tension within each candidate as well as within the system as a whole. While parties may scrutinize the nominating process for evidence of a contender's ability to win, the country also gets to observe that person's capacity to reunite what he or she has helped divide.[29] In representing those values, the president is charged with modeling them as well as speaking on their behalf. That office more than any other is charged with exemplifying a *civil* discourse, and its eloquence is to a considerable degree based on a capacity, even under duress, to retain a sense of civility. The bluster that dominates our political talk, whether the yellow-press journalism of nineteenth-century partisan newspapers or the present-day political shout shows that play so well on radio and television, may provide much of a democracy's amusement, but such theatrics substitute macho strutting for reason, and volume for logic. That form of rhetoric seeks not to persuade but only to excite already entrenched opinions. It plays to believers while deliberately antagonizing those of differing views. But the challenge of presidential eloquence is to move in precisely the opposite direction, to keep a constituency in community even when it cannot be kept in agreement, and by its own example to witness to our capacity, when consensus is impossible, to disagree rationally and respectfully. Its model must be familial rather than adversarial.[30]

The unique demands on the rhetoric of the presidency result not only from the practical pursuits of the office but from its special symbolic significance in our culture. The cycle of division and reconciliation in which the president performs has implications that are both cultural and psychological, at once public and personal. The nation's need to affirm uniqueness within a larger, shared identity parallels a struggle in which each individual is engaged, and certainly a part of the significance we assign to our political life grows from how profoundly it seems to imitate our own psychic existence.[31] Ralph Waldo Emerson and Walt Whitman, celebrants of both selfhood and transcendence, made little distinction between the individual and the Union and insisted that both were at once many and one. And so, in a different context, did such politicians as Daniel Webster and Henry Clay. Each denied that "self" and "union" were antithetical; each insisted that one was essential to the realization of the other. The very idea of union acknowledges, as well as subsumes, difference. Without separate states, political union is meaningless, and no useful conception of the self can deny the several competing forces that each of us attempts to contain in our larger sense of who we are. The conflicting experiences, emotions, and attitudes that threaten the synthesis we call the "self" are analogous to the political *plura* as they struggle both to be and not to be *unum*. But for both the psyche and the nation it is only by reconciling those competing tendencies—only as *unum*—that selfhood is achieved.

Implicit in nineteenth-century American culture was this analog between the union of the self and the union of the nation. What was being acted out in the American experiment was not just an exercise in political theory but an aspiration of human nature played on the grandest scale. The political and psychological challenges, now as then, mirror one another. As a result, the presidency's importance in American life extends far beyond the significance of mere partisan victories and defeats. It speaks to the struggle for personal integration that composes the psychic life of each citizen. We desire above all else to be whole.

But even as the presidency joins the paradigm of union to personal aspirations, so too does it represent, looking in the direction of national ambition, an equally strong desire for America to stand forth as "the city on a hill," to be the world's people. In the middle of the nineteenth century, when Walt Whitman wrote "Passage to India," most of his countrymen assumed that history was both a progressive and a Western movement. America was, then, necessarily in the vanguard, the last link in the great circle, the point at which the westward migration returned to civilization's starting point. From such a perspective the United States was the great integrating bond, not only geographically but politically and culturally as well. The rise of the American Union thus represented both completion and beginning in a drama much larger than a single nation or people. At the same time as this country's great continental journey was reaching its ultimate destination, there was other evidence of a world whose parts were more closely conjoined: Technology was almost daily reducing the time required for traveling either by sea or by land, and the new canal at Suez and the trans-Atlantic telegraph cable provided even more tangible links between the continents.

The aspiration elaborated in Whitman's poem was not just an indulgence of poets. It was also voiced by many politicians, including the powerful senator from Missouri, Thomas Hart Benton, who—as the West's self-appointed spokesman—represented this vision as he championed the construction of a national highway to Oregon that would bring the new world face to face with the old, completing the circle in history's climactic moment, a spiritual as well as a commercial triumph. In that context national union, just as it mirrored a personal, psychological aspiration, also reflected an ambition in which all humanity participated. In this romantic rendering of history the dispersal of the race was, in the fullness of time, to lead to a reunion of the wanderers and a synthesis of the knowledge they had acquired on their various journeys. That so many of America's leaders tolerated profound moral disagreements—including those generated by slavery—suggests the depth of their conviction that Union was the trust they served above all others.

When the national Union was at last contested and achieved, the larger preoccupations of Whitman and Benton were not forgotten. On the contrary, although the language in which they were expressed may sometimes seem naïve, those ambitions have determined much of the job description of twentieth-century presidents. Almost immediately after the

Civil War the word "peace" took on the preeminence previously reserved for "union." It, too, referred to the ongoing search for domestic tranquility, the continuing effort to perfect the relations between countrymen, but by the middle of the twentieth century American presidents routinely cast their ambitions in international terms; they spoke as leaders of the Free World, committed to an interdependent world community, free and harmonious.

THE WORK OF WORDS

July 4, 1826, was a day of enormous significance for both the nation and the presidency. In the midst of Jubilee festivities commemorating the fiftieth anniversary of the Declaration of Independence, Americans learned of the deaths of John Adams and Thomas Jefferson, the last surviving signers of the Declaration, the latter celebrated as its author and the former widely regarded as its greatest defender. The coincidence of their deaths on a date so full of national significance was the cause of great wonder among their countrymen and in the months that followed came to be regarded as a kind of divine seal on the American experiment. It fell to Daniel Webster to eulogize the dead presidents, and he noted how wholly the careers of both were the work of words. Unlike the general they followed to the presidency, neither had fought in the Revolution; they had instead helped create and defend and govern the new nation rhetorically. But, Webster insisted, their "talk" constituted a kind of action, unique and invaluable, and in describing their greatness, he defined the synthesis toward which all eloquence aspires. "True eloquence," he told his audience,

> does not consist in speech. It cannot be brought from far. Labor and learning may toil for it, but they will toil in vain. Words and phrases may be marshaled in every way, but they cannot compass it. It must exist in the man, in the subject, and in the occasion. Affected passion, intense expression, the pomp of declamation, all may aspire to it; they cannot reach it. It comes, if it come at all, like the outbreaking of a fountain from the earth, or the bursting forth of volcanic fires, with spontaneous, original, native force. The graces taught in the schools, the costly ornaments and studied contrivances of speech, shock and disgust men, when their own

lives, and the fate of their wives, their children, and their country, hang
on the decision of the hour. Then words have lost their power, rhetoric is
vain, and all elaborate oratory contemptible. Even genius itself then feels
rebuked and subdued, as in the presence of higher qualities. Then patriotism is eloquent; then self-devotion is eloquent. The clear conception,
outrunning the deductions of logic, the high purpose, the firm resolve,
the dauntless spirit, speaking on the tongue, beaming from the eye, in-
forming every feature, and urging the whole man onward, right onward
to his object,—this is eloquence; or rather it is something greater and
higher than all eloquence, it is action, noble, sublime, godlike action.[32]

What Webster praised in the lives and rhetoric of the second and third
presidents was a realization of the synthesis that the presidency serves, a
synthesis that can be thought of in terms of Aristotle's speaker, speech,
and audience, or as the office, the person, and the moment, or, in a
slightly different turn, the particular and the universal. The Union of
which nineteenth-century statesmen spoke and the peace that post–Civil
War presidents have persistently addressed both tell of our longing for
resolution. If there is a utopian strain in all this, then the chief executive
is also to connect that ideal with reality. Foremost among that office's responsibilities is to bring divergent elements closer together. The Constitution acknowledged that such efforts will always be incomplete and
asked only that we advance the cause of a more rather than wholly perfect union. Practically, presidents can hope only to connect and not to
synthesize. Their work, and the obligation of their eloquence, is to hold
an ever enlarging "us" together even as we lament the difference between
what we want and what we have.

———

The chapters that follow examine the different oratorical occasions that
define a presidential career. Inevitably, in announcing a candidacy,
would-be presidents emphasize Aristotle's "ethical" appeal, arguing their
appropriateness for the office they seek. No matter how strongly they
protest, their subject on these occasions is primarily themselves. To a
considerable extent that emphasis persists in acceptance speeches at nominating conventions, though increasingly the special audiences on these
occasions demand their own due, and the "ethical yields to emotional ap-

peals that provoke noisy demonstrations and avalanches of balloons. But inaugurals introduce new regimes and, appropriately, give secondary significance to the speaker as they lay the foundations for an incoming administration. Just as the emphasis shifts from speaker to audience in the course of a campaign, so in office does the logical argument gain precedence. In State of the Union addresses and special speeches presidents argue for policies that will, to their minds, promote a more perfect union. Through it all they struggle to conjoin their own person, the mood of their national audience, and the political agenda they promote. And at the end, when presidents offer a final assessment of the synthesis, they speak directly—and sometimes unwittingly—of how their ambitions came together with their historical moment, they speak in frustration or celebration of how things turned out.

Chapter Two

Conspicuous Presumption

The Declaration of Candidacy

> I have to tell you with complete candor that being elected President is not the most important thing in my life.
>
> There are many ... things that I would not do to be President.
>
> —Jimmy Carter, 1974 Announcement Speech

When the French sculptor Antoine Houdon carved his version of George Washington for the Virginia State Capitol, he presented the patriarch standing, one arm braced on a walking stick and the other resting on a chest-high bundle of thirteen rods. The bundle, upright and held together by two thick bands, is a *fasces*—from which comes "fascist"—a symbol of strength through unity and the emblem of a Roman magistrate. In war it would have provided the shaft for a battle axe, but in Houdon's sculpture it is crowned only by Washington's cloak and his sheathed sword. The great man is relaxed, his uniform coat unbuttoned, his body at ease, bent slightly so that his weight leans against the column/bundle by his side. From the front, just visible as it peeks out from behind Washington's right boot, is the blade of a plow. On the base the commissioning General Assembly has inscribed its praise to one who united "the endowments of the hero" with "the virtues of the patriot."

This theme, especially the plow that epitomizes it, appears frequently in the United States Capitol. In the east fresco of the House Committee on Appropriations Room is the noble farmer whose plow Houdon—and so many others—borrowed. Cincinnatus, his cultivating efforts interrupted by a party of statesmen and soldiers who have come beseeching him to save their beleaguered Rome, stands beside yoked oxen, his hand on his heart, listening to his petitioners.[1] Offered by Livy as the republican ideal, Cincinnatus embodies the citizen who serves civic virtue instead of personal ambition, who—when the commonweal is threatened—takes up public office or arms at the urging of others, and then, when his service is no longer required, retires humbly to his civilian vocation.[2]

The idea that public office is to be accepted as an obligation of civic virtue rather than pursued as a lucrative career pervades our idealized notions of democratic politics, and of all our offices the presidency is most deeply rooted in this tradition of reluctance. Like the notion of a two-term limit, this is largely a legacy of its first occupant, but it is also a consequence of the peculiar nature of the position.

The fifty-seven-year-old soldier and planter who assumed the presidency in 1789 was the most popular man in the country—a country that agreed about little except its reverence for him. Washington was the person most directly responsible for America's independence, and yet to his countrymen he seemed modest and retiring. In fact, following his success as commander-in-chief of the Continental Army and president of the 1787 Constitutional Convention, he had little to gain from this new and uncertain office, a post more likely to damage than enhance his reputation. The presidency needed him more than he needed it, and for a people with a republican fear of tyrants as well as a conservative apprehension of disorder, this made him perfect for the job. Personal ambition, as common sense and subsequent French experience argued, was a dangerous quality in a republic's chief executive, and yet the new nation needed someone already commanding respect and authority who was willing to lend those advantages to its new government. So perfectly matched to the challenge was Washington that he provided the enduring model for the office.

The process of selecting presidential candidates has undergone considerable change over the course of United States history and is changing

still. Washington was essentially chosen by acclamation without competing factions, but in the contests that followed the very parties Washington feared quickly rose to do the choosing. In 1796 party leaders consult-
ed among themselves and identified their candidates for Washington's
successor. Following that precedent, a system of congressional caucusing
soon emerged to do the nominating, since it was easiest to gather the
leadership already assembled in the capital. But that narrow and controversial method collapsed in 1824, when the congressional Republican
choice (the Federalists had virtually disappeared from the national stage
and did not name a candidate), William H. Crawford, found himself
competing with nominees from his own party put into nomination by
several state legislatures.[3] With four candidates splitting the vote, the
House of Representatives chose John Quincy Adams, even though he
had finished a distant second to Andrew Jackson in both popular and
electoral votes. Four years later the congressional caucus was abandoned,
and the states once again provided the nominees.

In 1832 the major parties introduced the modern nominating convention, assembling delegates from the states in a national meeting.
Under this system potential candidates were kept at a distance from the
nominating process, their cause represented on the convention floor by
home state delegates. Their removal from the political maneuvering not
only made the candidates seem more "presidential" but also presented
them as servants of the states that advanced their cause. The authority
behind the nominee thus was not his own judgment but that of his regional party leadership, and the convention contests became as much
jousts between geographical units as between individuals.

At the beginning of the twentieth century, however, "progressives"
challenged the domination of state leaders and party bosses by creating
primaries to register popular preference and to nationalize preconvention
campaigning. They sought in this fashion to involve the public more directly in the selection of nominees and to break the power of entrenched
party leaders. Their reforming efforts, while not immediately successful,
have had a profound long-term impact, which showed itself most dra-
maticly in the late 1960s. One of the notable consequences of primaries
has been the increasing need for some form of public, personal declaration from those seeking nomination, creating a new rhetorical challenge,
calling for a discomforting alliance between ambition and *civitas*.[4]

SEEMLY SEEKERS

Announcement speeches by definition draw attention to the speaker and seek to prove, in the candidate's own words, his or her fitness for the office. No matter how much the would-be nominees might wish to concentrate on the issues, their audiences inevitably focus on *them*, asking who they are and on what personal grounds they commend themselves for the nation's highest office. Retrospectively considered—after a winner has been decided—announcement speeches mark the beginning of a presidency. They are coming-out affairs in which a presidential persona begins its career. These addresses, except when given by an incumbent, introduce individuals who want to be seen as presidents and who are testing the public's capacity to imagine them in that role.

At work in transforming this aspect of presidential politics have been the technological advances that both bring the office closer to the people and generate early public interest in those who pursue it. When Stephen Douglas, the 1860 Democratic nominee, undertook an unprecedented national canvass in an effort not only to defeat Lincoln but also to denounce secession in the South, the campaign was sufficiently demanding to weaken his health and bring on his death a few months later.[5] The 1896 Democratic nominee, William Jennings Bryan, traveled 18,000 miles by rail, addressing more than 5 million people and retained enough strength to run again in 1900 and 1908.[6] What the transportation revolution made possible with travel, broadcasting did for communications, and by the time he wrote his autobiography in 1929 former President Coolidge, who scorned the indignities of speaking from "the rear of the train," could note with satisfaction that radio had made that practice unnecessary: "It is so often that the President is on the air that almost anyone . . . has ample opportunity to hear his voice."[7]

If the congressional caucus was made necessary by the difficulty of travel in the nation's early years, thus severely limiting the number of people involved, in less than a century technology had made it possible for progressives to imagine a nominating process that could include virtually the entire electorate. While the early reformers did not change the nominating conventions as quickly or profoundly as they had hoped, the transportation and media revolutions were steadily increasing public awareness and involvement. As a result the candidates' viability was tested well before the convention assembled, tested as voters shaped and voiced opinions even when they were not directly asked to do so.

The primaries also encouraged a wider range of candidates. Candidacies that conventional wisdom doomed because of religion, region, or personal obscurity could receive a preconvention tryout. No matter the size or importance of the state in which this audition was held, the media would involve the entire country in the contest. The Georgian Jimmy Carter established his electability this way in 1976, just as John Kennedy in 1960 had proved that a Catholic could win in predominately Protestant states. Strikingly, Kennedy set aside any claim of reluctance or any pretense to be serving some higher cause. "My candidacy," he frankly admitted, "is . . . based on the conviction that I can win both the nomination and election."[8]

The first campaign in which primaries played an important role was that of 1912, when Theodore Roosevelt tried to use this progressive innovation to wrest the nomination from the incumbent, William Howard Taft, Roosevelt's hand-picked successor four years earlier. In order to enter the contest and influence the makeup of the convention, Roosevelt had to declare his intentions without appearing unpresidential. In response to that challenge he pioneered the process by which coy candidates publicly reveal their ambition. At issue in the preceding months was whether and how Roosevelt was going to disentangle himself from his "no third term" pledge of 1904. Having served all but six months of the term to which McKinley had been elected in 1900, Roosevelt had declared shortly after his own election that he considered this a second term and affirmed his commitment to the custom of a two-term limit. His reconsideration, given his often declared contempt for dishonesty and obfuscation, created an embarrassing problem as he struggled to avoid becoming the very kind of politician he supposedly deplored. Through the months before his announcement, the issue of Roosevelt's candidacy, of whether or not he would run, dominated the news. Individual and group efforts to tempt him into the race were highly publicized; editorials regularly commented on the subject, and congressmen and governors took sides.

As the primaries approached, the tone of the Roosevelt queries grew more impatient. In early February seven Republican governors sent a letter, arguing that the former president was the people's choice and insisting that his candidacy was not a matter of "personal interests" but of "plain public duty." Sixteen days later Roosevelt answered in a letter that was immediately published. At issue was what he termed "the genuine rule of the people," and he opened with an insistence that he was responding—as he had previously refused to do—not because his petitioners were heads of states but because they were "men elected by popular vote." Accepting their premise that the "interests of the people as a whole" were at stake, he declared his willingness to accept the nomination if it was tendered and his resolve to "adhere to this decision until the convention has expressed its preference." But his announcement was not the final word in even that short note, and Roosevelt concluded by turning from the "preference" of the convention to the will of the public, offering his candidacy as "the chance" for the people, "through direct primaries, to express their preference as to who shall be the nominee of the Republican Presidential Convention." In throwing his hat in the ring, Roosevelt called for a nationwide contest conducted through primaries and represented his candidacy as an effort to unite the "preference" of the convention with that of the people.[9]

When Senator Warren G. Harding issued his 1920 "announcement," he did so in response not to a nationwide movement clamoring for his nomination—he had, in fact, little to recommend him other than a lackluster career, good looks, and a much-admired congeniality—but to the Republican Commitee of Miami County, Ohio. In a letter allowing his name to be entered in his home state's primary, he expressed regret that there was no other Ohio Republican to take up the challenge. That there were able and willing Republicans elsewhere—among them a popular former Army Chief of Staff, General Leonard Wood—passed unremarked, as did the possibility that the national party might somehow be able to manage without a contender from Ohio.

Having thanked the committee for its endorsement, Harding reminded its members: "A previous communication to our State organization and many letters to political friends have expressed my real reluctance to permit the use of my name in this connection, and it was genuinely sincere and expressed then my personal and political preference." What overcame his earlier resistance, he continued, was the conviction that it was not his prerogative to ignore the wishes of the state and party that had made him a Senator.

I do not forget, however, that my first obligation, politically, is to the Republicans of our State who have so generously honored me, and I cannot ignore the natural and laudable wish to maintain the large part Ohio has taken in the national councils of the party, and to invite the attentions of the Republicans in the nation to the availability of a candidate from our great state.

Had some other Ohio Republican among the many fitted for such distinction been submitted, I would gladly have joined in supporting him. But the fortunes of politics and the activities incident to official position have combined to suggest my name, and the primary election laws of Ohio require my assent to any definite efforts to choose a delegation favorable to me.

Harding's letter allowed the advancement of his candidacy under the pretense that his consent was a concession to the people he served and reflected his commitment to the greater glory of Ohio and its Republican organization. He presented himself as a sort of soldier under the command of his state, duty-bound to follow orders. But lest anyone think Harding's was not a serious candidacy (or that his intent was merely to give Ohio a favorite-son delegation that could at an opportune moment, and for negotiated advantages, push some other candidate over the top), the once-reluctant senator declared, "One thing must be stated. We are all agreed that a thing worth doing at all is worth doing with all one's might." In his case, he insisted, that meant winning the nomination and not just the Ohio delegation. Having revised the familiar maxim—"A thing worth doing at all is worth doing well"—to emphasize effort, Harding once more displayed his own reserve by letting it be known that the "might" required must come wholly from them:

> I cannot agree . . . to any personal activity in promoting a preconvention campaign, not alone because of my distaste for unseemly seeking, but any neglect of important official duties in the ensuing five months in the Senate would rightfully forfeit me the confidence which Ohio Republicans have so cordially expressed. (*New York Times,* 12/17/19)

Harding's solution to the announcement dilemma, like that of many subsequent candidates, was to "yield" to the desire and labor of others while expressing personal gratitude and asserting his dedication to his present office. By declaring himself faithful in the lesser labor of the Senate, of course, he argued his fitness for greater things, all the while avoiding "unseemly seeking" of the sort in which his progressive opponents were engaged as they conducted national campaigns. Harding's message, received by press and public as an announcement of his candidacy, he implied was merely a formality required by Ohio law and a courtesy to his state and party.[10]

Harding's announcement through acceptance rather than declaration contained the politically necessary denial of self-promotion while satisfying primary rules that require candidates to make themselves available before they have been officially "drafted." For half a century, even as formal announcements became more and more unavoidable, the messages remained much like Harding's: a relatively brief, formulaic consent for one's name, in deference to some body of supporters, to appear on a ballot. That a short letter rather than a major political speech was usually sufficient to this end helped contain the immodesty of the gesture. Even by midcentury, when the nature and length of those messages was changing, the old style persisted.

The terms of announcement, of course, depend on a candidate's situation. Incumbent presidents have an obvious advantage, and they routinely either make known their decision to run for reelection by means of a messenger—Hoover in 1932 and Truman in 1948—or deliver the sort of brief address that Ronald Reagan gave in 1984. Reagan's theme of "unfinished work" is typical of incumbent explanations and seems the only justification necessary for a second candidacy. A sitting president does not face the problem of "unseemly seeking"; rather, he treats the presidency as a responsibility already assumed but requiring more time to complete. The emphasis is on faithful stewardship, on staying the course, on not shirking the hard work that goes with the honor. Never do incumbents announce their desire to run again, only their obligation, even though—from the first days of their first term—they are obviously weighing every executive decision with an eye to its effect on reelection.

In 1940, when the issue was a precedent-violating third term, Franklin Roosevelt made no public declaration before the convention began and instead instructed the delegates to choose whoever they wanted. Well aware that he would be that choice, he was making it known he could not refuse their nomination, while yet avoiding the indelicacy of directly seeking what none of his predecessors had pursued. Later he explained that he had not announced because it had been his intention to retire, but he did not want knowledge of that plan to undermine America's influence in the growing international crisis. That crisis was also the reason he gave, the nomination in hand, for delaying retirement and running for a third term.[11]

Four years later Roosevelt did declare his intention to run still another time, first in a letter to the chairman of the Democratic National Committee and then, nine days before his actual nomination, at a press conference. Although he insisted he would prefer—as before—to return to his home on the Hudson River, he stressed that he was "a good soldier" and, with the nation at war, declared, "I will accept and serve in this office, if I am so ordered by the Commander in Chief of us all—the sovereign people of the United States." His was the opportunity civilian candidates covet—to run as a soldier rather than a politician and to portray a refusal to serve as the equivalent of desertion under fire. Significantly, Roosevelt humorously inverted General William T. Sherman's famous refusal, "If nominated, I will not run. If elected, I will not serve," to "If the convention should . . . nominate me for the Presidency, I shall accept. If the people elect me, I will serve" (*New York Times*, 7/12/44).

GOOD SOLDIERS

Given how easily the first president conveyed a public-spirited reluctance and how quickly soldierly analogies spring to the lips of even career politicians, it is no surprise that apart from presidents seeking second terms, generals enjoy the greatest advantage in offering themselves for national office. They most literally embody, after all, the Cincinnatus example.[12] In 1948 General Douglas MacArthur, hero of the Pacific campaign, sent a dispatch from Tokyo expressing his gratitude to those who, in a "spontaneous display of friendly confidence," were putting his name on the ballot for the Wisconsin primary, declaring, with typical extravagance, "No man could fail to be profoundly stirred by such a public movement in this hour of momentous import, national and international, temporal and spiritual." His actual announcement of candidacy, however, was couched in the language of willingness rather than desire.

While it seems unnecessary for me to repeat that I do not actively seek or covet any office and have no plans for leaving my post in Japan, I can say, and with due humility, that I would be recreant to all my concepts of good citizenship were I to shrink because of the hazards and responsibilities involved from accepting any public duty to which I might be called by the American people. (*New York Times*, 3/9/48)

MacArthur's declaration made of the White House a sort of hardship post in a theater of war. Thus he could suggest that to refuse the office would be cowardly, a betrayal of public trust, a barb directed at his arch-rival, Eisenhower, hero of the European war and courted by Democrats and Republicans alike, who had declared his noncandidacy a few weeks before.

During the nineteenth century generals were regularly nominated for the presidency (besides Jackson and Grant, nominees who had enjoyed that title included William Henry Harrison, Zachary Taylor, Winfield Scott, Franklin Pierce, John C. Frémont, George B. McClellan, Rutherford B. Hayes, James A. Garfield, Winfield Scott Hancock, and Benjamin Harrison), creating the impression, not altogether false, that the office of Commander-in-Chief pursues generals rather than the other way around.[13] The notion was strongly reinforced by General Sherman's 1884 rejection of efforts to make him, rather than the frontrunner and eventual standard-bearer, James G. Blaine, the Republican nominee. So defiant a refusal might seem the ultimate affront to the presidency, but in many ways, ironically, it makes the refuser seem all the more fit for the job. Consider the rarely mentioned fact that Sherman's brother, John, pursued the prize throughout the decade. His 1880 effort was managed by the eventual winner, James A. Garfield, and in 1884 both his and William's names were placed before the convention. In 1888 he led all Republican candidates in the early balloting. That we celebrate the older Sherman's uninterest while forgetting the younger's eagerness says much about the American attitude toward presidential ambition as well as our fascination with generals.

Military professionals—in contrast to the large number of Civil War generals who came from and returned to civilian life—seem incapable, even as they announce their candidacies, of avoiding a condescending tone when they speak of political office.[14] General Sherman held a typi-

cal military disdain for the frustrating inefficiencies of politics and politicians, while other generals, like MacArthur, have assumed that their previous commands amply prepared them for the less desperate work of
civilian leadership and have regarded national office as their just due
should they desire it. Despite Ulysses S. Grant's example of how ill-pre-
pared a commander of the armies may prove to be when elevated to
Commander-in-Chief, there is a persistent notion among generals and
their admiring public both that military office is the presidency's best ap-
prenticeship and that the service they are leaving is higher and nobler
than the one they are about to enter.[15] The result, as it often was with
MacArthur, can be more Coriolanus than Cincinnatus, evidence more of
a hero's pride than of civic virtue.

Four years after MacArthur's high-minded declaration that he would
not refuse a nomination that was never offered, Eisenhower advanced a
more artful variation on the theme. Following by one day a statement
from Massachusetts Senator Henry Cabot Lodge that the general would
accept a nominating draft, Eisenhower sent confirmation from Paris,
where he was serving as Supreme Commander of the North Atlantic
Treaty Organization. He began his brief message by declaring himself a
Republican, a matter of no small consequence if he was to appear on primary ballots. (A group of soldiers had petitioned him to be the candidate
for both parties and, like Washington, to unify the country under a non-
partisan executive.) But he continued to insist that he would "not seek
nomination to public office." Repeating the disinclination to enter politics he had expressed in 1948, Eisenhower suggested that he had a greater
responsibility to his office in Europe: "America's enlightened self-interest," he declared, "and the future of Western civilization alike demand
success in our collective effort to produce security against communistic
threat and to preserve peace." Eisenhower emphasized that he would not
ask for "relief from this assignment." Then, in his inimitable style, he
subtly encouraged those who were campaigning on his behalf, while elevating himself above their efforts. "I shall not," he insisted, "participate
in the pre-convention activities of others who may have such an intention with respect to me."

Unlike MacArthur, who at least admitted he was "stirred" by a "public
movement" to nominate him, Eisenhower conceded nothing, either to
the office or to the outpouring of popular support. He expressed no grat-

itude, offered no words of humble appreciation; merely an olympian disinterest in politics, albeit with the acknowledgment that he had consistently voted Republican and the disclosure, delivered through Senator Lodge, that in 1948 he had voted against his Democratic Commander-in-Chief. Nothing in word or tone suggested any enthusiasm for the position that he was, however expressed, now officially pursuing.

The crucial closing paragraph of Eisenhower's announcement implied that his disdain for politics and his reluctance to campaign would extend only through the nomination process; he was not another Sherman. But, again, his obliqueness kept that paramount point from appearing too important. What was most obvious was the lofty position from which he spoke. "Of course," he conceded,

> there is no question of the right of American citizens to organize in pursuit of their common convictions. I realize that Senator Lodge and his associates are exercising this right in an attempt to place before me next July a duty that would transcend my present responsibility.

Here, as with Harding, the announcement is presented as a concession to the efforts of others and a show of respect for their opinions rather than an acknowledgment of ambition. Eisenhower cleared the way for his candidacy with a defense, not of his personal interest, but of the right of supporters to work on his behalf, hinting with righteous indignation that those rights had actually been challenged. Thus in the rhetoric of his announcement Eisenhower became a defender of his friends and well-wishers rather than a petitioner seeking personal recognition.[16] Yet he finally confirmed his willingness to run, albeit in the most indirect manner, concluding, "In the absence, however, of a clear-cut call to political duty I shall continue to devote my full attention and energies to the performance of the vital task to which I am assigned" (*New York Times*, 1/8/52).

More than any other modern presidential candidate, Eisenhower managed to announce his intent and still play the role of Cincinnatus, to make himself available while maintaining something of Washington's reserve. In noting "the absence . . . of a clear-cut call," he effectively incited his supporters to rally such a mandate. His message, despite its disinterested tone, was a teasing invitation to greater efforts on his behalf, though without an overt commitment to personal participation. Senator

Robert Taft, his own candidacy already unequivocally declared, insisted that Eisenhower's statement was no announcement at all but an acknowledgment "that he is not and will not be a candidate." Not surprisingly, Senator Lodge heard a quite different message, "a forthright answer that [Eisenhower] will accept the Republican nomination." Eisenhower's studied ambiguity allowed him both to seek and to reject the presidency, to declare a willingness to serve without revealing too great an appetite for doing so.

The recurrent American interest in a "nonpolitical" candidate occasionally settles on a business rather than military leader, but the logic is much the same. Captains of industry are periodically presented, like generals, as more practically proven leaders than career politicians, managers tested under the real fire of performance and production. Despite the fact that no one has ever moved from a boardroom to the White House, we regularly give serious consideration to the possibility. In the not too distant past Lee Iacocca, former head of Chrysler Corporation, was thought by some to be a viable candidate, and in 1992 the Texas billionaire Ross Perot actually mounted a third-party campaign. Perot well understood that his appeal rested both on his amateur standing and on an apparent personal uninterest in the job, and to this end he managed to be, not once but twice, "drafted" by a popular movement he both organized and financed. He also understood the advantage of the military–business analogy, building his organizational leadership around retired military officers and presenting himself as a sort of corporate general, a no-nonsense commander—brush-cut hair and all.

Most presidents and presidential aspirants, of course, have not been generals able to sound the political themes established by Washington. They are undeniably those creatures of whom their countrymen are so suspicious—career politicians—and cannot, like Eisenhower and MacArthur, claim to have more pressing responsibilities in an alternative profession. Harding and his contemporaries, unable to effect the role of field commander, presented themselves as loyal soldiers in a partisan army, but as primaries became increasingly important for nomination and well-funded national organizations a necessity, such poses have become nearly impossible to maintain. In recent years party loyalty has become a quality much less admired than in Harding's day, and candidates go to great lengths to distance themselves from national politics.[17]

SOUNDING THE ALARM AND ANSWERING IT

The end of the Roosevelt era marked another dramatic transition in the way prospective candidates approached the nominating process. In 1948 announcements began to move away from the reticent Harding model toward more elaborate, significant rhetorical events. A new communications technology was broadcasting an increasingly dramatic and aggressive image of the presidency, facilitating a swing in the nominating process toward the direct involvement of the electorate that the old Progressives sought. The growing visibility of the convention itself led, after disruptive conventions in 1964 (Republican) and 1968 (Democrat), to reforms that shifted more and more power to state primaries. A review of candidates' announcements at twenty-year intervals reveals the dramatic nature of the transformation.

1948: Shaping the Cause

On March 8, 1948, Harry Truman, president since Roosevelt's death in 1945, confirmed through the Democratic National Committee chairman that he would seek another term—a matter of considerable uncertainty until that day—and in the same message declared he would not back down on the civil rights program he had delivered to Congress. His conjoining of seemingly unrelated topics anticipated a crucial issue for the coming political conflict. By linking his candidacy with his controversial policy, Truman indicated he would not soften his position to appease Southern Democrats.

At virtually the same moment, General MacArthur (with Eisenhower already out of the race) issued his brief statement from Tokyo allowing his name to be entered in the Wisconsin primary. The eventual Republican nominee, New York's Governor Thomas E. Dewey, had already announced, sending word on January 17 from the Albany statehouse—by way of an assistant—of his willingness to accept the nomination once again if it were offered (he had been the losing candidate in 1944). But he insisted that pressing duties as governor would keep him from actively campaigning. Dewey entered the fray as a known quantity, with little fanfare and without an extended statement. He also entered, so far as it remained possible, in the old deferring way (*New York Times*, 1/17/48).

In much the same fashion, California's Governor Earl Warren (the eventual vice presidential nominee and later Eisenhower's appointee to be Chief Justice of the United States) had "consented" the previous November to run in his home state's primary and, depending on the outcome, to consider entering races elsewhere. His announcement came amid relatively informal remarks at a Sacramento press conference and took the traditional tack of acknowledging efforts on his behalf while downplaying personal interest (*New York Times*, 11/14/47).

Only slightly more expansive, Senator Robert Taft ("Mr. Republican," son of William Howard Taft, and the favorite among conservatives) returned to his home state of Ohio and on October 24, 1947, informed the press of his own entry into the race. He too demurred when it came to actual preconvention campaigning, offering the usual excuse of more pressing business—in his case the special congressional session President Truman had called for the following month. In a letter addressed to the Ohio Republican Committee chairman, Taft provided a longer description of his plans and a clearer indication of his personal interest in becoming president, but he concluded with the refrain that his nomination prospects rested with his followers, because duty would keep him busy elsewhere (*New York Times*, 10/25/47).

Although these candidates were reluctant to trumpet their own cause, none suggested, as Harding had, that an active pursuit of the presidency would be in any way unseemly. Rather they unanimously attributed their avoidance of active campaigning to previous commitments. All, with the partial exception of MacArthur, appealed to the traditional nominating authority: the state organizations that knew them and their service best.

The first Republican to announce for the 1948 nomination, however, had been Harold Stassen, and his entry into the race more clearly anticipated the practice of later years. A former "boy governor" of Minnesota (elected in 1938 at the age of thirty-one, he was reelected, then resigned to serve in the Navy) no longer holding elective office, he could hardly feign lack of interest, nor could he avoid campaigning on the grounds that he had greater obligations somewhere else. Still less did he have a convenient corps of impatient supporters seeking to put his name on a primary ballot. His announcement came in December 1946, well before the primary season and nearly a year before any other competitor declared. Stassen did well, beating MacArthur in Wisconsin and winning in

enough other states to force the 1944 standard-bearer, Dewey, into an increasingly active campaign role, culminating in a radio debate before the
Oregon vote. Dewey carried Oregon, in part because of his success in
that exchange, but Stassen received sufficient encouragement to cause
him to announce in virtually every succeeding campaign for the rest of
his life, even when few Americans remembered his name or the role he
played in 1948.[18]

Although unorthodox at the time, Stassen's early announcement and
the preconvention platform that accompanied it established a precedent
for future candidates. More important, the reasons compelling Stassen to
start so soon led later contenders to follow his example. Lacking the excuse of the pressure of an impending primary, Stassen justified his early
announcement by asserting that his campaign was an effort to reshape
the GOP and not simply an attempt to win its nomination, reversing the
usual claim of acquiescing to party wisdom and judgment. His contribution in 1948 was to challenge the course Republicans were pursuing, and
consequently his announcement address was a fully developed campaign
speech.[19] The purpose of his candidacy, he declared, was "to move our
Republican party along the path of true liberalism," and the point of his
initial speech was to elaborate on one aspect of that effort—labor legislation—with other policy statements to follow over the coming year and a
half. To demonstrate the seriousness of his commitment to a reform
campaign, Stassen set aside the traditional clichés of reluctance and
launched into a detailed discussion of the appropriate relationship of
government to the control of unions and the right to strike, including
specific proposals in the area of labor law and enforcement policy (*New
York Times*, 12/18/46).

Stassen's announcement suggested that a prenomination campaign
could educate a political party and clarify policy alternatives, and like the
old progressives he sought to cast the primaries as a referendum on ideas
as well as on individual candidates. Thus he anticipated what would become by the 1980s the prevailing announcement model, introducing a
vigorous preconvention contest between the contenders and their ideas.
His enthusiasm for this process was so great that he kept on announcing,
entering primaries even in the 1980 race.[20]

Stassen's was not the only substantive declaration in the 1948 campaign. Henry A. Wallace, a former Roosevelt vice president turned third-

party presidential aspirant, ran on a peace and security platform that also required early and intense canvassing. Conservative Democrats had vehemently opposed his presence on the ticket in 1940 and had forced Roosevelt to dump him in 1944. A member of a distinguished Republican family—his father had been appointed Secretary of Agriculture by Harding—he had edited *Wallace's Farmer*, a leading agricultural magazine, and did pioneering work in developing hybrid seed corn. Concerned about the worsening plight of farmers, he switched parties and campaigned against his fellow Iowan, Herbert Hoover, in the 1928 election. FDR's Secretary of Agriculture for seven years before becoming vice president, he briefly served in Truman's Cabinet as Secretary of Commerce until he resigned in protest over the administration's foreign policy. He blamed Truman for the Cold War, arguing that America, by changing its policy of containment and assuming a more pacifist stance, could reduce international hostilities and lead the world toward peace.

While Stassen applied pressure to reform his party, Wallace set out to defeat his, denouncing his old colleagues in his nationally broadcast announcement as the agents of "war and depression" and proclaiming:

When the old parties rot the people have a right to be heard through a new party. They asserted that right when the Democratic party was founded under Jefferson in the struggle against the Federalist party of war and privilege of his time. They won it again when the Republican party was organized in Lincoln's day. The people must again have an opportunity to speak out with their votes in 1948.

Declaring the 1948 election a referendum on peace and a choice between "progress and reaction," Wallace announced his opposition to universal military training and all "programs which give guns to people when they want plows." He insisted that the United States, under an administration committed to international cooperation, could "organize for peace" at a much lower cost than it could for war and in so doing could stop what he described as a slide toward economic depression at home. "I fight," Wallace declared,

the Truman doctrine and the Marshall plan as applied because they divide Europe into two warring camps. Those whom we buy politically with our food will soon desert us. They will pay us in the base coin of temporary gratitude and then turn to hate us because our policies are destroying their freedom.

Wallace announced the entry of a cause rather than a person into the presidential contest, inviting voters to transform the political landscape as profoundly as had the followers of Jefferson and Lincoln. He offered his adherents the opportunity to engage in a "great fight," to be a people "on the march" against the "powers of evil," and so—although they might be maligned as "Russian tools and Communists"—to restore an Americanism betrayed by the forces of "monopoly capitalism, yellow journalism and racial bigotry." His exhortation ended with a call that can best be described as biblical populism conjoining all his campaign themes:

We have assembled a Gideon's army—small in number, powerful in conviction, ready for action. We have said with Gideon, "Let those who are fearful and trembling depart." For every fearful one who leaves there will be a thousand to take his place. A just cause is worth a hundred armies.

We face the future unfettered by any principle but the principle of general welfare. We owe no allegiance to any group which does not serve that welfare. By God's grace, the people's peace will usher in the century of the common man.[21] (*New York Times*, 12/30/47)

The issue raised by presidential self-promotion is that of the authority by which a candidacy is legitimated. In the days before primaries, state party organizations did the authorizing, backing their favorites with institutional experience and judgment. Not surprisingly, they nearly always based their support on previous political service. However, as individuals began in this century to make their own case, no matter how demurringly, authority and legitimacy subtly shifted to other sources. The primaries, by design, challenged the sovereignty of state committees and party organizations and asserted—as Teddy Roosevelt declared—that only the will of the people mattered. By that logic, parties were to take rather than give direction. But this did not change the need to identify candidates for voters to choose among; it simply added another level of elections as a means of narrowing the field. Candidates, stepping forward on their own, had to distinguish themselves from their competitors on the basis of either experience or ideology. While such an effort need not require inventing a new party, for the duration of the primary season it has something of the same effect. It divides Republicans and Democrats into smaller factions, special interest groups of diverse commitments who challenge each other during the preconvention period in a manner that resembles the conduct of contending parties after the nominating process has been completed. Stassen insisted, however, that a party could contain those conflicts, a conclusion shared in 1968 by Eugene McCarthy and Robert Kennedy and by Jesse Jackson in the 1980s. By contrast, efforts like those of Henry Wallace in 1948 and of Jerry Brown and Ross Perot in 1992 went beyond the intra-party approach and argued not just that an outsider can be an effective president but that *only* an outsider can be an effective president. Such candidates inevitably project the tone of a crusade and hold up everyday politics for condemnation, attacking the traditional parties as corrupt, incapable of change, and entrenched in self-interest. Sermonizing and evangelical in their fervor, they strike at the root of the party system.

1968: Dissent and Divide

In 1912 Teddy Roosevelt had seized upon the newly created state primaries to challenge a sitting president seeking reelection. He prevailed in nearly all of those contests, but Taft remained in the race, convinced that with his supporters in control of the party he would be renominated. He ran, he claimed, less to win than "to perform a great public duty—the duty of keeping Theodore Roosevelt out of the White House." Certain that his old friend and patron had become a dangerous radical, Taft, lacking any personal enthusiasm for the presidency, sought renomination to keep the GOP from becoming too liberal, and ran as a spoiler.

The mini-revolts of 1948 were conducted quite differently. In his effort to liberalize the Republican party, Stassen followed Teddy Roosevelt's strategy, but the GOP had been out of the White House for sixteen years, and he was not opposing a sitting president. Neither the Dixiecrat candidate, Strom Thurmond, nor Henry Wallace had pursued the Democratic nomination—Thurmond's entry was a sort of afterthought to the convention, and Wallace's a third party venture from the start.[22] It was not until 1968 that another serious effort was mounted to unseat a president from within his own party.

By the late 1960s the United States was embroiled in a level of domestic unrest and uncertainty as threatening as anything the country had experienced since the Civil War. There was still no glimmer of the long-promised "light at the end of the tunnel" in the Vietnam War, and the Tet offensive of early 1968 had undermined any lingering public credibility enjoyed by the president and the Pentagon. Growing rebellion among white middle-class college students over American involvement in Vietnam generally and the draft specifically divided the country along generational and class lines. Johnson's success with civil rights legislation had further alienated Southern states, and the attention he and the courts had given to the injustices endured by Black America was answered with a backlash in many Northern blue-collar communities. At the same time the nation's ghettos, their economic and political problems undiminished, had repeatedly erupted in televised displays of arson and violence that reached apocalyptic proportions in Los Angeles and Detroit. The rise of the mostly white and mostly young "New Left," together with the transition of power in the civil rights movement from ministers committed to passive resistance to younger and more militant leaders like Stokeley Carmichael and H. Rap Brown, dramatized the extreme unrest within those groups and, in turn, generated great anxiety in the rest of America. Then came a season of assassination unequaled in our history.

In 1948 the country, for all its profound disagreements about the future, had celebrated a past in which Germany and Japan had been defeated in a great world war, but twenty years later this consensus had been supplanted by division and unrest that called the very possibility of union into question.

A third-party effort of the "Southern" variety was initiated in February 1968 when former Alabama Governor George Wallace—best known at the time for his efforts to block the integration of the University of Alabama—announced his candidacy. Wallace took that occasion to oppose more than Lyndon Johnson and his policies; he condemned as well the Democratic party's position on civil rights, the Supreme Court appointments made by every president since World War II, and that most reliable of scapegoats, the federal bureaucracy. In his message and his subsequent responses to the press, he stated his aim of appointing a court with a "different intention" and insisted that Johnson's civil rights laws were "really an attack on the property rights of this country and on the free enterprise system and local government." He announced a plan of law and order to deal with urban unrest—"I would keep the peace if I had to keep 30,000 troops standing in the streets, two feet apart and with two-foot-long bayonets"—and proposed ridding government of "briefcase-toting bureaucrats" from the Department of Health, Education, and Welfare (*New York Times*, 2/9/68).

At no point did this Wallace echo Stassen's commitment to redirecting the party with which he had been previously affiliated, and in fact it would be the Republican Party of Nixon, Agnew, Reagan, and Bush that would prove most sympathetic to his views. Since the creation of a new party requires a divorce, Wallace was relieved of any concern about future reconciliation and therefore had no need to worry about how he might someday reunite what he now hoped to divide. Like Henry Wallace before him, he left a party which he declared irredeemable, and like all third-party candidates, he authorized his campaign on ideological grounds, legitimating it by discrediting all existing parties and their leaders.

Those who opposed Johnson for the 1968 Democratic nomination faced the difficult task of unseating an incumbent president without discrediting their party—of isolating Johnson and his supporters from the rest of the Democratic organization. They presented a more devastating critique—if only because it was personal—than Stassen had offered in 1948, but without following Henry Wallace's seceding example. The challenge to Johnson began with Eugene McCarthy, the Democratic Senator from Minnesota, who declared his opposition to the president over a single aberration in the administration's policies: its pursuit of the Vietnam War. McCarthy's entry into the race, he declared, came in response to continual escalation of a conflict whose cost had become catastrophic not only in lives and financial expenditure, but also in a general decline of domestic morale. After elaborating on the consequences of the war both at home and abroad, McCarthy came to the point on which the ultimate credibility of his candidacy rested:

. . . there is growing evidence of a deepening moral crisis in America—discontent and frustration and a disposition to take extralegal if not illegal actions to manifest protest.

I am hopeful that this challenge which I am making . . . may alleviate at least in some degree this sense of political helplessness and restore to many people a belief in the processes of American politics and of American government.

By depicting his campaign as an effort to redeem the existing political system, McCarthy emphasized that he was not opposing that system itself. Much as Henry Wallace invoked the founding of the Democratic and Republican parties to de-radicalize the creation of a third, McCarthy also attempted to bring his revolt into the political mainstream. His intent, he declared, was to provide a legitimate channel for dissent and thereby preserve rather than destroy the Democratic party. In that way he meant to "counter the growing sense of alienation . . . reflected in a tendency to withdraw from political action, to talk of nonparticipation, to become cynical and to make threats of support for third parties or fourth parties or other irregular political movements."

Precisely because he remained a Democrat, McCarthy's announcement, despite its central moral arguments, was more restrained than the fiery appeals of the two Wallaces. The challenge to all in-party dissenters is to voice extreme criticism without seeming themselves extreme. George Wallace's best hope, on the other hand, was to divide the electorate so badly (denying either of his opponents a majority vote in the Electoral College) that the election would be forced into the House of Representatives, thus giving the South a greater role in determining the outcome. McCarthy wanted the advantage of a major party nomination and with it the opportunity to win the election outright. To this end he adopted the respectful tone of a conserving traditionalist rather than of a destructive radical. "I do not see in my move," he insisted, "any great threat to the unity and strength of the Democratic party," implying that it was the president who posed such a threat as he continued, "whatever that unity may be today and whatever strength it may be." "I believe," he concluded, "we can restore to this nation a clearer sense of purpose and of dedication to the achievement of our traditional purposes as a great nation in the 20th century." This is hardly stirring stuff. There is little of the passionate intensity that elsewhere marked anti-Johnson, antiwar oratory, but it separated McCarthy from the president *and* from radicalism. His rhetoric signaled that while the government in power threatened public order, he—in opposition—stood for traditional party principles and the social harmony they sustain. In short, he sought to be legitimated by both principle and party (*New York Times*, 12/1/67).

New York Senator Robert Kennedy's entry into the race, announced after McCarthy's strong showing in New Hampshire, also displayed considerable restraint but was most memorable for the emotion it did reveal. Kennedy began, "I do not run for the Presidency merely to oppose any man but to propose new policies. I run because I am convinced that this country is on a perilous course and because I have such strong feelings about what must be done, and I feel that I am obliged to do all that I can." Implicit was Kennedy's explanation for the lateness of his declaration. Because of his troubled relations with Johnson (dating all the way back to his opposition to the Texan's being placed on the 1960 ticket and publically visible during the time after his brother's assassination that he continued on as Attorney General) and especially because he was a Kennedy, he argued, an earlier candidacy would have been perceived as a personal attack, a vendetta; but McCarthy's success in New Hampshire allowed him now to enter the contest on the basis of issues. His claim that he ran to "propose" rather than "oppose," like McCarthy's insistence that his purpose was to serve the traditional political system, was an effort to project a positive agenda over a negative critique. The reason he claimed for entering a race in which a dissenting candidate was already successfully at work was the intensity of both the national crisis and his personal conviction.

Those justifications, especially the latter, necessitated stronger emotional appeals than McCarthy had employed. Kennedy depicted the divisions in American society much more graphically and expansively than McCarthy, emphasizing the urban violence erupting across the country. He spoke with an urgency that, in the opening sections of his address, built forcefully through parallel constructions and strong emotional appeals, and throughout his remarks was the haunting echo of his dead brother's cadences and accent.

> I run to seek new policies—policies to end the bloodshed in Vietnam and in our cities, policies to close the gap that now exists between black and white, between rich and poor, between young and old in this country and around the rest of the world.

I run for the Presidency because I want the Democratic party and the United States of America to stand for hope instead of despair, for reconciliation of men instead of the growing risk of world war.

I run because it is now unmistakably clear that we can change these disastrous divisive policies only by changing the men who are now making them. (*New York Times*, 3/11/68)

Despite Kennedy's highly charged opening remarks, much of the speech stressed reconciliation and insisted on (not altogether convincingly) his regard for McCarthy as well as his appreciation for Johnson's kindness in the weeks following JFK's assassination. But its most memorable moments built on an emotion that he barely contained. In contrast to McCarthy, Kennedy's appeal emphasized his personal capacity for feeling, his ability and willingness to feel the pain of others—whether its source was the "ugly deprivation" endured by blacks in Mississippi and Watts, the frustration of Appalachian whites condemned to lives of "empty idleness," or the anger of the young against the war in Vietnam. The clear implication was that while Kennedy opposed Johnson because the president represented an old, discredited policy, he could not support McCarthy's candidacy because McCarthy lacked sufficient empathy with those whom the new policy must serve. The unspoken rationale for his entry into the race was, therefore, not that he alone possessed the needed knowledge and conviction, but rather that he was the candidate of right feeling, the one who, despite being rich and white and middle-aged, could claim a degree of credibility with minorities and the poor as well as with the young, white middle-class students fueling McCarthy's campaign. Thus Kennedy's passion complemented the more intellectual and academic qualities McCarthy brought to the race and, despite his insistence to the contrary, it was this passion, legitimated by its being on behalf of others, that in the end pushed him to the forefront. Though he stated that his differences with Johnson had nothing to do with personality, he hinted that it was precisely personality that distinguished him from McCarthy.

There were other candidates in 1968. George Romney, three-term governor of Michigan and former head of American Motors, offered himself to Republicans, announcing in November 1967 and running against a domestic policy that had made American society "aimless" and "flabby" and a foreign policy that had left the country "mired in an Asian land war which sacrifices our young men and drains our resources with no end in sight." Romney's attack on the Democratic administration was relatively conventional and included the usual laments about failed leadership and a country morally adrift. "We're becoming," he observed, "a house divided."

Notable was Romney's use of the outsider argument. Not only did he emphasize his lack of Washington connections, he also insisted that he really was—even after all his years as a governor—still just a businessman and that corporate experience was what recommended him. Introducing his wife, he said, "She excels in eloquence, the poetry of words, empathy, and graciousness. Well, I've given my life to the poetry of decisions and work." His criticism of "the present President" was primarily that he was "experienced only in the tools of government" (the implication being that Romney himself understood "real" tools) and would, therefore, "continue no matter what his intentions, to build greater and greater governmental control over our lives." Romney, on the other hand, claimed the ability to "decentralize our attack on problem-solving" because of quite different experience.

> I have worked in the fields, in construction, in independent and voluntary agencies during war and peace, in international trade and labor conferences, in two of the nation's largest corporations operating in three major industries and in state and Federal Government. (*New York Times*, 11/19/67)

While neither Romney's arguments nor his experience rallied Republicans to his cause, his claims bore a strong resemblance to those George Bush would offer the country twenty-five years later.

Governor Nelson Rockefeller of New York entered the race for the Republican nomination on April 30, 1968, shortly after the assassination of Martin Luther King, Jr. His announcement, like Earl Warren's twenty years earlier, came in a brief statement, followed by a press conference. In his opening remarks Rockefeller explained his decision in terms of "the dramatic and unprecedented events of the past week." The continuing escalation of domestic violence he offered as his explanation for reversing his March 21 declaration that he was "unequivocally . . . not a candidate campaigning directly or indirectly for the Presidency of the United States."

Rockefeller hinted at a role similar to the one Robert Kennedy had defined for himself, that of peacemaker and healer to a divided and wounded people, but his announcement was more constrained, the exact nature of his candidacy vague. "I am deeply disturbed," he declared, "by the course of events, the growing unrest and anxiety at home and the signs of disintegration abroad." But all he offered in response to this crisis was his conviction "that true unity is forged by full examination of the facts and the free interchange of honest convictions." In a telegram to party leaders, also released to the press at the time of his announcement, he stated as his purpose "to give the party a choice of candidates and programs." In his exchange with reporters he played down the ideological nature of that choice, ignoring the vitriolic denunciations of his liberalism that Goldwater conservatives had shouted during his appearance at the 1964 convention. "I have a feeling," he told his April 30 audience,

> that ideology is not as big a factor now as is the desire on the part of the party and the country to find unity and to find constructive action to meet the problems. I think there's more pragmatism in the feeling of the people than before. I think we recognize we cannot afford the luxury of ideological debates which are unrelated to the problems we face, which have tremendous reality and which are of deep concern to people. (*New York Times*, 5/1/68)

In entering the contest, Rockefeller offered nothing more specific, either in criticism of the candidates already in the field or in analysis of the problems at hand; nothing that would have made his late entry into the fray either exciting or unseemly.

The eventual 1968 nominees, Hubert Humphrey and Richard Nixon, both well-worn politicians known to the public from previous campaigns, announced in quite different ways. Nixon, who had been defeated in 1960 by John Kennedy, declared his candidacy in a letter addressed to the voters of New Hampshire and delivered at the end of January preceding that state's March primary. He declared the country's need for "new leadership" and, though somewhat less than new himself, he suggested that in his years out of office he had gained a different point of view.

> During fourteen years in Washington I learned the awesome nature of the great decisions a President faces. During the past eight years I have had a

chance to reflect on the lessons of public office, to measure the nation's tasks and its problems from a fresh perspective. I have sought to apply those lessons to the needs of the present, and to the entire sweep of this final third of the 20th century.

Vintage Nixon in its emphasis on learning from his personal frustrations (or "crises"), the letter presented him as the experienced candidate and yet one whose favorite word was "new" and whose campaign theme would be a "new beginning." The legitimacy of his candidacy was based on previous political experience combined with recent "reflections," the lessons of the latter preparing him for the leadership the future required. In form and tone, however, the message reached back to the first half of the twentieth century even as it looked to the future; but instead of being simply a note from the statesman whom others had urged into a primary, it was a personal promotion that strove to keep the traditional tone of statesmanship intact so far as circumstances would allow (*New York Times*, 1/30/68).

Humphrey—one of the candidates defeated by John F. Kennedy for the 1960 Democratic nomination, and in 1968 Lyndon Johnson's vice president—announced his candidacy in a televised speech delivered to a crowd of Washington, D.C., supporters. The *New York Times* observed, "Known for his enthusiasm, Mr. Humphrey had never seemed quite so exuberant as he was on the threshold of his greatest challenge." Given that the chief executive he served had already been driven from the race by McCarthy and Kennedy, the vice president's unfailing perkiness seemed somewhat out of joint with the times. "And here we are," he declared.

> just as we ought to be, here we are, the people, here we are in a spirit of dedication, here we are the way politics ought to be in America, the politics of happiness, the politics of purpose, and the politics of joy. And that's the way it's going to be, too, all the way from here on out.

Presenting himself as the candidate of positive thinking, the indefatigable champion of cheerfulness, Humphrey personally set himself against the visions of America offered by McCarthy and Kennedy, placing his own good nature and optimism against their dire depictions as well as in implied contrast to the gloom of LBJ's final year in power. And where Romney called for a president trained in the world of business, Humphrey offered, intermixed, the political and familial offices he had filled.

> My credentials? Well, they may be stated rather simply: of a loving family, teacher, Mayor of my city, Senator from my State, Vice President of my country, grateful husband, proud father, believer in the American dream and the concept of human brotherhood.

In his announcement address Humphrey cast the most promising light then available on each of the issues of the day; on Vietnam he spoke hopefully of the administration's most recent peace initiative; on the growing clamor of dissent he said, "We do not demand . . . an America of one mind. What we seek is an America of one spirit." Wherever there were problems Humphrey pointed to promise, and to the question, "What do these times call for?" he responded:

> Well, the time has come to speak thoughts deeply felt, but not often said by millions of Americans. The time has come to speak out on behalf of America—not a nation that has lost its way, but a restless people, a great nation striving to find a better way. . . .
>   The time has come for those who share a deep and abiding belief in the purpose and potentialities of this nation to say "I love my country."

Humphrey's announcement, in tone and sometimes in content, resembles less the rhetoric of subsequent Democratic candidates than the sunshine oratory Ronald Reagan would bring to preeminence a decade later. Just as the conservative leader of the 1980s decried the nay-sayers and declared it "morning in America," the archetypal liberal of the 1960s attacked the negativism of his opponents and preached the gospel of American confidence. What Humphrey delivered with an overcharged exuberance, intense and often bombastic, Reagan would present in a less excited, more mellowed manner.

At the close of his formal announcement Humphrey indirectly confronted his Democratic opposition. "But what concerns me," he said, "is not just winning the nomination, but how it is to be won. The man who wins the nomination must be able first to unite his party, and the man who unites his party must be able, above all, to unite and govern his nation." The implication was clear: in opposing Johnson, McCarthy and Kennedy had divided their party, and whereas Kennedy had offered himself as an empathetic link between dissenting groups, he could not bridge the gulf he had helped to create among Democrats. Only Humphrey, once much admired among Johnson's Democratic opponents and himself an unquestioned champion of the liberal causes that Robert Kennedy had adopted, could hope to unite a factionalized party. With friends in all camps—those who appreciated his support for the President as well as those who had admired him as a senator—Humphrey offered himself as the candidate of reconciliation (*New York Times*, 4/28/68).

1988: Early Birds and Primary Worms

"Once upon a time, not so long ago," the election scholars Nelson W. Polsby and Aaron Wildavsky remind us, "there was a gap between one presidential campaign and the next one four years later."[23] As candidates have become self-selecting they have not only needed longer messages to justify their presumption; but in order to compete with similarly motivated politicians, they have also required more time to build an organization and a public image. Polsby and Wildavsky attributed the disappearance of "breathing space" between elections to reforms in delegate selection instigated in part by the collision of McCarthy and Kennedy dissenters with the old political order at the 1968 Chicago convention.[24] The party's response to the riot that raged around the nominating proceedings was to institute delegate selection reforms that increased, through primaries and caucuses, the number and variety of people involved in the process. The systemic reform that progressive Republicans tried to impose upon their party in 1912, Democrats legislated for themselves after their Chicago fiasco. Those changes, by increasing the number and importance of state primaries, also pushed the Republicans in a similar direction.

The new rules for delegate selection immediately opened the field to a wider range of candidates. But they also made it impossible for all but the best known to wait as long as had the 1968 contenders to declare their entry into the race. Little known figures like George McGovern and Jimmy Carter had to make themselves nationally recognizable, a feat that required time, money, and publicity. The drama of the 1968 dispute among Democrats had already drawn increased attention to the announcement message, but by 1972 it had become even more important to be taken seriously from the start and to attract as much media coverage and money as possible. As a result, announcing ceremonies and speeches became far more significant events than had previously been the case in all but a few instances.[25] The fact that they were occurring before the usual election season meant they had to emphasize substance in order not to appear simply as displays of excessive ambition. They had become "events," staged, scripted, and scheduled with all the artful calculation of a Broadway production.

Before the 1972 primaries, when Democrat George McGovern's advisers met to choose the right moment for their candidate's announcement, they fretted about seeming "too early." They recognized both the time required to turn a relatively unknown Senator from South Dakota into a potential president and the dangers that come with increased media scrutiny.[26] They were well aware that the only game in town gets all the attention, an ambiguous advantage that has negative as well as positive consequences. When he eventually gave his formal announcement on January 18, 1971, according to Theodore White—who had forgotten Harold Stassen or had come, in light of Stassen's subsequent quixotic runs for the presidency, to dismiss him as a crank—McGovern's was the "earliest announcement of any major modern candidacy."[27] Jimmy Carter, the next time around, was even earlier, declaring his intention on December 13, 1974. A Gallup survey of nearly the same date had listed thirty-one individuals "mentioned" as potential candidates; Carter's name did not appear, an indication of why an early announcement was necessary if he were to have any chance at all.[28]

A motley crowd of contenders entered the 1988 presidential race— eight Democrats and six Republicans, including four senators, a former senator, two representatives, one governor, two former governors, one retired general, a vice president, and two Protestant ministers. The earliest announcement was that of one of the least known candidates, former Delaware Governor Pierre DuPont, coming in September 1986; the last was Senator Robert Dole's in November 1987. Eight others came during the spring of 1987. In several cases "preannouncement" statements gave a date for the "official" declaration,[29] and nearly everyone was aware that some late announcers, such as Vice President Bush, were already running serious campaigns.

All gave substantial speeches. Some, like DuPont and Senator Gary Hart, elaborated programs, offering mini-platforms in their announcing remarks. Others, like Representative Richard Gephardt and the Reverend Jesse Jackson, raised a single issue that would provide the theme of their campaigns. Each tried in one way or another to stake out a territory of his own, not just politically but also personally, offering autobiography as a significant argument for presidential legitimacy. Senator Albert Gore emphasized his youth and his identification with the Vietnam generation; Senator Dole stressed his World War II experience, his rural roots, and his record as a leader in the Senate. The eventual Democratic nominee, Governor Michael Dukakis of Massachusetts, based his appeal first on the prosperity his state had enjoyed under his administration; then on an implied connection with John Kennedy who, like Dukakis, was born in Brookline (the governor offered several rhetorical allusions as well, declaring at one point, "Ask more than what we are going to do; ask what we have already done.");[30] and, finally and most persistently, on the immigrant experience of his Greek parents. His stance in announcing suggested that he was at least as conservative as he was liberal, being concerned with the "economic growth that provides genuine opportunity for all Americans." A celebrant of the American dream, Dukakis offered his candidacy on the basis of "the passion I feel for these free shores, which welcomed Kitty's [his wife's] family and my own." Ironically it was his apparent *lack* of passion that plagued him throughout the campaign (*New York Times*, 4/30/87).

On Location

An important part of the new self-representation was the choice of an appropriate place from which to announce a candidacy. Location itself provided a statement about character and values. That was less the case when the announcement came, as it did with Bruce Babbitt, on the campaign trail in a primary state, but it was certainly the reason Hart chose Colorado's Red Rocks Park and "The Garden of the Titans" as the theatrical backdrop for his entry into the race. More typically the chosen place, as with Dole, was a hometown. The decision to begin the candidate's official journey toward the White House at the site of his own life's beginnings was more than a return to a friendly setting; it was an effort to create the context in which the country would see him. Dole described the crowd in Russell, Kansas, as the "people who know me best . . . people who have always accepted me, and believed in me." In the ceremony that preceded his speech, a local pharmacist presented Dole with a cigar box that once sat on the drugstore's counter for contributions to assist a grievously wounded veteran. Deeply moved, the Senator incorporated that piece of personal history into his speech, recalling his injury and the response of his community.[31]

> There are people standing here who long ago put quarters they couldn't spare in this cigar box. That generosity helped reshape my life.
>
> I remember the experience—many years ago—that began when I felt a sting in my shoulder. I remember the first thing I thought of was home.[32]
>
> The goodness of the people of Russell over the years has been the source of my inspiration and my strength. The people who settled this community, like so many others across America, were immigrants and frontiersmen and homesteaders who knew that grit and endurance and reliance on one's neighbors were needed to build a better life for their children. They were optimists and builders; they harnessed invention and hard work to carve a life out of the wilderness. I have carried the spirit of this place with me all of my life.
>
> That is why I have come back home today to announce before family and friends, that I am a candidate for my party's nomination to the office of President of the United States.

Robert Dole never enjoyed the reputation of being a particularly eloquent man. In fact he regularly frustrated his speechwriters by departing from the text and rambling off on his own; but in the first lines of his 1988 candidacy he achieved one of the few eloquent moments of a campaign that offered little apart from the high oratory of Jesse Jackson. The poignancy of Dole's response to the place and people of his youth went well beyond a segue into a political speech and became its first, best proof that in addition to political experience the Senator brought with him a compassion born of other people's generosity. Thereafter, a Republican's capacity for kindness and humanity became a central theme for him; surrounded by candidates who declared themselves self-made and who insisted they were generous on principle, Dole noted that he had learned generosity early in life as one who had benefited from the charity of others (*New York Times*, 11/10/87).

Gore presented his own hometown of Carthage, Tennessee, and not his seat in the Senate as preparing him for national office. He introduced himself as a child of "the New South," influenced by the postwar struggles for social justice and ready to "help build a new America." He made his remarks near the local veteran's memorial, and after reminding his audience of his own service in Vietnam, read the names of area men who had died in that conflict. Thus Gore implied that along with his youth came the two defining experiences of his generation, and that those were an important part of what he would bring to national office (*New York Times*, 6/30/87).

Jesse Jackson entered the presidential race in Raleigh, North Carolina, not far from where, as a college student, he had begun his career as a civil rights activist. Like Gore he held up the struggle that had taken place in the region of his birth as particularly pertinent to national service, arguing, "The New South has not only liberated itself but it will change the priorities of our nation." In contrast to Gore's privileged beginnings, Jackson's background was one of deep poverty—"I was born to a teenage mother. Nobody knew my name." Jackson stressed that such a past allowed him to identify with the vulnerable and dispossessed and informed his commitment "to bring justice in our land, mitigate misery in the world, and bring peace on earth." Jackson presented himself not only as a reminder of the nation's profoundest problems, but also as an emblem of its promise. "Only in America," he proclaimed, "is such a dream possible" (*New York Times*, 10/11/87).

While Dole emphasized the compassion that he, a white Midwestern farm boy, had learned from the generosity of others, Jackson cited the instruction that came from being not only poor and fatherless, but black in a segregated society, claiming that those experiences had prepared him to be a force for justice and inclusion. The message was similar to that of Robert Kennedy in 1968 as he attempted to reform his country and his party while working within the system.[33]

Perhaps the most unusual use of place by an announcing candidate was the Reverend Pat Robertson's choice of Brooklyn's Bedford-Stuyvesant neighborhood, hardly a bastion of the religious right (the televangelist Robertson's most reliable supporters) and far from his patrician

Virginia origins. Predictably, the candidate was heckled throughout his remarks—a fact perhaps intended to support his claim of being "a candidate who is willing to take risks." But the neighborhood had a more personal significance for the born-again Robertson, for it was there that he had moved twenty-seven years earlier in response to a divine call to serve the poor. The second birth of his religious conversion and his later commitment to political service reflected, he implied, the same sort of holy directive that first brought him to Bedford-Stuyvesant (*New York Times*, 10/2/87).

In his unsuccessful 1980 nomination bid, George Bush had announced in Washington, D.C., and promptly flown to his home state of Connecticut to give a follow-up speech. The message was clear: In contrast to the leading contender that year, Ronald Reagan, Bush was an insider, a man with a resume and an almost unprecedented range of experience in the Washington bureaucracy. When in 1988 he ran again, however, he emphasized a quite different personal history, announcing in his adopted home state of Texas which, like Robertson's Brooklyn, represented a second biography. In his Houston speech he dismissed traditional roots and presented himself as he would throughout the campaign as a self-made man shaped by the rough and tumble of the Texas oil business. Notably absent, given the emphasis his eventual opponent gave to family background, was any mention of his wealthy parents or his schooling at Andover and Yale University. He preferred to open his biography with the new life beginning in the school of hard knocks.

> I am a man who 40 years ago threw everything he had into the back of a Studebaker and tooled on out to west Texas—where I started a business and tried to meet a payroll and experienced the tensions and the satisfactions of having a business in America. I felt the deep joy of being able to provide for my wife and children; I felt a joy when I was able to give a fellow a job and know that his children would be cared for. And so I am a man who knows in his heart that it all comes down to family—that all our best endeavors come back to that core.

Bush showed no apparent concern that his statement, "it all comes down to family," would evoke the privileges provided by the affluence of his parents. Rather, the family referred to here is the archetypal 1950s model, heading west in a Studebaker. It is the kind of family that hovered over much of the 1988 campaign, one that Robertson as well as Bush sought to recover and that traditional liberals like Paul Simon were pledged to protect; but no one managed to capture it with the consistency or persistence of Bush, a nostalgia-laden television version starring Fred MacMurray as the father. Gone was Bush's own father, the Senator and millionaire so reverently recalled in 1979, replaced by the son, a typical young veteran with a growing family and an ambition to get ahead. Texas belonged to the younger Bush, while Connecticut and Washington, D.C., belonged to the elder. Abandoning the Northeast his second time around, the Vice President made Texas his place of origin, although, once elected, he turned his parents' Maine estate into the summer White House.

The Vice President's emphasis upon his military and oilfield experience was no doubt an effort to answer the peculiar charge of being a "wimp" that dogged him throughout the preconvention campaign. Just a few days after *Newsweek* made that issue the subject of its cover story, an announcing George Bush pointedly repeated ten times in a single page the phrase, "I am a man."

The *New York Times*'s report on Bush's announcement speech, in an unusual credit, indicated it had been written by Peggy Noonan, the ghost behind Ronald Reagan's more memorable presidential utterances and subsequently the principal author of Bush's acceptance and inaugural addresses. After Dole's victory in Iowa and a subsequent sluggish performance by Bush in his first days in New Hampshire, Ms. Noonan—or "The Poetry Lady," as she was called by some Reagan and Bush staffers—was called in again. The problem was the public's lack of any clear perception of who the Vice President was. The challenge, as he described it to Noonan was, ". . . we gotta get me out there, we gotta sort of get me out there, they don't know me."[34] Noonan had seen this from the start and had crafted his announcement to address that dilemma.

As both Noonan and Bush were well aware, this was not the sort of public recognition problem Carter had when he declared his candidacy in 1974. Bush was, as Noonan lamented, "famous" but not "well known." In part, this was because he had been standing in Ronald Reagan's shadow for eight years, but it also had to do with ideology and character. Having embraced Reagan's policies, policies Bush had derided during their 1980 primary skirmishes—especially his "voodoo economics"—the Vice President had not convinced Republicans so much of his conservatism as of his opportunism. Even the "wimp" charge referred to uncertain ideological convictions and suggested that he lacked principled courage.[35] To make himself better known he had to declare his candidacy in such a way as to distinguish himself from Reagan and project the "manliness" his opponents were suggesting he needed. At the same time, because of his predecessor's popularity, he had to avoid any hint of disagreement with the man he sought to succeed.

"A President," Bush suggested in his announcement, "must never intrude, but a President can set a tone, an atmosphere, a mood." Oddly this description matched the nation's prior perception of Bush and was the version his opponents had ridiculed. Even when Ronald Reagan lay gravely wounded after an assassination attempt and Bush was Acting Chief Executive, what captured the headlines was the presumptuous claim of the Secretary of State, Alexander Haig (a former general who announced his own 1988 candidacy by saying he was "throwing his helmet in the ring"), that *he* was in charge. But in 1987 the Vice President claimed being unobtrusive, something he had proved himself good at, was in fact "presidential" if it was combined with the ability to set an appropriate "tone," to generate an "atmosphere."

Bush further argued that his blandness was what post-Reagan America required since the nation had been "righted" in the previous eight years. "We don't need radical new directions—we need strong and steady leadership. We don't need to remake society—we just need to remember who we are." But to this point the Vice President had only identified his faithfulness to Reagan's accomplishments. It remained for him to assert his own personality, and he attempted to do so in terms of the atmosphere he could contribute.

"I mean," he continued, "to stand for a new harmony, a greater tolerance, and a renewed recognition that this country is and always has been a partnership." Specifically, he referred to racial harmony. "The sadness of racial tensions in America," he explained, "should have ended completely by now. We are on a journey to a new century, and we must, finally, leave the tired old baggage of bigotry behind us." Although inconsistent with the Republicans' repeated use of a campaign ad featuring Willie Horton, a black rapist who, released from a Massachusetts prison during Dukakis's governorship, had committed another rape and then murdered his victim, Bush's announced intentions offered, at the time, a small step away from the outgoing president. Reagan's presidency had been widely perceived as unresponsive to African-Americans, and that gave Bush an opportunity to distinguish himself without suggesting fundamental opposition to the Reagan revolution. ("I am proud to have been his partner; I am proud to have been part of his great work".)

While all this may have reassured Reagan loyalists, it did not offer much of an answer to the larger question shadowing Bush's candidacy—whether he was "man enough" for the job. In stressing "tone and "atmosphere" he had only confirmed the view of himself as timid, but in the final section of his announcement he declared himself. Insisting that "history is biography" he unrolled the impressive list Senator Dole ("I offer a record, not a resume") had mocked.

I am a man who, as a Navy flier in World War II, was shot down by the enemy . . .

I am a man who in two years in Congress learned that Democracy stays new by reinventing itself . . .

I am a man who was chairman of a great political party . . .

I am man who, as the head of the CIA, learned the world is full of danger for the decent . . .

I am a man who learned first hand in 7 years as Vice President that a modern president must be many things.

After enumerating a few of those "many things," Bush drew his biography and his office together in a declaration radically at odds with the deference he had displayed in earlier campaigns: "I know what it all comes down to, this election—what it all comes down to, after all the shouting and the cheers—is the man at the desk. And who should sit at that desk. I am that man" (*New York Times*, 10/13/87).[36]

1992 and 1996: I Want to Lead

The year 1992 confirmed trends readily apparent in the previous election; although the campaign began much more slowly, the announcement formulas were much the same. With an incumbent Republican secure in the White House, Democratic hopefuls—other than former

Senator Paul Tsongas, who, as an out-of-office Greek-American from Massachusetts, hardly seemed a likely contender so soon after the Dukakis defeat—were slow to present themselves. They finally began stepping forward in late September and early October 1991, sensing Bush's growing vulnerability over the sluggish economy and a general domestic malaise. Senator Tom Harkin declared himself in a small town in Iowa, insisting that his liberal politics were based on traditional values. But like JFK in 1960, he emphasized most his capacity to win. "I know there are those who say it's a long shot," he said, "that we might as well call the election off. I'm here today to tell you that George Herbert Walker Bush has got feet of clay, and I intend to take a hammer to them" (*New York Times*, 9/16/91).

Nebraska Senator Robert Kerry, Vietnam war hero and entrepreneur, announced that the American problem had become "our own pessimism" and offered himself as the embodiment of "prairie optimism." In addition to that Reaganesque approach he introduced a generational theme, the counterpart to Harkin's emphasis on class. "I want," he said, "to lead America's fearless, restless voyage of generational progress" (*New York Times*, 10/1/91). But despite what, prior to the campaign, many Democrats had expected to be a strong candidacy, the electorate never got a fix on Kerry, could never quite match the man and the message, could not find a sense of direction in those generalizations. Apart from his generational distinction, Kerry seemed intent on echoing Ronald Reagan's unflappable positive thinking. But Reagan always seemed an uncomplicated man sustained by a simple faith, while Kerry, who took time from his campaign to lecture Harvard students on Albert Camus, was clearly full of complexity, and the authority he could legitimately command was that of experience, not the innocence upon which the old actor relied.

Like the other governor in the race, Virginia's Douglas Wilder, Bill Clinton of Arkansas put heavy emphasis on fiscal responsibility and economic growth. But he also introduced the persistent themes of the younger Southern leadership: racial harmony and the lessons the South had learned that were applicable to the nation as a whole. Unlike Gore in 1988, he did not make Vietnam the great generational watershed—he himself had opposed and avoided the war—but drew the dividing line wholly along the route of freedom marches and desegregation struggles that ran through many Southern cities, including Little Rock.[37] Standing on the steps of the Old State House in Little Rock, the site of Arkansas's 1861 secessionist convention, he declared,

> For twelve years the Republicans have tried to divide us, race against race. Here in the shadow of this great building, all of us, we know all about race-baiting. They've used that old tool on us for decades now. And I want to tell you one thing: I understand that tactic, and I will not let them get away with it in 1992. (*New York Times*, 10/4/91)

Like his competitors, Clinton began his primary campaign with the warning that he, in contrast to the party's nominee in 1988, would not let negative Republican tactics of the Willie Horton kind go unanswered. And just as Tom Harkin accused Bush of dividing the country along class lines and Kerry had stressed generational divisions, Clinton—emphasizing race—criticized President Bush's inability to unite the country.

There was as well Republican opposition to George Bush. Both political commentator Patrick Buchanan and Louisiana's David Duke attacked him from the right. In his declaration of candidacy Buchanan offered "a new nationalism," a slogan and theme reminiscent of 1920s and 1930s politics even down to its promise, "We will put America first" (*New York Times*, 12/11/91). Duke, a former state legislator and Grand Wizard of the Ku Klux Klan, gave a more racist tinge to his nationalism, suggesting, "We must go to the Japanese and say, 'You no buy our rice, we no buy your cars,'" stating more extreme versions of political views that would grow in prominence in the following years. "This country," Duke insisted, "is overwhelmingly [of] European descent. It's overwhelmingly Christian. And if we lose our underpinning, I think we are going to lose the foundations of America" (*New York Times*, 11/19/91).

As Republican candidates lined up for the privilege of challenging President Clinton in 1996, they came on the wave of momentous congressional victories in the off-year campaign. Buchanan, buoyed by his modest success in challenging the Republican incumbent in 1992, reapplied for the nomination on the basis of his "America First" strategy and the claim of a major American swing to the right. He paid deference to the agenda of religious conservatives but much of his speech was populist, directed at workers and attacking both unfair foreign competition and corporate greed (*New York Times*, 3/21/95).

Former Tennessee Governor Lamar Alexander offered himself as an outsider running against professional politicians. "They are from Washington," he asserted, "I am from Maryville," referring to his Tennessee hometown, the setting for his announcement. Though a former Bush appointee as Secretary of Education, he promised as proof of his conservatism to abolish the Department of Education and to emulate Ronald Reagan. "Now is the time," he declared, "to give another Republican Washington outsider the same opportunity to help put a little humility into the arrogant empire in Washington" (*New York Times*, 2/29/95).

While other Republican outsiders, most notably California Governor Pete Wilson, were issuing similar appeals, insisting on the superior judgment of states and local communities in virtually all matters except national defense, the most interesting candidates were all Washington insiders. Indiana Senator Richard Lugar wryly noted that "the conventional wisdom of generous columnists seems to be that Dick Lugar would be a good president. That he is intelligent, has broad experience, exercises courage and prudence appropriately. But such a person is rarely nominated or elected" (*New York Times*, 4/20/95). He hoped to defy the last part of that opinion by promising a broad vision and a reduced federal government. The failure of his campaign to generate wide support may be due in part to the fact that his announcement came on April 19, the same day as the bombing of the Oklahoma City Federal Building.

Senator Arlen Specter of Indiana offered himself as a sort of Republican counterbalance to the likes of Pat Buchanan and was the only candidate to look beyond Reagan for a personal mentor. (Spector's choice was Lincoln and he announced at the Lincoln Memorial.) He took specific issue with the religious right, naming names and convictions: "When Pat Robertson says there is no constitutional doctrine of separation between church and state, I say he is wrong. . . . When Pat Buchanan calls for a holy war in our society, I say he is wrong. . . . When Ralph Reed says a pro-choice Republican isn't qualified to be our president, I say the Republican party will not be blackmailed" (*New York Times*, 3/31/95). There was, however, no groundswell of Republican confirmation for these views in the days that followed.

The early frontrunner among the most conservative GOP hopefuls was Texas Senator Phil Gramm, who saw the 1994 congressional elections as the most dramatic since 1932. This time their message was "to stop the taxing, stop the spending and stop the regulating" that the 1932 New Deal victories had introduced. Then in an assertion that was one part truism and one part a peculiar reworking of the past to which he had just alluded, he said that he was running for president "because I believe that if we don't change the policy of our government, if we don't change it soon, if we don't change it dramatically, in twenty years we're not going to be living in the same country we grew up in." As the basis for decision-making in the new Republican era, he offered the Dickie Flatt test, named for a hard-working printshop owner in Mexia, Texas. "As president," he said

> I will look at every federal program, think about the millions of people like Dickie Flatt who work hard for a living, and ask a simple question: will the benefits to be derived from spending money on this program be worth taking money from the Dickie Flatts of America to pay for it? And let me tell you something: There are not a lot of programs that will stand up to that test. (*New York Times*, 2/26/95)

Senator Dole, promoted to Senate Majority Leader by the 1994 election, gained the most visibility of all the announcing Republicans as a result of the GOP sweep, and yet in a campaign against old leadership he was the most entrenched of Washingtonians, having served in Congress since 1961. Born in 1923, he was also older than his opponents, older even than former President George Bush. In announcing his 1996 candidacy he offered a blend of the old and the new. Once more he returned to Kansas to enter the race (this time beginning in Topeka), and once more he stressed his connection with small-town values and his World War II experience. At the same time, he agreed to an agenda much like that promised by his opponents, vowing to rid the nation of "ineffective, burdensome, meddlesome" federal departments, starting with Education, Housing and Urban Development, Energy, and Commerce. He pledged to get rid of the Endowments for the Arts and Humanities ("Why is the federal government in the culture business?") and the Corporation for Public Broadcasting, and to yield to the states welfare and as much else as possible.

But the most telling part of Dole's presentation of his candidacy was, in fact, his appeal to experience, his underlying suggestion that America needed once more to be led by someone shaped by World War II. Just as he began by recalling his wartime experience, so at the end he returned, literally, as he described the fiftieth anniversary ceremonies in France and his return to North Italy where he had been wounded. In these memory-filled places, he recalled,

> I thought about why we had been sent there, about the America of our youth, the America we were risking our lives to protect, and about our hopes for the generations who would follow us. And then I thought about the America we live in now—still great and still the beacon of freedom around the world, but an America that is headed in the wrong direction.

In a campaign where "experience" was often regarded with suspicion, Dole concluded by insisting that this was necessary for the leadership America desperately required, and in a campaign in which his age would surely be an issue, he implied that only those of his generation, those who had served in the last great war, represented that experience. "I thought of why," he concluded,

> it is critical to have a president who knows what made America great, who knows what has been sacrificed to keep us free and who would do all in his power to lead America back to her place in the sun.

This is knowledge, given its special source, that none of his opponents or the incumbent president could claim, ironically, because of their relative youth. Dole emphasized the point, saying, "I have the experience. I've been tested in many ways. I am not afraid to lead and I know the way" (*New York Times*, 4/11/95).

UP TO THE JOB

Once would-be presidents overcame the traditional reluctance to declare themselves—once "modesty" had become less important than a quick start for a long campaign—candidates were forced to represent their self-promotion as somehow in the spirit of the office they sought. They now make little pretense that they enter the race at the insistence of others and instead offer themselves on the basis of self-knowledge and patriotic commitment. The wisdom that calls them out belongs to neither a proud state nor a national movement among concerned citizens. It is their own, as they claim to identify a public need that they, more than any of their contemporaries, can satisfy. And they do not altogether conceal their pride and ambition. Boasting their success in other work, they declare themselves up to this most demanding job. Thus John Kennedy, aware of how important it is for Americans to think themselves winners, proclaimed himself one too.

"Seeking" is no longer inherently "unseemly." The assumption of late-twentieth-century politics, one planted by the two Roosevelts, is that presidential boldness and presidential frankness and presidential ambition all reflect the unabashed attitudes of a bold, frank, and ambitious people. That is not to deny that all three must be moderately asserted, and ambition in particular remains problematic. If we no longer expect to discover Cincinnatus on our presidential ballot, neither do we want Napoleon. Candidates can seem too hungry for the position, too willing to cut their principles and policies to match the prevailing fashion—a suspicion that in recent years has damaged both Bush and Clinton. Acceptable ambition must appear principled. While it is no longer necessary to pretend that the leader is anything other than a reflection of the people he leads, it remains important that his version of us be deserving. If it remains unsettling for presidential hopefuls to nominate themselves, there is at least a poetic justification for calling as the first witness the candidate's "self." But to be effective the self presented must be more than an individual ego; it must be a "union" of family and community and professional experience, the "many" of which the person is composed.

Chapter Three

A Party's Choice

Accepting the Nomination

> . . . one topic would dominate all the rest. That topic is the
> future.
> —Dwight Eisenhower, 1956 Acceptance Speech

> We make history tonight, not for ourselves but for the ages.
> —Richard Nixon, 1968 Acceptance Speech

> Together, let us make this new beginning.
> —Ronald Reagan, 1980 Acceptance Speech

In 1932 Franklin Roosevelt began a new tradition in presidential politics. He appeared before the convention that had just chosen him as its standard-bearer and accepted the nomination. Previously nominators and their nominees had been kept apart like the nuptial pair before a wedding—in the political instance, as in the marital one, to project an aura of innocence around the bride. But following the radio broadcast of his convention triumph, Roosevelt flew from Albany to Chicago to deliver his formal acceptance in person. He began his address by observing:

The appearance before a National Convention of its nominee for President, to be formally notified of his selection, is unprecedented and unusual, but these are unprecedented and unusual times. I have started out

71

on the tasks that lie ahead by breaking the absurd tradition that the candidate should remain in professed ignorance of what has happened for weeks until he is formally notified of that event many weeks later.

This appearance marked a radical departure from nineteenth-century custom but was consistent with a decline of party and the rise of personality in presidential contests, a change served by the progressive reforms of the 1910s.

The essential work of a convention, in addition to drafting the party's platform, is to nominate presidential and vice presidential candidates and to reconcile rival factions to that ticket. Throughout the nineteenth century the double task fell almost wholly on party leaders, the bosses and chairs who oiled the state and local machines. The nominee remained as distant and aloof as possible. In the twentieth century, candidates became the contending parties, personalizing the conflict and thus making it necessary for the victor to take more direct responsibility for uniting and marshaling their parties.[1] Consequently, since FDR's break with tradition the acceptance speech has become an essential event in our national politics. Unlike the announcement message, it became *immediately* important and has been broadcast, printed, and scrutinized ever since its 1932 introduction.[2]

No matter how much outside attention focuses on the speaker, however, this is a speech that must focus on the audience, most especially on the party faithful. To serve the candidate it must serve the system, must tell his partisan colleagues who they are as Republicans or Democrats and what work their principles call them to perform in the present context. Even when, as in recent years, the address emphasizes personal biography, the details of that life must provide clear points of connection with the audience and must somehow encode the ideals and aspirations of the party. And the message, despite the distance it suggests we've traveled on the path from reluctance to ambition, must suggest a "seemly" humility, it must still be a message of "acceptance" rather than personal victory.

SPECIAL DELIVERY AND THE PARLOR RECEPTION

While the announcement message is almost wholly rooted in the primaries of the twentieth century, the acceptance grew from the emergence of nominating conventions in the 1800s. Andrew Jackson was the first president so nominated. But at the time (1832) he was already in the White House and firmly in control of his party. He simply assumed rather than accepted the nomination. Four years later, however, the party's nominee was neither so powerful nor so popular. Jackson's hand-picked successor was his vice president, Martin Van Buren, and in May 1835 (more than a year prior to the election) the party faithful, still very much under Old Hickory's command, confirmed his choice. What fol-lowed was a ritual that continued essentially unchanged through the end of the century, a formal betrothal ceremony in which the convention ten-dered its proposal and the candidate accepted, but far removed from the raucous and often promiscuous proceedings of nomination.

Van Buren received his official notification in a letter from the "Vice Presidents of the National Convention," who informed him: "We have been requested to communicate to you this nomination, and ask your ac-ceptance of the same. We take pleasure in performing this duty and re-spectfully solicit an answer at such time as may suit your convenience to give one." Within the week Van Buren had composed his reply: a pledge "to tread generally in the footsteps of President Jackson" and "to defend the Constitution and the national union," but he also included a convo-luted protest against charges that he had too zealously pursued the posi-tion. No man, he insisted, "can truly say, that I have solicited his political support, or that I have entered or sought to enter with him into any arrangement, to bring about the nomination which I have now received, or to secure my elevation to the Chief Magistracy of my country."[3]

Van Buren, like those pre–World War II candidates described in the pre-vious chapter, believed that actively seeking the office would be perceived by his countrymen not only as unseemly but as evidence of a dangerous ambi-tion. The energy with which he defended himself, even after the nomina-tion had been won, suggests how powerful he assumed the Cincinnatus par-adigm to be. Clearly what FDR would dismiss as an "absurd tradition" in 1932 was for nineteenth-century candidates an essential practice. James Polk asserted in his 1844 note of acceptance: "It has been well observed that the office of President of the United States should neither be sought nor de-clined." As evidence of his own qualification, he continued, "I have never sought it, nor shall I feel at liberty to decline it, if conferred upon me by the voluntary suffrage of my Fellow Citizens."[4] This refrain was regularly repeated by other pre–Civil War nominees. Typical was Buchanan's 1856 insistence: "Deeply sensible of the vast and varied responsibility attached to the station, especially at the present crisis of our affairs, I have carefully refrained from seeking the nomination either by word or deed."[5]

Convention leaders learned in 1848 the danger of depending upon the mail for notifying their nominees; their postageless letter languished among the dead letters for several days. While it was not uncommon at the time for the recipient to pay postage, Zachary Taylor, still basking in the national limelight as the hero of the Mexican War, was receiving so much mail that he had instructed his postmaster to deliver only prepaid letters.[6] Subsequently it became the custom not only to provide the stamp but to hand-deliver the message through a committee of convention delegates who traveled to offer the party's proposal in person. In 1860 Abraham Lincoln received such a delegation. He, of course, already knew of the convention's decision, having been immediately telegraphed the outcome by supporters on the scene, but the official word was delivered in person by the convention president and the chairs of the state delegations, a group sufficiently small to fit into the north parlor of Lincoln's Springfield home. The nominee received their message, then noted how "deeply and even painfully sensible of the great responsibility" he was and added that he could "almost wish" it had "fallen upon some one of the few more eminent men and experienced statesmen whose names were before the convention" (*New York Times*, 5/22/1860). He was not the first to plead inadequacy. Washington expressed similar fears in his first inaugural address, and Zachary Taylor, when he finally received his mail, wrote of his "sincere distrust of my fitness to fulfill the duties of an office which demands for its exercise the most exalted abilities and patriotism, and which has been rendered illustrious by the greatest names in our history."[7]

Ulysses Grant offered little in the way of self-deprecation or reluctance. Although virtually unopposed for the Republican nomination in 1868, he had no formal remarks prepared when the delegation arrived to deliver the party's message but promised "in a very short time to write . . . a letter accepting the trust you have conferred upon me."[8] The delay, he suggested, was to allow a careful reading of the party platform and the preparation of "some statement of views beyond the mere acceptance of the nomination." But Grant enlarged upon his preliminary remarks only to a length of seven sentences, written in a single sitting on the morning after his meeting with the announcement committee:

The proceedings of the Convention were marked with wisdom, moderation, and patriotism, and I believe, express the feelings of the great mass
of those who sustained the country through its recent trials. I indorse
[sic] their resolutions. If elected to the office of President of the United
States, it will be my endeavor to administer all the laws in good faith,
with economy, and with the view of giving peace, quiet and protection
everywhere. In times like the present, it is impossible, or at least eminently improper, to lay down a policy to be adhered to, right or wrong
through an administration of four years. New political issues, not foreseen, are constantly arising, the views of the public on old ones are constantly changing, and a purely administrative officer should always be left
free to execute the will of the people. I always have respected that will,
and always shall. Peace, and universal prosperity—its sequence—with
economy of administration, will lighten the burden of taxation, while it
constantly reduces the national debt. Let us have peace. (2:1274)*

As readers of his memoirs are aware, Grant, a master of eloquent, clear,
and direct writing was given neither to embellishment nor to wordiness.
"Moderation" and "economy," along with "peace," were the key words in
his message of acceptance and accurately characterized both the general's
politics and his rhetoric.

If there were in his remarks no protestations of personal inadequacy,
none of Lincoln's awe for the office, not even a sense of history, it is because Grant belonged more clearly to a Jacksonian tradition and was a
"small d" democrat, inclined to demystify leadership and make it a matter of common sense rather than genius. In accepting his party's standard, he declared his service not to narrow ideology, but to the will of the
people, which he suggested is neither hard to discern nor difficult to follow. In short, he saw nothing particularly daunting in the challenge.

Given his role in preserving the Union and the great popularity he enjoyed throughout the victorious North, it is hardly surprising that Grant
offered no deference to "more eminent and experienced statesmen." Nor
is it difficult to imagine that in the wake of Andrew Johnson's angry oratory and the often wild extravagance of Johnson's congressional opponents

---

*See Schlesinger, ed., *History of American Presidential Elections*. All subsequent page references in
this chapter, except where noted, are to this source.

that Grant's refusal to inflate either message or emotion would have seemed a welcome respite to his countrymen, a lull after the storm. Appropriately, "let us have peace," a line Grant added as an afterthought when he signed his acceptance, became the simple theme of his campaign, a postwar corollary of "let us have Union" and an introduction to the great presidential theme of the next century.

The ceremonies in which Lincoln and Grant received their party's highest honor were simple and plain, but they were ceremonies nonetheless, political rituals that were part Cincinnatus (the nomination coming to them rather than the reverse) and part public performance. In subsequent years that latter dimension grew, and the occasions became much more elaborate and formal. The ceremony accompanying the 1888 renomination of President Grover Cleveland, for example, was carefully staged and, according to a *New York Times* reporter much taken with it all, presented "a simple but impressive scene, long to be remembered by those who took part in it." The committee "met at the Arlington Hotel in the forenoon, and each member signed the letter of notification written by the Hon. Charles D. Jacob of Kentucky. At 2 o'clock the committee met again at the hotel and marched in couples to the executive mansion." There the procession filed into the East Room and waited "in a large horseshoe" as the presidential party entered. When all had taken their places the convention chair stepped forward to present the chairman of the notification committee. Dressed in their "close-fitting, tightly-buttoned Prince Albert coats," the party resembled either a formal wedding or a relatively casual coronation. The chair read the committee's brief message with a stiffness that prevailed throughout:

> SIR: The delegates to the National Democratic Convention, representing every State and Territory of our Union, having assembled in the city of St. Louis on June 5 inst., for the purpose of nominating candidates for the offices of President and Vice-President of the United States, it has become the honorable and pleasing duty of this committee to formally announce to you that without a ballot you were by acclamation chosen as the standard bearer of the Democratic Party for the Chief Executive of this country at the election to be held in November next.

He then presented Cleveland with the party's platform, and the nominee responded with remarks equally stylized and solemn:

I cannot but be profoundly impressed when I see about me the messengers of the national Democracy, bearing its summons to duty. The political party to which I owe allegiance both honors and commands me. It places in my hand the proud standard and bids me bear it high at the front in a battle which it wages bravely because conscious of right, confidently because its trust is in the people, and soberly because it comprehends the obligations which success imposes. (*New York Times*, 6/27/1888)

The officious presentation to Cleveland—made more so perhaps because it took place in the White House—no doubt reflects the tendency of ceremonies of any sort to become, with time, increasingly formal and ritualized, but it also demonstrates the inherent tension in being a candidate and still appearing presidential. The elaborate effort to separate the office and the nominee from the conflict and festivity of a national convention and the use of emissaries charged with carrying the nomination from the blatantly political context to the home of the chosen suggest a continuing concern to deny ambition and to pretend to a Washingtonian ambivalence. No matter how prolonged or contentious the nominating battle, the notification ceremony remained subdued and correct, an investiture untouched by the machinations of partisan politics. And since, prior to the late nineteenth century, nearly all nominees avoided the appearance of campaigning, the ritual observed with Grover Cleveland suggests America's undiminished need to separate its highest elective position from all others, to conceal beneath tight-buttoned Prince Albert coats the nature of the nomination process and the ferocious ambition that drives every successful contestant. The political realities of faction and special interest inherent in the democratic system were played out at the national convention, but they immediately yielded to America's romantic longings for a leadership that transcended such narrow concerns.

SETTING THE AGENDA

The turn-of-the-century candidates, William Jennings Bryan and Theodore Roosevelt, usurped the party's dominant role, openly courting the presidential prize and campaigning vigorously once the nomination was won. In preparation for their vote-seeking, they grew more aggressive in acceptance and exploited their messages to advance detailed political agendas. In 1904 President Theodore Roosevelt, though he dutifully awaited the appearance of the convention's messengers at his Oyster Bay home, went far beyond the brief acknowledgments typical of the previous century's candidates and plunged directly into the campaign with his reply. Instead of humbly answering the summons of his party, he took command and, in remarks that run to nearly fifty pages, instructed his fellow Republicans on how the coming contest should be approached. In this matter, as in so many others, the first Roosevelt pushed the presidency toward its modern construction.[9]

In contrast to Grant, Roosevelt was rarely moderate in either manner or style, and on occasion he wrote an exceedingly affected and overwrought prose. But he could be a master at clear and persuasive speaking of his own particular sort, and his acceptance letter shows him at his best. Although it continued the formal tradition of communicating with the party from a distance, it resembled Franklin Roosevelt's more radical approach twenty-eight years later in breaking through ceremony and coming directly to points of contention. In so doing it asserted the candidate's position as party leader rather than its servant. Whereas President Cleveland modestly accepted his party's wisdom as he received its nomination, Roosevelt instructed the Republicans who nominated him to be sure they accurately represented his opinions in the coming campaign.

Already in office after inheriting the presidency from the assassinated McKinley, Roosevelt urged the country ahead to complete the work begun during his first years in office. His message focused on matters of parties and policies, issues that he presented as a series of Democratic charges followed by the appropriate Republican rebuttal. Of foreign policy he asked, to what do the Democrats object? "Do they object to the way in which the Monroe Doctrine has been strengthened and upheld?" "Do our opponents object to what was done in reference to the petition of American citizens against the Kishineff massacre?" "Do our opponents object to the fact that the international tribunal at the Hague was rescued from impotence . . . ?" "Do our opponents object to the settlement of the Alaska boundary line?" With each question, followed by a terse response, Roosevelt not only implied that the Democrats stood against popular sentiment on those emotionally charged issues but also presented his own activist record on behalf of such "righteous" causes.

Throughout his letter he repeatedly insisted that the basic questions were simple and the answers apparent. Even when he acknowledged a complication, he found ways to make that matter seem easy, too. Thus, in the area of foreign policy, where increasing evidence of America's imperialistic designs had aroused criticism, he fixed on a single aspect of the complaint. "Alarm has been professed," he wrote, "lest the Filipinos should not receive all the benefits guaranteed to our people at home by the Fourteenth Amendment to the Constitution." After simply asserting that such was not the case, he moved to the domestic front for a counterattack, signaled by the phrase "guaranteed to our people at home." "This government has been true to the spirit of the Fourteenth Amendment in the Philippines. Can our opponents deny that here at home the principles of the Fourteenth and Fifteenth Amendments have been in effect nullified?" Insisting that Democrats had been overly accommodating in gathering their electoral support, Roosevelt turned the Philippines charge against them by exposing their own complicity in a Jim Crow South and blocked their effort to occupy the moral high ground.

Roosevelt himself laid claim to the path of principle and grandly proclaimed, "No other Administration in our history, no other Government in the world, has more consistently stood for the broadest spirit of brotherhood in our common humanity, or has held a more resolute attitude of protest against every wrong that outraged the civilization of the age at home or abroad." That assertion lay at the heart of his vision of the Republican party—the party of emancipation—as well as of his own administration. His most ringing phrases came when he described the uncompromising commitment to justice that he insisted must be the basis of all responsible politics, in labor and race relations or in foreign affairs. Repeatedly he declared his fundamental ideal of American government: "that each man, no matter what his occupation, his race, or his religious belief, is entitled to be treated on his worth as a man, and neither favored nor discriminated against because of any accident in his position."

This emphasis on equality (the "square deal") was, to some extent, standard Republican fare in the years after the Civil War, a reminder that the GOP had been born out of the antislavery movement and that the reemerging Democratic party had a history of moral accommodation on issues of race. Having first invoked the principle, Roosevelt admitted that "here at home there is painful difficulty in realizing this ideal," yet he went on to suggest that American failure in this area occurred at the state level, where Democrats exercised their greatest influence. With the federal government, where Republicans were in control, he insisted, "all that could be done has been done."

Roosevelt's 1904 acceptance letter marked a significant presidential transition not only because it took on substantial issues but also in the particular issues it addressed. Besides the domestic matters that had dominated America's past, the message acknowledged international concerns that loomed over the nation's future. It spoke of internal improvements in the West, the conflict over the gold standard, and pensions for Civil War veterans—old issues—but at the same time it argued that America must play an active moral role upon the world stage. From the moment that Washington warned his countrymen against foreign entanglements, presidents had been inclined to keep their distance from the rest of the world in all but practical matters—discussing issues of trade or piracy or, when it was safe to do so, speaking out against European imperialism in the New World. For the most part America's moral business in the international arena was, it was thought, best served by example, proving by our own success the superiority of democratic institutions. But Roosevelt called his party and his country to advance actively the revolutionary principles of freedom and equality abroad. In this he anticipated the ambitious internationalism of Woodrow Wilson and the post–World War II presidents.[10]

Theodore Roosevelt did not cast himself as the international Lincoln, a role to which Wilson later aspired (both Roosevelts, but Teddy in particular, were little inclined to emulate Lincoln, apparently considering themselves too alive, confident, and progressive to play such a self-doubting, brooding role), but he did describe a national mission that was increasingly interventionist, in which America—part policeman and part mentor—aggressively reshaped the world in its own image. That mission would govern our conduct in the Philippines, for example, where by his accounting we were guiding a people he depicted as irresponsible and childlike through their political and cultural adolescence in a "great stride forward in spreading the principles of orderly liberty throughout the world." The goal of such intervention was both "civic righteousness and national greatness," the twin purposes Roosevelt served, which, in his view, were inseparable. In his confident morality—and morality of confidence—virtue was always rewarded.

There was in Roosevelt's 1904 acceptance—and throughout his career—a peculiar mixture of the romantic and the practical, the plain-speaking American leader who comes to the complexities of governance convinced that all problems are solvable, but who is simultaneously the servant of high purpose, a kind of knight errant championing a democratic chivalry. His letter to his party made no suggestion of personal inadequacy and did not offer humble words of gratitude; instead it began boldly: "I accept the nomination for the Presidency tendered me by the Republican National Convention, and cordially approve the platform adopted by it." It was the candidate's approval that was paramount, not the party's.

No matter how great the differences in personality and manner, Teddy Roosevelt greatly influenced Woodrow Wilson's presidency. The Democrat responded to his 1912 nomination with a message as carefully composed as Roosevelt's and wholly unlike Cleveland's stilted remarks. In it he took command of the campaign and offered directions to his party similar to those the Republicans received in 1904. The difference lay in his contrasting language and voice. Far more professorial in style and less combative in tone, Wilson's acceptance sounded more like an academic lecture than—as was nearly always the case with the exuberant Roosevelt—the exhortation of a team captain rallying his fellow players. While the latter's leadership appeared the result of a natural vigor, the former's seemed always the product of study, of disciplined thinking and patient scholarship. In both instances, those were accurate characterizations: Wilson belonged in the classroom and library, while Roosevelt was a sportsman, cowboy, general enthusiast. Those personal qualities were also what each man thought most pertinent to America.[11]

Wilson's professorial voice conveyed his brilliance, but it imposed a certain distance from his listeners. Roosevelt's removal, by contrast, arose from the bursts of enthusiasm with which he tended to leap ahead of his audience, too energetic and involved to remain behind with the rest of the country. He seemed always beckoning from somewhere up ahead, dropping back only to prod his national teammates to a faster pace; his was the distance superior energy generates. Wilson's was that of superior learning, and he moved at the steady, deliberate gait born of years in the classroom, aware that there are no shortcuts and that audiences must be carefully and deliberately tutored. Like Roosevelt, he too posed a series of questions as a part of his acceptance strategy, but they were not Teddy's taunting rhetorical interrogatives. Wilson's were genuine inquiries, tutoral exercises designed to simplify not by reduction but by dividing matters into manageable parts. "What is there to do?" he asked, then instructed, "There are two great things to do." His queries functioned like headings in a study outline, and the argument that followed was similarly divided so that his audience would always know where they were in the lesson.

While Teddy Roosevelt sounded a wake-up call for an audience caught in either slumber or lethargy, Wilson declared the country "awakened." America, he suggested, did not need a rousing voice so much as a reflective one, so before calling his countrymen to action he first called them to thought. Wary of simple answers, he used syntax, in contrast to Roosevelt's shorter, punchier lines, that was more complex, slowing to qualify and redirect. "Our difficulty is not that wicked and designing men have plotted against us," Wilson declared, "but that our common affairs have been determined upon too narrow a view, and by too private an initiative." Here Wilson introduced one of his great themes—the constricting tendencies of special interest—but he was also describing a general principle, and his rhetoric, like good teaching, worked to expand and elaborate rather than reduce. He therefore accepted the nomination not as a repudiation of Teddy Roosevelt but as a kind of counterpoise.

But Wilson also opened for his immediate audience of convention representatives the issue of his and their relationship to the *national* audience. "You will expect me in accepting the honor to speak very plainly the faith that is in me. You will expect me, in brief, to talk politics and open the campaign in words whose meaning no one need doubt. You will expect me," he said, "to speak to the country as well as to yourselves." "We cannot intelligently talk politics," he added, "unless we know to whom we are talking and in what circumstances." Wilson's analysis of that audience instructed party officials on the complicated relationship between the many and the one, as well as between leaders and electorate. "We are servants of the people, the whole people," he declared. Even while challenging those "cynics" who doubted such altruism, he continued his lesson in distinctions:

> They do not, or will not, comprehend the solemn thing that is in your thought. You know as well as they do that there are all sorts and conditions of men—the unthinking mixed with the wise, the reckless with the prudent, the unscrupulous with the fair and honest—and you know what they sometimes forget, that every class without exception affords a sample of the mixture, the learned and the fortunate no less than the uneducated and the struggling mass. But you see more than they do. You see that these multitudes of men, mixed of every kind and quality, constitute somehow an organic and noble whole, a single people, and that they have interests which no man can privately determine without their knowledge and counsel. That is the meaning of representative government itself. Representative government is nothing more or less than an effort to give voice to this great body through spokesmen chosen out of every grade and class. (3:2227–36)

Wilson's lesson was multilayered. At one level he was arguing for a politics that would reach beyond special interest—a point "cynics" doubted—conducted by idealists who "see more" than any single constituency. But his advocacy for the "mix" within the American audience went beyond an assertion of pluralism among groups, suggesting a pluralism *within* groups and, by extension, within individuals as well. Implicit in his treatment of the audience are two different notions of how government represents the double sense of "mixture." While the legislature gives actual voice to the country's various interests and "represents" them in the most obvious and narrow sense, the executive leadership represents the "noble whole." That larger conception of the "multitude," Wilson implied, was not just the sum of all parts but a "single people," an aspiration running through the entire population and existing side by side with narrower interests. In that way, despite the contrast between his eloquence and common speech, Wilson justified his own claim to being representative; his was the voice of the nobler and wiser ideals of his countrymen.

PROSPERITY AND A GOVERNMENT OF COMMON SENSE

By the time Wilson left office in 1921, America had taken a giant step into the twentieth century and the modern world. American forces had fought on European soil for the first time, in a war where national interests were less than clear. Government expenditures had soared in rising to this occasion, and so too had the scale and power of federal bureaucracy. Wilson's Republican successors repudiated both his administration and his last great cause, the League of Nations. They played on a fear of foreign entanglements and a longing for simpler times. Theirs was a nostalgic turning back, a rejection not only of Wilson but also of Teddy Roosevelt and the progressive notion of the presidency. First Warren Harding, then Calvin Coolidge, and finally Herbert Hoover each began their acceptance messages by assuring GOP leaders of their loyalty and their approval of traditional, pre-Roosevelt nominating procedures. Harding stated the case most forcefully as he promised a "restoration" following Wilson and Wilson's war. "Let me be understood clearly from the very beginning," he told the 1920 convention's representatives and the crowd that had joined them. "I believe in party sponsorship of government. I believe in party government as distinguished from personal government, individual, dictatorial, autocratic, or what not." The promise to return government to the party was also a pledge to reduce the importance of both the executive branch and the personality of its occupant. "No man," Harding continued, "is big enough to run this great Republic. . . . Tranquility, stability, and dependability—all are assured in party sponsorship" (*New York Times*, 7/23/20).

Neither Coolidge in 1924 nor Hoover in 1928 spoke quite so strongly on that issue, but both began their candidacies with similar sentiments. Greeting the committee that had brought official word of his nomination, Coolidge—in the first acceptance to be nationally broadcast— agreed that the traditional way of nomination was best. "That method," he asserted,

is not the outcome of chance. It is the product of experience. Very early in their search for a sound method of self-government the American people discovered that the only practical way to secure responsible political action was by the formation of parties, which they adopted because reason pronounced it the most promising and continued because practice found it the most successful. (*New York Times*, 8/15/24)

Both Harding and Coolidge viewed innovation with suspicion and pejoratively described Wilson's policies as "fanciful," "imaginary," and, most extraordinary, "visionary." It is not, Harding insisted, that Americans lack vision, but that we are a "common-sensical people," our "feet on the earth," an obvious contrast to his image of the high-minded Princeton professor he hoped to succeed. Foremost among the "fanciful" notions attacked by Republicans was the League of Nations, that "visionary form" of "world super government." This threat to America's autonomy, Harding argued, had been blocked by patriotic Republicans in the Senate, who "halted the barter of independent American eminence and influence which it was proposed to exchange for an obscure and unequal place in the merged government of the world." Thus was saved "the heritage of American nationality unimpaired and unsurrendered." Never, under his leadership (and here he found a theme his party would rediscover in the 1990s) would any "world council" be granted authority to "summon the sons of our Republic to war."

Declaring Republicans to be the champions of nationalism, Harding promised a return to America's nineteenth-century approach to the world at large, that of example rather than involvement.[12] "The Republic," he proclaimed, "can never be unmindful of its power and must never forget the force of its example." That could be accomplished only by remaining apart and disinterested. "[W]e mean," he proclaimed in the most telling line of his speech, "to be Americans first to all the world." That meant reentrenchment in international affairs, but it had domestic implications as well, and Harding suggested in the rest of his remarks what being "American first" might mean. Mostly he argued for a reversal of trends that had begun in the twentieth century. He reassured labor that he did not want salaries that had increased during the war to shrink back to earlier levels, but he warned "that mounting wages and decreased production can lead only to industrial and economic ruin." He followed a pledge of economic justice with the promise "to crush sedition, to stifle a menacing contempt for law" and vowed "to stamp out . . . peril" of the sort that "destroyed all freedom and made Russia impotent."[13] While claiming to support collective bargaining, he denied the right of negotiating groups to prevent the hiring of replacement labor. "Any American has the right to quit his employment; so has every American the right to seek employment." While Teddy Roosevelt had devoted much attention to management's responsibilities, Harding's instruction was directed solely to wage earners with the bottom line that "we hold the majesty of righteous government . . . to be our avoidance of chaos and we call every citizen of the Republic to hold fast to that which made us what we are, and we will have orderly government safeguard the onward march to all we ought to be."

Reaching back to a time before the administrations of his principle antagonists, Harding called for a return to the traditional values practiced by the Midwestern farmers who founded the GOP: "Let us call to all the people for thrift and economy, for denial and sacrifice if need be, for a nation-wide drive against extravagance and luxury, to a recommittal to simplicity of living, to the prudent and normal plan of life which is the health of the Republic."

The message was much the same four years later, when Calvin Coolidge received the nomination, but the personality and style were different. Already president since Harding's death the year before, Coolidge grappled less with the Democrats than with the scandalous legacy of Harding's administration (it had become apparent that "denial and sacrifice" were qualities most valued in others). This he met largely with a simple style that contrasted sharply with his predecessor's more convoluted and sometimes imperious oratory.[14] After reviewing Republican success in restoring economic stability, Coolidge turned to the issue of corruption. "In all my studies of political history," he reasoned,

> I cannot recall an Administration that was desirous of a dishonest and corrupt Government that, for the purpose of checking extravagance, ever undertook to introduce a budget system, to cut down taxes, to purge the payrolls, to make enormous reductions in the public debt, and to lay firmer foundations for the peace of the world.

By reducing expenditures most vulnerable to abuse and through overall budget reduction, Coolidge insisted, government was proving itself responsible. Economic discipline "is not the way of dishonesty," he insisted. "The government is sound. But individuals charged with wrongdoing are being prosecuted. The people of this country hate corruption. They know my position. They know the law will be enforced."

Coolidge, whose considerable rhetorical skill has been largely ignored in the general fascination with his legendary "silence," projected both openness and sincerity. On the side of protective tariffs, his defense was simply that he knew no other way "to prevent the lowering of the standards of pay and living for the American wage earner toward the misery scale that prevails abroad." Raising the subject of the restrictive immigration laws Congress had recently passed, he admitted, "I would have preferred to continue the policy of Japanese exclusion by some method less likely to offend the sensibilities of the Japanese people. I did what I could to minimize any harm that might arise. But that law has been passed and approved, and the incident is closed." Neither playing to the popular prejudice that created the law nor denying his complicity in it, he acknowledged both what had been done and his discomfort. Coolidge spoke to his radio audience in short, direct sentences that seemed correct but conventional, a part of his effort to emphasize the "ordinariness" and honesty of the president. While he avoided overly familiar and colloquial talk—there was a "Yankee reserve—he was equally careful never to sound grandiloquent or pretentious. He spoke in what was emerging as his century's version of a "middling style."[15] "The people know the difference between pretense and reality," he concluded. "They want to be told the truth. They want to be trusted. They want a chance to work out their own material and spiritual salvation. The people want a government of common sense."[16]

More than either of his predecessors, Herbert Hoover acknowledged that the world and America had changed by 1928 and that at least part of the change was for the better. He exemplified part of the difference by pointing out that his nomination had been hand-delivered after a trip of 3,000 miles (from Kansas City to San Francisco) accomplished in four days. "I am reminded," he went on, "that in order to notify George Washington of his election, Charles Thompson, Secretary of the Congress, spent seven days on horseback to deliver that important intelligence 230 miles from New York to Mount Vernon." He noted, too, that millions had heard "by the magic of the radio" about his nomination and were now listening as he accepted. "We stand," he observed, "in their unseen presence."

In contrast to Harding and Coolidge, Hoover, the former engineer, celebrated progress. Instead of speaking for the virtues of austerity, he spoke approvingly of growing expectations. "Our workers," he boasted, "with their average weekly wages can today buy two and often three times more bread and butter than any wage earner of Europe. At one time we demanded for our workers a 'full dinner pail.' We have now gone far beyond that conception. Today we demand larger comfort and greater participation in life and leisure." Then, in the worst-timed prophecy in presidential history, he declared his grandest aspiration:

> One of the oldest and perhaps the noblest of human aspirations has been the abolition of poverty. . . . We in America today are nearer to the final triumph over poverty than ever before in the history of any land. The poorhouse is vanishing from among us. We have not yet reached the goal, but given a chance to go forward with the policies of the last eight years, and we shall soon, with the help of God, be in sight of the day when poverty will be banished from this nation.

One "innovation" that both Harding and Coolidge applauded also played an important role in Hoover's acceptance. "The womanhood of America," Harding had intoned in 1920, "always its glory, its inspiration, and the potent, uplifting force in its social and spiritual development, is about to be enfranchised."[17] Those new voters he then recommended on two counts: the fact that they were American-born and -educated and, therefore, carriers of traditional national values, and the expectation that they would bring the moral superiority of their sex into the political arena. Coolidge expressed similar sentiments, welcoming the guardians of the home and protectors of childhood into national service "as a great instrument of mercy and a mighty agency of peace." Hoover, similarly anticipating women's "keener" insight into the moral and spiritual issues facing the country, went much farther than his predecessors and recognized the presence of women in nearly every section of his speech. When his subject was the economy, he declared it every woman's right "to ask whether her life, her home, her man's job, her hopes, her happiness, will be better assured by the continuance of the Republican party in power." Discussing farm policy, he demanded for the farmer's wife "the same comforts in her home as women in other groups." In praising workers, he compared them favorably, "man for man and woman for woman," with their counterparts elsewhere. And in pledging his administration to equal opportunity, he promised to "hold open the door" to every girl as well as boy and thus to stimulate "endeavor" and "achievement" in women as well as men. Harding and Coolidge welcomed women to the electorate in the belief that they would prove a force for conservatism, but Hoover, whose own wife was an activist and a progressive, included them in discussions of social change and improvement.[18]

More forward-looking than either of his immediate predecessors and much more a product of twentieth-century experience and ambitions (he had headed the European relief effort after the war and was Secretary of Commerce under Coolidge), Hoover expressed a greater ambition for his countrymen as he accepted his party's nomination. Though careful not to separate himself from the prosperity America was enjoying and complimentary to the rectitude and fiscal responsibility of the popular Coolidge, he sometimes sounded more like his Democratic successor than the Republican he followed. Not only could he imagine the end of poverty, but he also advocated greater "equality of opportunity," declaring it the right "of every American—rich or poor, foreign or native-born, irrespective of faith or color," and argued that this was the only valid test of political policy or ideology. If Harding and Coolidge promised to undo the work of Roosevelt and Wilson and to take America back to what it had been, Hoover anticipated the themes that would dominate the future, and in domestic matters his announcement serves as a better bridge between the two Roosevelts than does even Wilson's. "Our purpose," he concluded, "is to build in this nation a human society, not an economic system. We wish to increase the efficiency and productivity of our country but its final purpose is happier homes" (*New York Times*, 8/12/28).

NATIONAL ACTION AND THE FIRST PERSON SINGULAR

In 1932 Franklin Roosevelt remarked not on the speed with which others—traveling by rail—had delivered his nomination, but rather on the lateness of his arrival at the convention, blaming his tardiness on "the winds of heaven" that had impeded his flight. Thus began the modern age of acceptance speeches. To a nation mired in depression, his gesture of coming to the convention signaled his readiness to act; to a world in which the rising tide of fascism challenged the very freedoms Wilson had championed, Roosevelt declared his faith in democratic institutions. The second Roosevelt not only acknowledged but boasted of his connection to the convention and the politics it embodied, and he dismissed the old reticence as a lie.

> My friends, may this be the symbol of my intention to be honest and to avoid all hypocrisy or sham, to avoid all silly shutting of the eyes to the truth in this campaign. You have nominated me and I know it, and I am here to thank you for the honor.
>
> Let it also be symbolic that in so doing I broke traditions. Let it be from now on the task of our party to break foolish traditions. We will break foolish traditions and leave it to the Republican leadership, far more skilled in that art, to break promises.

Far from a candidate humbled by the honor or the responsibility being offered to him, he presented himself as both confident and eager, indeed already "started out on the tasks that lie ahead." He did not hint at any reluctance. Instead he insisted that he knew precisely what needed to be done and was prepared to do it. Following the examples of Teddy Roosevelt and Wilson he did not defer to party but offered his own vision and energy to make his case.

The tone of Franklin Roosevelt's entire speech emphasized energetic leadership and no-nonsense, commonsensical action, a theme that would be carried through the campaign and would receive its most famous expression in his inaugural address. "This is," he said, "no time for fear, for reaction or for timidity." Neither was it a time to turn "toward the past," but rather an historical moment in which precedents must be broken, "absurd traditions" cast aside. By contrast the Republican leadership, faced with economic collapse, had become either "reactionary" or "inactive." From his opening words FDR projected his candidacy, in large things and in small, as direct and forward-looking. The first-person pronoun flew over his speech like a battle flag: "I have many things on which I want to make my position clear"; "I will leave no doubt." The "I" asserted confidence and boldness as he rallied, with his own conviction and vitality, a nation that had every reason to be dispirited and unsure.

Explicit in Franklin Roosevelt's 1932 message was the danger—at the height of a depression—of hesitation and self-doubt. Thus, while acknowledging catastrophic levels of unemployment, he immediately struck a positive note:

> Yes, I have a very definite program for providing employment. . . . I have done it, and I am doing it today in the state of New York. I know that the Democratic Party can do it successfully in the Nation. That will put men to work, and that is an example of the action that we are going to have.[19]

The simple declarative sentences, the repeated grammatical subjects, and the clipped, assertive delivery sound neither biblical nor Lincolnesque but rather like Mark Twain's Connecticut Yankee (another reformer who called his agenda a "new deal") battling the medieval ignorance of King Arthur's court.[20] FDR acknowledged no connection with the past. Instead he presented his candidacy as brash and new, freed from outmoded tradition. He displayed a good deal of Teddy's self-assurance, much of his energy and confidence, and yet FDR seemed more controlled and patient—almost as though the vigorous Teddy had been miraculously combined with the more meditative Wilson.

Near the close of his speech Roosevelt declared that what Americans wanted more than anything else was work and security, terms that paralleled his own agenda of "action" and "confidence." "Work and security," he declared, "—these are more than words." That telling phrase revealed a basic opposition running not only through his speech but through American culture generally, namely the opposition between the man of words and the man of action. In 1988 Vice President George Bush emphasized this theme, first in New Hampshire, when he seemed in danger of falling hopelessly behind Robert Dole, and again in his acceptance when he declared, after recounting his life's story in sentence fragments, "I may be, may not be the most eloquent, but I learned that, early on, that eloquence won't draw oil from the ground. And I may sometimes be a little awkward. But there's nothing self-conscious in my love of country."[21] Bush's implication was that eloquence and common sense were somehow incompatible, or that the absence of one provided evidence of the other. But FDR's assertion was more subtle and direct, since, in contrast to Bush, he had an already established reputation for eloquence and was generally admired as a man of words. For Roosevelt it was not eloquence but obfuscation that was suspect. Clarity in speech and purpose were subjects for Roosevelt's praise; the Democratic platform was, he claimed, "admirable" above all for being "clear," and he wanted his own words to be understood more than remembered. Artifice, no matter how hallowed by tradition, was part of the "hypocrisy and sham" he claimed to be attacking. "And you can "accept my pledge," he assured the convention, "that I will leave no doubt or ambiguity on where I stand on any question of moment in this campaign."

For a nation that most valued work and security but had found itself unemployed and uncertain, Roosevelt's character and his candidacy were calculated to inspire. But if his audience was to embrace his optimism, his rationale had also to be shared. That, Roosevelt insisted, was why he broke with tradition and set aside the exhausted conventions of political discourse—at least as practiced by the Republican leadership—in order to address issues directly and simply. "Out of all the tons of printed paper, out of all the hours of oratory, the recriminations, the defenses, the happy-thought plans in Washington and in every State, there emerges one great, simple, crystal-pure fact." And though the fact—that Republican policies on the tariff had wreaked havoc on the economy—was neither simple nor crystal-pure, the candidate made it seem that way, just as he made his own elaborate economic agenda appear commonsensical and easy to grasp. By suggesting that matters were simpler than despairing Americans had been led to believe, Roosevelt argued that the problems themselves were less intimidating. "Our Republican leaders," he said, "tell us economic laws—sacred, inviolable, unchangeable—cause panics which no one could prevent. But while they prate of economic laws, men and women are starving. We must lay hold of the fact that economic laws are not made by nature. They are made by human beings."

The Republican administration portrayed the depression as inevitable, the consequence of global economic forces beyond the control of any one nation and, as a result, a problem that must rectify itself. Roosevelt insisted it was a matter of "simple economics, the kind of economics that you and I and the average man and woman talk." In this vein he narrated the economic history of the past decade, describing it not as a mysterious process but as the predictable outcome when corporate managers squandered their surpluses in mindless speculation. Having rationalized the cause of the depression, Roosevelt could then insist that a program for recovery should follow commonsense principles of the sort well known to average citizens. This commonsensical basis would provide the foundation for the "new deal" he pledged for "the American people."

In contrast to the formal reverence of Cleveland's 1888 acceptance, Franklin Roosevelt's remarks were informal and relatively unadorned. Nowhere is this more evident than in his transitions. "I cannot take up all the problems today. I want to touch on a few that are vital"; "Just one word or two on taxes"; "And talking about setting an example"; "And now one word about unemployment"; "One more word about the farmer." Together with his tendency—shared with Teddy Roosevelt and Wilson—to ask and then answer questions, Roosevelt's artless shifts from point to point argued his commitment to clarity and openness. He presented himself as a self-assured leader but one whose confidence—as opposed to Wilson's and, ironically, more like that of Coolidge—came from common principles rather than privileged knowledge. In contrast to Wilson's professorial instruction, FDR directed his audience to trust their own wisdom and apply it to national as well as personal conduct. Where TR seemed intent on getting the nation up to his speed, and Wilson, up to his intellectual level, FDR was promising to bring the presidency up to where the people already were.

By appearing before the assembled convention, FDR lessened not only the distance between the presidency and the political process but also that separating the president from the American people. He demystified the office, approaching his audience on common ground rather than await it in an atmosphere of reverence. The voice he used was familiar, even jocular at times. He punned on the language of highly charged issues (after a brief aside calling for repeal of prohibition, he continued his remarks on the economy by saying, "To go back to this dry subject of finance") and threw sardonic barbs at the Republican opposition. The whole performance rested on Roosevelt's professed conviction that the general public could understand the most esoteric aspects of national governance and that the most desirable quality a presidential candidate could offer was everyday logic combined with common values. Throughout his remarks he suggested that a healthy irreverence was more to be trusted than debilitating awe or empty traditionalism.

FDR understood, even more than TR, the double-stranded nature of America's presidential politics. On the one hand we revere the Washington model of "special" leadership, special because divinely sanctioned and special by personal character, a political equivalent of the Romantics' "genius" (a favorite Wilson concept). On the other hand a democratized version of leadership requires a degree of shared identity—of the sort Coolidge enjoyed—between the president and the people. The obvious tension between those standards has sometimes been resolved, as with Lincoln, by presenting an uncommon man grown from common origins. Such a solution was hardly possible for either Roosevelt, but rather than trumpet his own special qualifications (as did Wilson and to a lesser extent TR), FDR insisted that he merely recognized and represented the genius and values of ordinary citizens.[22] In contrast to the reverential tendency of most nineteenth-century presidents and their emphasis on the president as a servant of Providence, FDR presented a chief executive who looked in the other direction for guidance. It is the people, he implied, and not God who determine America's future; it is the practical rather than the supernatural upon which the health of a democracy depends.

If Franklin Roosevelt spoke irreverently, it was consistent with his claim that he and his countrymen, through the application of common sense and ordinary virtue, were themselves capable of solving the nation's problems, just as in their day-to-day lives they met challenges similar in kind if not in scale. All this he argued with a logic appropriately simple and an unpretentious style. But he also understood the hunger, even in democracies, for the memorable phrase and the occasional sense of awe and destiny. "There is "a mysterious cycle in human events," he told the 1936 convention. "To some generations much is given. Of other generations much is expected. This generation of Americans has a rendezvous with destiny."[23]

In his address to the 1948 Democratic convention, Harry Truman took "commonness" farther than it had yet gone in the twentieth century. Brought into office three years earlier by FDR's death, Truman's standing in the polls had fallen to abysmal levels, the Dixiecrats had deserted to nominate their own presidential slate, and his party was in disarray. Truman presented his acceptance speech at a moment in which his candidacy was regarded by nearly everyone as hopeless. His response was not to justify himself but to attack the Republican congress, to taunt it, to dare it into a contest that could displace the race between nominees as the central activity of the campaign. In that way he took the combative spirit of Theodore Roosevelt, combined it with FDR's contempt for sham, and began his legendary "give 'em hell" crusade. With his small stature and spectacles, his mercantile background, and his identity as a middle American from Independence, Missouri, the impression he gave was that of a banty-rooster or a scrappy flyweight fighter. His speech was plain—though far less reserved than Coolidge's—often colloquial, and frequently biting and sarcastic ("Now listen to this one"). It was energized by anger, a righteous indignation directed at "special interests"— the Democratic theme of this century—that betray "the people." By refusing to be put on the defensive and by focusing on the shortcomings of Congress, the incumbent president presented himself as the underdog attacking privilege and wealth and the legislature that served them. His bold strategy of reversal owed much of its eventual success to sheer audacity (*New York Times*, 7/5/48).

In every aspect of his speech, Truman narrowed the distance between president and public more than anyone who had held the office before. Both Coolidge and FDR had emphasized clarity and had avoided obvious rhetorical embellishment, but they remained notably oratorical. Despite the relative plainness of their phrasing and the unpretentiousness of their language, neither allowed his talk to become truly common; with Coolidge there was always restraint, and with Roosevelt always eloquence. But Truman voiced everyday indignation in the cadences of everyday speech. "And I'll say to labor just what I said to the farmers. They are the most ungrateful people in the world if they pass the Democratic party by this year." "Now everybody likes to have a little surplus." "The first one of these tax bills they sent me was so rotten that they couldn't even stomach it themselves." "I wonder if they think they can fool the people of the United States with such poppycock as that?" Such talk—and it conveys the clear sense of "talk" rather than "oratory"—is that of an indignant small-town Midwesterner. It resonates with the vernacular, and its genius lies in the fact that it never sounds extraordinary, never sounds like any more than what regular folks might say among themselves, and in very nearly the same words.

When FDR drew his audience closer to him, it was an effort all the more apparent—and appreciated—because of the actual distance that separated them. An American aristocrat by virtue of education and wealth, his congenial regard for listeners and his respect for their intelligence was the more significant precisely because he was in so many ways *not* one of them at all. But Truman was. He did not merely accept them; he seemed to *be* them in thought, expression, and temperament. In 1932 Roosevelt's confidence set him apart as the bringer of hope to a broken nation, a confidence lacking in the people he sought to lead but desperately needed if they were to break free of their depression. That alone removed him from his audience as he beckoned them to advance toward him and toward recovery. They *needed* that distance, just as they needed to believe that the hope he offered was justified and that he was talking "straight" to them.

In 1948 Truman had been in office nearly an entire presidential term, and the final year of that term was being portrayed as the ineffectual winding down of twenty years of Democratic rule. He himself was being depicted as a little man unable to fill the large man's shoes. What he attempted in his acceptance speech (and what energized his campaign) was to take advantage of his "smallness" and to cross the gap between president and people. He accepted the GOP charge that he was nothing special and presented himself as a typical citizen voicing typical frustrations. That allowed him to direct attention away from the White House in which he sat and toward the Republican Congress. Truman's seemed less Wilson's symbolic voice of the country than its *actual* voice, and that voice tends—when it comes to politics—to be one of complaint.

SIMPLE HUMANITY AND THE AMERICAN "SPIRIT"

Because of his unprecedented tenure in office and his remarkable political success, Franklin Roosevelt influenced every post–World War II president's notion of audience and the eloquence appropriate to it.[24] Truman's more idiosyncratic rhetoric was nearly inimitable, but FDR provided an easily adaptable model. Jimmy Carter, running for office soon after the Vietnam War and the Watergate scandal, saw parallels between the malaise gripping America in the 1970s and the effects of the greater depression FDR had addressed. Carter also promised progress ("There is a fear that our best years are behind us, but I say to you that our nation's best is still ahead"), built on "the sound judgment and good common sense and the high moral character of the American people." And like Roosevelt he blamed America's predicament on the "powerful" who "always manage to discover and occupy niches of special influence and privilege" and affirmed that "[o]ur nation should always derive its character directly from the people."[25]

Since Americans doubted not their leaders' ability to act but the integrity with which they conducted themselves, the challenge in 1976 was one of trust rather than of confidence. In its Machiavellian maneuvers the Nixon administration, Carter argued, had lied and concealed, and so he promised truth ("we *just* want the truth again!") and openness ("It's time for us to take a new look at our government, to strip away the secrecy"). In contrast to Nixon, the Democratic nominee presented himself as committed to disclosure and to turning government away from "scandal and corruption and official cynicism."

Though much was borrowed from Roosevelt—the same basic problems, the same sorts of answers, the same villains—Carter's style was more akin to Coolidge's. Entering a political arena permeated by mistrust and cynicism, Carter presented himself as a relatively simple man, defined by his religious beliefs and a kind of political innocence that in a different time would have been unappealing. Even his rather homely appearance and the folksy Georgia drawl that would, four years later, contrast so strongly with the polish of a former Hollywood actor suggested a lack of sophistication Americans found reassuring. His answers to present-day dilemmas were to be found in conventional wisdom. "Justice," for example, whether in regard to the powerful ("I see no reason why big shot crooks should go free and the poor ones go to jail") or as a legal recourse for victims of racial or sexual discrimination, should, he insisted, be defined by simple humanity rather than complicated logic. In what would be the strongest positive legacy of his administration, he extended that concern from the domestic to the international level, arguing that national security—peace—meant more than an absence of war, meant as well "the unceasing effort to preserve human rights." Carter referred to the human rights issue as a matter of common dignity and embraced it as a presidential obligation, and here he recalled Wilson (as a Sunday School teacher Carter was as used to moralizing as the Princeton history professor had been). In combining his populist appeal with the abstract responsibilities of high office, Carter moved away from his audience even as he attempted to explain himself to them, a problem neither FDR nor Reagan created for himself. He brought a moral zeal to his rhetoric that contrasted sharply with the easygoing religiosity Americans favor in their leadership, a sometimes overwhelming depth of sincerity that could make people uncomfortable in a way that Roosevelt's patriarchal concern or Reagan's breezy piety never did. At the time of his 1976 acceptance speech, however, it all served rather than hindered Carter's appeal to the electorate.

No Democrat, however, took the rhetorical model of Franklin Roosevelt more to heart than did that Republican and fervent anti–New Dealer Ronald Reagan. The precedent FDR had established was so compelling that forty-eight years after he broke tradition by addressing the nominating convention, his Republican protégé strained for a similar effect. The practice Roosevelt initiated in 1932 called for the nominee to appear before the delegates on the evening following his nomination to make an acceptance speech. The other business of that day is the selection of a running mate. In 1980 Reagan appeared in the convention hall shortly after midnight—but before the close of the session in which he had been nominated—to declare, personally, his choice for a vice president, and as he did he cast his action in Roosevelt's terms:

> I know that I am breaking with precedent to come here tonight and I assure you at this late hour I'm not going to give you my acceptance address tonight.
>
> But in watching at the hotel the television, and seeing the rumors that were going around and the gossip that was taking place here, I felt that it was necessary to break with tradition just as probably in this campaign we're going to break with tradition a lot of times.[26]

Just what subsequent attacks on precedent Reagan had in mind was neither clear nor particularly important (though he would assert the same the following night as well); what was striking was his eagerness to be seen as a Rooseveltian iconoclast, even while running as a conservative of the very sort Roosevelt had attacked.

Reagan was not the first Republican nominee to consider making an early entrance. Richard Nixon in 1960 had similar inclinations: "May I say that I have been wanting to come to this convention," he noted in his acceptance address, "but because of the protocol that makes it necessary that a candidate not attend the convention until the nominations are over, I have had to watch it on television." By abiding by tradition Nixon left it for Reagan twenty years later to mimic FDR and break this lesser precedent (4:3549).

In his actual acceptance, Reagan placed himself at an economic cross-roads equal to the one Roosevelt had confronted and pointed toward the "unprecedented calamity which has befallen us." "Never before in our history," Reagan continued,

> have Americans been called upon to face three grave threats to our very existence, any one of which could destroy us. We face a disintegrating economy, a weakened defense and an energy policy based on the sharing of scarcity.[27]

While hyperbole is typically stronger than historical reliability in convention remarks, Reagan stretched after crises sufficient in number and seriousness to equal those FDR had confronted in three-plus terms. He chastised the Carter administration on the same grounds that the Democrats had challenged Republican leadership in 1932: for living in a world of "make-believe, self-deceit—and above all—transparent hypocrisy." He offered as the Republican promise the old New Dealer's refrain, "We will simply apply to government the common sense we all use in our daily lives." Even Roosevelt's twin themes of work and security were echoed, although with a subtle change. "Work and family," in Reagan's version, "are at the center of our lives; the foundation of our dignity as a free people. When we deprive our people of what they have earned, or take away their jobs, we destroy their dignity and undermine their families."[28] Security, too, was a Reagan priority, but it was not based on protection from corporate greed and certainly not committed to an activist role for government in determining the "distribution of national wealth;" it was, rather, security against hostile foreign powers, "adversaries large and small [who] test our will and seek to confound our resolve," as well as security against insidious domestic forces dedicated to undermining "the family."

Like the New Deal Democrat, Reagan wanted to break with the past, to make "a new beginning," and yet he also struggled to look back ("renew" was most often used in place of FDR's "new"), introducing historical scenarios and quoting historical figures.[29] Reagan nearly always used quotation with a twist. Echoing the eighteenth-century radical Thomas Paine, he declared, "We have it in our power to begin the world

over again," but the 1980s application of this message was a nostalgic return of the sort Harding had promised. Quoting Lincoln's assurance that
"no administration by any extreme of wickedness or folly can seriously
injure the government in the short space of four years," Reagan then offered a correction: "If Mr. Lincoln could see what's happened in these last
three and a half years, he might hedge a little on that statement." And, at
greater length, Reagan quoted FDR's appeal for fiscally solvent government even as he mounted an effort to dismantle Roosevelt's social legacy.
How aware Reagan was of the ironic implications of his rhetorical strategies is hard to guess, though in most things he seemed a man lacking in
irony. Lincoln, after the terrible carnage of his own first term, might not
have been much impressed with the damage done by the Carter presidency, but that thought seems not to have occurred to either Reagan or
his writers. Irony, however, lay at the heart of Reagan's message as he
sought simultaneously to emulate Roosevelt and to undo his legacy.

FDR called for discipline, especially within the business and financial
arenas. After describing the enormous corporate profits produced in the
1920s and noting that very little "was taken by taxation to the beneficent
Government of those years," he asked:

> What was the result? Enormous corporate surpluses piled up—the most
> stupendous in history. Where, under the spell of delirious speculation,
> did those surpluses go?. . . . Why, they went chiefly in two directions:
> first, into new and unnecessary plants which now stand stark and idle;
> and second, into the call-money market of Wall Street.[30]

Reagan, in contrast, championed in his acceptance the same corporate
powers his rhetorical mentor had attacked and attributed the "stark and
idle" plants of his own day to the very regulations and taxes Roosevelt
initiated. It was government that was spendthrift, and business that, released from excessive regulation and taxes, would lead the country to
greater prosperity. Roosevelt declared the need for a progressive conservation policy; Reagan insisted that most conservation efforts were merely
"obstructionist," asserting, in a peculiar co-optation, that "we are going
to reaffirm that the economic prosperity of our people is a fundamental
part of our environment." The need, Reagan argued, was to turn away
from "trust me" government to "faith" in the free enterprise system that
"helped us master a continent." Roosevelt's warning against the excesses

of that system (and even of continental conquest) Reagan dismissed in his attack on excessive government and regulation.

Roosevelt declared: "Today we shall have come through a period of loose thinking, descending morals, an era of selfishness, among individual men and women and among Nations," sentiments that Reagan endorsed forty-eight years later. But Roosevelt continued, his promise to speak bluntly applying even to his listeners' complicity: "Blame not Governments alone for this. Blame ourselves in equal share. Let us be frank in acknowledgment of the truth that many amongst us have made obeisance to Mammon, that the profits of speculation, the easy road without toil, have lured us from the old barricades."[31] By contrast, in 1980 Reagan asserted that America's economic woes did not result from having "lived too well," and he absolved his countrymen of all guilt. Like Roosevelt he assured them that, "we have to move ahead, but we're not going to leave anyone behind," yet his promise assumed that only government was a villain, and that once freed from federal regulations all other parties would behave honorably and sensibly.[32] Reagan's ambiguous use of "we"—one moment all those outside of Washington, in the next, the incoming administration—represented a somewhat conflicted doctrine of gaining power in order to eliminate power, implying that with his election the distinction between the two "we's," like that between the past and the future, would disappear entirely. Government, instead of being a policeman, would be policed, and private interests would be liberated. Mammon in this scenario is not the devil New Dealers took him for, and speculation is an activity, at the very worst, benign. The public, Reagan argued, was best served by trusting rather than suspecting its material desires.

Reagan's attachment to Roosevelt seems to have been, as much as anything else, an admiration of will, of the confidence with which, in the later president's sentimentalized history, the earlier one reenergized a broken country. That his own diagnosis of social ills and economic forces diametrically opposed that of his predecessor mattered less to Reagan than sheer force of personality. If he tended to oversimplify Roosevelt's gifts, to reduce him to a sort of political Norman Vincent Peale, that was because he himself believed more in confidence than in ideology, understood character better than ideas. In contrast to Roosevelt's relatively detailed elaboration and defense of his political program, Reagan's acceptance agenda consisted of cutting taxes, deregulating the energy business, and increasing military spending. What he offered as analysis was vague and formulaic, largely because he conceived of issues in terms of determination rather than expertise. "We are going to put an end to the money merry-go-round"; "we are going to put an end to the notion that the American taxpayer exists to fund the government"; and "None of this will be based on any new form of monetary tinkering or fiscal sleight of hand. We will simply apply to government the common sense we all use in our daily lives."[33] The *how* that Roosevelt had to clarify for the public in 1932 was less pertinent in 1980 than simply the determination to act. During the Great Depression the president needed, or so Roosevelt thought, to convince people that the crisis could be solved with new policies, but he also believed that such conviction could grow only from an understanding of those policies and the logic behind them; in 1980 Reagan insisted the crisis of his own time would go away, not if new policies were instituted but if, in fact, "new" policies were abandoned and the country were allowed to do, individually and collectively, what came naturally.

Reagan aspired to Roosevelt's demystifying plain speaking, regularly employing colloquial language, contractions, and such folksy phrases as "they formed what they called a compact," "[Lincoln] might hedge a little on that statement," and "monetary tinkering." But he seemed also inclined toward something resembling reverence, not so much for the presidency as for the historical pageant surrounding that office. As a consequence, nostalgia and sentimentality played a role in his address that was virtually absent from FDR's speech, and always with a drift toward melodrama. References to "the American spirit"—"the spirit that burned with zeal in the hearts of millions of immigrants from every corner of the earth who came here in search of freedom," the spirit that the campaigning Reagan felt "all across the land; in the big cities, the small towns, and in rural America . . . ready to blaze into life if you and I are willing to do what has to be done"—like his emotional and idealized historical generalizations, tended toward an excessiveness Roosevelt attacked rather than indulged.

In Reagan's stretch to be both Roosevelt and a conservative, he staged one of the more peculiar moments in the history of acceptance speeches. Having brought his 1980 address to a perfectly conventional and appropriate closing line, he lingered and said, "I have thought of something that is not part of my speech and I'm worried over whether I should do it." Having titillated his audience with this hint of a break with tradition and propriety even more daring and spontaneous than his early arrival the night before, he then launched into what was clearly a composed and rehearsed description of God's covenant with America.

> Can we doubt that only a Divine Providence placed this land, this island of freedom, here as a refuge for all those people in the world who yearn to breath freely: Jews and Christians enduring persecution behind the Iron Curtain, the boat people of Southeast Asia, of Cuba and Haiti, the victims of drought and famine in Africa, the freedom fighters of Afghanistan and our own countrymen held in savage captivity.

On this emotional peak he returned to that worrisome something—not a part of his speech—that it had occurred to him to say. "I'll confess that I've been a little afraid to suggest what I'm going to suggest—I'm more afraid not to—that we begin our crusade joined together in a moment of silent prayer. God bless America."[34]

Even in the atmosphere of 1980s politics, a period enthusiastic for elaborate gestures of patriotism and popular religiosity, this confession seemed absurdly inflated—never mind that two conventions later it would be remembered by the religious right as an act of moral courage.[35] But its tone was deeply conflicted. Quite obviously scripted, Reagan's "spontaneous" act of piety was inappropriately coy, seemed to trivialize piety with its peculiar teasing manner. And of what was he afraid? What, here among his enthusiasts, was the cause of his worry? If this was a tongue-in-cheek attack on the ACLU, a spoofing of liberal objections to public prayer, then the praying itself would be facetious, a near blasphemous joke. If Reagan was being serious and sincerely thought of his call to prayer as an act of political daring, then he was revealing a naïveté and historical ignorance. The convention he was addressing, like every convention that preceded it, had heard public prayers almost beyond counting, and far from being unusual in calling for yet another, he was merely joining a long line of nominees who had moved their remarks to a prayerful close.[36] Just as Franklin Roosevelt opened his 1932 acceptance by declaring himself a breaker of empty traditions, a rejector of insincere gestures and political sham, so his 1980 admirer sought to close his own acceptance remarks. But Reagan's obliqueness in his conclusion contrasted with FDR's call for direct speaking, and his closing "innovation" was merely a repetition of a convention commonplace.

THE EXEMPLARY "I"

One of the most dramatic developments since 1950 has been an increasing emphasis on personal biography in all presidential politics, but especially in acceptance speeches. Predictably, given the move away from false modesty and self-deprecation, the candidate and the details of his life have grown increasingly prominent in acceptance remarks. As close as earlier candidates came to personal emphasis were Harding's observation that he spoke "as one who has counted the contents of the pay envelope from the viewpoint of the earner as well as the employer" and Hoover's claim to "having earned my living with my own hands."

Dwight D. Eisenhower began his acceptance speech by emphasizing his lack of political experience, noting that this was his first convention and reminding his audience that he had not gotten there by the usual path. He then congratulated them on choosing as his running mate Richard Nixon, a consummate politician (a point Nixon emphasized a short time later when he noted how hard the convention chairs were— "I've been in one because I've been a delegate") and with an exquisitely chosen infinitive and a completely straight face, praised his running mate's "ability to ferret out any kind of subversive influence wherever it may be found and the strength and persistence to get rid of it." Eisenhower's larger message, however, was built on personal military experience so well known that he could continually allude to it without being explicit. "Ladies and Gentlemen," he intoned with the same Cincinnatian language he had used during the primary season, "you have summoned me on behalf of millions of your fellow Americans to lead a great crusade—for freedom in America and freedom in the world." "I know something," he continued, "of the solemn responsibility of leading a crusade. I have led one" (*New York Times*, 7/12/52).

Eisenhower's own account of the war years was entitled *Crusade in Europe* (1948), and the message with which he had launched D-Day and the Allied invasion contained the declaration, "Soldiers, sailors, and airmen of the Allied Expeditionary forces! You are about to embark on the great crusade." His own reputation, then, added special significance and authority to his use of relatively conventional images of politics as battle (in contrast with the politics of "ferreting"), and he presented himself as a kind of righteous knight coming to the rescue of a people suffering "the bitter fruit of a party too long in power." Marshaling his forces, he called for "total victory" and insisted that the struggle for Republican success would be a "great battle," the campaign "a fighting road," and, he assured his followers, "In this fight I will keep nothing in reserve."

Most telling was the way Eisenhower explained his own approach to battle and the model of leadership it provided. "Before this," he assured the convention, "I have stood on the eve of battle. Before every attack it has always been my practice to seek out our men in their camps and on the roads and talk with them face to face about their concerns and discuss with them the great mission to which we were all committed." Even as he promised some analogous approach to political campaigning and national governance, he comforted Americans with his version of the great leader mingling with his troops, paternal in his reassurance and authoritative in his instruction, calling to mind Shakespeare's Henry V and a host of movie commanders.

The party Eisenhower addressed in 1952 had been out of power for twenty years and had managed four years earlier to lose the first post-Roosevelt election, despite being heavily favored. To that body the newly retired general promised leadership that would bring victory. To the country at large, listening and now watching in unprecedented numbers, Eisenhower offered the military and international experience it needed both to disentangle itself from the Korean conflict and to respond to the challenges of the "Cold War" and the nuclear age. Accepting his party's nomination the Republican candidate, above all, presented himself as a father figure, agreeing to shepherd his country as he had once shepherded America's troops, and he closed with an image that recalled his military past. As the nominee, he promised to end each day

> thinking of millions of American homes, large and small; of fathers and mothers working and sacrificing to make sure that their children are well cared for, free from fear; full of good hope for the future, proud citizens of a country that will stand among the nations as the leader of a prosperous world.

Picturing himself circulating among civilian neighborhoods as he had once moved among military campfires, Eisenhower saw his job as unchanged: to give comfort and reassurance and to protect his "family" from a hostile world. Appropriately he concluded with a call to prayer, not in the manner of Reagan's defiant religiosity, but in a pastoral tone of humility and dedication, an appeal for blessing and guidance. In all of this he stepped away from FDR's model and stressed the difference between himself and his audience. Like Wilson he acknowledged a superior position, but his, unlike the academic's, carried a victorious general's authority.

Eisenhower's successor, John Kennedy, had no choice but to confront biography, and he began his acceptance speech by addressing the most obvious characteristic separating him from a sizable portion of the Democratic constituency, his Catholicism. "I am fully aware of the fact," he told the 1960 convention, "that the Democratic party, by nominating someone of my faith, has taken on what many regard as a new and hazardous risk—new at least since 1928." Having directly raised the religious issue, Kennedy just as directly affirmed his commitment to the separation of church and state. "I am telling you now what you are entitled to know: That my decisions on every public policy will be my own—as an American, a Democrat, and a free man." Later in his remarks he made the biblical injunction "Be strong and of good courage" his own, and in his conclusion he drew a homiletic application of a text from Isaiah, as though, having addressed the issue of religious difference, he could now appeal to a biblical culture shared by Protestants and Catholics alike (*New York Times*, 7/16/60).

But there was a second matter that, according to the conventional wisdom, cast doubt on the viability of Kennedy's candidacy. Still only forty-three, he was considered by many too young and inexperienced for the presidency. In a sense his entire acceptance speech addressed this issue, both through its emphasis on change and in its own liveliness of thought and expression. The address was punctuated throughout by the words "change" and "new" as well as by a recurrent use of "old" as a pejorative term: "Today our concern must be with that future. For the world is changing. The old era is ending. The old ways will not do." A few paragraphs later he concluded, "but now this is a new generation," and a little farther on he expanded that notion and placed himself in relation to that reality, the "now" he had been describing, the "now" that was his principle subject:

> It is time, in short, for a new generation of leadership. All over the world, particularly in the newer nations, young men are coming to power. Men who are not bound by the traditions of the past, men who are not blinded by the old fears and hates and rivalries, young men who can cast off the old slogans and the old delusions.
>
> The Republican nominee, of course, is a young man. But his approach is as old as McKinley. His party is the party of the past, the party of memory. His speeches are generalities from Poor Richard's Almanac. Their platform, made up of old left-over Democratic planks, has the courage of our old convictions. Their pledge is to the status quo, and today there is no status quo.

Kennedy's rhetoric was a lively mix, full of reversals and intellectual play, all of which embodied "change" and the "new," in stark contrast to what even Eisenhower's most devoted followers conceded was a plodding tendency in the older president's talk.

As with Teddy Roosevelt (that other boyish Commander-in-Chief), Kennedy used rhetorical energy as part of his argument, evidence of a capacity for leadership based less on experience and age than on quickness and wit. There was, as well, learning displayed throughout the speech (references to English and American history, biblical references, and literary allusions), but none of it was delivered with Wilson's professorial tone. Rather, it was all made to seem at once playful and serious, making important points at the same time as it amused. Even the often quoted rhetorical figures of Kennedy's inaugural had their preview here, though with a lighter touch: "It sums up not what I intend to offer to the American people, but what I intend to ask of them." The play or wit at work in his words served both to entertain and to persuade; it presented an argument but did so in a manner that engaged more than just the audience's understanding. Even in his attacks on his opponents, the negative was undercut by humor so that the charges would seem less mean-spirited, an important strategy, since a mean spirit was precisely what he criticized in the Republican nominee. "We know that our opponents will invoke the name of Abraham Lincoln on behalf of their candidate," he told his audience, "despite the fact that his political career has often seemed to show charity towards none and malice for all."

When Kennedy's Republican opponent, Richard Nixon, responded at his own convention, he tended to confirm rather than refute the caricature Kennedy had sketched. Nixon's ponderous but simplistic style ("I have also been asked by my friends in the press, 'Mr. Vice President, where are you going to concentrate? What States are you going to visit?'") seemed laboring after clarity, as though he were struggling to be understood by a convocation suddenly stricken with senility—all the more so when contrasted with the sophisticated verbal wit of his Democratic opponent (4:3551). The implication was not merely that Kennedy was a younger man, but that he was addressing a younger audience (he called it at one point "the young in heart, regardless of age"), an impression that his Inaugural would confirm. At the same time, Nixon seemed intent on defending the old, not just the departing Eisenhower, but an entire generation of aging leadership. "It is true," he admitted,

> that youth does bring boldness and imagination and drive to leadership, and we need all those things. But I think most people will agree with me tonight when I say that President de Gaulle, Prime Minister MacMillan, and Chancellor Adenauer may not be young men—but we are indeed fortunate in that we have their wisdom and their experience and their courage on our side in the struggle for freedom today in the world. (4:3554)

Thus Nixon accepted Kennedy's characterization of the parties—one being of the past, the other of the future, one of memory and one of hope—in order to stay close to the powerful legacy of his predecessor. In doing so he conceded the powerful words, repeated so regularly by Democratic challengers—"new" and "change"—to his opponent, who was in this vocabulary justifying his biography as well as his political agenda.

Kennedy's address marks at least an interruption in the Roosevelt tradition of acceptance in that he, more than any other president since Wilson, made elaborate use of rhetorical tropes and figures, gave clearly composed, literary speeches rather than a more conversational address. The oratorical blandishments familiar to nineteenth-century audiences were frequent in his remarks, although they lacked the solemnity that had formerly accompanied them. He directed his oratory toward play rather than bombast. His acceptance speech was, in fact, a form of serious fun, his a campaign energized by excitement more than anger or indignation. Kennedy built upon a lesson learned from FDR, the value of undercutting stuffiness and official pretensions, but he did not reject the "artificial" techniques of an older rhetoric. Rather he employed those techniques after the fashion of poets and playwrights, turning them away from grandiloquence and toward wit and amusement. The result was not the biblical style perfected by Lincoln and sometimes pursued by Wilson and Adlai Stevenson, but instead a version of the classical style favored by many nineteenth-century orators and best represented in the Oval Office by John Quincy Adams.

Richard Nixon, perhaps even more than Kennedy, was a captive of his biography, though more for personal than for public reasons. He stressed his membership in the rank and file, but unlike Truman or Reagan seemed inclined to think of everyday people as something less than bright, a group to be talked down to like a second grade class. "Now I am sure that many of you in this hall and many of you watching on television, might well ask, 'But Mr. Nixon, don't our opponents favor just such goals as this?' And my answer is, 'Yes, of course.' All Americans regardless of party want a better life for our people" (4: 3552). Such remarks, typical of Nixon during his 1960 run for the presidency, sounded like neither a Roosevelt nor a Truman, but like Mr. Rogers calming a group of preschoolers. Although Reagan would address his audience simply and sometimes simplistically, he never seemed condescending, but Nixon often sounded patronizing; his approach to his audience was full of ambivalence and sometimes smacked of insincerity.

But his point of connection was his past, and he turned to that personal history whenever his career was at a crossroads. The problem in 1968 was recent history—a failed 1960 presidential bid, a subsequent loss in a gubernatorial contest, a televised exercise in self-pity that concluded, "you won't have Nixon to kick around any more"—and so he used his second acceptance speech to introduce a new version of himself, albeit one rooted in his earliest years. Although most of his speech, one in every way more effective than his 1960 effort, elaborated his vision of America (a nation that he, Eisenhower-like, promised to extricate from a messy Asian war) as it approached the millennium (the millennium looms large in this speech both as a quirk of the calendar and as a kind of cosmological benchmark), his remarks were also a reenvisioning of Nixon the man. After describing a child of poverty and despair in present-day America, Nixon continued:

> I see another child tonight. He hears a train go by. At night he dreams of faraway places where he'd like to go. It seems like an impossible dream. But he is helped on his journey through life. A father who had to go to work before he finished the sixth grade sacrificed everything so his sons could go to college.
>
> A gentle Quaker mother with a passionate concern for peace, quietly wept when he went to war but she understood why he had to go.
>
> A great teacher, a remarkable football coach, an inspirational minister encouraged him on his way. A courageous wife and loyal children stood by him in victory and also in defeat.
>
> And in his chosen profession of politics, first there was scores, then hundreds, then thousands, and finally millions who worked for his success.
>
> And tonight he stands before you, nominated for President of the United States of America.
>
> You can see why I believe so deeply in the American dream. (4:3840)

This was not identification with party but an explication of self, the introduction of an "I" that is emblematic of America's promise, a living proof of what one can become in this country. Nixon believed in America because it had nominated him for the presidency.

In 1988 George Bush continued the effort to tell who he was. Picking up where he had left off in his Houston announcement, he sketched the life of a postwar middle-class everyman:

> We moved to west Texas 40 years ago, 40 years ago this year. And the war was over, and we wanted to get out and make it on our own. And those were exciting days. We lived in a little shotgun house, one room for the three of us. Worked in the oil business, started my own.
>
> And in time we had six children. Moved from the shotgun house to a duplex apartment to a house. And lived the dream—high school football on Friday nights, Little League, neighborhood barbecue. (*New York Times*, 8/18/88)

Earlier he had mused, Reagan-like, "I wonder sometimes if we have forgotten who we are," and his response was a sort of TV sitcom answer to that question, one in which the "I" and the "we" are interchangeable. In this version of himself (and his countrymen) he insisted that the clichéd nature of his story be readily apparent in order to confirm his own "ordinariness" rather than draw attention to the extraordinary background that had actually produced him.[37]

By 1992 the transformation of the acceptance speech from a pledge of fidelity to party to an unveiling less of the candidate's ideas than of his life was so complete that the Democratic nominee, Bill Clinton, simply assumed, as did nearly every television commentator, that biography should be his primary concern. "Tonight I want to tell you, as plainly as I can, who I am, what I believe in, and where I want to lead America," he said. He continued with a description of his widowed mother's struggle to raise her family, of his shopkeeper grandfather who taught him by example to see beyond race and poverty in his relations with others, and of his wife, who instructed him on the needs of children. Like Nixon and Bush before him, he offered his life as a kind of American exemplum, a movie script and morality tale (*New York Times*, 7/17/92).

In contrast to Bush's 1988 emphasis on his experience as a business-man taking a family to a new state, or even Dukakis's sketch of his immigrant parents, Bill Clinton's autobiography emphasized family as a direct connection with popular concerns and problems. His mother's fight with cancer and his stepfather's alcoholism were offered as critical to his preparation for the presidential labors. If Bush emphasized the postwar success story popular in the 1950s, Clinton stressed the family traumas familiar to 1990s talk show viewers and readers of self-help books. Where Bush's plot hinged upon work, Clinton's turned on sensitivity and how to empathize with those in pain. But both told the politically correct stories of their generations.

ETHICAL ACCEPTANCE

The remarkable transition that has taken place in the ways nominees accept their party's favor indicates radical changes in presidential politics and rhetorical conventions. The political context, the carefully catalogued lineage (Roosevelt begets Truman, Truman begets Kennedy,

Kennedy begets Johnson) has in recent years ceased to be very important, and party hagiography has been almost wholly replaced by a more personal and idiosyncratic one. Reagan recognized no debt to Eisenhower or Nixon (though he did acknowledge the 1964 Republican nominee, Barry Goldwater) and stressed instead his background as a disgruntled Democrat; Bush ultimately identified Harry Truman as his mentor (though he had given Teddy Roosevelt an earlier whirl) in an effort to claim Truman's ordinariness for himself. What matter most to recent candidates are the experiences that have shaped them personally rather than those that have influenced their party.

Of course the "ethical" argument—centered on the speaker—has always played an important role in acceptance speeches, even in acceptance letters and remarks made to convention messengers. Van Buren, for example, tried in his note to overcome his image as a Machiavellian. Similarly, FDR was presenting himself as much as a political agenda when he took the stage at the 1932 Democratic Convention, portraying in the nature of his speech and argument the kind of president his countrymen could expect him to be. But the "ethical" is not necessarily autobiographical, and while some aspects of personal history have always received attention—military service, log cabin births, rail-splitting youths—those were in the past symbolic to the point of impersonality and hardly compare to such intimacies as the kind of home one owned or substance addictions by family members.

Just as the efforts to lessen the gap separating president from public have led to an increasingly colloquial language and in its extreme, the use of slang and ungrammatical constructions, so has it led to an insistence that the presidents we elect are not that much different from ourselves in wisdom, taste, or experience. The personalizing of acceptances represents a direct effort, increasingly explicit, to cast the country in the image of a particular candidate and to assert a vital correspondence between the nation's mood and experience and the autobiography of the person seeking its highest office. The occasion blends humility and hubris in a daring concoction designed to prove a unique fitness for the presidency, and in its audacity, as in its modesty, it offers a glimpse into both the office itself and those who would occupy it.

Chapter Four

Reuniting the Country

Inaugurals I

In the discharge of these duties my guide will be the Constitution, which I this day swear to "preserve, protect, and defend."
For the interpretation of that instrument I shall look to the decisions of the judicial tribunals established by its authority and to
the practice of the Government under the earlier Presidents, who
had so large a share in its formation. To the example of those illustrious patriots I shall always defer with reverence, and especially to his example who was by so many titles "the Father of his
Country."

—Zachary Taylor, Inaugural Address, 1849*

Franklin Roosevelt oversaw the cold, wet festivities for his second
presidential inauguration from what appeared to be a small portico on the front of a colonial mansion. The structure, pulled nearly to the curb of Pennsylvania Avenue, was two-dimensional, a piece of
movie-style scenery that from the street resembled the quiet elegance of
Andrew Jackson's home outside Nashville, the Hermitage. With that
backdrop Roosevelt set the stage for his second term. Having declared in
his address at the Capitol that his listeners were a generation about to

---

*See *Inaugural Addresses of the Presidents of the United States from George Washington 1789 to George Bush 1989*. All such quotations here, except for Clinton's, are taken from this source.

113

keep a "rendezvous with destiny," he retreated at the close of his remarks to a mock-up of the seventh president's residence.

The elaborate front provided—literally—a "stand" for reviewing the Inaugural parade, a façade that concealed the president's braced legs as well as a heater to warm his lower body and a bar he gripped to maintain his balance. He was to have been protected by a panel of bullet-proof glass as well, but the president ordered it removed, declaring it an unnecessary obstruction between him and his countrymen. While his companions sat safely sheltered, farther back on Old Hickory's porch, FDR took the brunt of a wet, blustery morning, holding himself upright before the crowd.

Had the reconstruction of the Hermitage's portico been intended simply to conceal the reelected president's infirmities, *Life* magazine's photographers would not have been encouraged to take pictures of the support apparatus and, in the published account of the ceremony, to explain both its function and its cost.[1] The structure was a political statement, a declaration of official lineage and ideological kinship. Roosevelt identified with Jackson's conflict with the "monied" interests and saw in the old Democrat's battle over the national bank an equivalent to his own Depression-era struggle for economic reform. He had presumed this kinship with the nineteenth century's most celebrated Democrat from the moment of his first election. Soon after his arrival at the White House in 1933 he asked to see a tree that Jackson had planted on the grounds. Later, on a trip to the Tennessee Valley, he made a pilgrimage to the real Hermitage and enthusiastically recounted the experience to his vice president.[2]

No president since George Washington has stood alone on the inaugural platform. All have, consciously or not, been attended by predecessors, most obviously those with a special hold on their own understanding of the office. Thus, while declaring his refusal to be bound by tradition, FDR found in Andrew Jackson a reassuring precedent for his own belligerency.

LOOKING AHEAD WITH A BACKWARD GLANCE

An inaugural address, particularly one that marks a change in administration, is the most carefully written and elaborately rehearsed speech of any president's career, and it provides a remarkably reliable indication of what matters to a new president and how he wants to be perceived. Written over the months separating election from inauguration, it is delivered before the executive burden has taken its toll on strength and vision. These first words announce the beginning of a new regime and provide a foundation upon which the incoming executive can build, a perception of the idiosyncrasy of his own time contained in some larger vision of America and its purpose. They pave the way for what is to come by reminding all Americans of their union with one another now that the electoral contest has passed and of the historical and spiritual continuities that join them to both past and future generations.

In modern politics inaugurals mark the transition from candidates talking about themselves to presidents—who are presidential precisely to the extent that they can talk about something other than themselves—who give shape to national aspiration. During this act of disruption and continuation, the sense of history is all-pervasive, testifying to the country's capacity to survive changes in leadership and judging the incoming executives' understanding of the challenge ahead.

Viewed from the inaugural platform, history is defined by great events in the nation's life—together with the individuals who played a part in them—that tower over succeeding generations as standards of both accomplishment and faithfulness. In the first two hundred years of inaugurations three landmarks dominated the national skyline. The first was the Revolution and founding; the second the Civil War; the third the Great Depression and World War II. Each held the national imagination for more than half a century before drifting off into a past too remote to seem real. The last of the landmarks began to lose its influence in the early 1990s. Both George Bush, whose public career began in that last "great" war, and Bill Clinton, the first president born after it, recognized the loss and the need for some subsequent locating influence. Bush feared it would be Vietnam but hoped that instead the void could be filled by the end of the Cold War. Clinton made a case for the civil rights movement, but what in fact the country might endorse remained uncertain.

LAYING THE FOUNDATION

America's first president began his first term (1789) by declaring the reluctance and anxiety he brought to the occasion, describing the presidency of the United States—an office so eagerly sought in subsequent times that it seems there is virtually no limit to what men will do to possess it—as simply one of "the vicissitudes incident to life," notable only for being, in his case, the most troubling of those vicissitudes. The speech that followed began and ended with appeals to the "Almighty Being who rules over the universe," "the benign Parent of the Human Race." Not the perfunctory "God bless you's" of our theologically more casual age, those were supplications that recognized the enormous improbability of the nation's very existence and the threat posed by internal dissent. The reverential tone was directed not toward the office Washington was assuming but toward the Providence that had brought the new government into being and that must safeguard it in the future.

> No people can be bound to acknowledge and adore the Invisible Hand which conducts the affairs of men more than those of the United States. Every step by which they have advanced to the character of an independent nation seems to have been distinguished by some token of providential agency; and in the important revolution just accomplished in the system of their united government the tranquil deliberations and voluntary consent of so many distinct communities from which the event has resulted cannot be compared with the means by which most governments have been established without some return of pious gratitude, along with an humble anticipation of the future blessings which the past seems to presage. (pp. 2–3)

Tranquility among "distinct communities"—rather than victory in war—Washington offered as evidence of God's favor, and "public harmony" he identified as the central and revolutionary obligation of the new government.

Having said midway through his remarks that it would be inappropriate on Inauguration Day to offer legislative recommendations, the new president focused instead upon the character appropriate for those legislators seated before him, qualities that he congratulated them in advance for cultivating. "In these honorable qualifications," he instructed his congressional listeners,

> I behold the surest pledges that as on one side no local prejudices or attachments, no separate views nor party animosities, will misdirect the comprehensive and equal eye which ought to watch over this great assem-

blage of communities and interests, so, on another, that the foundation of our national policy will be laid in the pure and immutable principles of private morality, and the preeminence of free government be exemplified by all the attributes which can win the affections of its citizens and command the respect of the world. (p. 3)

In making that pledge on behalf of an audience already severely divided, Washington sought to move these representatives of jealous districts and states toward a national view, asserting throughout his remarks the concept of "united" states and stressing wholeness rather than mere association as the nature of their connection. From "great assemblage of communities" he moved toward "national policy," and throughout he presumed a common identity to which they were more obligated than to their separate and distinct ones. In that way he called the representatives of multiplicity to the responsibilities of union, called them to the task of building "affections" and international respect, duties more typically assigned to the executive branch. But, in fact, the conjoining of offices typifies the way in which Washington used his inaugural address to run things together rather than to sort them out, to synthesize rather than to analyze. Asserting a continuity between public and personal virtue and insisting that moral obligation does not change in the shift from one context to the other, he did more than argue standards of conduct for representatives; he presented them for government itself. That effectively lessened the difference between the individual and the nation, making the state comparable to a person. As such, it could be the object of affection, deserving of the same care and devotion as a beloved family member.

Before a body preoccupied with distinction, he persistently emphasized commonality. Mingling his calls to harmony and civic responsibility, he declared,

I dwell on this prospect with every satisfaction which an ardent love for my country can inspire, since there is no truth more thoroughly established than that there exists in the economy and course of nature an indissoluble union between virtue and happiness; between duty and advantage; between the genuine maxims of an honest and magnanimous policy and the solid rewards of public prosperity and felicity. (p. 3)

Here are his great themes combined—love of country and "indissoluble union"—and though they are presented as the sort of abstract virtues his audience could hardly reject, Washington attempted to shift his listeners' primary loyalty from the states to the nation and to undercut their localized patriotism. The union he affirmed was not just that of "virtue and happiness" but a political and social community—*the* Union—in which lay all prospects for happiness, and the virtue he praised served that concept over all narrower interests. To his own considerable personal authority he added a more daunting source of moral intimidation, calling again upon that "Great Author of every public and private good," the "providential agency" that had guided the American cause through its revolutionary trials, and he warned his countrymen "that the propitious smiles of Heaven can never be expected on a nation that disregards the eternal rules of order and right which Heaven itself has ordained" (p. 3). Since the Union, in Washington's view, was ordained by God, it would be blasphemy for its leaders to serve anything less.

Throughout his presidency Washington not only anticipated the party animosity that would prevail in American politics but also identified his own difficult role in keeping such conflicts from tearing the infant nation apart. He recognized the mundane, even the corrupt, which frustrates the work of governance—the fight for public honors, for power and monetary rewards (he renounced for himself "every pecuniary compensation")—but he acknowledged as well a profounder purpose beyond the muddle of politics and self-interest: "the preservation of the sacred fire of liberty and the destiny of the republican model of government," which have been "*deeply . . . finally*, staked on the experiment entrusted to the hands of the American people" (p. 3–4). Washington's solemnity, his tone of awe in accepting the nation's highest office, has influenced nearly all subsequent presidential beginnings, the consequence of a fearful burden recognized even in the moment of celebration. His articulation of the presumption and obligation inherent in the presidency resonated not only for those few gathered to witness his own swearing-in but as well for those who would follow him. His message was that of a more perfect union, and the eloquence of his words and his example in the very first utterance of the office defined the nature of the presidency for succeeding generations.

OUT OF THE SHADOW

There was no second Washington. Only he was elected unanimously, and the issue of his successor was hotly contested. John Adams gained seventy-one electoral votes to Thomas Jefferson's sixty-eight. Much of the disagreement in 1796 concerned precisely the issue Washington tried to settle—the influence of the federal government—and the division of the vote followed geographical as well as ideological lines.[3] In his 1797 inaugural Adams attempted to calm partisan disputes by focusing on the Constitution. Unlike modern declarations of love for America, his looked neither to the place nor to its people as the beloved but to an abstract and idealized government. "Employed in the service of my country abroad during the whole course of these transactions," he reminded his audience,

> I first saw the Constitution of the United States in a foreign country. Irritated by no literary altercation, animated by no public debate, heated by no party animosity, I read it with great satisfaction, as the result of good heads prompted by good hearts, as an experiment better adapted to the genius, character, situation, and relations of this nation and country than any which had ever been proposed or suggested. (p. 8)

And then, a little later: "What other form of government, indeed, can so well deserve our esteem and love?" (p. 9) Among those "forms" of government less deserving of our affection, besides those of foreign powers, he included those of the separate American states.

Principle, Adams insisted, was to be loved more than region or party, thus the Constitution must prevail over every other claim on a true American's loyalty. To that end the second president emphasized that the ultimate pursuits of this new nation were to be virtue and education, and those would be measured by the citizenry's capacity to understand and sustain principle: "If national pride is ever justifiable or excusable it is when it springs, not from power or riches, grandeur or glory, but from conviction of national innocence, information, and benevolence" (p. 10).

Adams acknowledged Washington's peculiar status, the "immortal glory" that he had attained among Americans, noting that his "example has been recommended to the imitation of his successors by both Houses of Congress and by the voice of legislatures and the people throughout

the nation" (p. 10). Not all the commendations lavished on the departing first president were endorsements of his federalist views, but Adams
made them such and argued that he would be obeying the states and
their representatives only by scrupulously emulating the beloved Washington. In a page-long sentence comprising eighteen clauses beginning
with the word "if" and followed by a political or moral principle, he presented his interpretation of what such obedience would entail. Significantly, given the attacks on his republicanism, he headed his list with "a
preference, upon principle, of a free republican government," a position
he insisted was based not on popular opinion but "upon long and serious
reflection, after a diligent and impartial inquiry after truth" (p. 11). Responding to claims that he would erode the influence of states, he
promised "a constant caution and delicacy toward the state governments"
and "an equal and impartial regard to the rights, interest, honor, and
happiness of all the states in the Union" (p. 11). To the Francophiles,
who believed him to be anti-French, he expressed "a personal esteem"
based on a seven-year residency in France and a "sincere desire to preserve their friendship." By that "apology" he attempted to reassure his
countrymen on issues of greatest controversy, but always in the context
of his highest obligation, upholding the Constitution. Without backing
away from the federalist principles he shared with Washington, Adams
attempted to calm fears that persisted after the election.

Four years later Jefferson won, and the country, along with its incoming president, had to contend with the defeat of an incumbent and the
yielding of power by one party to another. In the uncertainty of such a
transition, Jefferson appealed, as had Adams, to principle as the foundation of national unity. "During the contest of opinion through which we
have passed," he suggested,

> the animation of discussion and of exertions has sometimes worn an as-
> pect which might impose on strangers unused to think freely and to
> speak and to write what they think; but this being now decided by the
> voice of the nation, announced according to the rules of the Constitu-
> tion, all will, of course, arrange themselves under the will of the law, and
> unite in common efforts for the common good. (p. 14)

Jefferson's "of course" spoke—as "of courses" so often do—more of hope
than of certainty, but it pointed to fundamental lessons about obligation

in a democracy, obligation that applies to victors as well as to the defeated. Those who have lost must accept peacefully the will of the majority. Those who have won must honor the principle—"the sacred principle"—"that though the will of the majority is in all cases to prevail, that will to be rightful must be reasonable; that the minority possess their equal rights, which equal laws must protect" (p. 14).

If Washington's most important message had to do with the danger of partisan conflict, Jefferson's concerned itself with how the Union could survive such rancor. It is, he argued, a matter of political tolerance, since "every difference of opinion is not a difference of principle. We have called by different names brethren of the same principle. We are all Republicans, we are all Federalists" (p. 15). Though he certainly knew the limits of such a claim, he understood that the acceptance of majority rule and the observance of minority rights were possible only so long as neither political side became wholly "other" to its rival. If we are not all, to some degree, at once republican and federalist, liberal and conservative, if our minds and natures do not contain elements of both, then the failure of one side in any election will lead to a holy war, a confrontation between zealots lacking any common ground except the shared conviction of personal righteousness. It is likely that in 1801 neither Jefferson nor anyone else knew for certain whether Americans could see themselves, in their differences, as "brethren of the same principle," but his first presidential message argued that if such were not the case, all would be lost. He staked political union on a trust in what he would term in his second inaugural a "union of sentiment." Washington had been concerned with creating the bonds of affection—still largely more hoped for than realized—that allowed union. Jefferson, head of an opposition party, in victory had to explain the limits of enmity and hope that sufficient common feeling existed to allow the transition.[4]

STEWARDSHIP AND PRESERVATION

The United States had never been so prosperous as when James Madison came to office in 1809. This good fortune Madison attributed to the "benign influence of our republican institutions, and the maintenance of peace with all nations whilst so many of them were engaged in bloody and wasteful wars" (p. 26). As the retiring Secretary of State, the incoming president knew well how quickly that situation could change. Britain continued to impress American sailors (claiming them as British subjects), and the embargo Madison had encouraged against both that country and France had proved more hurtful at home than abroad. While Madison had reason to believe that the Union was growing more secure in the minds and habits of Americans, he could not know how it would fare against an external foe. Like John Adams he gave as his source of confidence and strength the principles he brought to office, and, like Adams he listed these in a long sentence of parallel clauses—this time beginning with "to." The first clause, pointing toward the source of his greatest concern, was "to cherish peace and friendly intercourse with all nations, having corresponding dispositions" (p. 27).

The first three presidents benefited from their association with America's heroic past and easily assumed the role of instructing their countrymen, explaining national purpose and propriety even as they accepted the reins of its leadership. But the tone of inaugural remarks—and more especially the basis of authority such instruction implies—subtly changed as the country moved farther away from Washington's administration. Incoming presidents took note of generational change and recognized the distance separating themselves and the founders.

Even Madison, whose founding credentials were as impeccable as those he succeeded, confessed to being intimidated by their examples. Already the burden was shifting as a new office gained a tradition and accumulated precedents to be upheld, examples to be honored. And for Madison, the first American chief executive to be tested by war, the possibility of failure, of being the last president, brought a burden different from any assumed by his predecessors. As a tradition lengthens, so does the weight of its responsibility increase. By Madison's time it did not matter that he was as much, if not more, a founder than either of his immediate predecessors (neither Adams nor Jefferson had been members of the Constitutional Convention, which Madison dominated). As president he had to prove himself by an established standard; executive performance was now a subject for comparison.

This is not to say Madison's inaugural was doubt-filled or insecure, or even that Madison was particularly concerned with expectations that might have been aimed too high. Rather it is to suggest that the office was being changed not only because the world and America were chang-ing, but because the presidency was evolving into a position charged more with stewardship and preservation than with the innovative and self-defining work that had earlier preoccupied it. "It is my good for-tune," Madison reported, "to have the path in which I am to tread light-ed by examples of illustrious services successfully rendered in the most trying difficulties by those who have marched before me" (p.27).

James Monroe reiterated that theme eight years later, when "conscious of [his] own deficiency," he praised "the illustrious men who have pre-ceded me" and recommended them as "instructive" "examples" to all fu-ture presidents (p. 40). As evidence of their wisdom he pointed to Amer-ica's success in the second war with Britain and its continuing prosperity. But even more compelling evidence of the founders' good judgment was the nation's remarkable physical growth accompanied by an equally im-pressive increase in familial feeling. The experiment had succeeded; the Union was secure. "Discord does not belong to our system," he declared. "The America people have encountered together great dangers and sus-tained severe trials with success. They constitute one great family with a common interest." "If we look to the history of other nations, ancient or modern," he continued, "we find no example of a growth so rapid, so gi-gantic, of a people so prosperous and happy." The executive task, he ar-gued, was now a conserving one:

> In contemplating what we have still to perform, the heart of every citizen must expand with joy when he reflects how near our Government has ap-proached to perfection; that in respect to it we have no essential improve-ment to make; that the great object is to preserve it in the essential princi-ples and features which characterize it, and that is to be done by preserving the virtue and enlightening the minds of the people; and as a security against foreign dangers to adopt such arrangements as are indispensable to the support of our independence, our rights and liberties. (p. 40)

"Preserve and protect" are ever the watchwords of second generations. Monroe declared the revolution accomplished, and the work of the chil-dren would be to keep intact what the fathers had joined together.

The presence of the fathers was especially poignant in John Quincy Adams's 1825 inaugural address. Besides praising his predecessor, James

Monroe, Adams deliberately took up the banner his own father carried twenty-four years earlier. He extolled the Constitution and then noted, "Since the adoption of this social compact one of these generations has passed away," anticipating by only slightly more than a year the deaths of the last survivors of that group of statesmen, his father and Jefferson. This, the younger Adams concluded, "is the work of our forefathers" (p. 54).

To the legislators assembled for his inauguration, John Quincy issued the same call Washington had once delivered to the Revolutionary army, to witness by example to the national union, claiming that by their generation the

> prejudices . . . against distant strangers are worn away, and the jealousies of jarring interests are allayed by the composition and functions of the great national councils annually assembled from all quarters of the Union at this place. Here the distinguished men from every section of our country, while meeting to deliberate upon the great interests of those by whom they are deputed, learn to estimate and do justice to the virtues of each other. The harmony of the nation is promoted and the whole Union is knit together by the sentiments of mutual respect, the habits of social intercourse, and the ties of personal friendship formed between the representatives of its several parts in the performance of their service in this metropolis. (pp. 57–58).

But Adams had a more immediate and practical interest in the old message. The good feeling that Monroe enjoyed came at a time when his election was virtually unopposed. In 1816 he had carried sixteen states and lost only three. The demise of the Federalist party was nearly complete, and in 1820, of 232 electors, only one voted against Monroe. Adams was not so fortunate. Elected by the House of Representatives after finishing second to Andrew Jackson in both the popular vote (115,696 votes to 152,933) and the Electoral College (84 to 99) he came to office without any claim to a national mandate. Four nominees—selected by geographical regions—received electoral votes in 1804, with Adams carrying only New York and New England. Since no one had received a majority, the election was thrown into the House. Only the top three vote-getters remained eligible, and the eliminated candidate, Henry Clay, gave his support to Adams in order to defeat the popular Jackson.[5]

With those events shadowing his election, the new president, already attacked by the Jacksonians as a conspirator circumventing the public will, called upon the memory of the fathers while acknowledging the uniqueness of his own situation. He began his closing paragraph by referring directly to "the peculiar circumstances of the recent election" and then acknowledged: "Less possessed of your confidence in advance than any of my predecessors, I am deeply conscious of the prospect that I shall stand more and oftener in need of your indulgence." For himself he pledged "upright" intentions and a "devoted" heart. In turn he asked, in the name of the founding fathers, for his countrymen's "liberal support." In concluding Adams asserted his own "humble but fearless confidence" in providence and "the future destinies" of the country (pp. 59–60). The fathers loomed large over the second Adams inauguration both because John Quincy *was* the second Adams and because he called upon their ghostly presences as witnesses for the Union in an uncertain time.

Adam's successor, Andrew Jackson, was a man disinclined to personal comparison and seemed, at first glance, not to suffer from generational complexes. In fact, in his 1829 inaugural he mentioned no earlier president by name and was generally disposed to speak only of himself, the people, and the "Almighty Being." But in his inaugural conclusion even he called upon old feelings and suggested that a "diffidence, perhaps too just, in my own qualifications will teach me to look with reverence to the examples of public virtue left by my illustrious predecessors, and with veneration to the lights that flow from the mind that founded and the mind that reformed our system" (p. 64). Proud as he was to assert his membership in the revolutionary generation (he had enlisted at thirteen and had been a prisoner of war) and eager, as the hero of America's second war with England, to be thought of as the second Washington, it is not surprising that Jackson would plead reverence to the "light" and "mind" of that founder of the "system." But almost immediately he turned to the subject of change and the reforming mind of Jefferson.

In a speech formally modeled after Washington's first inaugural, but advancing a quite different, even antifederalist message (which Vice President John C. Calhoun, a South Carolinian, helped write), Jackson promised the states that he would be "animated by a proper respect for those sovereign members of our Union, taking care not to confound the powers they have reserved to themselves with those they have granted to the Confederacy" (p. 62). In reexplaining the executive duties, he placed greater emphasis upon confederation than on union, emphasizing that legitimate power emanated from the consenting states. His quick transition from "the mind that founded" to the one "that reformed" was an effort to defend change by appealing to precedent. Insisting that he had been elected to transform the system, Jackson justified his own position as both preserver and innovator and announced his reforming agenda ("The recent demonstration of public sentiment inscribes on the list of Executive duties, in characters too legible to be overlooked, the task of *reform*" [p. 63]).

Four years later, at his second inauguration, Jackson's remarks were far more Washingtonian in their emphasis, and the word "union" assumed a more prominent role. Calhoun, having resigned because he found Jackson less a state rights advocate than the first inaugural implied, and with South Carolina threatening secession after trying to nullify federal tariff laws, the president quoted Washington's farewell address (though without identifying the source) with its admonition "to think and speak of the Union as of the palladium of your political safety and prosperity, watching for its preservation with jealous anxiety!" To this he added his own injunction: "Without union our independence and liberty would never have been achieved; without union they never can be maintained." Then, to make sure he was understood, he repeated the assertion: "The loss of liberty, of all good government, of peace, plenty, and happiness, must inevitably follow a dissolution of the Union" (pp. 66–67). If South Carolina had doubted his commitment or his will, Jackson used his second inaugural to declare his intention to "exert" all his "faculties to maintain the just powers of the Constitution and to transmit unimpaired to posterity the blessings of our Federal Union" (p. 67). Shortly thereafter South Carolina "nullified" its Ordinance of Nullification.

Martin Van Buren, who in 1837 followed the popular and magisterial Jackson, felt the full weight of Old Hickory's legacy and made little distinction between him and the founding fathers. Van Buren's words were laced with awe and humility, not simply because of the larger-than-life dimensions of his "illustrious predecessor" but also because he clearly belonged to another generation. "Little Van" (he stood 5 feet, 6 inches tall alongside Jackson's 6 feet, 1 inch) in the first moments of his tenure sounded almost plaintive, virtually ready to concede the inevitability of disappointment. He began, echoing a now familiar refrain: "I tread in the footsteps of illustrious men, whose superiors it is our happiness to believe are not found on the executive calendar of any country." In a speech that began and ended in the shadow of the "illustrious," Van Buren quickly pointed to the dwarf-ing distinction that marked his lesser place. Those that went before were

> the earliest and firmest pillars of the Republic—those by whom our na-tional independence was first declared, him who above all others con-tributed to establish it on the field of battle, and those whose expanded intellect and patriotism constructed, improved, and perfected the ines-timable institutions under which we live. (pp. 69–70)

Perhaps Van Buren was reminding the imperious Jackson that greatness preceded him as well, that even Old Hickory stood in shadows, but mostly he was concerned with the problematic position of the sons as they assumed the offices of their heroic fathers, the inheritors who en-joyed the rewards the previous generation had won.

> If such men [the founding heroes] in the position I now occupy felt themselves overwhelmed by a sense of gratitude for this the highest of all marks of their country's confidence, and by a consciousness of their in-ability adequately to discharge the duties of an office so difficult and ex-alted, how much more must these considerations affect one who can rely on no such claims for favor and forbearance! (p. 70)

Then Van Buren told his audience,

> Unlike all who have preceded me, the Revolution that gave us existence as one people was achieved at the period of my birth; and whilst I contem-plate with grateful reverence that memorable event, I feel that I belong to a later age and that I may not expect my countrymen to weigh my actions with the same kind and impartial hand. (p. 70)

In addition to the genuine respect expressed for the fathers, there is also regret, an apology for having been born too late and the practical recog-nition that Van Buren, unlike those who were "there" could not trade on a personal connection to the heroic past.

A MATTER OF AGE

For the inaugurals immediately following Van Buren's, age more than generation became the subject. William Henry Harrison—in 1841 the oldest man elected to the presidency—began his excessively Roman inaugural oration (Daniel Webster claimed to have edited the text and in the process to have "killed seventeen Roman proconsuls as dead as smelts"[6]) by pointing out that he had been called to the office from a retirement he had "supposed was to continue for the residue" of his life. The speech that followed—the longest of its kind—seemed designed to prove he still had the stamina for the work, although it turned out he did not and was dead within the month. But Harrison's remarks were more than an endurance test; he was more outspokenly critical of America's government than any of his predecessors had been in their first day on the job. He began by pointing out that democracies have flaws (the difference between what politicians promise as candidates and what they deliver as officeholders) and moved on to what he termed the "defects of the Constitution." In part, the length of his speech and the frequency of his classical allusions were an effort to place American government in a broader context than its own brief history and to use the ancient republics to provide cautionary warnings.

If Harrison's tone differed from Monroe's respectful remarks, it was not because the old man wanted to challenge the first presidents, but rather because he objected to the innovations that came after Monroe. During the campaign Harrison had been presented as the Whig repudiation of Jackson even more than the conqueror of Van Buren. Like Old Hickory a hero of the wilderness wars—nicknamed for leading the victory over the Indian confederacy at Tippecanoe Creek—and only six years Jackson's junior, Harrison had run as a champion of the West and a log cabin candidate.[7] And Jackson was the target of his inaugural complaints, all of which centered on the growing influence of the executive branch and the potential of that influence "essentially and radically" to change the "character" of American government. Offering as a given "the never-failing tendency of political power to increase itself," Harrison argued that the control of patronage (one of the reforms Jackson had presented in his first inaugural) led as well to control of "the whole revenues of the country," and he continued with a list of other abuses that follow from excessive executive influence. He proposed a single-term limit on the presidency and claimed that this "correction" of the Constitution would bring it into line with the founders' intention.[8]

In his earnestness Harrison invoked Roman consuls, Athenian democrats, Helvetic confederates, former U.S. presidents, Caesars, Cromwells,

Bolívars. All of those and more he called as witnesses to the profound implications of the occasion and to the remarkable nature of the democratic
venture. In the end his oration boiled down to the recurrent warning and
affirmation at the core of America's political life and, most especially, of
its presidency:

> Always the friend of my countrymen, never their flatterer, it becomes my
> duty to say to them from this high place to which their partiality has exalt-
> ed me that there exists in the land a spirit hostile to their best interests—
> hostile to liberty itself. It is a spirit contracted in its views, selfish in its ob-
> jects. It looks to the aggrandizement of a few even to the destruction of the
> interests of the whole. The entire remedy is with the people. Something,
> however, may be effected by the means which they have placed in my
> hands. It is union that we want, not of a party for the sake of that party,
> but a union of the whole country for the sake of the whole country. (p. 96)

The man who followed Harrison, the Democrat James K. Polk, began
his inaugural address with a confession that contrasted sharply with
Tippecanoe's plea of age:

> Honored with this distinguished consideration at an earlier period of my
> life than any of my predecessors, I cannot disguise the difference with
> which I am about to enter on the discharge of my official duties.
>
> If the more aged and experienced men who have filled the office of
> President of the United States even in the infancy of the Republic dis-
> trusted their ability to discharge the duties of that exalted station, what
> ought not to be the apprehensions of one so much younger and less en-
> dowed now that our domain extends from ocean to ocean, that our peo-
> ple have so greatly increased in numbers, and at a time when so great di-
> versity of opinion prevails in regard to the principles and policy which
> should characterize the administration of our Government? Well may the
> boldest fear and the wisest tremble when incurring responsibilities on
> which depend our country's peace and prosperity, and in some degree the
> hopes and happiness of the whole human family. (pp. 99–100)

The burden acknowledged here differs sharply from that described by
Van Buren. Polk expressed no regret at belonging to a generation that
had not witnessed the Revolution. But age was not Polk's actual concern—surely Harrison's recent example would have made youth seem de-

sirable in a president—rather it was the increasing demands of the office, the unanticipated transformation of the country in the fifty-six years since the first executive had declared its leadership a source of anxiety. If "Father of his Country" Washington could find the office intimidating in 1789, what was "young" Polk to make of it in 1845? That which in Washington's day had been virtually a coastal nation spanned a continent by Polk's election and was being challenged internationally over its western boundaries and domestically on the limits of slavery.

Jefferson had argued in his second inaugural that growth was good for America, that "the larger our association the less it will be shaken by local passions" (p. 19). Despite his complaint, Polk agreed. Urging the annexation of Texas and promising to fight vigorously for America's western territorial claims, Polk suggested that expansion could ameliorate the geopolitical issues troubling the nation and make the country more rather than less governable. "As our population has expanded, the Union has been cemented and strengthened. As our boundaries have been enlarged and our agricultural population has been spread over a large surface, our federative system has acquired additional strength and security." Having declared those advantages, he concluded:

> It may well be doubted whether it would not be in greater danger of overthrow if our present population were confined to the comparatively narrow limits of the original thirteen States than it is now that they are sparsely settled over a more expanded territory. It is confidently believed that our system may be safely extended to the utmost bounds of our territorial limits, and that as it shall be extended the bonds of our Union, so far from being weakened, will become stronger. (p. 108)

The generation denied the experience of Revolution could still achieve heroism, not only through Monroe's conservative work of preserving the Union but also in the innovative business of increasing it.

FATHERS AND SONS

The inaugural address which, in retrospect, most tellingly bridges the gap between those that looked back to the Revolution and those influenced by the Civil War was delivered in 1853 by Franklin Pierce. It began rather strangely, even ominously: "It is a relief," he said, "to feel that no heart but my own can know the personal regret and bitter sorrow over which I have been borne to a position so suitable for others rather than desirable for myself" (p. 115). Given the decade in which Pierce spoke and the terrible turmoil and uncertainty over which he was to preside, that might have sounded like a comment on the political reality of the times.[9] In fact it was a reference to the death of his son two months earlier, the only fatality when a railway car in which he and his parents were riding broke loose and virtually disintegrated.[10] It may also have referred to the continuing anguish the event brought to the Pierce marriage; it drove Mrs. Pierce into deep depression and often alienated her from her husband whose ambition she believed was responsible for their loss. The speech that followed that troubled beginning was noteworthy for a number of reasons, most especially the melancholy that lingered throughout.

Pierce spoke to the traditional themes of hope, of past travail successfully managed, and of the model of the fathers as they overcame dissent and adversity, but an autumnal air persisted throughout. Although he echoed Polk's faith in expansion (an effort to which he had personally contributed as an officer in the Mexican War), claiming the additional stars on the national flag as evidence both of the founders' wisdom and their successors' faithfulness, Pierce's enthusiasm rang less loudly, his tone seemed older, even though he was younger than Polk had been when he had assumed office. Where Polk began by emphasizing the limits of his experience, Pierce began by lamenting the extent of his. The fact that Polk was speaking in political terms and Pierce in personal ones, measuring their lives by very different calendars, did not change the general impression in Pierce's address that the hour was late, that youth had been spent.

Death was the dominant presence at the end as well as the beginning of his 1853 inaugural, that of the son at the start and of the fathers at the close. "Standing, as I do," he said in his peroration,

almost within view of the green slopes of Monticello, and, as it were, within reach of the tomb of Washington, with all the cherished memories of the past gathering around me like so many eloquent voices of exhortation from heaven, I can express no better hope for my country than that the kind Providence which smiled upon our fathers may enable their children to preserve the blessings they have inherited.

Standing at the threshold of an undistinguished presidency, one note-worthy primarily for its inability to break free of its own malaise, Pierce could not have known that the son he mourned, a child who would have turned twenty in 1861, prefigured the fate of unthinkable numbers of that child's generation, a generation that would suffer violent deaths by the tens of thousands. And that massive loss would call to judgment the heroic grandfathers as well as the ineffectual fathers.

Shortly before concluding, Pierce said, speaking of political union, "Let it be impressed on all hearts that, beautiful as our fabric is, no earthly power or wisdom could ever unite its broken fragments" (p. 122–23). But his words applied as well to the "impressed" heart whose own breaking was as much the new president's subject as was the rending of national institutions, and the longing for its union would become (perhaps always was) the "one" that America continually struggles after, the broken self and the inner multitude that we most yearn to reconcile. Whatever Pierce saw in his own grief—the loss of the child, the growing threat to a generation entrusted to his care—provided the experience that aged him beyond Polk without summoning the wisdom the nation desperately required. So fearful of the fathers were Pierce and the others of his political generation, so afraid were they of not living up to expectations established by their predecessors, that they did not see the terrible judgment the young would silently deliver, the young whose graves would grow so numerous on the hills of Arlington that they would constitute a virtual city of the dead across the river from the nation's capital. No matter how great the burden that fell on Pierce and his contemporaries in the 1850s, its weight would be exceeded by that awaiting their children in the next decade.

REBELLION AND REDEMPTION

The great legacy of Abraham Lincoln's two inaugurals (1861 and 1865) is their commitment to reconciliation even after the national fabric had been torn, their insistence that, contrary to traditional reasoning, all Americans were inextricably bound to one another. Lincoln was in those addresses laying the foundation for a new union even as the old one lay in tatters around him. Though he agreed with Pierce that reunion is a goal beyond "earthly power" to realize, he argued that such is the case with union of any sort. *His* conception of wholeness came more from the

Hebrew Bible than Enlightenment philosophy, and his union demanded more in humility and pain than his predecessors had ever suggested. The trial of secession required a profounder and more subtle understanding than that required of any previous president.

Unlike Daniel Webster or even Henry Clay, the most admired orators of his youth, Lincoln's formal style was more biblical than classical, deftly using tropes and figures and yet remarkably clear and simple. Thus he could open a speech with an archaic phrase like "Four score and seven" without seeming pretentious or ridiculous, but sounding appropriately solemn. The key to his rhetorical genius was his employment of a language and cadence drawn from the King James version of the Bible, a text that he understood to be—at least for his generation—the best model for a democratic sublime. While quite different from his audience's everyday speech, its images were the closest they had to a common literary experience, and the use of that model could elevate an occasion and satisfy his listeners' need for dignity, even poetry, while reaffirming their kinship with the speaker.

The work of secessionists had already begun by the time Lincoln took his first oath of office in March 1861, and rumors of plots and assassins forced the president-elect into a secretive arrival at the nation's capital. With Lincoln's election the executive office had become antithetical to its own purpose as the person of the president became the excuse for disunion, and the Southern states began to secede. At his inauguration just two weeks after Jefferson Davis had been installed as the president of the Confederate States of America, Lincoln spoke of the terrible ironies of his situation, pointed out that he swore an oath to a Constitution that required him to preserve the Union *and* to protect the rights of the states. He stressed the limits on presidential power that controlled every executive, regardless of party or ideology. Addressing those "who really love the Union," he delivered a concise but finely argued interpretation of American constitutional government, emphasizing on the one hand that his election represented no fundamental change in the presidency and, on the other, that secession was unacceptable. "I trust that this will not be regarded as menace, but only as the declared purpose of the Union that it *will* constitutionally defend and maintain itself" (p. 136).

The reassurance Lincoln offered to the dissatisfied South was the promise that the president, any president—as the Southerner Zachary

Taylor had in 1849 assured the North—was required to enforce *all* laws and could not select among them according to his own conscience. On the other hand, the promise to "preserve, protect, and defend," the essence of the oath of office prescribed by the Constitution, warned secessionists that they had no more power in those matters than did the chief executive; they could no more dismantle the union than could he. Only the people, not Lincoln or the states individually, could change the Constitution or the Union. "This country," Lincoln declared, "with its institutions, belongs to the people who inhabit it. Whenever they shall grow weary of the existing Government, they can exercise their *constitutional* right of amending it or their *revolutionary* right to dismember or overthrow it." He insisted, as Ronald Reagan would playfully recall more than a century later, that "the frame of the Government under which we live" insures that "no Administration by any extreme of wickedness or folly can very seriously injure the Government in the short space of four years."[11] The principle in question, one intended both to calm fears over a particular presidency and to give secessionists warning, Lincoln described crisply:

> The Chief Magistrate derives all his authority from the people, and they have referred none upon him to fix terms for the separation of the States. The people themselves can do this if they choose, but the Executive as such has nothing to do with it. His duty is to administer the present Government as it came to his hands and to transmit it unimpaired by him to his successor. (p. 140)

"I hold," he declared,

> that in contemplation of universal law and of the Constitution the Union of these States is perpetual. Perpetuity is implied, if not expressed, in the fundamental law of all national governments. It is safe to assert that no government proper ever had a provision in its organic law for its own termination. Continue to execute all the express provisions of our National Constitution, and the Union will endure forever, it being impossible to destroy it except by some action not provided for in the instrument itself. (pp. 135–36)

Just as the president, in his service of the "one," is not allowed to threaten the Union by attacking the states, neither are the states allowed to destroy the Union in the service of their own special interests—the "many." Neither party is granted such power by the Constitution, a document that can be changed only by the many acting as one (or as near to that as three-fourths make it), and not by the one acting arbitrarily or any of the several acting independently.

But there was another understanding of the United States, one prevalent among the champions of state rights, that regarded the nation as no more than an association of states existing at their individual pleasures. Even that view, Lincoln argued, did not legitimize secession. "If the United States be not a government proper, but an association of States in the nature of contract merely, can it, as a contract, be peaceably unmade by less than all the parties who made it? One party to a contract may violate it—break it, so to speak—but does it not require all to lawfully rescind it?" Lincoln, of course, believed it to be a "government proper," and he insisted that the Union predated even the Constitution, extending back to the 1774 Articles of Association, and that the constitutional self-explanation, "in order to form a more perfect Union," acknowledges this fact, assuming a previously existing union to be perfected. "But if destruction of the Union by one or a part only of the States be lawfully possible," he argued, "the Union is *less* perfect than before the Constitution, having lost the vital element of perpetuity" (p. 136).

Lincoln's inaugural addresses are tough-minded and logically coherent as well as eloquent, their beauty simultaneously that of thought and expression. The unconstitutionality of secession had to be understood as an argument and not received merely as a conclusion. The president's explanation, even as it warned separatists, had to affirm a basis for Union sufficient to sustain those who would take up the moral challenge of its preservation. The legal and moral foundation that Lincoln constructed in his first inaugural brought him to the conclusion he hoped would persuade his audience to commit themselves, knowingly, to a course that was both physically dangerous and, otherwise considered, at odds with their most basic notions of legality and virtue. Having outlined his constitutional position, Lincoln declared:

It follows from these views that no State upon its own mere motion can lawfully get out of the Union; that *resolves* and *ordinances* to that effect are legally void, and that acts of violence within any State or States against the authority of the United States are insurrectionary or revolutionary, according to circumstances. (p. 136)

But separation was not just an issue of law, any more than union was simply a matter of political and commercial expedience; it also had to do with the fundamental assumptions about human community and self-governance on which the nation was founded. Lincoln's assertion that the Constitution's first loyalty was to union represented more than a legal opinion; it was also a statement about the very concept of union. To reject union is, he told his countrymen, to affirm disunion, and that, once chosen, will contaminate everything else. "If a minority . . . will secede," he argued, "rather than acquiesce, they make a precedent which in turn will divide and ruin them, for a minority of their own will secede from them whenever a majority refuses to be controlled by such a minority. . . . All who cherish disunion sentiments are now being educated to the exact temper of doing this" (p. 138). When the newly elected president declared the "central idea of secession is anarchy," he was enlarging the implications of brokenness beyond the political sphere, treating it as pervasive, involving all those areas in which we long for wholeness, including that of the self. In his 1858 debates with Stephen Douglas, he had stressed how slavery divided not only parties and sections but also religious denominations and families. Confronting actual secession, he treated the failure as more than political: a spiritual disintegration and a despair fed by brokenness.

Appealing to geography but speaking as much of individual Americans as of their nation, Lincoln insisted that "we cannot separate," not because our union is a marriage but precisely because it is not. "A husband and wife may be divorced and go out of the presence and beyond the reach of each other, but the different parts of our country cannot do this. They cannot but remain face to face, and intercourse, either amicable or hostile, must continue between them" (p. 139). But if a political union is not a marriage, as the word's common usage would suggest and Southerners would argue, not an agreement between independent "adults" to conjoin their identities, Lincoln had to offer an alternative definition. The answer he provided, one consistent with his geographical analogy, was that Union is itself one thing, *the* thing, singular and inviolable. It most resembles, then, not two—or several—parties contractually united but one party that cannot be divided without the destruction of the entirety. It is a self, and no matter how aware we may be of the self as several—mind and body, thinking and feeling, etc.—it is in some transcendent sense either one or nothing at all. He concluded reluctantly, affirming in the midst of secession a surviving union of love as well as one of constitutional imperative, and stressing not the collision of states but familial discord and the conflicted feelings within individuals. "I am loath to close," he said, his repetition of the "lo" sound prolonging and softening the line.

> We are not enemies, but friends. We must not be enemies. Though passion may have strained, it must not break our bonds of affection. The mystic chords of memory, stretching from every battlefield and patriot grave to every living heart and hearthstone all over this broad land, will yet swell the chorus of the Union, when again touched, as surely they will be, by the better angels of our nature. (p. 141)

There is a sad lyricism to his final lines, one built on an echoing alliteration ("mystic chords of memory," "heart and hearthstone"), as Lincoln affirmed the common memories and feelings that bind Americans internally no matter their external separation.

Four years later Lincoln, at his second inauguration, looked back, across a gulf no other American president had ever witnessed, to his first:

> While the inaugural address was being delivered from this place, devoted altogether to *saving* the Union without war, insurgent agents were in the city seeking to *destroy* it without war—seeking to dissolve the Union and divide effects by negotiation. Both parties deprecated war, but one of them would *make* war rather than let the nation survive, and the other would *accept* war rather than let it perish, and the war came. (p. 142)

There is something terrible in the economy of this statement, in the inevitability, so simply stated. If secession is, as Lincoln insisted in 1861, anarchy, then dissolution is its only end and not a means to some nobler purpose. And if the Union is, as he argued in the same speech, irreducible, in fact *the* end and not—as the confederationists argued—merely a means, then disunion is not just the withdrawal of one part and the continuation of the other, it is an act of self-annihilation. The many, in Lincoln's 1865 address, narrowed to these two—those who would save the Union at any cost and those who would destroy it at any cost. The first affirmed oneness above all else, and the second asserted precisely the opposite. No longer Washington's parties or Jefferson's Federalists and Republicans or Buchanan's states or Henry Adams's special interests, the many became in Lincoln's psychodrama of secession simply the conflicting forces of union and disunion. It was not traditional Good battling traditional Evil, though for him it was very nearly the same: wholeness against brokenness, solution against dissolution.

That bifurcation quickly led Lincoln to the recognition of another—although ultimately all these divisions are expressions of the same distinction—that of colored slaves and free whites. Jefferson had been able, at the end of a heated campaign in which party differences had become all-important, to diminish public division. He could assert that in their profoundest political commitments Americans were one. But when the distinctions are slave and free, or even pro- and antislavery, common ground becomes, ultimately, impossible to claim. For generations the appeal of "union" had held the one together despite the contradiction American slavery embodied, but largely because the division was represented as regional rather than moral, a matter of North and South instead of slave and free. By the 1850s that thin veil of deception had fallen away, and the unifying claims of the past became more difficult to sustain. While all "official" Americans might in some sense see themselves as both Federalist *and* Republican, and thus fundamentally one, they could not claim—though, ironically, of course they did—to be both slave and free, both abolitionist and pro-slavery. And if the Union must be one thing, applying Jefferson's paradigm and Lincoln's logic, it must all be free since it cannot all be slave.

Unlike Jefferson, Lincoln did not suggest that the divisions of his time were neither "real" nor important; rather he declared that, real and important as they were, they could not change the obligation toward union. From the moment he advanced the "House Divided" thesis in 1858, he had made it obvious that he believed change inevitable, that the country would move to consolidate the interests of either slavery or its opposition, but that change could not involve disunion and had to be the work of the people through the constitutionally defined process.[12] On that principle the remnant nation had been at war with secession since the first months of his first term. By 1865 the military advantage having only recently swung decisively to the Union side, the complementary truths offered in the House Divided speech and the first inaugural had been validated by blood: The "house" which had either to fall or to "become one thing" had moved definitively toward singularity.

There is in the long, sad statement that is the body of Lincoln's four-paragraph Second Inaugural a concession to inevitability, the product of an Old Testatement perspective on America's history in which the war is divine judgment, not merely on the South but on the whole of the nation, not on slavery alone but on the inherent presumption, shared by all Americans, that had allowed slavery to survive and prosper. The style is simple and straightforward, the emotion restrained. The impression conveyed is of a recitation of facts.

> One-eighth of the whole population were colored slaves, not distributed generally over the Union, but localized in the southern part of it. These slaves constituted a peculiar and powerful interest. All knew that this interest was somehow the cause of the war. To strengthen, perpetuate, and extend this interest was the object for which the insurgents would rend the Union even by war, while the Government claimed no right to do more than to restrict the territorial enlargement of it. (pp. 142–43)

Having insisted that slavery be seen as the sole cause of the war and the desire to increase and perpetuate it the motive for secession, Lincoln turned from difference to likeness.

> Neither party expected for the war the magnitude or the duration which it has already attained. Neither anticipated that the *cause* of the conflict might cease with or even before the conflict itself should cease. Each looked for an easier triumph, and a result less fundamental and astounding. Both read the same Bible and pray to the same God, and each invokes His aid against the other.

The issue of divine sanction, of which side God favored, turned Lincoln briefly to the Northern point of view: "It may seem strange," he acknowledged, "that any men should dare to ask a just God's assistance in wringing their bread from the sweat of other men's faces." He continued, pushing beyond this conventional wisdom to add, "but let us judge not, that we be not judged." Here lies the terrible complication; judgment could not be avoided, and it was the weight of that fact that dominated the rest of the paragraph.

The prayers of both could not be answered. That of neither has been answered fully. The Almighty has His own purposes. "Woe unto the world because of the offenses; for it must needs be that offenses come, but woe to that man by whom the offense cometh." If we shall suppose that American slavery is one of those offenses which, in the providence of God, must needs come, but which having continued through His appointed time, He now wills to remove, and that He gives to both North and South this terrible war as the woe due to those by whom the offense came, shall we discern therein any departure from those divine attributes which the believers in a living God always ascribe to Him? Fondly do we hope, fervently do we pray, that this mighty scourge of war may speedily pass away. Yet, if God wills that it continue until all the wealth piled by the bondsman's two hundred and fifty years of unrequited toil shall be sunk, and until every drop of blood drawn with the lash shall be paid by another drawn with the sword, as was said three thousand years ago, so still it must be said "the judgments of the Lord are true and righteous altogether." (p. 143)

In some ways Lincoln's Second Inaugural is the most astonishing utterance of the American presidency, and yet it is the ultimate declaration of the common theme of all presidencies, the paradigm for the office itself. The man whose person had, four years before, divided the country, in this address rhetorically restored the Union to a wholeness it had never previously attained. What had been torn asunder, by war North and South, was in his words reunited on the basis not of conquest but of common suffering and common judgment. In this reinterpretation of America neither side is innocent; the nation in its entirety has been presumptuous to the point of disaster, and the consequence of that arrogance has been distributed across the entire country. The God who judges all is the God of the Old Testament prophets (and of Herman Melville's Calvinist priest in *Moby Dick*, Father Mapple), the God whose words begin with "Woe," the God who tramples out vengeance. This deity in Lincoln's vision grants advantage to neither side but judges all as one, one in guilt and one in punishment, one before God even in the moment that, divided, they made war on each other. The impossibility of separation to which Lincoln pointed in his first inaugural had, by the time of his second, been confirmed by both divine judgment and the war's sufficient anguish.

But the other division, the other expression of the "many," which no president prior to Lincoln even thought to reconcile, was slave and free, or now black and white, and his second inaugural presented the groundwork for that new inclusion. The man who in 1861 still looked hopefully to Liberia and racial separation seemed to recognize in 1865 that black and white Americans were as profoundly inseparable as North and South.[13] The perverse bonding of master and slave, even at slavery's end, had joined the fates of both—like those of the states—in perpetuity. They, too, were one, their identities mutually inclusive. The war of unthinkable cost was, Lincoln argued, just payment, demanded of white America for black America's long agony. By that logic the redemption of white America could be achieved only through that of black America.

In the end what allowed the reaffirmation of a more fully realized American Union, one that goes beyond states and parties, was Lincoln's reading of the war as the whiplash of slavery turned upon the society that would presume and tolerate the concept of human bondage, and the shared mark of that lash had become the nation's common bond. The triumphant epiphany of the Second Inaugural comes from the terrible realization that union is at last achieved, not because of common economic interests or a shared political system, but because of a common and shared pain. From the start, no matter how intently white Americans tried to imagine otherwise, it was slavery that provided the most devastating image of the nation's division; at the end it would be the communion of suffering that linked black to white as well as North to South. What a righteous God demanded of white America was, in Lincoln's formulation, defined by black anguish, even unto a war that could consume all the profit accumulated through slavery and that drew by shell and bayonet sufficient blood to match that previously drawn by the master's lash.

The Second Inaugural vindicated no other American ideal or virtue save Union. And in this it radically reconceived the oneness toward which the United States could now advance. Through a triumphant but apocalyptic progression that included the Gettysburg Address, Lincoln reconstructed the Union as both a political and a psychological entity, reclaimed it from the fathers and their enlightened thought, and reconceived it in Old Testament terms. The biblical tone, the scriptural allusions, which became increasingly dominant in his oratory, had, by the second inauguration, defined a common political culture as well as a shared literary one. In time America would accept, to a considerable extent, the implications of this remarkable revision of itself, placing in a low-roofed Greek temple the brooding figure of the man who had been translated into the American Christ. There, nearly within the shadow of our soaring tribute to reason and George Washington, Lincoln's less lofty memorial sits in enduring judgment of America's hubris. Ironically, the base originally planned for Washington's obelisk—the one belittled by Horatio Greenough as contradicting the singularity of the primary structure with its columned multiplicity—found its proper place a reflecting pool away and completed the symbolic representation of the American paradox. But it is the statue within that temple which is definitive, for in the context of Lincoln's Second Inaugural (unique among such addresses because it actually dealt with a profoundly different nation from the one addressed in the first) and the Gettysburg Address, Americans are not, as an earlier generation had perceived it, citizens of a new Greece or a new Rome but are instead children of Abraham—an identity, as Isaac discovered, fraught with its own terrors.

In the final words of his Second Inaugural, Lincoln called for a profounder reconciliation than the zealots of either side desired—"with malice toward none, with charity for all, with firmness in the right as God gives us to see the right . . ." The only way "to finish the work we are in" he argued, is "to bind up the nation's wounds," sharing both victory and defeat. Only by caring, without distinction, "for him who shall have borne the battle" and becoming the family for the widow and orphan can the country move from the oneness of shared anguish to a oneness of mutual responsibility, united in "charity" as it had been in the death grip of "malice." Suffering, he suggested, can generate an intimacy more profound than any attending prosperity, can provide a stronger basis for union than can rational argument and "considered alliance" (p. 143). Radical Republicans might have scoffed at a restored national Union that denied advantage to the victorious North, and unreconstructed Southerners hardly embraced the idea of that reconciliation or of a Union that consisted of black and white races equally free and empowered, but such was the only basis the Second Inaugural found acceptable to God and consistent with America's constitutional ambitions.

Chapter Five

Beyond Secession

Inaugurals II

The oath taken in the presence of the people becomes a mutual covenant. The officer covenants to serve the whole body of the people by a faithful execution of the laws, so that they may be the unfailing defense and security of those who respect and observe them, and that neither wealth, station, nor the power of combinations shall be able to evade their just penalties or to wrest them from a beneficent public purpose to serve the ends of cruelty or selfishness.

—Benjamin Harrison, 1889 Inaugural Address

A MORE AND LESS PERFECT UNION

The Civil War replaced the Revolution and the founding as the great model of patriotism, dominating inaugural thinking through the rest of the nineteenth century and the beginning of the twentieth. Except for Grover Cleveland, all postwar presidents up to Teddy Roosevelt had served in the Union army and were particularly mindful of the unfinished business still at hand. As with earlier executives, union remained their defining concern, but it was a union rescued from secession rather than one drawn up at a constitutional convention. At his first inauguration,

Ulysses S. Grant recognized that the most pressing concerns facing his new administration were the result of the "great rebellion" and were unprecedented in America's history. "In meeting these," he counseled, "it is desirable that they should be approached calmly, without prejudice, hate, or sectional pride, remembering that the greatest good to the greatest number is the object to be obtained" (p. 146). Especially troubling were the nation's debt and the inability of the defeated states to contribute to its payment. But Grant encouraged his countrymen with the promise of yet unexploited natural resources. "Why, it looks as though Providence had bestowed upon us a strong box in the precious metals locked up in the sterile mountains of the far West, and which we are now forging the key to unlock" (p. 147).

He addressed more directly the most troubling human issues in his second inaugural. "The effects of the late civil strife," he bluntly told his 1873 audience, "have been to free the slave and make him a citizen. Yet he is not possessed of the civil rights which citizenship should carry with it. This is wrong, and should be corrected" (p. 150).

Four years later, in 1877, Rutherford B. Hayes addressed the enormous social change the war had begun while at the same time reassuring white Southerners that Reconstruction was coming to an end.[1]

> The sweeping revolution of the entire labor system of a large portion of our country and the advance of 4,000,000 people from a condition of servitude to that of citizenship, upon an equal footing with their former masters, could not occur without presenting problems of the gravest moment, to be dealt with by the emancipated race, by their former masters, and by the General Government, the author of the act of emancipation.

Wryly, he observed: "That it was a wise, just, and providential act, fraught with good for all concerned, is not generally conceded throughout the country." What he insisted was beyond question was the "moral obligation" that remained with the national government "to employ its constitutional power and influence to establish the rights of the people it has emancipated, and to protect them in the enjoyment of those rights when they are infringed or assailed." He described the fates of all Southerners, black and white, as inseparable and argued that this shared condition of theirs could improve only with "the united and harmonious efforts of both races, actuated by motives of mutual sympathy and regard" (p. 155).

To this James Garfield added in 1881: "The elevation of the negro race from slavery to the full rights of citizenship is the most important political change we have known since the adoption of the Constitution of 1787." Endorsing the inclusionary principle of Lincoln's 1865 inaugural, he enthusiastically described its political contribution to a healthier, wealthier America. "No thoughtful man can fail," he continued,

> to appreciate its beneficent effect upon our institutions and people. It has freed us from the perpetual danger of war and dissolution. It has added immensely to the moral and industrial forces of our people. It has liberated the master as well as the slave from a relation which wronged and enfeebled both. It has surrendered to their own guardianship the manhood of more than 5,000,000 people, and has opened to each one of them a career of freedom and usefulness. It has given new inspiration to the power of self-help in both races by making labor more honorable to the one and more necessary to the other. The influence of this force will grow greater and bear richer fruit with the coming years. (p. 163)

But Garfield also acknowledged efforts in the Southern communities to prevent black inclusion, especially in the exercise of voting rights, and he recommitted his office to serving the Union of Lincoln's Second Inaugural, identifying ignorance as the principal hindrance in his own time. While implying on one hand that Southern repression resulted from white fear of uneducated blacks, he argued on the other that racism was itself a consequence of white ignorance. Appalled by the level of illiteracy throughout the population, he called for major efforts in education, specifically linking that concern with the larger issues of race and civil rights.

> To the South this question is of supreme importance. But the responsibility for the existence of slavery did not rest upon the South alone. The nation itself is responsible for the extension of the suffrage, and is under special obligations to aid in removing the illiteracy which it has added to the voting population. For the North and South alike there is but one remedy. All the constitutional power of the nation and of the States and all the volunteer forces of the people should be surrendered to meet this danger by the savory influence of universal education. (p. 165)

The issue of union—particularly in the context of race—has never been removed from the presidential agenda. It was an inaugural theme of Republican presidents as late as 1909. William Howard Taft included in his remarks a long section on the civil and social rights of black Americans:

> The negroes are now Americans. Their ancestors came here years ago against their will, and this is their only country and their only flag. They have shown themselves anxious to live for it and to die for it. Encountering the race feeling against them, subjected at times to cruel injustice growing out of it, they may well have our profound sympathy and aid in the struggle they are making. We are charged with the sacred duty of making their path as smooth and easy as we can. (p. 223)

Although admirably struggling with the problem of race discrimination, Taft unintentionally represented the contradiction that would haunt twentieth-century America: the principled recognition that we are all one, all Americans, and—simultaneously—the persistent usage of "we" and "they." Taft accepted the presidential chore of greater inclusion, of pushing toward more perfect union, but he came to that work unwittingly testifying, with his vocabulary of distinction, to the very powers of division he was sworn to oppose.

As much an issue as the inclusion of African-Americans was a concern for the reunification of the states themselves. Benjamin Harrison conjoined those topics when he argued in 1889 that the war had liberated not only the slaves but also the Southern economy, which had previously been built solely around agriculture. "Mill fires," he asserted, "were lighted at the funeral pyre of slavery. The emancipation proclamation was heard in the depths of the earth as well as in the sky; men were made free, and material things became our better servants." The application of "emancipation" to the developing mining and manufacturing industries of the reconstructing South, according to Harrison, promised to draw the old slave states, their economies newly diversified, into a union of common economic interests. The South's prewar emphasis on geographical expansion—a natural preoccupation for an exclusively agricultural society—would now be replaced by a concern for new forms of commercial growth: "Every new mine, furnace, and factory is an extension of the productive capacity of the State, more real and valuable than added territory" (p. 178). The fact that he also celebrated in the same speech the "near prospect of the admission into the Union of the Dakotas and Montana and Washington Territories" (p. 183) indicated Harrison's appreciation for the advantages of physical growth, but not for the reason offered by Polk and Pierce—allowing room in which both slave and free interests could expand. To the contrary, he argued, the war and abolition were necessary to bring the South into the modern age and to a point where, more industrialized, it could more fully participate in an enlarged and more prosperous Union. Previous presidents tended to see economic diversity among the several states as contributing to a desirable interdependence, but Harrison's model called for each region to be itself diversified, both to lessen its vulnerability to market fluctuations and to create production communities that were nationwide. He declared "the consequent development of manufacturing and mining enterprises in the States hitherto wholly given to agriculture as a potent influence in the perfect unification of our people" (p. 179). But true to the old Republican values, he chided white Southerners for allowing "the prejudices and paralysis of slavery . . . to hang upon the skirts of progress" and warned those benefiting from economic change that "the free ballot of the working man, without distinction of race," was important to the general welfare. "I do not doubt," Harrison continued,

> that if those men in the South who now accept the tariff views of Clay and the constitutional expositions of Webster would courageously avow and defend their real convictions, they would not find it difficult . . . to make the black man their friendly and safe ally, not only in establishing correct principles in our national administration, but in preserving for their local communities the benefits of social order and economical and honest government. (p. 179)

Perhaps because he alone of his generation of presidents had avoided military service, hiring a replacement to serve in his stead, Grover Cleveland made only vague reference to the Civil War in his 1885 and 1893 inaugurals. As the first Democrat elected since Buchanan, he called on Americans "from this hour" to "cheerfully and honestly abandon all sectional prejudice and distrust" (p. 170). In remarks much like those of presidents a half-century earlier, he held up the founders as models of "patriotic devotion," committing himself to the Constitution and the policies of Washington, Jefferson, and Monroe. Still, perhaps *because* he was a Democrat, he felt it necessary in his first address—after promising fair treatment to Native Americans and lamenting the offensiveness of Mormon polygamy—to affirm his obligation to the rights and security of the freedmen. "All discussion as to their fitness for the place accorded to them as American citizens," he warned, "is idle and unprofitable except as it suggests the necessity for their improvement" (p. 173). Eight years later, after a defeat and a reelection (although he won in the popular vote in 1888, he lost to Benjamin Harrison in the Electoral College; then he defeated Harrison in 1892), he focused almost entirely on civil service reforms, fiscal responsibility, and the danger posed by business aggregates. Then he reaffirmed the right of "equality before the law." "The enjoyment of this right," he reminded, "follows the badge of citizenship wherever found, and, unimpaired by race or color, it appeals for recognition to American manliness and fairness" (p. 190).

In the last inaugural of the nineteenth century, William McKinley closed his 1897 remarks by congratulating the country on "the fraternal spirit of the people and the manifestations of good will everywhere so apparent," insisting that the recent election had "demonstrated the obliteration of sectional or geographical lines" and "to some extent also the prejudices which for years have distracted our councils and marred our true greatness as a nation." "The North and the South," he continued, "no longer divide on the old lines, but upon principles and policies; and in this fact surely every lover of the country can find cause for true felicitation" (p. 201). Despite such good feeling, McKinley had cause to chastise his countrymen for acts that were distinctly lacking in fraternity. "Lynchings," he declared, "must not be tolerated in a great and civilized country like the United States" (p. 198). He noted as well the "industrial disturbances" from which the country was suffering.

PEACE AND A GREATER UNION

Beyond the issues of slavery's domestic legacy, however, were the first stirrings of a tendency to interpret America's liberating responsibility in international terms. Evidence of that came as early as Ulysses S. Grant's 1869 inaugural.

The young men of the country—those who from their age must be its rulers twenty-five years hence—have a peculiar interest in maintaining the national honor. A moment's reflection as to what will be our commanding influence among the nations of the earth in their day, if they are only true to themselves, should inspire them with national pride. All divisions—geographical, political, and religious—can join in this common sentiment. (p. 147)

This new union, a generation removed from slavery and civil violence, would, Grant predicted, serve traditional American aspirations in an even larger arena, a notion he returned to in his second inaugural as he took up questions of further expansion. Focusing on inhabitants rather than land, he insisted he would promote only acquisitions that were requested by the people of the place in question (some Santo Domingans had made such a request). Then he added:

I say here, however, that I do not share in the apprehension held by many as to the danger of governments becoming weakened and destroyed by reason of their extension of territory. Commerce, education, and rapid transit of thought and matter by telegraph and steam have changed all this. Rather do I believe that our Great Maker is preparing the world, in His own good time, to become one nation, speaking one language, and when armies and navies will be no longer required. (p. 150)

Blending the practical with the visionary, seeing new technologies in the service of grander union, the plainspoken, no-nonsense Grant issued a challenge that would be accepted by Teddy Roosevelt and Woodrow Wilson, both children of the 1850s who, "twenty-five years hence," would be thirty-six and thirty-eight years of age, respectively.

Though it would be Wilson who most directly addressed Grant's nation of nations prophecy, the first Roosevelt perhaps spoke most clearly for their generation. Already by 1905 nearly four years in office as a result of McKinley's assassination, he was well aware of the challenge of being "a great nation, forced by the fact of . . . greatness into relations with the other nations of the earth." "We have duties to others," he declared, "and duties to ourselves; and we can shirk neither." Looking ahead, he noted that "modern life is both complex and intense" (p. 210). Looking back, he recalled "the memories of the men of the mighty past" who "did their work" and "left us the splendid heritage we now enjoy." In bringing their example to the twentieth century, America would necessarily, in Roosevelt's view, assume international leadership.

> Upon the success of our experiment much depends, not only as regards our own welfare, but as regards the welfare of mankind. If we fail, the cause of free self-government throughout the world will rock to its foundations, and therefore our responsibility is heavy, to ourselves, to the world as it is today, and to the generations yet unborn. There is no good reason why we should fear the future, but there is every reason why we should face it seriously, neither hiding from ourselves the gravity of the problems before us nor fearing to approach these problems with the unbending, unflinching purpose to solve them aright. (p. 211)

"We are provincials no longer," Wilson declared in his second inaugural (1917). War in Europe had given America a special role, or rather had—in Wilson's formulation—expanded its traditional charge to include all the world. As he called his countrymen to this new challenge, he declared that their union was being perfected by the demands of a new age:

> We are being forged into a new unity amidst the fires that now blaze throughout the world. In their ardent heat we shall, in God's Providence, let us hope, be purged of faction and division, purified of the errant humors of party and of private interest, and shall stand forth in the days to come with a new dignity of national pride and spirit. (pp. 234–35)

The language of purgative fire and purification drew on imagery strongly associated with the nation's war over slavery, and Wilson seemed intent on making the European conflict, from which American armies were still disengaged, an extension of that earlier struggle for liberation, only this time a purer and more unified America would include the whole world in a global union. That too would be—according to the president as he established a vocabulary for the century—a struggle against "slavery," only on a greatly expanded theater and with the entire human race as its beneficiary.

In Wilson's first inaugural the key word as he elaborated on his domestic agenda was "restore." Clearly he celebrated his party's victory both in the presidency and in Congress, but he concentrated on some broader and less specific "restoration" of morals and justice and fair play. His lan-

guage and vision continually harked back to a historical moment less ambiguous than his own, that of 1865, one in which "restoration" could
clearly be the central business. What diminished America both in a slave
economy and in the new industrial state was "inexcusable waste," production gains won at the cost of "lives snuffed out," and a government
that had become the instrument of "private and selfish purposes." Wilson's immediate concern in 1913 was with industrial justice, with freeing
government from the control of special interest. He devoted one paragraph to a brief summary of specific reforms—the tariff, banking, natural
resources—but the greater portion of his speech lacked such specificity
and, in fact, seemed to be reaching for something commensurate with
Lincoln's war, some higher moral challenge where a more dramatic conflict of Good against Evil could be fought.

> Here muster, not the forces of party, but the forces of humanity. Men's
> hearts wait upon us; men's lives hang in the balance; men's hopes call
> upon us to say what we will do. Who shall live up to that great trust?
> Who dares fail to try? I summon all honest men, all patriotic, all forward-
> looking men, to my side. God helping me, I will not fail them, if they
> will but counsel and sustain me. (p. 231)

The immediate task may have been unclear, but the earnestness, the fer-
vency of the address (reminiscent in this regard as well as in its "crusading" language of William Jennings Bryan and Teddy Roosevelt) awaited
its mighty cause.

Four years later, with war raging across Europe, Wilson defined that
cause more clearly in his second inaugural. "We are a composite and cos-
mopolitan people," he noted in 1917. "We are of the blood of all the nations that are at war" (p 233). Wilson's America was united in the moral
resolve he had emphasized in 1913—and "united" is a word again receiving great emphasis in his second inaugural—but it was also a paradigm
of the world, elsewhere torn apart by its differences, yet at home, despite
our varied origins, unified in a commitment to liberty and justice. Wilson's America *is* the world, both in its pluralism and in its example; and
in this inclusionary leap Wilson found the cause that he believed could
make his age and his presidency as momentous in their service to the
founders' ideals as the Revolution and the Civil War.

Wilson's effort to extend Lincoln's war and Lincoln's model into the twentieth century prevailed, but through international affairs rather than domestic policy. The presidency, previously preoccupied with the precarious Union of American states, became increasingly inclined—with a few notable exceptions—to find its work in the world at large.[2] In part that was because, on the superficial level at least, the issues of domestic union, those of the "united states," had been settled. But there had been as well an expansion of the old commission, a worldwide extension of the American ideal that had been introduced as early as Washington's First Inaugural with its image of a torch for all nations. In the 1800s America served this ideal passively, as an exemplary model, a city on a hill. In this century, mirroring a phenomenon that James Monroe had emphasized in his annual messages nearly a century earlier, political consolidation at home and political conflict abroad allowed a more active American role, one which most twentieth-century presidents, apart from Harding and Coolidge, have wholeheartedly embraced. The old continental expansionists like Polk had seen growth as a kind of domestic balm and as a manifest destiny; Wilson saw in moral imperialism an ideal at least as attractive and, in some principled way, superior. His internationalist instincts, the aspiration to lead a world to freedom, would be most fully realized by Eisenhower, who was the only president to come to the office with globally recognized credentials in the international arena.[3]

What Wilson sought to restore and extend was severely tested by World War I and by his unsuccessful efforts for the League of Nations; his immediate successors were far more cautious about America's international responsibility. Warren G. Harding opened his 1921 inaugural message with the declaration,

> When one surveys the world about him after the great storm, noting the marks of destruction and yet rejoicing in the ruggedness of the things which withstood it, if he is an American he breathes the clarified atmosphere with a strange mingling of regret and new hope. We have seen a world passion spend its fury, but we contemplate our Republic unshaken, and hold our civilization secure. (p. 237)

Harding suggested that in the great test just concluded, America had passed while the world had failed, and in anticipating the work of his administration he turned more inward than had Wilson four or even eight years earlier. "The recorded progress of our Republic," he declared, repeating the central themes of his acceptance message,

> materially and spiritually, in itself proves the wisdom of the inherited policy of non-involvement in Old World affairs. Confident of our ability to work out our own destiny, and jealously guarding our right to do so, we seek no part in directing the destinies of the Old World. We do not mean to be entangled. (p. 238)

This did not mean that America intended to ignore international alliances and responsibilities. But it did mean that the United States government had grown wary of a leading role on the world's stage and was more inclined to pursue the old domestic business of building internal strength and unity. "Our supreme task," Harding insisted, "is the resumption of our onward, normal way. Reconstruction, readjustment restoration, all these must follow" (p. 241).

Harding and his successor, Calvin Coolidge, repeatedly emphasized the unselfish spirit that had led America into the first world war. They insisted that our participation in that conflict grew out of humanitarian concerns and not from any imperialistic ambitions, that whatever future involvement we had with the international community could be trusted because our interests were narrow. Harding acknowledged a readiness "to associate ourselves with the nations of the world, great and small, for conference, for counsel," but then stressed America's refusal to be drawn into any more restrictive association. A "world supergovernment is contrary to everything we cherish . . . This is not selfishness, it is sanctity. It is not aloofness, it is security. It is not suspicion of others, it is patriotic adherence to the things which made us what we are" (p. 239).

Coolidge repeated that message in his 1925 inaugural, "We have been," he said,

> and propose to be, more and more American. We believe that we can best serve our own country and most successfully discharge our obligations to humanity by continuing to be openly and candidly, intensely and scrupulously, American. If we have any heritage, it has been that. If we have any destiny, we have found it in that direction. (p. 249)

Implicit in that analysis was a conservative suspicion of idealism. Because American involvement in the war was unselfish, it was also, conservatives hinted, unnecessary. A part of the presidential responsibility—and this is where they thought Wilson was dangerously irresponsible—is to protect a humane and generous people from being victimized by their own virtues. Harding and Coolidge were born after the Civil War and were less to be influenced than their predecessors by calls to personal sacrifice for the liberation of others. They discarded chivalric romanticism that pervaded the speeches of Theodore Roosevelt and Wilson in favor of a rhetoric of practical self-interest. "There has been something crude and heartless and unfeeling in our haste to succeed and be great," Wilson had warned (p. 229). But Harding and Coolidge offered a more benign version of prosperity, "We want an America of homes," Harding insisted,

> illumined with hope and happiness, where mothers, freed from the necessity for long hours of toil beyond their own doors, may preside as befits the hearthstone of American citizenship. We want the cradle of American childhood rocked under conditions so wholesome and so hopeful that no blight may touch it in its development, and we want to provide that no selfish interest, no material necessity, no lack of opportunity shall prevent the gaining of that education so essential to best citizenship. (p. 244)

Having declared that noble social goal, he spoke cautiously of its realization:

> There is no shortcut to the making of these ideals into glad realities. The world has witnessed again and again the futility and the mischief of ill-considered remedies for social and economic disorders. But we are mindful today as never before of the friction of modern industrialism, and we must learn its causes and reduce its evil consequences by sober and tested methods. Where genius has made for great possibilities, justice and happiness must be reflected in a greater common welfare. (p. 244)

Coming after a year of mass arrests—communists, anarchists, and labor agitators—some of Harding's "ill-considered remedies" had been highly publicized during the "Red Scare," but the vagueness of his phrase implied a suspicion not only of the extreme left but of reform efforts in general. "We cannot finance the country," Coolidge declared four years later, we cannot improve social conditions, through any system of injustice, even if we attempt to inflict it upon the rich. Those who suffer the most harm will be the poor. This country believes in prosperity. It is absurd to suppose that it is envious of those who are already prosperous. (p. 254)

Such a view seemed, by the time Herbert Hoover took office in 1929, to have been vindicated by economic accomplishment. And Hoover could celebrate in his inaugural America's "liberation" from widespread poverty, along with the "new race" emerging on its soil. He reassured the rest of the world (which included a Stalinist Soviet Union, an Italy ruled by Mussolini, and a Germany in which, the following year, the Nazi party would gain a majority in national elections) "that the American people are engrossed in the building for themselves of a new economic system, a new social system, a new political system," and had no interest in any territory they did not already occupy. (p. 263)

ALL WE HAVE TO FEAR

Franklin Roosevelt recognized the historic calendar by which Americans located themselves, and in 1941 he began his third inaugural by noting the two great benchmarks of America's past: "In Washington's day the task of the people was to create and weld together a nation. In Lincoln's day the task of the people was to preserve that Nation from disruption from within." To those he added his own time as a third: "In this day the task of the people is to save that Nation and its institutions from disruption from without" (p. 279). His intuition those few months before Pearl Harbor was correct. What the Revolution and the Civil War had meant for succeeding generations, the war Roosevelt anticipated in 1941—together with the Great Depression—would be for Americans during the fifty years that followed his remarks. Like the Revolution, this landmark struggle was against "tyranny"; like the Civil War, it attacked "slavery."

But those words and that conflict came in FDR's unprecedented third and fourth terms, and because of his long tenure the thirty-second president himself became a historical dividing line. World War II *and* Roosevelt defined the presidency for all who held office until 1993. In his first two inaugural messages (1933 and 1937) he set the domestic agenda that would hold center stage through the rest of the century, and in his second two (1941 and 1945) he paved the way for the postwar approach to international affairs.

First coming to office in a time of national despair and uncertainty, when the prosperity that his recent predecessors had offered as evidence of the superiority of the American system had collapsed in the 1929 stock market crash and the Depression that followed, Roosevelt spoke to a "stricken nation in the midst of a stricken world." Yet he began his 1933 inaugural with the words "I am certain," and in the lines that followed asserted his confidence in his countrymen and himself even as he acknowledged the crisis at hand. In a speech that followed logically and rhetorically his acceptance message, FDR's short, no-nonsense sentences called for an end to "paralysis"—his image—(malaise, like complication, always speaks in long sentences) and a commitment to action.[4] "This is preeminently," he declared, "the time to speak the truth, the whole truth, frankly and boldly." "So, first of all, let me assert," he began, introducing one of the most famous lines in inaugural history, "my firm belief, that the only thing we have to fear is fear itself" (p. 269).[5]

Typical of FDR's genius for building morale was his quick transition from monetary collapse to "social values." He began his list of the nation's terrible difficulties with the comment, "They concern, thank God, only material things." Later, after his attack on the "money changers" responsible for the Depression, those whom his election had driven from the "temple," Roosevelt declared, "Happiness lies not in the mere possession of money; it lies in the joy of achievement, in the thrill of creative effort" (p. 270). The losses served as a reminder of what was essential, revealing what the president would, in the face of another crisis eight years later, call the "spirit of America." The litany of disasters served, finally, as a series of spiritual and creative challenges, an opportunity for new achievement.

FDR's cousin Teddy had built a political career around notions of vigor and manliness, the idea that Americans welcomed a demanding life as a proving ground for character and will. In 1933 the next political generation of the family, himself physically constrained, assumed similar national traits and called for their application to a new crisis. In the midst of suffering and panic, he called for perspective. "Only a foolish optimist can deny the dark realities of the moment," he declared.

Yet our distress comes from no failure of substance. We are stricken by no plague of locusts. Compared with the perils which our forefathers conquered because they believed and were not afraid, we still have much to be thankful for. Nature still offers her bounty and human efforts have multiplied it. Plenty is at our doorstep, but a generous use of it languishes in the very sight of the supply. Primarily this is because the rulers of the exchange of mankind's goods have failed, through their own stubbornness and their own incompetence, have admitted their failure and abdicated. (p. 270)

It was this forcefulness, combined with confidence, that the conservative Ronald Reagan, years later, would recall as admiringly as any liberal Democrat. Those were the qualities that gave Roosevelt credibility at a time filled with suspicion and provided the basis, in the midst of economic peril, for preserving a union that as recently as four years earlier Hoover had suggested was, above all, rooted in national prosperity. Even more, they were qualities that supported his intention to "act and act quickly" through direct federal intervention, "treating the task" of creating jobs "as we would treat the emergency of war." In concluding he extended the analogy, suggesting that, if the Congress should fail to cooperate, the need for action would require "broad Executive power to wage a war against the emergency, as great as the power that would be given to me if we were in fact invaded by a foreign foe" (p. 273).

Roosevelt's "union" was threatened by economic distinctions, disparities dividing rich and poor. "If I read the temper of our people correctly," he declared in 1933, "we now realize as we have never realized before, our interdependence on each other" (p. 272). This above all else was the central message of his second inaugural, perhaps the most eloquent of the four. Although corporate gains were evident as early as 1934, only toward the end of FDR's first term had employment figures, aided by the 1935 creation of the Works Progress Administration and the massive financing of public projects, begun to rise. Exploiting discontent among those whose condition had worsened rather than improved, such organizations as Huey Long's Share-the-Wealth movement and Father Charles Coughlin's National Union for Social Justice demanded a redistribution of wealth and incited class hatred among the poor. As some of the unrest was being calmed with federal relief efforts, conservatives and the wealthy grew increasingly unhappy with the growth of socialist programs.

In that volatile context Roosevelt assumed a prophetic posture at his second inauguration, speaking in visionary terms of a promised land ("our happy valley") beyond the present suffering. Defending his policies and the "new chapter in our book of self-government," which together they were writing, he insisted that Americans had discovered "the truth that democratic government has innate capacity to protect its people against disasters once considered inevitable, to solve problems once considered unsolvable." "We refused," he continued, "to leave the problems of our common welfare to be solved by the winds of chance and the hurricanes of disaster" (p. 274). Out of that awareness, FDR insisted, had come the enlarged government of his first administration. "Nearly all of us," he argued following his landslide 1936 reelection, "recognize that as intricacies of human relationships increase, so power to govern them also must increase—power to stop evil; power to do good." As he urged his listeners forward in the "new order of things," he reminded them that progress was to be measured in terms of the general welfare and that "the new materials" they were bringing to "the old foundations" were those of social justice. "We have always known," he asserted, "that heedless self-interest was bad morals; we know now that it is bad economics" (pp. 275–76).

On that basis Roosevelt called for those whose economic conditions had improved not to forget those still left behind. "The test of our progress is not whether we add more to the abundance of those who have much; it is whether we provide enough for those who have too little." The promised land he "envisioned" (one in which, "under democratic methods of government . . . national wealth can be translated into a spreading volume of human comforts"), could be entered, he told his countrymen, only through the gate of economic justice (p. 277). That would require restricting the liberties of the "callous and selfish" ("democracy" was a more important concept in early FDR speeches than was "freedom") and, at the same time, resisting class conflict. "Today," he concluded,

> we reconsecrate our country to long cherished ideals in a suddenly changed civilization. In every land there are always at work forces that

drive men apart and forces that draw men together. In our personal ambitions we are individualists. But in our seeking for economic and political progress as a nation, we all go up, or else we all go down, as one people. (p. 278)

Arguments concerning that domestic vision would define both liberalism and conservatism for the rest of the century; it would be praised and extended by liberal Democrats—most especially Lyndon Johnson—and vilified by the Republican right—most successfully Ronald Reagan.

But the last two of FDR's inaugurals, necessarily, were preoccupied with international politics, and here, reasserting views advanced by Teddy Roosevelt and Wilson, his position would be endorsed by postwar Republicans as fervently as by Democrats. In 1941 the message concerned keeping democratic values alive in a world elsewhere caught by a wave of antidemocratic feeling. Despite the spread of Fascism and Communism in Europe and the claims of many, even in free countries, "that for some unexplained reason, tyranny and slavery have become the surging wave of the future—and that freedom is an ebbing tide. . . . We Americans know that this is not true." Having survived the Depression with their democratic values intact, citizens of the United States knew "democratic aspiration is no mere recent phase in human history. It is human history" (p. 279).

Four years later, with the war that had justified Roosevelt's faith nearing an end, the ailing president reviewed the lessons America had learned:

We have learned that we cannot live alone, at peace; that our own well-being is dependent on the well-being of other nations far away. We have learned that we must live as men, not as ostriches, nor as dogs in the manger.

We have learned to be citizens of the world, members of the human community. (p. 284)

During the post–World War II period, Wilson's great theme of fighting "slavery" throughout the world reemerged as a dominant preoccupation of inaugurals. What in the wake of the first war was repudiated by Harding and Coolidge—entangling foreign alliances—in the aftermath of the second would be embraced by both parties. The Republican

Eisenhower, fresh from his service as leader of the Western alliance, came to the presidency already a practical and practicing internationalist, prepared by vision and experience to bring world leadership to his inauguration. Richard Nixon found his own great inspiration in the person and policies of this century's first Democratic president and staked his entire presidential career on his success in donning Wilson's mantle. Even the ascent of 1980s conservatism under Ronald Reagan resulted in an increase rather than a lessening of international activism. Only in the 1990s did that tendency slacken.

THE TWILIGHT STRUGGLE

In 1949 Truman described a world divided between democracy and communism and, having enumerated the differences between those ideologies, he outlined the Cold War strategy: support for the United Nations, support of European economic recovery, defense pacts with other "freedom-loving nations," and "making the benefits of our scientific advances and industrial progress available for the improvement and growth of underdeveloped areas" (p. 289). There was no question of retreating into fortress America, only the issue of restoring "peace, stability, and freedom to the world" (p. 287). His plan was to assist other nations in imitating the American example and to offer a global version of the New Deal, both from a sense of moral responsibility and as a strategy for containing communism.

Dwight D. Eisenhower aptly represented the postwar view in his 1953 inaugural, a message he opened with a prayer that called more for solemn soul-searching than for civic celebration. Depicting a world where the "forces of good and evil are massed and armed and opposed as rarely before in history," he described the event of inauguration not merely as one man's "swearing his oath of service, in the presence of God," but as the whole nation's "testimony in the sight of the world to our faith that the future shall belong to the free" (p. 249).

The entirety of Eisenhower's remarks sustained this tone of moral struggle. Meditative from its opening prayer to its benedictory close— "This is the work that awaits us all, to be done with bravery, with charity, and with prayer to Almighty God (p. 299)"—Eisenhower's remarks focused on the awesome power America controlled in the postwar, nuclear age. His remarks drew on the special regard in which he had come to be held; the General home from the world's most terrible war, he reflected a wisdom won from experience, an awe for the task ahead that stemmed from lessons learned in previous trials. As a result his speech, more than that of any of his predecessors, resembled George Washington's both in its reverential solemnity and in its effort to instruct the audience.

His focus was historical, an assessment of America at midcentury, and his perspective elevated. He spoke of the arrogance that can come with victory as well as the sense of uncertainty that accompanies change. First he summarized the previous fifty years:

> Since this century's beginning, a time of tempest has seemed to come upon the continents of the earth. Masses of Asia have awakened to strike off shackles of the past. Great nations of Europe have fought their bloodiest wars. Thrones have toppled and their vast empires have disappeared. New nations have been born.
>
> For our own country, it has been a time of recurring trial. We have grown in power and responsibility. We have passed through the anxieties of depression and of war to a summit unmatched in man's history. Seeking to secure peace in the world, we have had to fight through the forests of the Argonne, to the shores of Iwo Jima, and to the cold mountains of Korea. (p. 294)

Meditating on those momentous events, he turned to the profound questions they raised, not to offer answers so much as simply to legitimate the queries themselves:

> In the swift rush of great events, we find ourselves groping to know the full sense and meaning of these times in which we live. In our quest of understanding, we beseech God's guidance. We summon all our knowledge of the past and we scan all signs of the future. We bring all our wit and all our will to meet the question:
>
> How far have we come in man's long pilgrimage from darkness toward light? Are we nearing the light—a day of freedom and of peace for all mankind? Or are the shadows of another night closing in upon us?

Eisenhower's opening prayer—for complete dedication, for the ability to discern right from wrong, and for unity among those of different political views—had been preparation for this contemplative inquiry into meaning and purpose. The "crusade" of the war completed, he looked to an ongoing spiritual pilgrimage. Both troubled and hopeful, aware of the darkness as well as the light, Eisenhower had been made prayerful by the uncertainty of the times and by the unprecedented power available to an American president in the nuclear age. In the years after Hiroshima, when science "seems ready to confer upon us, as its final gift, the power to erase human life this planet," the office needed to be approached with awe and humility (p. 295).

Eisenhower's prayer spoke of inadequacy and began by "beseeching" God to complete the new president's own dedication and that of those who would share the work of governance. The central assertions of his speech were that (1) America, at midcentury, held previously unimaginable power, and this power would provide the nation's most demanding test; but (2) it could bring to this test, if faith in its oldest values were maintained, confidence and conviction. He then elaborated the principles, generated by the old values in the face of new circumstances, that would govern his administration's approach to world leadership and thereby fulfill a more humbled version of the old Wilsonian ambition—reconciling a divided world.

In his second inaugural Eisenhower returned to the same theme. "In the heart of Europe," he said, "Germany still stands tragically divided. So is the whole continent divided. And so, too, is all the world." As victor in the war little more than a decade past and as the most prosperous nation on earth, the United States cannot rest on its laurels but must take up the challenge issued by "International Communism," the "divisive force," which seeks "to seal forever the fate of those it has enslaved" and "break the ties that unite the free" (p. 301). This is Lincoln's old work of holding the Union against the slave powers, but World War II gave Eisenhower's America the global power and the global opponent Wilson lacked. The truth revealed by that conflict, one which "must rule all we think and do," was that "[n]o people can live to itself alone. The unity of all who dwell in freedom is their only sure defense" (p. 303).

The most celebrated of recent inaugurals, certainly the only one accorded much literary acclaim, was that of John F. Kennedy in 1961, a speech often quoted and admired though most often treated as a display of verbal virtuosity, a collection of catchy phrases. It was, as well, an address that marked a decisive turning in Cold War rhetoric, less restrained than Ike's tempered words and impatient with the older generation's slowness to act, embracing Ike's analysis of the conflict with communism but chafing under his cautiousness.

The 1961 inaugural was, above all, a declaration of generational change, an announcement of the passing of the torch to those

> born in this century, tempered by war, disciplined by a hard and bitter peace, proud of our ancient heritage—and unwilling to witness or permit the slow undoing of those human rights to which this Nation has always been committed, and to which we are committed today at home and around the world. (p. 306)

Implicit—often explicit—throughout Kennedy's inaugural was the perennial complaint of the young about their elders. Kennedy's own youthfulness, regarded by many during the campaign as a considerable handicap, was flaunted in his inaugural remarks, presented as a bold revitalizing force of the sort Americans had once so greatly admired in Teddy Roosevelt, and his address—in its elegant flourishes and memorable phrases ("Let the word go forth from this time and place"; "And if a beachhead of cooperation may push back the jungle of suspicion")—illustrated a verbal energy that sharply contrasted with the more ponderous style generally associated with Eisenhower. But more than anyone realized at the time, Kennedy's remarks were spoken both about and to the truly young, the high school and college students who would fuel his programs. In pledging to help those "peoples in huts and villages across the globe struggling to break the bonds of mass misery" (p. 306), no less than in promising a military presence that would allow America "never to negotiate out of fear," Kennedy committed the youth of 1961 to his Cold War version of the old Wilson mission. The world would be redeemed by America's young (whose numbers were larger than at any previous time in the nation's history), in the Peace Corps as well as the Green Berets, and it was they who were being called upon to "pay any price, bear any burden, meet any hardship, support any friend, oppose any foe, in order to assure the survival and the success of liberty" (p. 306). Kennedy's tone resembled Wilson's, but the historical irony, viewed from the vantage point of subsequent events, was more akin to that of Franklin Pierce.

Kennedy called those young people to the "long twilight struggle" against "tyranny, poverty, disease, and war itself," enlisting a "new generation" in causes familiar from earlier presidential oratory. Like Wilson he asked for America to sustain the "revolutionary beliefs for which our forebears fought" in struggles around the globe; like Hoover he declared it within human power "to abolish all forms of human poverty," but like Eisenhower he also observed that we have the capacity "to abolish all forms of human life." The address moves continuously between promise and danger, between the national past and a global future, sustained throughout by balanced sentences and parallel clauses. Kennedy's apparent ease in making such connections, his ability to describe a fearful challenge with such exhilaration ("I do not believe than any of us would change places with any other people or any other generation") suggested that he was at once clearsighted and visionary.

For all the emphasis on change, Kennedy's language and style were more than a little archaic: "Let us never negotiate out of fear. But let us never fear to negotiate"; "ask not what your country can do for you. Ask what you can do for your country." More blatantly oratorical than any inaugural speaker since Wilson and more obvious in his use of rhetorical tropes and figures than even the old Princetonian, Kennedy introduced an administration built on the young but enamored of old notions of elegance and dignity. His popularity stemmed in large part from what was celebrated as the Kennedy "style": an ease with both the casual and the ceremonial, a style both regal and common.

While his inaugural address reflected the intrinsic formality of the occasion, it contrasted sharply with the banter of his press conferences. The rhetorical success of his administration grew from his ability to present the public with two versions of his presidency and himself, one official and eloquent in an old-fashioned sort of way and the other personal, relaxed, unintimidated by office or responsibility. Though not so great a contrast as the prophetic Lincoln of the great speeches and cracker-barrel Abe, this duality (the formal more Roman than biblical, the informal more urbane than cracker-barrel) was a primary cause of the enormous hold the Kennedy presidency had, and continues to have, on the national imagination.

RICH IN GOODS, RAGGED IN SPIRIT

Nearly alone among the post–World War II presidents, Lyndon Johnson measured the office more by the standard of New Deal domestic reforms than by internationalism. His legacy of choice was the Great Society, and that was the subject he expounded in his 1965 inaugural message. Though he affirmed his commitment to "the liberation of man," it was liberty at home that was uppermost on his mind. Taking up the message of an earlier generation of Republican presidents, he concentrated on issues of racial and economic justice. "Justice requires us to remember," he instructed his countrymen, "that when any citizen denies his fellow, saying, 'His color is not mine,' or 'His beliefs are strange and different,' in that moment he betrays America, though his forebears created this nation" (p. 310). Johnson offered the Great Society as the means to a more perfect union, one in which poverty and discrimination would be eliminated, one "not without differences of opinion but without the deep and abiding divisions which scar the union for generations" (p. 312).[6] Ironically, the foreign policy that he barely mentioned in his inaugural message, the ongoing struggle to stop the spread of communism, drove him from office and cut short his domestic agenda.

Richard Nixon's instincts were precisely opposite to Johnson's. International affairs defined his presidential aspirations, but he came to office at the height of the Vietnam controversy and with urban violence at its zenith.[7] In 1969 he saw the irony of his position and, looking back to FDR's first inaugural, he recognized how different was his own situation.

> Standing in this same place a third of a century ago, Franklin Delano Roosevelt addressed a Nation ravaged by depression and gripped in fear. He could say in surveying the Nation's troubles: "They concern, thank God, only material things."
>
> Our crisis today is the reverse.
>
> We have found ourselves rich in goods, but ragged in spirit; reaching with magnificent precision for the moon, but falling into raucous discord on earth. (p. 317)

Like Kennedy ("Now the trumpet summons us . . .") he offered the global challenge of "peacemaking" ("This is our summons to greatness"), but that role must first be filled at home, where "[w]e are torn by division, wanting unity." Nixon called on his countrymen to "lower" their voices in the interest of domestic peace. "America has suffered," he argued, "from a fever of words; from inflated rhetoric that promises more than it can deliver; from angry rhetoric that fans discontent into hatreds; from bombastic rhetoric that postures instead of persuading." Only if the "shouting" stops can "our words be heard as well as our voices" (p. 317). Victorious in an election in which race had been a powerful issue (a third-party candidate, the segregationist George Wallace, won forty-six electoral votes) and in a year when Robert Kennedy and Martin Luther King were assassinated, Nixon reminded America, "No man can be fully free while his neighbor is not. To go forward at all is to go forward together" (p. 318). "I know America," he added. "I know the heart of America is good" (p. 319). This he offered not only as evidence that we could solve our problems at home but that his country would also assume the "sacred commitment" he accepted for himself. "I shall consecrate my office, my energies, and all the wisdom I can summon to the cause of peace among nations" (p. 320). This was the postwar business he longed to complete and for which he was, he believed, especially prepared. "I also know," he said, "the people of the world."

In 1973, with American troops withdrawn from Vietnam and the nation's cities somewhat calmer, Nixon devoted himself more fully to the subject he preferred and assured his audience that "we stand on the threshold of a new era of peace in the world" (p. 321). In the end, in another reversal of Johnson, Nixon was brought down by his failures at home, resigning his office in 1974. Jimmy Carter, coming to office in 1977 with the humiliations of Johnson and Nixon still fresh in the public's mind, returned to the 1969 emphasis on spiritual crisis. Taking both strands of the FDR legacy, he affirmed America's international obligations *and* a commitment to human rights and equal opportunity at home, but he recalled "our recent mistakes"—both Vietnam and Watergate—and warned that " 'more' is not necessarily 'better' " and "that even our great nation has its recognized limits" (pp. 328–9). That admission, surely as much a statement about the Great Society as one about Nixon's petty failings, aroused the ire of conservative Republicans (who hated LBJ's domestic programs but loved FDR's style) and was the object of Ronald Reagan's contempt four years later.

As his acceptance speech made obvious, no one felt the weight of

Franklin Roosevelt's presidency more than Reagan. He more than any of his Democratic predecessors measured the office against FDR. Even his attacks on Carter echoed the New Dealer's scorn for the conservatives of his day, as Reagan represented his own election in terms as similar to those of 1933 as he dared. "We suffer," he said in an effort to create a crisis comparable to that faced by FDR, "from the longest and one of the worst sustained inflations in our national history" (p. 332). He, like Roosevelt, promised recovery generated by the "creative energy" of the American people. Like FDR, Reagan, too, placed the blame not on the general citizenry but upon an elite serving narrow personal interests.

Again, as with their acceptances, the differences are as instructive as the similarities. Significantly, 1933's "unscrupulous moneychangers" had disappeared by 1981, and the villains were government bureaucrats, including those who were appointed to keep the moneychangers under control. There was in Reagan's speech no denigration of "material things," none of Roosevelt's insistence that the primary concern was "social values," but rather emphasis upon the promised "bounty of a revived economy." Where FDR insisted that he had been called to provide "discipline and direction" and to prevent self-interest from destroying the common good, Reagan declared himself elected to "unleash" the individual, to liberate him from burdensome taxes and restrictive regulations. Carter, reminiscent in this respect of Eisenhower, had opened his inaugural with a biblical call for humility, preparation for his warning that "we cannot afford to do everything," but Reagan regarded such a cautionary tone as little less than blasphemy. He castigated Carter for small-mindedness and liberalism for losing its daring.

But despite Reagan's obvious admiration for FDR's presidential voice, the most telling difference between the two in their first inaugurals is their respective styles. Roosevelt's short sentences were forceful and clear, indicative of one who had taken charge and knew exactly where he was going. The speech did not concern itself with amiability and gave little indication of FDR's charm and personal warmth. Consistent with its prophetic stance, it set the speaker apart from the audience, identified him as the leader, and in that role permitted him to judge and scold as well as to encourage. In every way, the 1933 inaugural was more a call to battle than an invitation to be friends. By contrast Reagan's longer sentences took much of the urgency out of his 1981 message, made it more conversational in tone; despite its message of danger, the speech's refusal to be hurried offered reassurance. Things were bad, Reagan suggested, and yet there was no need to rush, at least not at his inauguration, the most lavish in American history. The voice was relaxed and friendly, that of a speaker both sympathetic and approachable; where Roosevelt wasted no time moving from one point to the next, reinforcing through the cadence of his speech a sense of action already begun, Reagan moved at a more leisurely pace, allowing time for anecdotes and musings.

Typical of the difference is the contrast between Roosevelt's declaration, "This nation asks for action, and action now," and Reagan's, "We are going to begin to act, beginning today." Reagan's recurrent use—unique in inaugural addresses—of the word "well" as a transition ("We hear much of special interest groups. Well, our concern must be . . .") was consistent with this verbal tendency to delay. It became a frequently noted Reagan quirk, much abused by impersonators, that gave a folksy tone to his talk. But its primary effect was to slow all movement and delay the issue at hand. In unscripted situations, interviews and press conferences, it was often a filler word, a sound to fill a gap and a means of masking uncertainty, confusion, even—as Nancy Reagan inadvertently revealed—a hearing problem. But Reagan's oratorical "well" was a good deal more. Not the rural one-word sentence, the "well" that says there is nothing more to say, his seemed rather a gathering of strength, an intake of breath needed for the utterance that would eventually follow. Instead of generating impatience among the listeners, it seemed to reassure them precisely because it did delay, softening the crisis being described, belying its urgency, and making the new president seem less radical than his supporters and opponents claimed.[8]

A NEW ORDER

Reagan very nearly marks the close of the period dominated by FDR and World War II. His vice president and successor, George Bush, himself profoundly influenced by those examples, anticipated the historic change in his 1989 address.[9] The "time of tempest" of which Eisenhower spoke had by Bush's inauguration quieted to a "breeze" as "the totalitarian era" with which his predecessors had contended came to an end, and "free markets, free speech, free elections, and the exercise of free will unhampered by the state" promised "a more just and prosperous life for man on earth" (p. 346). As the Cold War ended he recognized the successful resolution of an obligation passed on since the 1940s. Communism had been defeated, and, while the world was not wholly liberated, Bush believed a "new order" was at hand.

Bush anticipated the transition, which would in fact occur with his defeat four years later, when he declared, "And the generation born after the Second World War has come of age" (p. 348). Then, almost immediately, he turned not to *his* war but to the one that he feared influenced this new generation. Struggling to explain the suspicions separating political parties, he complained, "It has been this way since Vietnam. That war cleaves us still" (p. 348). Even as he announced the passing of the World War II generation he sought to prolong its influence and to erase the Asian conflict, which loomed large for those coming to power at century's end. "[S]urely," he said, "the statute of limitations has been reached. This is a fact: The final lesson of Vietnam is that no great nation can long afford to be sundered by a memory" (p. 348). Vietnam, he declared, was an inappropriate marker in the chronology of the country.

The age difference between William Jefferson Clinton when he was inaugurated and George Bush was twenty-two years, a generational gap only slightly less than that separating Eisenhower and Kennedy. Accordingly, the 1993 inauguration represented more than a transition between persons and parties. It meant a dramatic shift in the culture and experience that shape an individual president. Clinton *had* come of age in Vietnam America, a country divided rather than unified by war. While he could not be expected to measure himself by FDR or to understand his country in terms of Eisenhower's "Great Crusade," it was not altogether clear what the next benchmark should be. The Vietnam War, which Clinton as a college student had opposed and avoided, was hardly appropriate either personally or culturally. Bush was right to argue that a country cannot usefully measure itself by so divisive and troubling an experience. It can be warned by its mistakes but not defined by them.

Clinton suggested a certain ambiguity in his situation when he opened his address with the image of a "forced spring," reference to the gardener's way of bringing a generation to bud before its anticipated time. Though his immediate subject was "American renewal," "spring reborn in the world's oldest democracy," he soon turned directly to the generational issue. "Each generation," he observed, "must define what it means to be an American." Then he thanked his predecessor for "his half-century of service" and with him "the millions of men and women whose steadfastness and sacrifice triumphed over Depression, fascism, and Communism." Coming to office after the collapse of the Soviet Union, Clinton could point to the great postwar challenges as being completed, but in so doing he was implying an America no longer motivated by the agenda that had guided it for nearly fifty years. "Today," he announced, "a generation raised in the shadows of the Cold War assumes new responsibilities in a world warmed by the sunshine of freedom but threatened still by ancient hatreds and new plagues."

Clinton's word of thanks to those who had won both the World War and the Cold War was not merely an effort to be gracious to those he was displacing. It was a reminder that since 1933 Americans had known who or what was the enemy. Before the Depression's end there was fascism to fight, and no sooner was it defeated than communism declared itself as the foe. In 1993, however, the familiar antagonist had disappeared. Bush could speak hopefully in 1989 of a new world order that lay just beyond Communism's crumbling walls, but by the time Clinton spoke Americans were no longer so confident that a collapsing Soviet empire ensured international harmony. The exact nature of the contemporary threat was unclear.

When Clinton's political hero, John F. Kennedy, dismissed the old leadership of his day, he did so without yielding their central work. The message of 1961 had been militant, the voice that delivered it full of aggressive confidence in the old Wilsonian assurance that the world could be changed as the wisdom and wealth of democracy were empowered by the energy and boldness its of youth. In 1993, despite all the echoes of that earlier address, Clinton's message could not be the same, in large part because the postwar era had ended and the incoming president could not rely on the Depression and World War II to locate himself or his country.[10] Even though he reached back to Kennedy rhetorically, it was to close rather than to continue an era. Recalling "the trumpet" that summoned Americans in 1961, Clinton declared "we have heard the trumpets" and immediately added "we have changed the guard." And so he dismissed Kennedy as well as Bush. But there remained, as Bush had anticipated, the need for some great locating event that could tell us who and where we were, and like FDR in 1941 Clinton confronted the issue of national chronology, adding his alternative to Vietnam: "From our revolution to the Civil War, to the Great Depression to the civil rights movement, our people have mustered the determination to construct from these crises the pillars of our history."

He was not alone in seeing in Civil Rights movement as the exemplifying experience, the great moral conflict of his own youth, that embodied American purpose and ideals. This view had been offered by many Southern Democrats, including his vice president, Al Gore. Jimmy Carter's concern in the 1970s had been to extend to the rest of the world the human rights lessons of America's 1950s and 1960s. In 1993 Clinton asserted that it was what America had learned in its own struggles against racism that replaced the war against fascism in guiding our world leadership. In a world still threatened by "ancient hatreds" the United States once more could turn to its own experience in providing guidance to other nations. "Communism's collapse," Clinton observed, "has called forth old animosities and new dangers." In Eastern Europe, Somalia, and the Middle East division and alienation were the operative realities of the day. With the demise of the Soviet empire there came in that vast region an eruption of suspicion, an explosion that rejected difference—whether of religion or race or ethnicity or clan—and declared likeness the only viable basis for community. In this context Clinton offered, as his country's credentials for international leadership, "the faces we show the world," the multihued array of persons assembled in his audience, the participating presence of women as well as men, African and Asian Americans, Latinos, and Native Americans as well as whites of European descent (*New York Times*, 1/21/93).[11]

RENEWAL AND REMEMBRANCE

The interaction of incoming presidents with both their immediate audience and their predecessors is itself an important service of inaugural messages. The need Adams and Jefferson acknowledged to assure Americans of the comfort of continuity as well as the excitement of change is the first duty of a president. This is a moment in which members of the audience need to be reconciled with one another, but also need to find a connection with the generations on either side. Even during secession and as the country prepared for a war within itself, Lincoln did not ignore this duty. The "mystic chords of memory" to which he appealed, while they did not prevail in 1861, were there for future presidents as the states were reunited.

In the anthologies of our political literature inaugural speeches appear more frequently than any other genre of oratory. They do so because presidents, regardless of their rhetorical gifts, recognize a poetry implicit in the occasion. It is a moment in which disruption must be incorporated into a larger sense of harmony, and that is the primary purpose of eloquence.

Chapter Six

The State of the Union

The closing year has been replete with blessings, for which we owe to the Giver of All Good our reverent acknowledgment. For the uninterrupted harmony of our foreign relations, for the decay of sectional animosities, for the exuberance of our harvests and the triumphs of our mining and manufacturing industries, for the prevalence of health, the spread of intelligence, and the conservation of the public credit, for the growth of the country in all the elements of national greatness—for these and countless other blessings we should rejoice and be glad.

—Chester A. Arthur, 1883 Annual Message

"Throughout the year since our last meeting," James Buchanan reported to Congress in December 1860, "the country has been eminently prosperous in all its material interests." Hardly an inventive opening, considering that presidents since Washington had regularly begun annual messages with descriptions of what John Adams termed "flattering prospects of abundance." Buchanan's introductory sentence nevertheless had an ominous tone, one foreshadowed by the conspicuous presence of the qualifying "material." "The general health has been excellent," he continued, our harvests have been abundant, and plenty smiles throughout the land. Our commerce and manufactures have been prosecuted with energy and industry, and have yielded fair and ample returns. In short, no nation in the tide of time has ever presented a spectacle of greater material prosperity than we have done until within a very recent period. (I:1025)*

Again the burdensome adjective "material" lay heavily on the subject, compromising the very notion of "prosperity" as the president—less than four months from the end of his term—plodded on toward his inevitable point. "Why is it, then, that discontent now so extensively prevails, and the Union of the States, which is the source of all these blessings, is threatened with destruction?"

That was the moment presidents had feared since Washington's administration. What Buchanan saw was the brink of not only a personal failure but a failure of the office he served. In the month in which he spoke South Carolina left the Union, and a few weeks later the ship he sent to support the garrison at Fort Sumter was fired upon as it entered Charleston harbor. That was the moment all previous reports on the state of the union had declared to be *not* at hand, and Buchanan's predecessors, even in the most difficult times, could claim at least this success. His "Why is it, then?" echoed the traditional query of those occasions, but in previous messages the "it" had referred exclusively to America's prosperity, and the answer that followed had always been, "because of the Union and God's favor." Now the "it" referred to failure, and the president looked elsewhere for his answers.

Buchanan alternated between blame and reassurance, between reckless indictments and desperate cajoling. The fault, he first asserted, lay solely with the North and its "long-continued and intemperate interference . . . with the question of slavery in the Southern states." The result, he insisted, was "natural," and the "different sections of the Union are now arrayed against each other, and the time has arrived, so much dreaded by the Father of his Country, when hostile geographical parties have been formed." Sectional conflicts, he claimed, resulted not from efforts to ex-

---

*Unless otherwise noted, all references in this chapter are to Fred C. Israel., ed., *The State of the Union Messages 1790–1966* (New York, 1966).

clude slavery from the territories, nor even from Northern defiance of the Fugitive Slave Law. "All or any of these evils," he insisted,

> might have been endured by the South without danger to the Union (as others have been) in the hope that time and reflection might apply the remedy. The immediate peril arises not so much from these causes as from the fact that the incessant and violent agitation of the slavery question throughout the North for the last quarter of a century has at length produced its malign influence on the slaves and inspired them with vague notions of freedom. Hence a sense of security no longer exists around the family altar. This feeling of peace at home has given way to apprehension of servile insurrections. Many a matron throughout the South retires at night in dread of what might befall herself and children before the morning. (I:1025–26)

Civil strife resulted, in this peculiar view, from encouraging slaves to believe they could be free and from the fear felt by Southern whites not of Northern abolitionists but of Southern blacks. In this accounting an action like that of John Brown at Harpers Ferry became an assault on the women of the South, not on the governments of the slave powers.

Buchanan's was a plea for time—the slavery question, he promised, would "have its day"—and was coupled with a warning to a successor that no seceding state could be held by force. In his first message to Congress in 1857, he had lingered long on what to do with a rebellious Brigham Young and his threats to challenge with force the federal government's right to name anyone other than himself Utah's territorial governor. "This is the first rebellion," Buchanan told the legislature,

> which has existed in our Territories, and humanity itself requires that we should put it down in such a manner that it shall be the last. To trifle with it would be to encourage it and to render it formidable. We ought to go there with such an imposing force as to convince those deluded people that resistance would be vain, and thus spare the effusion of blood. (I:961)

Through such action, he insisted in a logic peculiarly his own, "We can . . . best convince them that we are their friends, not their enemies." In dealing with a rebellious territory in 1857, especially one populated by the "frenzied fanatics" of an unpopular religious sect, Buchanan felt justified in proposing military intervention. He did not apply that principle, however, to the Southern states in 1860. "The fact is," he insisted,

> that our Union rests upon public opinion, and can never be cemented by the blood of its citizens shed in civil war. If it cannot live in the affections of the people, it must one day perish. Congress possesses many means of preserving it by conciliation, but the sword was not placed in their hand to preserve it by force. (I:1036)

If the Union failed—and that failure was becoming obvious even as he spoke—then the blood of the fathers was shed in vain, and humanity's best hope would be destroyed, yielding the world to "a long night of leaden despotism." The American example, for eighty years a beacon of promise, "would be quoted as a conclusive proof that man is unfit for self-government."

"This advice," he told Congress, "proceeds from the heart of an old public functionary whose service commenced in the last generation, among the wise and conservative statesmen of that day . . . and whose first and dearest earthly wish is to leave his country tranquil, prosperous, united, and powerful" (I:1002). "Powerful" and "prosperous" he had managed, but "tranquil" and "united" had evaded him. The state of the union in Buchanan's final reading was disunion, and his message was a response to personal repudiation, despair, and the conviction that he would be the last to retire as president of united states.

A VISION OF THE WHOLE

Buchanan reported all that to Congress because he was required to. The Constitution stipulates that it is an executive obligation to report to that body "from time to time" "on the state of the union." Called the "annual message" until it became the "State of the Union" in 1945, it presumes that the representatives of the states need the executive to explain to them their collective condition. To speak of the state of the states united suggests how profoundly aware were the founders of the constant difficulty special interests have in seeing beyond their own narrow limits to a more inclusive view. Those who serve the individual states, in their singularity, the Constitution regards as unreliable at discerning the condition of the states in their entirety. Special interest is conditioned always to see the particular and to find its own preoccupations wherever it looks, but the leader of the Union, by the nature of that office, sees more largely, has a vision of the whole, and is charged to bring that vision to the representatives of America's constituent parts.

In 1792, when George Washington told congressmen that the greatest contribution they could offer their country was "the careful cultivation of harmony combined with a due regard to stability, in the public councils," he delivered the message (as he did each year) in person. He came to the chambers in which they so zealously represented their lesser districts to remind them of the larger body they also served. The Republican Jefferson considered those appearances to be too kingly, too much like the English monarch's ceremonial address before Parliament, and he substituted written reports, refusing to intrude his own presence on the legislative business. When Woodrow Wilson, 112 years later, renewed Washington's and Adams's practice of delivering the message in person, he was—as Arthur M. Schlesinger has noted—affirming an aggressive approach to "presidential leadership," one in which Congress has to deal with the person of the president as well as with the office he holds.[1] The presidents of the 1920s, concerned with reversing the prominence Teddy Roosevelt and Wilson had brought to the executive role, only rarely spoke their messages (Harding did so twice, Coolidge once, and Hoover never), but their successors, Republican and Democrat alike, have followed Wilson's example.

Prior to the Civil War the annual reports were, understandably, preoccupied with how tenuous were the ties of national union. Madison complained in 1812 that the governors of Massachusetts and Connecticut had refused "to furnish the required detachments of militia toward the defense of the maritime frontier" (I:117–18) so desperately needed in the second war with Britain. John Quincy Adams lectured the states in his 1828 message about the limits of their powers and the danger should they challenge the authority of Congress. But almost without fail presidents began with signs of promise. The good news with which Washington opened his 1790 report was that of North Carolina's endorsement of the federal Constitution, "the rising credit and respectability of our country, the general and increasing good will toward the Government of the Union, and the concord, peace, and plenty with which we are blessed" (I:2). Even in 1794, when he felt it necessary to open with less happy news, an act of rebellion against the national government, the first president prefaced his remarks as positively as possible. "When we call to mind," the address began,

> the gracious indulgence of Heaven by which the American people became a nation; when we survey the general prosperity of our country, and look forward to the riches, power, and happiness to which it seems destined, with the deepest regret do I announce to you that during your recess some of the citizens of the United States have been found capable of an insurrection. It is due, however, to the character of our Government and to its stability, which cannot be shaken by the enemies of order, freely to unfold the course of this event. (I:21)

The "event" that so shocked Washington was the armed resistance offered by a group of Pennsylvania distillers and their allies against the collection of a federal whisky tax. The indignant Commander-in-Chief elaborately recounted the history of that confrontation for the listening legislators. But even such an affront was not wanting in "substantial consolations":

> It has demonstrated that our prosperity rests on solid foundations, by furnishing an additional proof that my fellow-citizens understand the true principles of government and liberty; that they feel their inseparable union; that notwithstanding all the devices which have been used to sway them from their interest and duty, they are now as ready to maintain the authority of the laws against licentious invasions as they were to defend their rights against usurpation. It has been a spectacle displaying to the highest advantage the value of republican government to behold the most and the least wealthy of our citizens standing in the same ranks as private soldiers, preeminently distinguished by being the army of the Constitution. (I:24)

Washington's last two messages, in the absence of riotous distillers, reverted to cataloguing those signs of well-being that he and his successors took as evidence of divine favor.

The prefatory piety that has become commonplace in annual messages does not always make it clear whether God loves America because it is free or America is free because God loves it, but clear enough is the conviction that the two go together and that American prosperity—agricultural, commercial, political—is the result of the ultimate "most privileged" status. "Let us be grateful," Jackson instructed Congress in 1831, "for these blessings to the beneficent Being who has conferred them, and who suffers us to indulge a reasonable hope of their continuance and extension, while we neglect not the means by which they may be preserved." Explaining the ways of God to his congressional audience, Jackson described the divine intention: "He has made our national prosperity to depend on the preservation of our liberties, our national force on our Federal Union, and our individual happiness on the maintenance of our State rights and wise institutions" (I:345). Having it both ways in politics and theology, Jackson's explanation of America's success was an affirmation of both federalism and state rights, of both works and grace.

Providence on occasion was not so beneficent. John Adams noted in opening his first two annual messages (1797 and 1798) the "destructive pestilence" raging in America's coastal cities.[2] Still, the "reverence and resignation" with which he began those addresses did not include the suggestion of divine sanction, but yielded instead to gratitude for other favors, including a lessening of the disease in time for Congress to assemble in Philadelphia, one of the afflicted cities (I:44).

Similarly, Martin Van Buren "regretted" in 1839, another year of disease, that he could not "congratulate" the country on a year of "unalloyed prosperity." He, too, quickly turned to thanksgiving for a more general well-being "bestowed upon us by the Author of All Good," most immediately evident in the "exuberant harvests" of the past summer (I:517). The lesson, Adams and Van Buren implied, was that God and nature were doing their parts to sustain and strengthen America, and that only domestic conflict could bring the failure of Union. "In the example of other systems founded on the will of the people," Andrew Jackson had noted in 1835, "we trace to internal dissentions the influences which have so often blasted the hopes of the friends of freedom. The social elements, which were strong and successful when united against external danger, failed in the more difficult task of properly adjusting their own internal organization" (I:415).

AN AMERICAN DECLARATION

While the presidents preceding Jackson expressed similar sentiments, the external frequently dominated their annual reports, as they provided

Congress with detailed analyses of world happenings and the implications for America. In part this was a consequence of their own international experience, for all but one of the five executives separating Jackson from Washington had previously served as Secretary of State, and that one exception, John Adams, had spent ten years in foreign service before being elected vice president.[3] But it was also a reflection of the tenuous status of a vulnerable young nation in a world of colonizing superpowers. Concluding his 1797 report, Adams noted: "We are met together at a most interesting period. The situations of the principle powers of Europe are singular and portentious. Connected with some by treaties and with all by commerce, no important event there can be indifferent to us."

James Monroe explicitly linked the issues of internal harmony with Europe's political condition in all his annual messages—addresses coauthored by his Secretary of State, John Quincy Adams—and on that connection issued in his seventh report the most famous of all state of the union pronouncements, the Monroe Doctrine. The "era of good feeling" that had produced Monroe's unopposed reelection was also a period of an unprecedented increase in the number of states. From the nineteen states participating in the 1816 election, the Union had grown to twenty-four by 1820.[4] This combination of national growth and apparent political harmony presented Monroe with a strong foundation in dealing with the rest of the world. At the same time conditions in Europe were much changed since John Adams had found them so "singular and portentous" in 1797, when Napoleon was just beginning his campaigns. The French emperor had been sent to his second and final exile the year before Monroe's first election, but the consequences of his European campaigns were still being felt around the world, most especially among the colonial possessions of Spain. While the mother country had been distracted by its war with France, independence movements had swept across Spanish America, and in 1823 rumors spread that Spain, allied with the post-Napoleonic French government, planned to restore its former empire. The Monroe Doctrine responded to that threat by declaring America's opposition to further European colonization of the New World. It specifically included efforts to reclaim former possessions. Thus America announced its determination to be the dominant influence in the Western Hemisphere and a self-appointed guardian of emerging American republics. The doctrine—augmented by Teddy Roosevelt's

1904 corollary asserting the right to intervene in Latin America whenever disorder threatened—has continued to be enforced down to such recent events as the Reagan-ordered invasion of Grenada and Clinton's Haitian intervention.

Monroe had been preparing the case he presented in 1823 since his first year in the White House, building on the reasoning of his predecessors. In 1809 James Madison had closed his first annual message by congratulating his countrymen "on the prosperity and happiness flowing from our situation at home" despite "wrongs and vexations experienced from external causes." He attributed that achievement to the growth of domestic production and a lessening dependence on imports. "This revolution in our pursuits and habits," he wryly concluded, had come about precisely because the quarreling European powers had so obstructed United States foreign trade as to force development of America's own manufacturing (precisely the commercial direction the agrarian Jefferson had hoped, along with the ills of urbanization, to avoid). Madison closed with a brief benediction of thanksgiving that began, "Recollecting always that for every advantage which may contribute to distinguish our lot from that to which others are doomed by the unhappy spirit of the times we are indebted to . . . Divine Providence" (I:105). European troubles could be as providential and fortuitous as American prosperity.

Monroe refined and expanded the twin themes of "happiness" at home and a complementary "unhappiness abroad" in his first six annual messages. In each he surveyed Europe's misfortune—wars between neighboring states and rebellion in the South American colonies—and argued that even as the imperial powers were losing territory and wealth the United States was growing larger and richer. The lesson he drew from these circumstances was that, while empires are inevitably destabilized by the very acquisitions that define them and eventually fall apart, America was proving that a republic could greatly expand and be strengthened by the addition.

In his first annual message in 1817, Monroe assured Congress that America was militarily secure—"in case of future wars"—and financially strong. Even more important, he observed: "Local jealousies are rapidly yielding to more generous, enlarged, and enlightened views of national policy" (I:148). By contrast, Europe was in disarray, its "local jealousies" increasing in fervor and intensity. Since Spain's New World intentions were America's deepest concern, the president focused on that country's troubles, presenting it as a power being challenged by independence-minded colonies and incapable of maintaining control even of insignificant places like Amelia Island, a spot off the Georgia coast that had been captured by "adventurers" and turned into a smuggling center.

Monroe renewed this indictment the following year, extending it to Spanish Florida, where, he insisted, "the Government of Spain has scarcely been felt" (I:157). Apart from Pensacola and St. Augustine, with their small garrisons, the territory was essentially ungoverned, "the theater of every species of lawlessness" (I:158). He offered this as evidence not only of Spain's failing strength but also of the growing threat—on America's doorstep—from unrestrained "buccaneers," "fugitives from justice," and "adventurers." In that context the president reported two military actions in Spanish territory. Since his last annual message American forces had successfully dislodged the invaders of Amelia Island (an action Monroe justified as self-defense since it had been directed not against Spain but rather against a "force" that had "wrested" the island *from* Spain), and, on a different front, an ever zealous General Jackson had pursued Seminoles into Spanish Florida, again "not to encroach on the rights of Spain," but to deprive those savages . . . of the protection on which they had relied in making the war" (I:160). "Protection" was something Spain seemed incapable of providing (the Seminoles supposedly were benefitting from the absence of civil order); all authority in the area, Spanish or otherwise, Monroe reported, had collapsed.

For some years the United States had sought possession of the lands in question, and Monroe annually suggested they would be appropriate payment for American claims that the Spanish government had officially acknowledged in the 1795 treaty establishing the Florida boundary. "If the embarrassments of Spain," he chided in 1818, "prevented her from making an indemnity to our citizens for so long a time from her treasury for their losses by spoliation and otherwise, it was in her power to have provided it by the cession of this territory" (I:158).

In his third annual message (1820), Monroe resumed his depiction of an "unsettled" Europe and an increasingly "settled" America and report-ed that while a treaty had been negotiated providing some of the cessions he had called for the previous year, Spain was now refusing to proceed with ratification. An envoy was, as Monroe spoke, on his way to explain his government's objections. "Shall we act," Monroe asked Congress, "by taking the ceded territory and proceeding to execute the other conditions of the treaty before this minister arrives and is heard?" Acknowledging the insult in Spain's behavior, the president advised restraint. "By a short delay we lose nothing, for, resting on the ground of immutable truth and justice, we cannot be diverted from our purpose" (I:169). America's magnanimity, he implied, was evidence of its strength in comparison with an "embarrassed" Spain.

Monroe's 1820 address, coming in the midst of an economic depression, began with a peculiarly constructed assertion of "happiness" at home. "In communicating to you a just view of public affairs at the commencement of your present labors," he told Congress, "I do it with great satisfaction, because, taking all circumstances into consideration which claim attention, I see much cause to rejoice in the felicity of our situation" (I:174). The chain of prepositional delays and the hint of qualification—"taking all circumstances into consideration which claim attention"—lengthens the sentence and defers the expected "felicity" just a little longer. When he elaborated on the "circumstances" requiring "consideration," he was equally slow and convoluted. "In making this remark," he continued,

> I do not wish to be understood to imply that an unvaried prosperity is to be seen in every interest of this great community. In the progress of a nation inhabiting a territory of such vast extent and great variety of climate, every portion of which is engaged in foreign commerce and liable to be affected in some degree by the changes which occur in the condition and regulations of foreign countries, it would be strange if the produce of our soil and the enterprise of our fellow-citizens received at all times and in every quarter an uniform and equal encouragement. This would be more than we would have a right to expect under circumstances the most favorable. (I:174)

Still hesitating as he repeated the obvious, demurring that of course not all Americans were equally prosperous and happy, Monroe finally concluded: "Pressures on certain interests, it is admitted, have been felt." Only after a further delay of seven lines did the president finally raise the pertinent question, "From whence do these pressures come?" Not to be blamed on "a government which is founded by, administered for, and supported by the people," they were rather the doing of

> the peculiar character of the epoch in which we live, and . . . the extraordinary occurrences which have signalized it. The convulsions with which several of the powers of Europe have been shaken and the long and destructive wars in which all were engaged, with their sudden transition to a state of peace, presenting in the first instance unusual encouragement to our commerce and withdrawing it in the second even within its wonted limit, could not fail to be sensibly felt here. (I:175)

America's problems, such as they were, Monroe traced to overseas causes.[5] A warring Europe needed and encouraged American trade to make up for the loss of commerce among its own nations, but during periods of peace—and 1820 was such a time—it ignored and even penalized the United States in favor of its more immediate neighbors.

Embedded between these broad generalizations and Monroe's more specific report on foreign relations was a return to the conventional thanksgiving, praise for the "Supreme Author of All Good" responsible both for individual rights and the "Union blessed with plenty." But Monroe (echoing Madison's 1809 claim) also suggested that God was responsible for the "pressures" America felt, not as harsh judgments but as "mild and instructive admonitions, warning us of dangers to be shunned in future, teaching us lessons of economy" (I:175). Since the "pressures" were of European origin, it was presumed that the divine instruction concerned foreign policy, and a part of the lesson was that American happiness was not wholly separable from it.

One year later, not surprisingly, Monroe described an increased assertiveness in America's dealings with Europe, designed to alleviate the "pressures" he had discerned in 1820. The divine instruction was being followed. His administration was being firm in negotiations with both Britain and France and insisting on equal status in commercial affairs. He explained at some length the trade restrictions his envoys were fighting—the prohibition on direct trade with British colonies and inequalities in French trade regulations—then told the story of the *Apollo*, a French merchant ship that had tried to evade paying duties by anchoring on the Spanish side of the St. Mary's River, the boundary line between the United States and Spanish Florida, even though the only settlements with which it could do business were in the United States. The United States had subsequently seized the ship, and the government of France had protested. This little narrative, more than a gratuitous anecdote, suggested that America need no longer be intimidated by the old powers. The administration's refusal to tolerate the *Apollo*'s cavalier attitude toward American law, like its demands for equal treatment in trade, indicated it was willing and able to stand up for its interests.[6]

Over the course of six annual messages, Monroe laid the logical and emotional foundations for his 1823 address and the doctrine it advanced. His argument depended upon successfully portraying the contrasting fortunes of the United States and the old imperial powers and the degree to which his countrymen and the world at large accepted the notion of a shift in relative advantage. On that basis he drew the conclusion implicit in his earlier reports, issuing America's warning to Europe not once but three times.

First mention came as he discussed negotiations with Russia and Great Britain over conflicting claims in the Pacific Northwest. In this context, he told Congress

> the occasion has been deemed proper for asserting, as a principle in which the rights and interests of the United States are involved, that the American continents, by the free and independent conditions which they have assumed and maintain, are henceforth not to be considered as subjects for future colonization by any European power. (I:205)

Eight pages later, after listing the ambassadors to the new South American republics and reporting the growing readiness of America's armed forces, he returned to his doctrine and the social unrest in Europe. First he reiterated the country's commitment to nonintervention: "In the wars of the European powers in matters relating to themselves we have never taken any part nor does it comport with our policy to do so."[7] But, he continued, with "the movements in this hemisphere we are of necessity more immediately connected, and by causes which must be obvious to all enlightened and impartial observers." The first of those "causes," Monroe argued, was the inherent difference in assumptions about government that distinguished the United States from countries like Spain and Portugal. Americans' devotion to their political system ("which has been achieved by the loss of so much blood and treasure") leads them to oppose the further expansion of an antagonistic colonial model in the New World. "We owe it, therefore, to candor and to the amicable relations existing between the United States and those powers," Monroe warned, "to declare that we should consider any attempt on their part to extend their system to any portion of this hemisphere as dangerous to our peace and safety." He argued that this was a reasonable position both through the obviousness of the self-interest involved and the restraint that America would practice, but he made the limits of that restraint and the determination to pursue that self-interest clear and precise.

> With the existing colonies or dependencies of any European power we have not interfered and shall not interfere. But with the Governments who have declared their independence and maintained it, and whose independence we have, on great consideration and just principles, acknowledged, we could not view any interposition for the purpose of oppressing them, or controlling in any other manner their destiny, by any European power in any other light than as the manifestation of an unfriendly disposition toward the United States. In the war between those new Governments and Spain we declared our neutrality at the time of their recognition, and to this we have adhered, and shall continue to adhere, provided no change shall occur which, in the judgment of the competent authorities of this Government, shall make a corresponding change on the part of the United States indispensable to their security.

Determined to be understood, he repeated his doctrine more succinctly and even more emphatically a paragraph later, concluding,

> It is impossible that the allied powers [Spain and Portugal] should extend their political system to any portion of either continent without endangering our peace and happiness; nor can anyone believe that our southern brethren, if left to themselves, would adopt it of their own accord. It is equally impossible, therefore, that we should behold such interposition in any form with indifference. (I:213)

"Our peace and happiness" provides the second strand in Monroe's argument, evidence of America's ability to play a more assertive international role and of Providence's larger geopolitical design. "If we compare the present condition of our Union with its actual state at the close of our Revolution," he reminded the Congress, "the history of the world furnishes no example of a progress in improvement in all the important circumstances which constitute the happiness of a nation which bears any resemblance to it." Those circumstances he then enumerated in a half-page catalog of the statistics of national growth. But for an American republic, in contrast to a European empire, those numbers alone were not a sufficient measure. The truer standard was the advancement of the Union toward perfection, and Monroe declared that the

> expansion of our population and accession of new States to our Union have had the happiest effect on all its higher interests. That it has emi-nently augmented our resources and added to our strength and re-spectability as a power is admitted by all. But it is not in these important circumstances only that this happy effect is felt. It is manifest that by en-larging the basis of our system and increasing the number of States the system itself has been greatly strengthened in both its branches. Consoli-dation and disunion have thereby been rendered equally impractical. . . . To what, then, do we owe these blessings? It is known to all that we derive them from the excellence of our institutions. Ought we not, then, to adopt every measure which may be necessary to perpetuate them? (I:213–14)

With this question—or rather with its understood answer—Monroe closed his most famous message. Union, institutional coherence, harmo-ny, and public happiness were what vindicated America's claims over "un-settled" Europe, the signs of a superior system in sharp contrast to the failing Spanish and Portuguese empires and the flawed Russian behe-moth. Abroad, imperialistic expansion contained the seeds of destruc-tion, weakened the system both in the mother country and in its colonies, but at home growth, "native" (i.e., natural) growth, gave the strength to demand full respect from the older powers.

The annual messages of 1817 through 1823 did much more than summarize this country's diplomatic business; they argued the case for domestic expansion. While American growth would inevitably bring conflicts with the colonial powers (such as the boundary disputes in the Northwest), that prospect was no longer so daunting if Monroe's geopo-litical analysis was correct. And beyond the geographical collisions, this country was now prepared to enter—in this hemisphere—ideological contests. Neutrality toward European nations did not require the United States to be neutral in the New World. As other former colonies prevailed in their struggles for independence, this country would be calling into doubt the legitimacy of it own sovereignty if it did not censure efforts at recolonization. According to Monroe's formulation, the United States was morally and politically bound to affirm a natural and irreversible progression from colony to independence. And here he was speaking simultaneously of a Latin American future and an American present as he linked southern struggles for independence with his own country's struggle for full recognition in the community of nations.

Monroe's successor, John Quincy Adams (the Secretary of State who authored Monroe's foreign policy), happily announced in his 1825 message plans for a gathering of the American republics "to deliberate upon objects important to the welfare of all." This "congress," to assemble at the Isthmus of Panama, had been called, Adams reported, at the invitation of Colombia and Mexico, which had invited the United States to participate within the limits of "that neutrality from which it is neither our intention nor the desire of the other American states that we should depart." The most notable section of Adams's message, however, came as he completed the more conventional business and turned away from the physical growth and improvement that sustained Monroe's confidence in America's superiority. Those were important, he agreed, but even more so was "moral," "political," and "intellectual improvement." "Knowledge," he argued, was both the means and the measure of individual and social growth. Though he presented, as might be expected, a plea for "seminaries of learning," he quickly moved on to call for more explicit support of scientific research. He reminded his audience of their country's debt to Renaissance voyages of discovery, then asked whether "we are not bound by obligations of a high and honorable character to contribute our portion of energy and exertion to the common stock?" (I:244). In answer he proposed funding more thorough exploration of America's Pacific coast, renewed efforts to establish standards of weights and measures, improving the Patent Office, and erecting an observatory. Of the last he wryly noted,

And while scarcely a year passes over our heads without bringing some new astronomical discovery to light, which we must fain receive at second hand from Europe, are we not cutting ourselves off from the means of re-turning light for light while we have neither observatory nor observer upon our half of the globe and the earth revolves in perpetual darkness to our unsearching eyes? (I:246)

Arguing with an enthusiasm and an eloquence as great as any his father or Jefferson had mustered on behalf of learning, the second Adams de-clared that "liberty is power" and asserted a Monroe Doctrine of the in-tellect: "the nation blessed with the largest portion of liberty must in pro-portion to its numbers be the most powerful nation on earth, and . . . the tenure of power by man is, in the moral purposes of his Creator, upon condition that it shall be exercised to ends of beneficence, to improve the condition of himself and his fellow men" (I:248). In the alliance between liberty and learning he emphasized the ways in which knowledge would bring strength to America. But he well knew that this principle cut two ways and that with education came the demand for greater personal free-dom. Intellectual growth, while benefiting national security with inven-tions and technological development, also challenges constraints placed on the liberty of individuals. As a result, not all subsequent presidents were as enthusiastic as Adams on this subject.

A MATTER OF INCLUSION

From the beginning of independence and the earliest discussions of union, America's political thinkers had fretted over the appropriate size for a republic. Their common sense and classical models argued for rela-tive smallness, for a nation of neighbors whose interests and beliefs were sufficiently similar to allow a shared understanding of the commonweal. Since notions of republicanism are inseparable from ideas of community, it seemed reasonable that a viable republic could not encompass too much distance or too much difference. Monroe, following Madison's lead, argued that increased size and diversity could actually strengthen the United States, offering as his principle proof the nation's successful incorporation since 1800 of new land and new states. But his evidence, at best, only suggested that a republic could tolerate the growth already achieved by the United States and not that its capacity for inclusion was unlimited. Monroe's was an optimistic view, one not always shared by his successors, but the fundamental measure of the Union's health—in every age—is what and whom Americans believe it can include.

The issue of limits has always been a prominent feature of annual messages, a vulnerability suggested by excessive claims of prosperity and well-being as well as by more direct warnings. John Tyler's last annual message in 1844 contained a little of both as he congratulated his countrymen on having passed through a presidential election "without the commission of any acts of violence or the manifestation of a spirit of insubordination to the laws" (I:613). For two pages he continued his hymn to national harmony, insisting that the country with its ample territorial reserves could "invite the lover of freedom of every land to take up his abode among us." That was not simply an indication of exuberant confidence; even Tyler had his agendas and his fears. "Lovers of freedom" in Texas had recently (1836) gained independence after a revolution against Mexico, and the American president had an interest in their future. But more to the point, his assertions about the well-being of the union, like most such protestations when so emphatically declared, masked a concern over disunion, a concern that the Texas rebellion surely brought to mind.

At the end of his praise for the civic virtues of his countrymen—and just prior to a discussion of foreign relations—Tyler disingenuously turned to theoretical matters. He noted that, according to some political thinkers, confederacies were subject to divisions fostered by "foreign governments or the people of foreign states." Here was a way to introduce "opinions entirely abstract in the States in which they may prevail" that "may become the foundation of political parties, until at last the conflict of opinion, producing an alienation of friendly feeling among the people of the different States, may involve in general destruction the happy institutions under which we live" (I:615). Coming on the heels of an open invitation to emigrants and a celebration of America's capacity to absorb vast numbers of new settlers, the sudden turn to a warning against outside ideas and imported abstractions hinted at a conflicting suspicion of things foreign. Whatever specific evil influence Tyler had in mind, clearly his enthusiastic claims for America's stability in a time of enormous growth served as preparation for a call to vigilance and its attendant implication that his praise for the absence of violence in the recent past was a thinly veiled warning against future disorder.

Though Tyler's language was carefully ambiguous, the "foreign governments" and "people of foreign States" to whom he referred would appear to be not so much other nations as certain American states. Abolitionism was the "foreign opinion" whose dividing power the Virginian most feared. By asserting a general principle rather than a particular complaint, Tyler made a point that was—and is—more widely applicable, but whose most immediate example would have been the fear within slave states of antislavery sentiment. At issue was whether the invisible lines defining states within a "confederacy" could be successful barriers against outside thinking and differing values. A corollary issue concerned the terms America was offering its "freedom-loving" emigrants, apparently extending the invitation with the stipulation that the newcomers alone be transformed and brought into conformity with what was already here. In light of the changes emigrants from the United States had brought to Texas, changes Tyler applauded, his notion that nations—or even states—could be open to new members without also being open to change seems naïve, but it indicates a profound tension in America resulting from its simultaneous desire for more (land, people, wealth) and for less (difference and controversy).[8]

Amid America's confidence in physical growth and political expansion, the striking insecurity, the most persistent limit applied to Union, was generated less by *what* it could include than by *whom* it could include. Who could become "the American, this new man?"[9] To some extent our first political parties were formed around this question. Andrew Jackson's thundering assertion in 1839 "that the majority is to govern" implied an expansion by class and condition of political "membership" as applied to white males. But even so great a democrat as "King Andrew" held, by modern standards, a very narrow notion of the Union's inclusionary capacities and intended, one suspects, that his would be the last word, that he was defining "terminus" for this most critical area of his nation's growth.

Tyler's fear of the "foreign" and its subversive power has its specific application in every period of our history, as we redefine who we are, and inevitably the distinction between insider and outsider shadows most annual messages. "Outsider," of course, has never been simply a geographical designation since, even in the nation's first years, the most obvious "outsiders" were already on the "inside"—residents regarded as aliens. Most notably, but not exclusively, those were slaves and native peoples, "insiders" who lived in a perpetual estrangement from the dominant culture, "foreigners" who were American by birth.

EXCLUDED NATIVES

In Washington's 1790 message Indians were introduced as aggressors, a frontier threat whose incursions against white settlers made necessary constant military preparedness. Throughout his presidency Washington regarded Native Americans either as separate nations to be dealt with through treaty and diplomacy or as "banditti" (I:5) testing the new nation's resolve and discipline. John Adams, in his first annual message, described efforts by European countries to spread dissent among Western tribes and warned that, in addition to efforts "to preserve entire their [native people's] attachment to the United States" (I:42), stern disciplinary action might be required. In his four years that was virtually all he had to say on the subject.

But Jefferson was another matter, neither a disinterested observer nor a lawman with an eye for troublemakers. He had definite ideas about most things, including indigenous populations and what was best for them, and as chief executive he actively pursued those notions. In 1801 he happily reported that "a spirit of peace and friendship generally prevails" between the United States and its "Indian neighbors" and, even more happily, that the latter were adapting to the practice of husbandry and other household arts." As a consequence, their numbers—previously dwindling because of "their wars and their wants"—had begun to increase (I:58). It is not clear how many of his white countrymen greeted that news with the enthusiasm expressed by their president, but Jefferson's eagerness to prove that the benefits of civilization could be extended to native populations and that they, as a result, could become allies and "neighbors" proved resilient. Where Washington saw danger, Jefferson observed progress. Each of the latter's annual messages enthusiastically reported land purchases from tribes, agreements that he represented as conventional commercial exchange and as evidence that natives were taking up the white man's ways. The Delawares, Jefferson informed Congress in 1804, had relinquished their claim to more than 300 miles fronting the Ohio River and nearly 150 miles on the Wabash. Their motive, he insisted, was a desire "to extinguish in their people the spirit of hunting and to convert superfluous lands into the means of improving what they retain" (I:76). He brought similar news in 1805:

> Our Indian neighbors are advancing, many of them with spirit, and others beginning to engage in the pursuits of agriculture and household manufacture. They are becoming sensible that the earth yields subsistence with less labor and more certainty than the forest, and find it in their interest from time to time to dispose of parts of their surplus and waste lands for the means of improving those they occupy and of subsisting their families while they are preparing their farms. (I:82)

Jefferson followed this observation with notice of major acquisitions from tribes in the North, the South and the West, all presumably "surplus and waste lands" that prevented native peoples from learning the pleasure of a more restricted life. So far had the Cherokee nation progressed down this cultivating path, the president reported in 1808, that they might soon solicit the United States for citizenship and "be identified with us in laws and government in such progressive manner as we shall think best" (I:96).

Madison was preoccupied during his presidency with the War of 1812. When he noticed Indians at all, he tended to see them in terms of that conflict, "merciless savages" "seduced" by England (I:117). In Madison's atrocity-minded accounts Andrew Jackson, Indian fighter as well as confounder of the British, made his first appearance in the annual messages. In 1829, when Old Hickory himself reported the state of the union, he took up the Indian question with a different perspective from that of any of his predecessors. He could not regard the tribes—as Washington had—simply as a frontier nuisance, outsiders to be dealt with like other foreign powers, nor did he share Jefferson's idealistic anticipation of their eventual inclusion as fellow farmers and democrats. Jackson cast a colder eye on the subject and saw Indians as internal problems that needed to be literally externalized.

Jackson's analysis grew from a sense of his countrymen's limits as much as, if not more than, those of the Indians. "It has long been the policy of Government," he told Congress in 1829,

> to introduce among [the tribes] the arts of civilization, in the hope of gradually reclaiming them from a wandering life. This policy has, however,

been coupled with another wholly incompatible with its success. Professing a desire to civilize and settle them, we have at the same time lost no opportunity to purchase their lands and thrust them farther into the wilderness. By this means they have not only been kept in a wandering state, but been led to look upon us as unjust and indifferent to their fate. Thus, though lavish in its expenditures upon the subject, Government has constantly defeated its own policy, and the Indians in general, receding farther and farther to the west, have retained their savage habits. (I:308)

A repudiation of the old Jeffersonian strategy, Jackson's view was that where Indians had remained within state boundaries and even "made some progress in the arts of civilized life," the independent status of the tribe collided with the sovereignty of the state that contained it. Since, he insisted, there could not be the equivalent of one state within another (an ironic position given the national design), Jackson concluded that native populations must either give up tribal status and abide wholly by the laws of the state or "emigrate beyond the Mississippi" (I:309).

What Jackson recommended, and carried out, was a policy that linked removal with preservation. To remain in the same precincts with white settlers would cause, he argued, an inevitable destruction of native populations, and thus their only hope for survival was emigration. He sought to eliminate the obstruction to white settlement within the states by creating in the territories a sort of red Liberia, with the same disregard for diversity of origins and cultures.[10] In the removal of a troubling people to a place outside existing state boundaries, all that mattered was race.

Jackson conceded the disturbing implications of this policy but treated it as a necessary evil, even humane, considering the alternatives. His strategy was to make it a matter of sympathy rather than justice, insisting that the legitimate claims of Native Americans were relatively few. "[I]t seems to me," he reasoned in his first annual message, "visionary to suppose that . . . claims can be allowed on tracts of country on which they have neither dwelt nor made improvements, merely because they have seen them from the mountain or passed them in the chase" (I:310). Full of ironies, Jackson's principle for shrinking land entitlement differed little in *fact* from Jefferson's, although greatly in the explanation and application. Both accepted as a standard of Indian inclusion the shift from a hunting, migratory life to an agricultural one. Both viewed wandering as regressive. Jefferson's policy was to force civilization upon the tribes by buying the expanses of land that allowed their unsettled life. Jackson, convinced that Indians were making the transition too slowly or not at all, based the legitimacy of all land claims on a kind of homesteading principle; where there was no evidence of cultivation or when tribal loyalty had been maintained, he forced Indians onto the neutral ground west of the Mississippi. "There," he allowed, "the benevolent may endeavor to teach them the arts of civilization, and, by promoting union and harmony among them, to raise up an interesting commonwealth, destined to perpetuate the race and to attest to the humanity and justice of this Government" (I:310).

But Jackson's guiding philosophy was simply a more aggressive version of one Monroe had presented in 1817—a theoretical and chronological midpoint between Jefferson and Old Hickory. Still emphasizing buyout, Monroe had detailed to Congress purchases of Indian lands from the Michigan Territory to Alabama. "In this progress," he insisted,

> which the rights of nature demand and nothing can prevent, marking a growth rapid and gigantic, it is our duty to make new efforts for the preservation, improvement, and civilization of the native inhabitants. The hunter state can exist only in the vast uncultivated desert. It yields to the more dense and compact form and greater force of civilized population; and of right it ought to yield, for the earth was given to mankind to support the greatest number of which it is capable, and no tribe or people have a right to withhold from the wants of others more than is necessary for their own support and comfort. (I:152)

The "natural right" that legitimates this assertion, the right of the greatest number of potential occupants a given place can support over the ownership claims of the fewer immediate inhabitants, was acceptable when applied to an unpopular minority, an excluded "tribe," but not when applied to white landowners with large holdings. Or, most probably, Monroe meant it in the abstract, another grand geopolitical concept that justified the displacement of "uncivilized" peoples by civilized ones, of unsettled peoples by settled ones, the latter measured by the number of persons per acre. The bottom line was the same as Jackson's—"that independent, savage communities cannot long exist within the limits of a civilized population" (1818) (I:163).

Washington, with his narrow coastal country, maintained a rhetorical distance. In his annual messages he described Native Americans as foreigners to be courted with treaties and kept at bay with a strong militia. Jefferson refused from the start to confine his notions of territory and purpose, and so saw Native Americans as the subject for an interesting social experiment, savages who, under white tutelage, could make a great leap forward to a civilized state. He imagined a Union in which they, remade as republican yeomen, could find a place. But the nation over which Jackson presided, while geographically larger, was smaller in the difference it was prepared to contain. The native populations therefore were to be removed in order that the physical continuity of the states would not be broken by tribal lands, and in order to provide the surviving tribes with an opportunity either to imitate the dominant culture and become its ally or to go their savage way for a while longer.

But Indian policy was itself divisive, Jackson's plan a cause of dissension among whites. In his second annual message, with the work of removal already under way, he therefore attempted to justify the strategy, defending its moral correctness to a suspicious opposition. "Humanity has often wept over the fate of the aborigines of this country," he began, then argued that the displacement of one people by another is simply a fact of history. He offered as proof evidence of earlier tribes that had been pushed aside or annihilated by later Indian invaders and declared such social destruction no different from "the extinction of one generation to make room for another." "Nor is there anything in this," he continued

> which, in the general interests of the human race, is to be regretted. Philanthropy could not wish to see this continent restored to the condition in which it was found by our forefathers. What good man would prefer a country covered with forests and ranged by a few thousand savages to our extensive Republic, studded with cities, towns, and prosperous farms, embellished with all the improvements which art can devise or industry execute, occupied by more than 12,000,000 happy people, and filled with all the blessings of liberty, civilization, and religion? (I:335)

Jackson described the debate over his relocation policies as a conflict between sentiment and reason, soft-headed philanthropy and practical realism. Despite the complaints of his critics, his was a progressive policy—far more so than that of "annihilation" by which the Eastern states (where most of those critics resided) were opened to white settlement—a milder process of accommodating the "waves of population and civilization . . . rolling to the westward." The favored exchange, he insisted, was a "fair" one in which, for lands the tribes currently occupied, the United States promised—all expenses paid—"to send them to a land where their existence may be prolonged and perhaps made perpetual."

Responding to the charge that the Indian loss was not simply that of real estate as a commodity, Jackson acknowledged: "Doubtless it will be painful to leave the graves of their fathers, but," he chided,

> what do they more than our ancestors did or than our children are now doing? To better their condition in an unknown land our forefathers left all that was dear in earthly objects. Our children by thousands yearly leave the land of their birth to seek new homes in distant regions. Does Humanity weep at these painful separations from everything, animate and inanimate, with which the young heart has become entwined? Far from it. (I:336)

In his enthusiasm the president moved from the sympathizing view of the relocated tribes as necessary victims whom the government was protecting from more devastating harm to a view of them as beneficiaries of a federal largess that white citizens did not enjoy. "Our children," he reminded his audience—ignoring both the value of the lands being confiscated and the increasing government support of white settlement to the west—make this move "at their own expense."

> Can it be cruel in this Government when, by events which it cannot control, the Indian is made discontented in his ancient home to purchase his lands, to give him a new and extensive territory, to pay the expense of his removal, and support him a year in his new abode?

Then, completing the now familiar strategy of presenting the white majority and not a disadvantaged minority as the uncompensated victim, Jackson asked, "How many thousands of our own people would gladly embrace the opportunity of removing to the West on such conditions! If the offers made to the Indians were extended to them, they would be hailed with gratitude and joy."

Stung by critics for doing what he acknowledged as the nation's dirty work, Jackson flailed out at bleeding-heart philanthropy with a sort of

pre-Darwin social darwinism. At the same time he defended his "enlightened" government as presiding compassionately and humanely over
those events to the point of treating the problem race "better" than its
own citizens. Jackson presented a peculiar mixture of a tragic view of a
"primitive" people sacrificed to progress and an antisentimental insistence that all Americans advance by leaving the ancestral home behind in
search of a better life. He chastised those who wept for the forced migration of Indians even as he held up as exemplary the voluntary movement
of white Americans. Ironically, Jackson called for removal of Indians on
the basis of their "difference" from white settlers and then, to justify the
policy, argued from assumed likeness that the relocation of one was analogous to that of the other.

The challenge Native Americans offered to the concept of union was
answered with exclusion. In 1837 Van Buren celebrated the "happy results" of his predecessor's relocating efforts and concluded that they had
been not only "enlightened" but philanthropic. He supported that claim
the following year by asserting that the "condition of the tribes which occupy the country set apart for them in the West, is highly prosperous and
encourages the hope of their early civilization." He declared the "recent
immigrants" no longer reluctant but accepting of their "unavoidable destiny" because of the "abundance in comforts" of their new homes. Eight
years later James Polk agreed. He announced that the Menomonies had
ceded all their Wisconsin territory, about 4,000,000 acres, to the United
States and then declared: "The title to all Indian lands within the several
States of our Union, with the exception of a few small reservations, is
now extinguished, and a vast region opened for settlement and cultivation" (I:754). An administration later (1852), however, Millard Fillmore
warned that Texas, four years a state, had retained ownership of all its
"vacant lands" and showed no intention of giving them over to native
populations. Thus the nation's efforts to preserve frontier peace by separation of the races was being jeopardized. But, Fillmore declared,

> I trust . . . that a due regard for her own interests, apart from considera-
> tions of humanity and justice, will induce that State to assign a small por-
> tion of her vast domain for the provisional occupancy of the small rem-
> nants of tribes within her borders, subject, of course, to her ownership
> and eventual jurisdiction. (I:846)

The provisional nature of that request foreshadowed much about future conflicts in Western states and the general acceptance of the eventual extinction of all tribal life. The westward growth of the country and the continuous organization of territories into states meant the fulfillment of Jackson's prophecy that relocation deferred rather than defeated the inevitable. Increasingly there was no America remaining in which to indulge the luxury of exclusions.[11]

A BARBAROUS TRAFFIC

The other "alien" presence in the United States, which more subtly tested its capacity for inclusion than did even Native Americans, was that of black slaves. Although by the 1850s slavery had become a regular subject of annual messages, it was only rarely discussed by earlier presidents and then almost always discreetly, obliquely. It was more "presidential" to address the end of the African slave trade, prohibited by Congress (under the terms of Article I, Section IX of the Constitution) after 1807, than to confront the divisive issue of human bondage within our own borders.

Again, as with the early response to Native Americans, the inclination was to make the matter somehow foreign, an issue more akin to those of defense and international trade than to questions of what, internally, was American. The inner and outer distinctions so fundamental to political and psychological life, the "us" and "them" that allow people to locate themselves and their interests, pervade every aspect of rhetoric, especially when the subject is union. To be one of "us," if one started as an Indian, Jackson assumed was possible only if the person in question stopped being culturally Indian. To what extent that could be managed he never decided, though he was always skeptical. But the distinction between slave and free was, in the United States, first and foremost a distinction of color. A black person, even one legally free, who stayed in one place and cultivated land could not join the "us" of white citizens.[12] At the same time, however, America could not very well argue that American slaves were not "American," were somehow detachable from the national experience. The South stressed the importance of slavery to its own self-image; its states were identified as slave-owning not only by abolitionists but by Southerners as well. It was, above all, slavery that distinguished them from their Northern brethren. And certainly Southerners did not believe that by removal of the "them" from their midst, the "us" would—as with Indian removal—be more perfectly realized.

The illegal slave trade, however, identified a black "them" for presidents to exclude, but only by indirectly affirming the American-ness of the black population already living in the United States. The African slave trade was condemned as an abomination in annual reports from Madison's to Buchanan's, but the evil involved—if the indictment was not to be extended to domestic slavery—had to be narrowly defined. As early as 1810 Madison listed this crime "among the commercial abuses still committed under the American flag" (I:108) and indignantly announced "that American citizens are instrumental in carrying on a traffic in enslaved Africans, equally in violation of the laws of humanity and in defiance of those of this country." The emphasis placed on the designations "American" and "African" carried special significance, in the first instance because American law applied only to American citizens in this matter and in the second because not all slaves or all blacks were the objects of the wrong in question—only those identified as "Africans." Both the moral and the legal issues hinged on the determination of who belongs where, even of what persons belong *to* what place. Since interdiction at sea provided the only practical means of stopping the illicit commerce, the American government classified the trade "under the denomination . . . of piracy" (I:204), henceforth placing presidential discussions of the matter in the section of annual messages devoted to naval issues.

Van Buren termed the pursuit of the slave trade by any United States ship a "prostitution of the American flag." In 1840 he declared the activity "an outrage on the rights of others and the feelings of humanity" and labeled the "slave factories" on the African coast "dens of iniquity" (I:560–61). In 1844, John Tyler took pride in the fact that only the United States among the nations of the world prescribed the death penalty (the usual punishment for piracy) for those engaged in the trade (I:627). Zachary Taylor agreed (1849) that it was a "barbarous traffic" (I:779), but it was Buchanan who lingered longest on the subject, addressing it at considerable length in each of his last three reports to Congress. In 1858 the matter came up in his criticism of colonial Cuba, "the only spot in the civilized world where the African slave trade is tolerated," and Buchanan insisted that this anomaly was cause for a host of problems that could best be solved by America's purchase of the island.

Despite the acquiring eye on Cuba, the most striking concern of Buchanan's remarks was with Africa itself:

As long as this market shall remain open there can be no hope for the civilization of benighted Africa. Whilst the demand for slaves continues in Cuba wars will be waged among the petty and barbarous chiefs in Africa for the purpose of seizing subjects to supply this trade. In such a condition of affairs it is impossible that the light of civilization and religion can ever penetrate these dark abodes. (I:981–82)

Later in the same message he returned to the topic, this time as he told of the American capture of a slaver and the subsequent dilemma of what to do with its cargo of more than three hundred captives. "When the Africans from on board the *Echo*, were delivered to the marshal at Charleston," he explained, "it became my duty to consider what disposition ought to be made of them under the law." That they were to be returned to Africa was obvious but insufficiently precise. "Where to send them was the question. There was no portion of the coast of Africa to which they could be removed with any regard to humanity except to Liberia" (I:999).

The following year the subject of the trade arose again, this time following a broad discussion of slavery that anticipated the concerns of his 1861 address. Having voiced his hope that the Dred Scott decision had settled the issue for the territories, Buchanan, in a deflecting maneuver, attacked calls for renewing the African trade.[13] After recounting the history of that prohibition, he turned to the evils that would accompany its repeal. First in Buchanan's view would be the harm to "our domestic slaves." For a period of fifty years, he asserted, there had been no imported addition to their number, and "[d]uring this period their advancement in civilization has far surpassed that of any other portion of the African race. The light and the blessings of Christianity have been extended to them, and both their moral and physical condition has been greatly improved." All of those benefits, he claimed, would be put at risk by introducing "wild, heathen, and ignorant barbarians among the sober, orderly, and quiet slaves whose ancestors have been on the soil for several generations."

Considering the fear of rebellion and atrocities Buchanan elaborated elsewhere in this same speech and repeated more emphatically a year later, his confidence in the quiet orderliness of American slaves was not always so strong, but it is striking that he insisted they were American both by acculturation and by birth. They belonged to this place just as surely as the would-be captives of a renewed slave trade belonged to Africa. On that distinction rested the argument that could simultaneously condemn the trade and accept the institution.

The danger of reopening the African commerce, as Buchanan explained it, extended beyond the regression that American slaves might suffer in the presence of heathen barbarism. It included a parallel regression that would imperil the souls of masters. Rather than the "humane" system presently practiced, one resulting from a combination of philanthropy and self-interest, he argued, a much more ruthless exploitation would come into being. Again, Cuba provided the evidence:

> Let this trade be reopened and what will be the effect? The same to a considerable extent as on a neighboring island, the only spot now on earth where the African slave trade is openly tolerated. . . . There the master, intent upon present gain, extorts from the slave as much labor as his physical powers are capable of enduring, knowing that when death comes to his relief his place can be supplied at a price reduced to the lowest point by the competition of rival African slave traders.

The danger of religious and moral backsliding was great for both parties should the African trade be reopened—the slave as a consequence of dangerous outside influences, the master because of equally dangerous internal weakness.

The third victim, again, would be "unhappy Africa." The pandemonium already endemic on the "slave coast" would spread. "All hopes of African civilization would thus be ended," and inevitably the country that promoted such evil "would be held responsible in the eyes both of God and man" (I:1006). A country that annually paid homage to "the beneficent Author of All Good" could hardly expect continued providential support if it served such iniquity.

The African slave trade gave American presidents an opportunity to take a moral stand, to claim for their country a position of international leadership in eradicating a vicious and inhuman commerce. That is not to underestimate the more purely political and practical considerations implicit in any matter of "trade," but the need to claim some moral high ground, to present Americans as both civilized and Christian, certainly contributed to the recurrence of the subject in presidential reports. Dividing the subject of slavery into two discrete categories and then assigning all the evil to the category no longer applicable to the United States allowed presidents the luxury of condemning the sin their country was not committing while ignoring the sin that it was. The true evil of slavery, according to this explanation, was already accomplished on these shores at the time the United States came into existence and was therefore a European crime, a part of colonial corruption—like that still being committed in Cuba in 1858. The "benevolent" aspect of slavery was what had happened—as a consequence of American virtue—since the introduction of that institution: Pagans had been redeemed through exposure to Christianity and barbarians civilized by association with an enlightened people.

At issue, as with Jackson's Indian policy, was the question of who belongs where and why. Ironically, the answer in the one instance was the reverse of the other. Indians belonged somewhere else and so were removed, but slaves belonged where they were, and the government's primary concern was to make sure they did not "relocate." Slaves were, by the logic of all arguments against the African trade, African by descent but American by birth and, if Buchanan is to be believed, by religion and culture. Even the Liberian movement, so helpful in taking the *Echo*'s African cargo off Buchanan's hands, treated the relocating of freedmen to Africa, not as an effort to return them to their homeland but as a sort of missionary effort in which the agents of Christianity and civilization were "American" but black.

TRUE PROGRESS AND FAIR FAME

The endless inconsistencies and contradictions that swirl around issues of race and inclusion in State of the Union messages results from a confusion not only over what race means but also over what union is all about. From a relatively simple notion of cooperating states at one extreme to more complex concepts of a pluralistic community, a considerable range of interpretations compete for our loyalty in defining the ideal Americans are constitutionally committed to serve. In the expanding geographical and political entity that Monroe championed—as well as the language of "a more perfect union"—are hints of a future place and condition that are our greatest responsibility, an America we are helping bring into being. In that implied dedication to what lies ahead, what we are literally—in annual messages—growing into, can be seen a morally subversive influence. When Polk argued for expansion as a means of defusing the crisis over slavery, he deferred rather than addressed the immediate moral issues so that the Union could continue, compromised perhaps, but intact. In the same way Jackson openly acknowledged that Indian relocation simply put off an inevitable confrontation, but it removed a present obstacle to national growth. The frustration and annoyance that marked so many pre–Civil War discussions of slavery reflect a presidential priority that overrides immediate moral objections on behalf of a larger, future good. Even when they were labeled "annual messages," these reports were often future-oriented, concerned with the union that still lay ahead as America's destiny.

In his third annual message (1852) the cautious Millard Fillmore noted that this was a country "full of enterprise," then—echoing Tyler—warned that in such an environment some people mistook "change for progress and the invasion of the rights of others for national prowess and glory." The offending party was, of course, the antislavery movement, "ever ready to engage in any wild crusade against a neighboring people, regardless of the justice of the enterprise and without looking at the fatal consequences to ourselves and to the cause of popular government." The "victim" of those consequences was not an abused South but the future, and Fillmore concluded his warning with the declaration, "These reprehensible aggressions but retard the true progress of our nation and tarnish its fair fame" (I:853).

Fillmore's successor, Franklin Pierce, described that "true progress" in his first annual address: "The growth of our population has now brought us, in the destined career of our national history, to a point at which it well behooves us to expand our vision over the vast prospective." Based on past statistics, Pierce predicted in 1853 a numerically glorious future that included among its wonders a population, by century's end, of more than 100,000,000. This he elaborately and long-windedly explained:

A large allowance for a diminished proportional effect of emigration would not very materially reduce the estimate, while the increased average duration of human life known to have resulted from the scientific and hygienic improvements of the past fifty years will tend to keep up through the next fifty, or perhaps hundred, the same ratio of growth which has been thus revealed in our past progress; and to the influence of these causes may be added the influx of laboring masses from eastern Asia to the Pacific side of our possessions, together with the probable accession of the populations already existing in other parts of our hemisphere, which within the period in question will feel with yearly increasing force the natural attraction of so vast, powerful, and prosperous a confederation of self-governing republics and will seek the privilege of being admitted within its safe and happy bosom, transferring with themselves, by a peaceful and healthy process of incorporation, spacious regions of virgin and exuberant soil, which are destined to swarm with the fast-growing and fast-spreading millions of our race. (I:872–73)

Pierce's enthusiasm for increase and growth overwhelmed any specific information, despite his fascination with numbers. He did not explain the long-term arrangements he anticipated for the Asian "masses" on America's western shore or the South American countries he seemed to be inviting into the union of states. Neither did he clarify what would happen in a "transfer" that is simultaneously an incorporation, or what, in those conditions, he meant by "our race." He did not deem such details important. All that truly mattered was growth, both the productions of "exuberant soil" and the population increases that would unfailingly come if the Union was preserved. Nothing mattered more than "the realization of that magnificent national future," and so the president called his people to a "mutual forbearance, respect, and noninterference in our personal action as citizens and an enlarged exercise of the most liberal principles of comity in the public dealings of State with State" (I:873–74).

Two years later, in 1855, Pierce declared the necessity (apparent to all who had read his previous addresses) "to speak . . . plainly" and to identify the threat to America's future. "If the passionate rage of fanaticism and partisan spirit did not force the fact upon our attention," he argued,

it would be difficult to believe that any considerable portion of the people of this enlightened country could have so surrendered themselves to a fanatical devotion to the supposed interests of the relatively few Africans in the United States as totally to abandon and disregard the interests of the

25,000,000 Americans; to trample under foot the injunctions of moral and constitutional obligation, and to engage in plans of vindictive hostility against those who are associated with them in the enjoyment of the common heritage of our national institutions. (I:917)

Obliterated without hesitation or apparent notice was the distinction so many other presidents worked hard to draw in separating slavery from the African trade. America's destiny was not be deterred by a "few Africans," regardless of their place of birth. To take so small a view was to be "fanatical" and unenlightened, and so the distinction central for forty years of opposition to the slave trade dissolved. All blacks were declared Africans, and their cause, like their numbers, was reduced to insignificance when compared with the greater interests of "Americans."

THE HOUSE DIVIDED

After the Union had come apart, after the unthinkable had been not only thought but enacted, the issues of inclusion were redirected, applied not so much, for the moment, to races or territory as to rebellious states. While Buchanan warned that once dissolved the Union could not be restored, Lincoln—doing what his predecessor insisted a president could not do—acted to save that connection by force, all the while laying the groundwork for defying the old logic and rejoining that which had been torn asunder. In this latter effort he called as his primary witness America's geography. "A nation," he declared in his second annual message, "may be said to consist of its territory, its people, and its laws. Its territory is the only part which is of certain durability. 'One generation passeth away and another generation cometh, but the earth abideth forever'" (II:1075). There is no way, he insisted, to divide the physical space occupied by the United States, "no line, straight or crooked, suitable for a national boundary upon which to divide" (II:1076). While his "no line, straight or crooked," provided a powerful metaphor for the events of his day, the statement was literally intended, and he argued that any division would be, even were the federal government to accept it, unnatural and would invite a future of conflict and violence. Inherent in his argument were enduring Western convictions and suspicions, views that reached back to Senator Thomas Hart Benton and ahead to William Jennings

Bryan. The "great interior region," "the great body of the Republic," central to Lincoln's personal perspective as well as his argument, could not be severed from either North or South, nor could it be itself divided. It was rather a unit—large as it was—that defied reduction and could not be politically separated from those states that gave it access to the sea. Thus Lincoln's larger claim, which vindicated the expansionist policies of earlier executives as well as his own resistance to secession, was that the "national homestead" "demands union and abhors separation" (II:1077). "That portion of the earth's surface which is owned and inhabited by the people of the United States," Lincoln told Congress, "is well adapted to be the home of one national family, and it is not well adapted for two or more" (II:1075).

Andrew Johnson, arguing from law rather than landscape, also insisted that dissolution was impossible, declaring "the true theory . . . that all pretended acts of secession were from the beginning null and void." He continued in explanation:

> The States can not commit treason nor screen the individual citizens who may have committed treason any more than they can make valid treaties or engage in lawful commerce with any foreign power. The States attempting to secede placed themselves in a condition where their vitality was impaired, but not extinguished; their functions suspended, but not destroyed. (II:1115)

But Johnson was arguing, after victory, against Northern rather than Southern presumption. The Republican Congress, he insisted, in its efforts to "reconstruct" the South was violating the Constitution, since states, which could not legally secede, could not forfeit their constitutional rights. Opposed especially to disfranchising portions of the white population while empowering freed slaves, he accused the legislature of attempting to "Africanize the half of our country" (II:1152). Johnson annually declared the nation still in disarray and, typically, opened his final state of the union message in 1868 with the declaration: "Upon the assembling of Congress it again becomes my duty to call your attention to the state of the Union and its continued disorganized condition under the various laws which have been passed upon the subject of reconstruction" (II:1167).

No doubt partly motivated, as his enemies were quick to suggest, by his Southern roots, Andrew Johnson's sense of lingering "disunion" and the difficulty of political and psychological restoration was all too accurate, and the issue of reinclusion provided a central concern for subsequent annual messages, as did the effort to bring African-Americans into the Union. And as Johnson's position made clear, those paired concerns would often seem antithetical and would, to a considerable extent, remain antagonistic until the second half of the twentieth century, when race became a national issue, increasingly provoking as much division in the North as in the South, if not more.

THE ENEMY WITHIN

Ulysses Grant's eighth annual address came near the close of a presidency that historians have labeled a failure. Perhaps, as Woodrow Wilson would assert, Grant "himself knew that he had failed," and perhaps this weighed heavily on him in December 1876.[14] "History shows," Grant had reminded his audience,

> that no Administration from the time of Washington to the present has been free from . . . mistakes. But I leave comparisons to history, claiming only that I have acted in every instance from a conscientious desire to do what was right, constitutional, within the law, and for the best interests of the whole people. (II:1319)

His message offered, in his defense, his positive contributions, not the least of which, in his own mind, was furthering Reconstruction. Referring to Johnson's administration as "filled up with wranglings between Congress and the new Executive," Grant argued that the real issue was

> whether the control of the Government should be thrown immediately into the hands of those who had so recently and persistently tried to destroy it, or whether the victors should continue to have an equal voice with them in this control. Reconstruction, as finally agreed upon, means this and only this, except that the late slave was enfranchised, giving an increase, as was supposed, to the Union-loving and Union-supporting votes. If *free* in the full sense of the word, they would not disappoint this expectation. Hence at the beginning of my first Administration the work

of reconstruction, much embarrassed by the long delay, virtually commenced. (II:1319)

This was, in Grant's view, what redeemed his troubled presidency: that he had finally gotten the stalled work of reinclusion under way and that he had done so with a commitment, first and foremost, to union and emancipation. But while insisting that under his leadership the country had solved the problem of how to return formerly rebellious states to the national fold, he identified more subtle and confounding signs of "disunion."

The great weakness of Grant's administration was corruption among his appointees, a fault he acknowledged in his last report to Congress, admitting that "it is impossible . . . that the right parties should be chosen in every instance." Throughout his remarks he commented bitterly on the devious ways the greedy infiltrate the national system and pervert it for their own gain. Recalling the war, he added to those states in open rebellion an "enemy in the rear," one "almost as dangerous as the more honorable enemy in the front."

> The latter committed errors of judgment, but they maintained them openly and courageously; the former received the protection of the Government they would see destroyed, and reaped all the pecuniary advantage to be gained out of the then existing state of affairs, many of them obtaining contracts and by swindling the Government in the delivery of their goods. (II:1319)

To this age-old complaint about wartime profiteers Grant added another version of government-shaking greed when he turned to Indian affairs. Noting that hostilities had ended everywhere except "the Black Hills region and approaches thereto," he placed blame for the violence in that region on "the avarice of the white man who has violated our treaty stipulations in his search for gold." To the rhetorical question of "why the Government has not enforced obedience to the terms of the treaty" and forcibly removed whites from the region, he responded by saying that troops sent to enforce the order would themselves fall to temptation and desert so that they might seek their own fortunes (II:1320).

Grant's dismay at the depravity of the human race and its capacity to subvert liberal institutions severely tried his democratic convictions, and he saw that the most pernicious threat to "more perfect union" was the corrupt pursuit of self-interest by individual citizens. For all his enthusiasm over the 1876 Centennial Exposition's display of technological and scientific advancement (he called for the exhibit's permanent display at the Smithsonian), he found little improvement in human nature. He closed his message with yet another indictment, this one in reference to his long-standing recommendation for the annexation of Santo Domingo. He offered the usual geopolitical claims, then followed with the suggestion that many of the nation's freedmen would have found a better home there. His argument was not that African-Americans lacked either the right or the talents to prosper in the existing states, and he admitted that "their labor is desirable—indispensable almost—where they are now," but rather that the fault lay with the communities in which they lived. Pointing to the "great oppression and cruelty . . . practiced upon them in many places within the last eleven years," Grant despairingly suggested that in Santo Domingo former slaves could at least escape white Americans who deny them civil rights and a "congenial home" (II:1331).

Even after the cause of Union had officially carried the day, Grant reflected anew on how subtle are the other forces of disunion. If he gave a simplistic accounting, focusing on personal expressions rather than corporate manifestations, he nonetheless indicated the magnitude of the problem by locating its source in human nature. The "self" whose interests—whose selfishness—were ultimately most threatening to the whole was the individual. The struggle for a more perfect union was not limited to the old opposition of seceding and loyal states but, as Grant discovered, was a division within every American, a conflict between the desire to be whole, "members one of another," and the selfish impulses of our own secessionist hearts.

GRANDEUR AND DECAY

In the final annual message of his first administration, Grover Cleveland, echoing Grant in tone and critique, looked back over a century of national life and compared the Republic in its earliest days with what, by 1888, it had become. The frugal people who had created this country had been secure "in the enjoyment of the remaining recompense of [their] . . . steady and contented toil." "The pomp and glitter," he continued,

> of governments less free offered no temptation and presented no delusion to the plain people who, side by side, in friendly competition, wrought for the ennoblement and dignity of man, for the solution of the problem of free government, and for the achievement of the grand destiny awaiting the land which God had given them. (II:1598)

In this romanticized version of a less complicated and more virtuous past, Cleveland ironically planted the seeds of America's "fall": service to that "grand destiny" Pierce had so eagerly anticipated. What had been purchased by the frugality of those "plain people" who came before was the America over which Cleveland presided. "A century has passed," he told Congress.

> Our cities are the abiding places of wealth and luxury; our manufactories yield fortunes never dreamed of by the fathers of the Republic; our business men are madly striving in the race for riches, and immense aggregations of capital outrun the imagination in the magnitude of their undertakings.

Commingled in his description are elements of grandeur and decline, of wealth madly pursued, and just as he had identified the past with simplicity, he characterized the present with excess. "We note with pride and satisfaction this bright picture of our country's growth and prosperity," he continued, then added his darker refrain, "while only a closer scrutiny develops a more somber shading." His America is one torn by extremes, its cities divided with "wealth and luxury" on the one hand and "poverty, wretchedness and unremunerative toil" on the other. Rural areas are being depopulated as "the farmer's son, not satisfied with his father's simple life, joins the eager chase for easily acquired wealth."

At the heart of America's failure, as Cleveland reported it, was a disjunction between work and reward that did not exist in his more idyllic past; that is what lay at the heart of his apparent despair and brought contempt to his every mention of gilded age excess. The economic realities that distinguish his America from that of previous generations were, in his rendition, wholly incompatible with traditional values. "We discover," he lamented, "that the fortunes realized by our manufacturers are no longer solely the reward of sturdy industry and enlightened foresight, but that they result from the discriminating favor of the Government and are largely built upon undue exactions from the masses of our people." Thus he identified a new threat to the concept of union, the "gulf between employers and the employed," a division that "is constantly widening," splitting the population into opposing classes, "one comprising the very rich and powerful, while in another are found the toiling poor." The magnitude of the dilemma he embodied in the immensity of the new commercial structures, organizations for which he could find no other analogy except the monarchies from which our ancestors had escaped. Those provided the most frightening element in the scenario he painted. "As we view the achievements of aggregated capital," he declared,

> we discover the existence of trusts, combinations and monopolies, while the citizen is struggling far in the rear or is trampled to death beneath an iron heel. Corporations, which should be the carefully restrained creatures of the law and servants of the people, are fast becoming the people's masters. (II:1598–99)

Here was the population Pierce had so eagerly anticipated, the incredible economic growth he had promised as a reward for ignoring slavery; here was his America of ultimate promise. But, filled with melancholy and anger, Cleveland complained that the "grand destiny" previous generations had served was at century's end little more than the extravagances that our ancestors had contemptuously denounced in the aristocracies of Europe. Speaking a language of polarities, he divided his words into opposing camps, placing on one side "plain" together with "ennoblement," "dignity," and "free," and on the other, "pomp and glitter," "temptation," "delusion," and "less free." In the same way he associated the America of 1888 with words like "madly," "crowded," "discontent," "impoverished," and "wretched." The vocabulary of "master" and "iron heel" he applied to America rather than to Old World tyrannies. Like the narrator in John Dos Passos's *U.S.A.*, Cleveland mourned the existence of two Americas and saw in that polarization a terrible mockery of what he believed union to mean.[15]

The implication was that America could not be so divided and still be America. In a remarkable pairing he labeled as "communism" not only the action of those oppressed by "poverty and toil," who, "exasperated by injustice and discontent" attack "with wild disorder the citadel of rule," but also those who combine "wealth and capital, the outgrowth of over-weening cupidity and selfishness" (I:1601). The disorder of privilege *and* the disorder of deprivation preoccupied the outgoing president. He saw in both an equal danger to free institutions and saw in the gulf that separated them a threat to union as profound as those leading to civil war.

Cleveland's despairing glimpse of the new America came just as the old was passing from view and pointed toward two of the more significant forces of division in modern America: class and urbanization. The former would be addressed most forcefully by the two Roosevelts, both concerned with containing the drift toward economic factionalism. The split between urban and rural touched on a fear as old as Jefferson that cities—and the industries they favored—restricted personal freedom and generated precisely the kind of society America had chosen not to be. From the Enlightenment perspective the most free of citizens (not counting plantation-owning philosophes) was the yeoman farmer, cultivating his land and his character simultaneously. But wars in Europe, with their consequent interruptions of trade, taught even Jefferson that a self-sufficient nation had to manufacture its own heavy goods, and such industry required an urban workforce. It was development in this area that cheered Madison in 1809. But by the last years of the century Cleveland could suggest, and William Jennings Bryan insist, that necessary or not, cities were dangerous to America's morality and its health. Of course, much of the urban dilemma in any age matches Cleveland's description: the obvious disparity between rich and poor, and the consequences of that disparity when it exists in such close proximity.

THE ECONOMIC UNION

"On the sixth of September," Theodore Roosevelt reminded Congress in 1901, "President McKinley was shot by an anarchist while attending the Pan-American Exposition at Buffalo, and died in that city on the fourteenth of that month." With that beginning the new Commander-in-Chief presented his own political polarities, opposites represented by McKinley's republican virtue and the criminal depravity of his assassin. The virtues Cleveland identified with an earlier, truer America, Roosevelt depicted in McKinley, a man, he argued, of "tender affections and home virtues," a patriot loved by his countrymen, but also "a man of moderate means . . . whose stock sprang from the sturdy tillers of the soil, who had himself belonged among the wage workers, who had entered the Army as a private soldier" (II:2014). "Wealth," Roosevelt declared, "was not struck at when the president was assassinated, but the honest toil which is content with moderate gains after a lifetime of unremitting labor. . . . The blow was not aimed at tyranny or wealth. It was aimed at one of the strongest champions the wage-worker has ever had" (II:2015).

The new president, himself born into privilege, eulogized McKinley by offering "modest means" as evidence of virtue and suggested his murder was all the more outrageous because neither "tyranny [n]or wealth" was its victim. Opposite the late president's good example Roosevelt placed the anarchist, more terrifying than the passion-driven assassins who killed Lincoln and Garfield because he belonged "to that body of criminals who object to all governments, good and bad alike, who are against any form of popular liberty if it is guaranteed by even the most just and liberal laws, and who are as hostile to the upright exponent of a free people's sober will as to the tyrannical and irresponsible despot" (II:2014).

It is telling that, following a long and elaborate indictment of anarchism, Roosevelt turned abruptly to his next subject: "During the past five years business confidence has been restored, and the nation is to be congratulated because of its present abounding prosperity" (II:2018). The connection between anarchism and business in Roosevelt's address was much the same as that between Cleveland's two "communisms," the one of "wealth and capital," the other of "exasperated" poverty (I:1601), the same opposition Roosevelt virtually legitimated when he implied that McKinley's assassination would have been less repugnant if the victim had been a wealthy man. But Roosevelt was not so damning of those who had reaped the enormous profits of industrial development. Rather he praised "the captains of industry who have driven the railway systems across this continent, who have built up our commerce, who have developed our manufactures, have on the whole done great good to our people," all the while acknowledging that "much antagonism" had been aroused, and that old laws and customs, once "sufficient to regulate the accumulation and distribution of wealth," were inadequate for governing this new age of production.

Teddy Roosevelt, having cried anarchism over the dead McKinley and suggesting by innuendo that frustrated labor was being tempted by radical and insidious forces, warned the very industrial captains he praised that the shot fired at his predecessor would have found a more likely target, given the emotions of the day, in one of them. He denied that the "wage-worker" had ever been better off but conceded the danger in a popular perception that "the rich have grown richer" while "the poor have grown poorer" (II:2019).

What followed was a skillful navigation of the gulf between the classes, a word of support offered first on one side and then on the other, labor praised and then management, something good said about trusts *and* unions. But the purpose of all Roosevelt's spinning was to tie his threads to both constituencies, to remind all sides of the "fundamental rule in our national life" that, "on the whole and in the long run, we shall go up or down together." After reassuring business leaders that he understood the "delicate mechanism of modern business" and knew that "extreme care must be taken not to interfere with it in a spirit of rashness or ignorance," he continued, "and yet it is also true that there are real and grave evils." Roosevelt offered his own proposed regulations in response not to indictments of his own devising but to "widespread conviction[s] in the minds of the American people," and chief among those, he argued, was an animosity toward "the great industrial combinations which are popularly, although with technical inaccuracy, known as 'trusts.'" Being "technically inaccurate" did not lessen the "hatred and fear" that those combinations had generated in the public mind, and Roosevelt reminded his audience that those "two emotions, particularly when combined with ignorance. . . . unfit men for the exercise of cool and steady judgment" (II:2019–20).

The continued warnings against the danger of too great a division between classes, the suggestion that such alienation gives "anarchy" a space in which to ply its antagonizing trade, prepared the way for Roosevelt's own efforts to "update" eighteenth-century institutions so that they could accommodate twentieth-century economics. To that end he promised to serve both wage-workers, who thought themselves abused by unrestricted corporate power, *and* the corporations that would become the targets of increasing violence if the public continued to believe they were insufficiently regulated.

The economic union that Roosevelt championed contained the worker as well as the capitalist; he reminded both that they were members of an interdependent community and were responsible for one another. "When all is said and done," he reminded each side,

> the rule of brotherhood remains as the indispensable prerequisite to success in the kind of national life for which we strive. Each man must work for himself, and unless he so works no outside help can avail him; but each man must remember also that he is indeed his brother's keeper, and that while no man who refuses to walk can be carried with advantage to himself or anyone else, yet that each at times stumbles or halts, that each at times needs to have the helping hand outstretched to him. To be permanently effective, aid must always take the form of helping a man to help himself; and we can best help ourselves by joining in the work that is of common interest to all. (II:2024)

In subsequent addresses to Congress, Roosevelt delivered the same message, each time more forcefully, and always offering reassurance coupled with warning. He continually insisted that his position was not antagonistic either to workers or to capitalists and that in regard to corporations and trusts, "we are not hostile to them; we are merely determined that they shall be so handled as to subserve the public good." We are, he declared, "endeavoring to do away with the evil in them" (II:2055).

The New Deal responded to Teddy Roosevelt's warning against anarchy and revolution with economic reforms and social programs intended to narrow the gap between classes and to keep social inequities within acceptable bounds. Whether underwriting efforts in public health or in rural electrification, all presidents—following FDR—have tried to define and provide what they considered a minimum level of services and opportunities for Americans regardless of class. Their concern has been partly humanitarian, but it has been practical as well in recognizing that when distinctions become too great radicalism will flourish. As a consequence, post–World War II State of the Union messages have confronted a wide range of social issues largely unmentioned in the nineteenth century as they have struggled with the consequences of a union and a world more complex than any Cleveland could have imagined.

A DETERMINED OMISSION

The silences in presidential oratory, particularly in reporting on the state of the Union, may themselves represent efforts to exclude. The most striking omission—striking because of both the numbers and the issues that went unmentioned—has been women. Even in the years surrounding passage of the Nineteenth Amendment (1920), no notice was taken either of the suffrage movement or of the complicated ways in which sexual identity affects participation in American life. The index of *The State of the Union Messages* identifies only three presidents prior to 1967 mentioning "women" in their annual reports, one fewer than referred to the Mormon Church and twelve fewer than discussed Denmark.

The preeminent concern of the three presidents, Teddy Roosevelt, Calvin Coolidge, and Herbert Hoover, was with women in the workplace. Each treated women's labor issues in a section separate from their discussion of male wage-earners, most typically linking them with consideration of child labor, and their preoccupation was with protecting the weaker sex rather than economic equity. What was acknowledged, though begrudgingly, was the important role women were playing in the workforce, but what was implied was that this was largely undesirable. In Roosevelt's case—and he was the only one to deal with the issue in more than just a cursory way—the phenomenon was even unnatural. "It is very desirable," he wrote to Congress in 1904, "that married women should not work in factories. The prime duty of the man is to work, to be the breadwinner; the prime duty of the woman is to be the mother, the housewife." In his enthusiasm for the subject, Roosevelt declared the proper exercise of those gender-specific "duties" the most important element of America's progress and happiness. "All questions of tariff and finance," he exclaimed, "sink into utter insignificance when compared with the tremendous, the vital importance of trying to shape conditions so that these two duties of the man and of the woman can be filled under reasonably favorable circumstances."

Roosevelt's overriding interest in this discussion, however, was less women than children. He focused on proposals concerning "the vital matter of taking care of children" and calls for reform in child labor laws and the juvenile courts. Culminating his description of the feminine obligation, he made clear that childbearing and childrearing are the entire story. "If a race does not have plenty of children," he warned, "or if the children do not grow up, or if when they grow up they are unhealthy in body and stunted or vicious in mind, then that race is decadent, and no heaping up of wealth, no splendor of momentary material prosperity, can avail in any degree as offsets" (II:2114). A year later (1905) Roosevelt, obviously fearing the degeneration for which he held insufficient mothering responsible, called for a study of the effect of having 5 million women "engaged in gainful occupations." "There is need of full knowledge on which to base action looking toward State and municipal legislation for the protection of working women," he explained. But his primary concern was to protect the country from the consequences of women's "working." "The introduction of women into industry," he continued, "is working change and disturbance in the domestic and social life of the Nation. The decrease in marriage, and especially in the birth rate, has been coincident with it." If Roosevelt's preoccupation with increasing and improving the "race" (a term he employed variously, but generally in reference to nationality and the "American race") seemed aimed at removing women from the workplace and restoring the traditional family, he did acknowledge both the unlikeliness of such a reversal and the need to reform the work environment to lessen the conflicts among a woman's several obligations. "We must face accomplished facts," he conceded, "and the adjustment of factory conditions must be made, but surely it can be made with less friction and less harmful effects on family life than is now the case" (II:2155).

If Roosevelt's preference for a society in which women stay at home and raise children was unrelenting, he recognized that in twentieth-century America work was not likely to be the exclusive province of men. In this context he called for "exhaustive" study that could suggest policies accommodating family life. Inclined to see the phenomenon as purely the result of poverty—to believe women worked only because of financial need—he did not look beyond the factory in surveying the problem. Nevertheless, he anticipated two competing themes in the politics of the 1980s and 1990s, both claiming the high ground of "family values." The political and religious right echoed Theodore Roosevelt's claim for woman's moral and natural obligation to make a home and raise children, and liberals—including a growing number of Congresswomen—emphasized the need to reform the workplace to allow employees also to be parents. As a result, women's issues broke into State of the Union messages at the end of the century Roosevelt introduced. Issues like childcare became increasingly important as personal career commitments, along with poverty, greatly increased the number of females joining what he called "one of the greatest sociological phenomena of our time."

PURSUING THE GREAT SOCIETY

Harry Truman summarized the postwar challenge in his annual message of 1953, dating the modern presidency from "that great white flash of light, man-made at Alamogordo," and the opening of the "doorway to the atomic age." He asked the Congress and his national audience to consider "the great questions that were posed for us by sudden, total victory in World War II." Those, as Truman presented them were:

1. Would there be another depression here—a repetition of 1921 or 1929?
2. Would we take up again, and carry forward, the great projects of social welfare . . . that the New Deal had introduced into our national life?
3. What we would do with the Nation's natural resources—its soils and water, forests and grasslands?
4. Would we continue, in peace as well as war, to promote equality of opportunity for all our citizens, seeking ways and means to guarantee for all of them the full enjoyment of their civil rights?
5. Could the machinery of government and politics in this Republic be changed, improved, adapted rapidly enough to carry through, responsibly and well, the vast, new, complicated undertakings called for in our time?
6. Could there be built in the world a durable structure of security, a lasting peace for all the nations, or would we drift, as after World War I, toward another terrible disaster—a disaster which this time might be the holocaust of atomic war? (III:2995–97)

Economic security, social welfare, conservation, civil rights, political reform, and peace—while hardly new concerns—provided the framework
for post–World War II politics and the basic subheadings of State of the
Union messages for the next half-century. All had, as Truman noted, an
urgency increased by America's continued "growth" not only in influence
and wealth but in social and political complexity. A war with racist fascism and an ongoing struggle with totalitarian communism reinvigorated the nation's continuing civil rights debate and fueled a massive reconsideration of inclusion; an explosion in world population and
technological advancement put unprecedented demands on natural resources and the environment; and the cities that so troubled Cleveland
and Teddy Roosevelt were dwarfed by the vast and ill-defined urban cen-
ters of the century's second half.

Truman was right. It was all as new as the bomb and "as old as recorded history" (III:2998). The challenges to union in the second half of the
twentieth century were the consequences of a costly Cold War and a nation caught in a tumultuous struggle for justice, not just a securing of
rights already promised by law but an exploration of the very concept of
rights. The old terms of "self" and "union" remained at the heart of
things, but both were pushed farther than ever before as we struggled to
achieve union amid so much diversity.

When Eisenhower followed Truman in 1953, he agreed to the terms
his predecessor had outlined. In his first State of the Union message he
addressed all six of Truman's questions. Though his consuming interest
and greatest expertise concerned international affairs, he called for civil
rights legislation as well as support for education and health care, and in
1954 declared it his responsibility "to sense the deepest aspirations of the
people, and to express them in political action" (III:3038). In 1957 he
summarized what he considered the nation's guiding principles, those
qualities by which the state of the Union should be assessed: "A vigilant
regard for human liberty. A wise concern for human welfare. A ceaseless
effort for progress" (III:3068).

But the president who most presumed to bring the Union toward fulfillment was Lyndon Johnson, a practical, pragmatic Senate leader who
came to the White House with a near-utopian idealism. He maintained
that 1960s America had the scientific knowledge, the material prosperity,

and the liberal commitment to achieve its ultimate promise. He summarized this perspective in his second State of the Union (1965):

> We are entering the third century of the pursuit of American union.
>
> Two hundred years ago, in 1776, nine assembled colonies first joined together to demand freedom from arbitrary power.
>
> For the first century we struggled to hold together the first continental union of democracy in the history of man. One hundred years ago, in 1865, following a terrible test of blood and fire, the compact of union was finally sealed.
>
> That struggle has often brought pain and violence. It is not yet over. But we have achieved a unity of interest among our people unmatched in the history of freedom.
>
> And now, in 1965, we begin a new quest for union. We seek the unity of man with the world he has built—with the knowledge that can save or destroy him—with the cities which can enrich or stifle him—with the wealth and machines which can enrich or menace his spirit.
>
> We seek to establish a harmony between man and society which will allow each of us to enlarge the meaning of his life and all of us to elevate the quality of our civilization. (III:3162)

Like Wilson's, Johnson's vision did not stop at national boundaries—"the unity we seek cannot realize its full promise in isolation"—and like Eisenhower and later Reagan, he gave the struggle with communism an apocalyptic dimension.

> Our own freedom and growth have never been the final goal of the American dream.
>
> We were never meant to be an oasis of liberty and abundance in a worldwide desert of disappointed dreams. Our nation was created to help strike away the chains of ignorance and misery and tyranny wherever they keep man less than God means him to be.

Here was the old talk of destiny mingled with "Battle Hymn of the Republic," here was America in its ultimate manifestation, God's terrible swift sword *and* the New Canaan. Appropriately, Johnson's first subheading in his second annual message was entitled "State of the World" (III:3163).

What made that view credible to Americans was an unrestrained belief in science and technology and the progress both had achieved. In the years after World War II there had been a monumental proliferation of goods in this country (the point of Nixon's "Kitchen Debate" with Khrushchev), a revolution in medicine with "miracle drugs" and lifesaving surgeries, and equally dazzling advances in communications and transportation—in short, a radical transformation of what average Americans expected for themselves and their families and a general conviction that much more was on the way. The accomplishments of the recent past provided bold paradigms for the future: All disease would yield to research, travel would be swift and easy, unpleasant labor would be given over to machines. Ironically, all this promise of plenty and of magical solutions coexisted with deep fears, most especially of nuclear war and a host of social ills. But still there was an eagerness to believe, to believe that the nuclear age could prove beneficent despite its awful start, that Communism would either recede or become more friendly, that want and deprivation could be overcome by a growing economy, that bigotry and violence would yield to education. Perhaps because of the depth of their anxiety, Americans began to believe in salvation by technology and social engineering.

The rhetoric of both Kennedy and Johnson, in contrast to that of either Eisenhower before or Nixon after, was evangelical and homiletic. Johnson's especially was dense with prophetic intensity, his Great Society a vision that was to be all-compelling. The national agenda he offered in his second State of the Union was presented as a proposal but sounded like an imperative:

I propose we begin a program in education to insure every American child the fullest development of his mind and skills.

I propose we begin a massive attack on crippling and killing diseases.

I propose we launch a national effort to make the American city a better and more stimulating place to live.

I propose to increase the beauty of America and end the poisoning of our rivers and the air we breathe.

I propose we carry out a new program to develop regions of our country now suffering from distress and depression.

I propose we make new efforts to control and prevent crime and delinquency.

I propose we eliminate every remaining obstacle to the right and opportunity to vote.

I propose we honor and support the achievements of thought and the creations of art.

I propose we make an all-out campaign against waste and inefficiency. (III:3166)

While elements of those items can be found in messages by both Eisenhower and Kennedy, Johnson announced his program more grandly. His, "I propose we begin a program in education to insure every American child the fullest development of his mind and skills" contrasts sharply with Eisenhower's "Our school system demands some prompt, effective help" (III:3024), or Kennedy's "If this country is to grow in wisdom and strength, then every able high school graduate should have the opportunity to develop his talents (III:3136). Where Eisenhower pointed to the need for "some . . . help" and Kennedy called for giving "every student" the opportunity "to develop his talents," Johnson called for more, called for *ensuring* every child, not "help" or an "opportunity," but "the fullest development of his mind and skills." He did not qualify, did not suggest that those benefits might be impossible to deliver but called instead for bold guarantees. He concluded his message with what amounted to a priestly benediction, his elective authority reinforced by a liturgical cadence.

This then is the state of the Union: Free, restless, growing, and full of hope.

So it was in the beginning.

So it shall always be, while God is willing, and we are strong enough to keep the faith. (III:3171)

Three years later, in his 1968 annual message, he summarized the nation's impressive achievements in science, foreign aid, domestic programs, and productivity—all the building blocks of his earlier optimism. He pointed to eighty-three months of economic growth, "higher paychecks, humming factories, new cars moving down new highways," noted increases in home ownership, the creation of new colleges to serve more and more of the nation's young. Then he asked, "Why, then, this restlessness?" (PP, Johnson, 1968:27).*

His answer that year, just weeks before he announced he would not seek reelection, was both simple and profound:

> Because when a great ship cuts through the sea, the waters are always stirred and troubled.

> And our ship is moving. It is moving through troubled and new waters; it is moving toward new and better shores.

> We ask now, not how can we achieve abundance?—but how shall we use our abundance? Not, is there abundance enough for all?—but, how can we all share in our abundance? (p. 28)

What Johnson called "restlessness" or, in another place, "questioning" was an angry national division that grew more threatening with every escalation of violence, whether in urban riots or anti-Vietnam protests. He refused to concede that it was more than the turbulence that inevitably attends progress. He did not take a love-it-or-leave-it attitude, did not sort out "true" Americans from their disloyal opponents. He remained presidential—inclusive—insisting that the "restless" were also a part of the national union, that their "questioning" was legitimate.

Looking back over a year of ghetto riots across the nation, LBJ argued that "we saw how wide is the gulf for some Americans between the promise and the reality of our society." He acknowledged the obligation of a president to locate such gulfs and prevent their widening to unbridgeable distances. But he confessed that "we cannot change all of this in a day. It represents the bitter consequences of more than three centuries" (p. 28).

In closing he called upon the legislature and the campaigning candidates to debate these great issues, not as "subjects for narrow, partisan, oratory" but as matters central to the progress of the American Union. He concluded,

> If ever there was a people who sought more than mere abundance, it is our people.

---

*The abbreviation PP refers to *Public Papers of the Presidents of the United States.*

If ever there was a nation that was capable of solving its problems, it is this Nation.

If ever there were a time to know the pride and the excitement and the hope of being an American—it is this time.

So this, my friends, is the State of our Union: seeking, building, tested many times in this past year—and always equal to the test. (p. 33)

This was the old liberal at his best, holding out for the better society that social and economic justice will deliver, seeing the problems much as FDR had seen them thirty and more years before and focusing his attention on those who had been left out, the cultural outsiders, limited by poverty and by race. But absent from Johnson's formulation was the group whose energy and innocence Kennedy had called upon, the young essential to postwar social reforms. By 1968 they had disappeared from LBJ's liberal army; they were in Vietnam or evading the draft or protesting the war or campaigning for the antiwar candidate, Eugene McCarthy.

In 1969 Johnson reported to Congress after a trying year in which deep splits within his own party had prevented him from seeking reelection and in which deeper divisions within the country kept his hand-picked successor from winning the presidency. He represented a Union as disunited as it had been at any time since Reconstruction. Just days from the inauguration of Richard Nixon—the symbol of a politics Johnson had thought to eliminate—he spoke at a time of double humiliation: the personal repudiation of a proud, often arrogant man and the special judgment that civil conflict places on the person entrusted with the work of unification.

Johnson's speech began by proclaiming once more the "challenges and opportunity," the "commitments that all of us have made together that will, if we carry them out, give America our best chance to achieve the kind of great society that we all want," but quickly he began the qualifications that were absent from his early addresses, offering that "[e]very President lives, not only with what is, but with what has been and what could be" (p. 1263). His wording, an anticipation of the speech that followed, was haunted by time—"what has been and what could be"—and even more by "what might have been." That was the specter tormenting the departing president, a vision generated by the conjunction of terrible failure with extraordinary success. The programs central to the "Great Society," those dearest to his ambition, had largely been established, and if they could stand alone they would have ensured his reputation. But the very liberals whose domestic programs he had implemented with breathtaking success had been alienated by his expansion of the war in Vietnam. The young, whose idealism might have flourished with Johnson's War on Poverty or his historic leadership on civil rights, marched in protest around the White House and chanted personal insults. The war had strained all the bonds upon which union depends, and Johnson had become inseparable from that war, his name or initials often used to identify it. Thus the inevitable ghost of what might have been that drifted over his final meditation on the Union and its condition.

In acknowledging that every presidency is rooted in earlier events, "part of a larger sequence extending back through several years and extending back through several other administrations," LBJ did more than share the blame; he admitted as well a degree of impotence, a confession that spoke not only of what he had inherited but of what he was leaving to his successor, a catalog of presidential inadequacy.

> Urban unrest, poverty, pressures on welfare, education of our people, law enforcement and law and order, the continuing crisis in the Middle East, the conflict in Vietnam, the dangers of nuclear war, the great difficulties of dealing with the Communist powers, all have this much in common: They and their causes—the causes that gave rise to them—all of these have existed with us for many years. Several Presidents have already sought to try to deal with them. One or more Presidents will try to resolve them or try to contain them in the years that are ahead of us. (p. 1264)

This was, of course, the same catalog he had offered in his second State of the Union, then a list of promises, now a summary of uncompleted chores. The man who, at moments in his presidency, had presumed to complete the great unfinished work of other executives, who had thought to fulfill the unkept promise of "The Emancipation Proclamation," and who believed he could complete the New Deal in his Great Society—this man came at last to confess his limits and those of the office he had held.

Near the close of his address, Johnson spoke inevitably of Vietnam, insisting, defensively that the war had not limited spending for his major social programs, because "our prosperity is broad and it is deep." Yet Southeast Asia loomed over all his remarks: "Americans, I believe, are united in the hope that the Paris talks will bring an early peace to Vietnam" (p. 1267); "[t]he quest for peace tonight continues in Vietnam, and in the Paris talks"; and finally, "I regret more than any of you know that it has not been possible to restore peace to South Vietnam" (p. 1269). His tentativeness—the hesitant "I believe" that qualified all American hope for peace—the idea of an "early peace" when it was already too late, too late for Johnson and too late for his country—all these suggested the humbling nature of recent events. And when he called the Congress to support the troops who had served his policies, despite a brief burst of hawkish rhetoric, the effort at belligerency was undercut by the fact that only he was being discharged; our soldiers remained, mired in a conflict he could not conclude.

In a final assessment of his nation's health, a nation torn by civil strife, divided (as Robert Kennedy had proclaimed) into rich and poor, young and old, black and white, hawk and dove, Johnson did not pretend otherwise, but neither did he concede that those divisions could not be resolved. Rather, he merely conceded that the work was larger than he, that others would have to carry on.

THE TIES THAT BIND

When Woodrow Wilson brought the presidency back to the congressional chambers for his first annual message, he did it not merely to defy precedent but also because he was a teacher and disinclined to give his instruction by correspondence. It was a service, perhaps inadvertent, to an America that in the twentieth century would find its capacity for union tested in ways wholly different from those of the previous century. The troublesome "others"—native Americans and African-Americans in particular—that divided us East and West and North and South still challenged the nation but not in the old sense, not as the intruding outsider but as a part of a community that we had affirmed in law if not in practice.

Americans continued to use the language of "us" and "them", but apart from the forever prickly business of immigration, these distinctions now referred to equally legitimate parts of the national community. In the last decades of the twentieth century the divisions were not between states or alien enclaves—they were not for the most part external—but were "familial," literally so when the issue was gender or the country's youth, but also when the rights of Asian Americans or African Americans or Hispanic Americans were at stake. In this century the issues of union were close at hand, personal, and intimate, no matter how much we pretended otherwise. Because of that it was appropriate that presidents came to deliver their assessment of our mutual condition in person and, with advances in communications technology, to the members of that Union themselves.

Monroe picked his moment and challenged the Old World; Jefferson and Polk enlarged America's physical dimensions—the nation grew in power and resources and numbers. Through it all, presidents dutifully assessed the progress and the damage, cajoled and warned and comforted. For all their differences in temperament and abilities and for their widely contrasting views of what their country could contain, they have been of remarkably similar minds as to the nature of their elected duty. The job is always, as Washington foresaw, the difficult business of building affection, affection for one another and for the Union itself. This continuity of purpose, despite the never ending disappointment, argues for a greater degree of faithfulness and success than we might have expected.

Chapter Seven

Articulating History

The Rhetoric of Special Occasions I

But the White House is not only the center of political leadership. It must be the center of moral leadership—a "bully pulpit," as Theodore Roosevelt described it. For only the President represents the national interest and upon him alone converge all the needs and aspirations of all parts of the country, all departments of government, all nations of the world.

It is not enough merely to represent prevailing sentiment—to follow McKinley's practice, as described by Joe Cannon, of "keeping his ear so close to the ground he got it full of grasshoppers." We ... need ... a President who is willing and able to summon his national constituency to its finest hour—to alert the people to our dangers and our opportunities—to demand of them the sacrifices that will be necessary.

—John F. Kennedy, Speech Before the National Press Club,
1960

In 1812 that master of Lockean clarity James Madison addressed a group of chiefs freshly arrived from the frontier to meet the president of the United States.[1] Tailoring his remarks for that special audience, Madison strove to imitate the conventional white notion of Indian eloquence. "The red people," he said, "who live on this same great Island with the White people of the 18 fires are made by the Great Spirit out of the same earth, from parts of it differing in colour only." Madison's primary purpose was to limit the mischief the British could generate among the Western tribes, but he seized as well upon the opportunity to instruct his audience on the benefits of imitating white culture.

> You see how the Country of the 18 fires is filled with people. They increase like the corn they put in the ground. They all have good houses to shelter them from all weathers, good clothes, suitable to all seasons, and as for food of all sorts, you see they have enough and to spare. No man, woman, or child of the 18 fires ever perished of hunger. Compare all this with the condition of the red people. They are scattered here and there in handfuls. Their lodges are cold, leaky, and smoky. They have hard fare, and often not enough of it. Why this mighty difference? The reason, my red children, is plain. The white people breed cattle and sheep. They plow the earth, and make it give them everything they want. They spin and weave. Their heads and their hands make all the elements and productions of nature useful to them. Above all the people of the 18 fires live in constant peace and friendship. No tomahawk has ever been raised by one against another. Not a drop of blood has ever touched the chain that holds them together as one family. All their belts are white belts. It is in your power to be like them.[2]

While an extreme example, Madison's comments suggest how profoundly rhetoric is influenced by a speaker's understanding—or misunderstanding—of the audience. Obviously assuming that his listeners were intellectually childlike and incapable of abstraction, the president invented concrete euphemisms for abstract entities—eighteen fires for the eighteen states—and converted his own title from president to father ("I say to you, my children, your father does not ask you to join his warriors"). But in all this he strained after a recognizable eloquence, imitating an Indian oratory that white writers had long represented as the formal speech of New World natives.

And yet in his efforts at cultural translation, Madison extended his usual commission. He affirmed the Union as a family model, one in which the president, like a good father, worries that all his children are adequately fed and sheltered and are living in harmony with one another. Although he invited his "red children" only to imitate his white sons and daughters and not to join them as members of the same household, still he asserted that the strongest evidence of cultural maturity is the "chain" that holds a people together "as one family," the sense of connection that makes the well-being of each the concern of all. Thus he offered his executive paternity to two cultural lines, one red and one white, and urged both to seek union, though implicitly in communities defined by race.

Addressing the chiefs, even as he called upon them to change, Madison recreated himself and his office with images he thought his listeners might better understand. His stretch to find an appropriate idiom grew out of the vast rhetorical distance that separated him from his audience, and in his efforts to cross that chasm he provided dramatic evidence of the process of mutual redefinition that persuasion requires. Not content to allow the occasion to be merely ceremonial, Madison presumed a responsibility to "improve" his audience through his remarks, but his effort to "Americanize" his Indian guests also meant that he himself had to be remade.[3]

In speaking to the Western chiefs, Madison took advantage of their visit to express and expand the presidential message. Over the years such opportunities have increasingly been the occasion for important messages and have provided a more varied test of eloquence than the more set "pieces" that mark every administration. Executive messages that are not dictated simply by the presidential calendar represent either a dramatic intrusion—a crisis that cannot be ignored—or an opportunity seized by the president to speak for a particular cause or conviction. In the latter case they are often commemorative events that allow presidents to recast history and the audience according to their own interpretation and, by their presence, to make a connection between the past and some aspect of their own time. On other occasions, more obviously of their making, their concern is to influence the future, to set America on a different course. In this context the subject is less likely to be a remembered event than a desired policy. Such "special" messages seek to educate and change the audience.

Special addresses, however, that respond to "intrusive" events, matters that *require* executive comment, represent a more subtle challenge, one in which—ostensibly—the main intention is *not* to be changed but to protect our values and identity against some invasive power. In varying degrees calls to military action, and most especially requests for declarations of war, are of this sort, demanding that the president explain how, in such dramatic circumstances, the nation will both act and not be undone.

TO PROTECT AND DEFEND

On Behalf of War

Five times in American history, in response to a formal request from the president, [Congress] has passed a declaration of war. Complex rhetorical challenges, the speeches urging such actions must justify morally and practically putting at risk the lives and property Americans expect their government to protect. Perhaps because the basic elements of such occasions are unchanging, the messages themselves follow a recurrent pattern, and in their study of presidential calls to war, Karlyn Kohrs Campbell and Kathleen Hall Jamieson identify those common characteristics of presidential war rhetoric:

> (1) every element in it proclaims that the momentous decision to resort to force is deliberate, the product of thoughtful consideration; (2) forceful intervention is justified through a chronicle or narrative from which argumentative claims are drawn; (3) the audience is exhorted to unanimity of purpose and total commitment; (4) the rhetoric not only justifies the use of force but also seeks to legitimate presidential assumption of the extraordinary powers of the commander in chief; and as a function of these other characteristics, (5) strategic misrepresentations play an unusually significant role in its appeals.[4]

The first two elements follow necessarily from the gravity of the decision. No matter how emotionally charged the evidence the president offers in a narrative of grievances, the argument must grow from something more than mere anger and must demonstrate that the dangerous course proposed is both reasonable and carefully considered. To that end in 1812 James Madison, calling the United States to its first war since the Revolution, proceeded calmly and carefully through a catalog of British wrongs. "Without going back," he told Congress, beyond the renewal in 1803 of the war in which Great Britain is engaged, and omitting unrepaired wrongs of inferior magnitude, the conduct of her Government presents a series of acts hostile to the United States as an independent and neutral nation. (MP, 1:499–500)*

Though Madison's charges grew increasingly inflammatory ("British cruisers . . . have been violating the American flag," "thousands of American citizens . . . have been torn from their country and from everything dear to them," British ships "hover over and harass our entering and departing commerce") (1:500), the president never wholly abandoned the cadences of his opening, and his longish sentences testify to executive calm and judiciousness, the reasoned measures of self-control. In contrast to an enemy that was "wanton," "belligerent," and "insincere," Madison projected a United States that conscientiously sought reconciliation even in the face of such effrontery and that moved toward war only after exhausting all diplomatic possibilities.

The juxtaposition of American reasonableness with Britain's malicious and erratic behavior provided the basic structure for Madison's speech. "It has become, indeed, sufficiently certain," he told Congress,

> that the commerce of the United States is to be sacrificed, not as interfering with the belligerent rights of Great Britain; not as supplying the wants of her enemies, which she herself supplies; but as interfering with the monopoly which she covets for her own commerce and navigation. (1:502)

The directness of the opening charge with its subject/predicate construction, its emphatic wording ("It has become, indeed, sufficiently certain"), and its dramatic alliteration ("sufficiently certain that . . . commerce . . . is to be sacrificed") carries emotional conviction, but emotional conviction shaped by the careful consideration that the narration outlines. The work of reason and not simply passion, it nonetheless is full of righteous indignation prompted by British hypocrisy and dishonor as much as American suffering.

In the American paragraph, however, the writing is less direct, less clear.

---

*The abbreviation MP refers to James A. Richardson, ed., *A Compilation of the Messages and Papers of the Presidents* (Washington, DC, 1897).

Anxious to make every experiment short of the last resort of injured nations, the United States have withheld from Great Britain, under successive modifications, the benefits of a free intercourse with their market, the loss of which could not but outweigh the profits accruing from her restrictions of our commerce with other nations. And to entitle these experiments to the more favorable consideration they were so framed as to enable her to place her adversary under the exclusive operation of them. (1:502)

Before stating what the United States had done, Madison offered a qualification ("Anxious to make every experiment short of the last resort of injured nations") and thus deferred describing the action his administration had actually taken against Great Britain. Even in presenting that action, the statement unfolds slowly, deflected by extra verbiage and intruding phrases, the syntactical equivalent of America's painstaking quest for a diplomatic solution and a sharp contrast to the abrupt and bullying ways of the arrogant British. As with the explanation offered by the Declaration of 1776, it is the older nation that is portrayed as disregarding law, as pursuing its least honorable ambitions without regard either to the rights of other sovereign states and peoples or the honor of nations. The younger country, on the other hand, has followed to no avail the course of "moderation and conciliation." At the end Madison can no longer defer, and so he succinctly declares: "We behold, in fine, on the side of Great Britain a state of war against the United States, and on the side of the United States a state of peace toward Great Britain" (1:504).

Presenting the "history" of the executive branch's handling of British affronts, Madison suggested to the Congress a perspective that was at once interested and disinterested, one that objectively reviewed the evidence and then was stirred, as it suggested any impartial observer would be, by the results of that inquiry. In closing he indicated that this was his constitutionally defined role, to bring to the Congress the results of his diplomatic labors and allow its members to judge the case for themselves:

Whether the United States shall continue passive under these progressive usurpations and these accumulating wrongs, or, opposing force to force in defense of their national rights, shall commit a just cause into the hands of the Almighty Disposer of Events, avoiding all connections which might entangle it in the contest or views of other powers, and preserving a constant readiness to concur in an honorable reestablishment of peace and friendship, is a solemn question which the Constitution wisely confides to the legislative department of the Government. In recommending it to their early deliberations I am happy in the assurance that the decision will be worthy the enlightened and patriotic councils of a virtuous, a free, and a powerful nation. (1:504–5)

Intent on demonstrating America's capacity to act maturely and honorably in an international arena that it had only recently entered and on proving that it was an "enlightened" as well as a "patriotic" country, Madison was, as well, conscientiously following constitutional law even under extreme conditions. This he interpreted as requiring the executive to make a remarkable move from disinterest to interest, from objective viewer to partisan. Madison's presentation of British provocation and American restraint depended upon the appearance of an initially dispassionate leadership even as it justified a passionate indignation from representatives of "a virtuous, a free, and a powerful nation." Ending as he began with tangible evidence of America's disciplined response to the outrages of another nation, the first president to preside over a war provided a model for subsequent executives.

In making his case Madison adhered to the paradigm outlined by Campbell and Jamieson, satisfying their fifth criterion ("strategic misrepresentation") by what he did *not* mention in regard to popular feeling and motive. His was not, until its conclusion, a war that enjoyed great support. Free trade and sailors' rights, the primary issues he emphasized in his appeal to Congress, were not held by all of his countrymen as sufficient cause given the risk, and perhaps that is why his call for "unanimity of purpose" (the third ingredient in Campbell and Jamieson's formula) and extraordinary powers for the Commander-in-Chief (their fourth) were relatively subdued. The eventual favorable vote, the numbers lowered by a large number of abstentions among legislators from Madison's own party, was badly divided (79 to 49 in the House and 19 to 13 in the Senate) and reflected strong sectional disagreement. Though most of the president's presentation of just cause grew from maritime abuses (interception of commercial ships in international waters, the removal of sailors for "impressment" into British service, and the seizure of American goods), war had little support in the Northern maritime states, whose commerce it would ruin even more surely than Britain's refusal to honor the neutrality of their shipping.

Support for war came from Southern and Western states and had little to do with crimes at sea. The closest Madison came to referring to the immediate object of those "war hawks," as they were called, was a brief mention—almost a footnote—near the end of his address when, as further evidence of Britain's immoral conduct he accused that country of supporting the warfare of "savages on one of our extensive frontiers—a warfare which is known to spare neither age nor sex and to be distinguished by features peculiarly shocking to humanity" (I:504). That was a Western issue, the conflict between America's expansionist interests and Europe's commitment to contain those ambitions. War would allow both retribution for old wrongs and the chance to win territory, in particular Canada. Such aspiration, however, does not so neatly serve the stark distinctions between good and evil, noble and ignoble, so central to all war rhetoric, and so it was British greed rather than American ambition that Madison emphasized.

In 1846 the expansionist-minded James K. Polk presented his case for war with Mexico in much the same way as Madison had against the British in 1812, emphasizing a similar concern for the constitutionally distributed powers and the same attention to America's enlightened and diligent pursuit of peace in the face of repeated provocation. The tone of his message throughout its first paragraphs was carefully controlled, the sentences (like Madison's) often lengthened by qualifications and seldom blatantly emotional. When the sentences were shorter ("The redress of the wrongs of our citizens naturally and inseparably blended itself with the questions of boundary. The settlement of the one question in any correct view of the subject involves that of the other") (4:438), the object seemed to be clarity rather than passion.

Long-suffering in its desire to be reasonable and deliberate in all its responses, the United States, Polk insisted, found itself rebuffed and, through no fault of its own, at war with Mexico. In contrast with Madison's condemnation of Britain, an old nation whose outrageous behavior must result from contempt and disregard for a younger country, Polk suggested that Mexico did not know how to behave as a government. "Our forbearance has gone to such an extreme as to be mistaken in its character," he told his audience. "But now, after reiterated menaces, Mexico has passed the boundary of the United States, has invaded our territory and shed American blood upon the American soil. She has proclaimed that hostilities have commenced, and that the two nations are now at war" (4:442). The emotions that remained subdued in the opening paragraphs are at last brought directly into play, even to an expression of regret that the United States had not acted earlier, but central to the indignation is a righteousness vindicated by Polk's chronology of the events and efforts that preceded the irrevocable "now." Only when his narrative had been laid out before the legislature did the president call upon Congress to pursue a war he insisted had been thrust upon their country, first by insult and finally by invasion.[5] He did not mention that the ultimate affront, the shedding of "American blood upon the American soil," took place on disputed territory, that portion of Texas claimed by both sides, or that, from a Mexican perspective, the troops Polk had sent to occupy that contested region were the invading force.

Thus virtually all calls for war are formulaic, and for every country the narration of offenses by a dishonorable foe, no matter how credible, must precede a formal declaration of one's own intent. In this America has been no different, and yet each of our war calls has borne the clear stamp of its time and speaker. There was less restraint in Polk's call for war with Mexico than in Madison's earlier indictment of Britain, more eagerness to get on with it, more a tone of frustration that action had been so long delayed, and in his speech he pressed the legislature, flexing his presidential muscles a great deal more than had Madison. But his war, despite the opposition of a few Whigs, was more popular (the vote was 174 to 14 in the House and 40 to 2 in the Senate) and involved a much weaker opponent.

In 1898 President McKinley moved even more hurriedly down the same rhetorical path as he urged Congress to declare war on Spain. He reached an emotional pitch by the third paragraph, and only then calmed sufficiently to provide—as if it were an afterthought—the prerequisite historical narrative. The preparation for this war began in the days of Monroe and the regular depiction of Spain as a brutal but failing imperial power. Animosity had been fanned for months by a hawkish American press that, responding to the outbreak of rebellion in Cuba, featured daily atrocities. Conflicts between Spain and Cuba had long troubled the

United States, McKinley reminded his audience, and the present insurrection in particular had "caused enormous losses to American trade and commerce, caused irritation, annoyance, and disturbance among our citizens, and, by the exercise of cruel, barbarous, and uncivilized practices of warfare, shocked the sensibilities and offended the human sympathies of our people." From the inconvenience at home he turned to the effect on Cuba, his prose growing increasingly florid:

> Since the present revolution began, in February, 1895, this country has seen the fertile domain at our threshold ravaged by fire and sword in the course of a struggle unequaled in the history of the island and rarely paralleled as to the numbers of combatants and the bitterness of the contest by any revolution of modern times where a dependent people striving to be free have been opposed by the power of the sovereign state. (13:6282)

Then, returning the point of view to "our people," he reported without explanation losses that under Cuba's colonial economy would surely have been suffered by the oppressor as well as the oppressed as Americans "beheld a once prosperous community reduced to comparative want, its lucrative commerce virtually paralyzed, its exceptional productiveness diminished, its fields laid waste, its mills in ruins, and its people perishing by tens of thousands from hunger and destitution" (13:6282).

Acknowledging America's impotence so long as the struggle remained Cuban (the Hearst papers had ridiculed McKinley for his refusal to act), the president explained, "We have found ourselves constrained, in the observance of that strict neutrality which our laws enjoin and which the law of nations commands, to police our own waters and watch our own seaports in prevention of any unlawful act in aid of the Cubans" (13:6282). But the sinking of the battleship *Maine*, the climactic moment in McKinley's narration, had delivered the United States from the shackles of neutrality. Though, as the president admitted, responsibility for the calamity had not yet been fully established, it had made America the object rather than the mere observer of Spanish insult.

Madison's grievances in 1812, while largely commercial, had centered on insults directed more against U.S. citizens—blockading American ports, harassing coastal traffic, and impressing American seaman. Polk's charges, questionable as they may have been, also involved threats to American persons, culminating in a violent "invasion." But McKinley's rhetoric was most indignant when property was the issue, albeit property on which there was only an indirect American claim (the "enormous losses" he attributed to unrealized trade). For the most part, in his account, Americans suffered only "irritation," "annoyance," and "disturbance" until the sinking of the *Maine*. Most grievous of the ravages of "fire and sword" was, the president declared, the lost productivity of a "fertile domain." He lavished his most indulgent adjectives on matters of property ("lucrative commerce," "exceptional productiveness"), and his catalog of atrocities grew most impassioned when the object of violence was production (commerce paralyzed, productiveness diminished, fields laid waste, mills in ruins). His remarks, in fact, implied that a rich and productive land "at our threshold" was now available as the spoils of a just war, and while he never addressed America's potential gain, neither did he allow the wealth of Cuba to slip from view.

McKinley argued that given the destructive nature of the conflict between Cuba and Spain and the unlikelihood that either side would permanently prevail, American intervention would be beneficial to all concerned and would reflect, more than self-interest, a humane concern for the antagonists. He sought the weight of precedent—the recognition of insurrectionist Texas during the Jackson administration—but in the case of Cuba he could identify no functioning government for the United States to endorse, so he called, in effect, for an alliance with a future government, one that had yet to be established. By invoking Texas he legitimated the possibility of expanding American interests without compromising American principle. "The only hope of relief and repose from a condition which can no longer be endured," he concluded, "is the enforced pacification of Cuba. In the name of humanity, in the name of civilization, in behalf of endangered American interests which give us the right and the duty to speak and to act, the war in Cuba must stop" (13:6292). This was his great moral triad—humanity, civilization, and American interests—that legitimized American involvement, principles that together convey the "right and the duty to speak and act," and the greatest of these was "interest."

In 1917 Woodrow Wilson, like his warring predecessors, reminded Congress of the Constitution's assignment of responsibility and then proceeded to make the case for America's entry into the World War. Like Madison and McKinley, Wilson depicted America's dilemma in terms of a wronged neutral whose ships were being attacked by a European belligerent (a point so questionable that his Secretary of State, William Jennings Bryan, resigned over it),[6] but, unlike those earlier presidents, he quickly deemphasized property and commerce as the matter of concern:

> I am not now thinking of the loss of property involved, immense and serious as that is, but only of the wanton and wholesale destruction of the lives of non-combatants, men, women and children, engaged in pursuits which have always, even in the darkest periods of modern history, been deemed innocent and legitimate. Property can be paid for; the lives of peaceful and innocent people cannot be.
>
> The present German submarine warfare against commerce is a warfare against mankind. (17:8227)

Wilson called for his country to enter a war that would determine the future of the world, a war between "free," "self-governing peoples" and "selfish and autocratic power"—in short, a war *for* the world. Indirectly he extended the premise of the Monroe Doctrine to the entire globe, casting America as the international guardian of democracy and freedom. In joining the struggle against European autocracy, Americans were merely acting on the principles of their own revolution, a point Wilson reinforced by echoing the final lines of the Declaration of Independence in his own conclusion.

> To such a task we can dedicate our lives and our fortunes, everything that we are and everything that we have, with the pride of those who know that the day has come when America is privileged to spend her blood and her might for the principles that gave her birth and happiness and the peace which she has treasured. (17:8233)

The war the United States joined in 1917 was, in Wilson's explanation, to be the third act in the drama that had begun in 1776, an assertion of the universal rights of all persons that followed the logic of America's revolution and Civil War to its inevitable conclusion. "Neutrality," this country's shield against European wars since the nation's founding, Wilson declared "no longer feasible or desirable where the peace of the world is involved and the freedom of its peoples. . . . We have seen the last of neutrality in such circumstances" (17:8229).

Wilson assured the country that this was a conflict between a regressive government and the disinterested principles of democracy and suggested its end would not be the humiliation of the German people but their liberation; he celebrated the recent overthrow of the Russian monarchy as evidence that history, together with the American example, was pushing the whole world toward freedom.

> The world must be safe for democracy. Its peace must be planted upon the tested foundations of political liberty.
> We have no selfish ends to serve. We desire no conquest, no dominion. We seek no indemnities for ourselves, no material compensation for the sacrifices we shall freely make. We are but one of the champions of the rights of mankind. We shall be satisfied when those rights have been made as secure as the faith and the freedom of nations can make them. (17:8231)

The noble mission to which Wilson had called his countrymen in his first inaugural had now found specific expression; the great act of faithfulness for his generation had now been identified.

Of all presidential calls to war, only Franklin Roosevelt's in 1941 broke the prevailing pattern—in form, in emotion, and in length. Little more than a page long, it made no mention of constitutional duties and its rehearsal of wrongs surveyed little more than the previous twenty-four hours. It opened in censure and outrage and concluded in the same tone. Because he alone among the presidents who have asked Congress to declare a war could refer to a clear and uncontrovertible act of aggression, he did not have to interpret a history of lesser offenses or justify his indignation. He could speak with the sure knowledge that Americans shared his shock and outrage. "Yesterday," he began, "December 7, 1941—a date which will live in infamy—the United States of America was suddenly and deliberately attacked by the naval and air forces of the empire of Japan." Underlining the deceit and hypocrisy of the enemy, Roosevelt continued by pointing out that, one hour after the bombing had commenced in Hawaii, the Japanese ambassador in Washington delivered a diplomatic communiqué that made no mention of hostilities, and then he emphasized the elaborately premeditated nature of the incursion by reminding his audience of the distance separating Japan from the Hawaiian Islands.

By stressing Japanese perfidy, Roosevelt sought to increase the moral revulsion incited by the attack; not only was the bombing deadly ("I regret to tell you that very many American lives have been lost"), but it was also unprovoked and cowardly. The president in 1941, as in no other time in American history, had to rally people grievously wounded and stunned by the magnitude of the assault on their security. He need not convince them of the justice of war, but he had to unify them, retrieve them from the demoralized state produced by the attack. He did so by outlining the enormity of what had just happened, narrating the actions of a single day. In addition to the attack in Hawaii, he reported:

> Yesterday the Japanese Government also launched an attack against Malaya.
>
> Last night Japanese forces attacked Hong Kong.
>
> Last night Japanese forces attacked Guam.
>
> Last night Japanese forces attacked the Philippine Islands.
>
> Last night the Japanese attacked Wake Island.
>
> Japan has therefore undertaken a surprise offensive extending throughout the Pacific area. The facts of yesterday and today speak for themselves. The people of the United States have already formed their opinions and well understand the implications to the very life and safety of our nation. (*New York Times*, 12/9/41)

The apparent directness with which the president described the scope of the aggression, the insistence—as in his first inaugural—that he concealed nothing, was oddly reassuring, as though in all the panic and confusion of a seemingly endless chain of disastrous reports, simply knowing how truly bad the news was would be a step forward. By speaking briefly and economically, by enumerating the losses without further elaboration (and the full extent of the harm was his "strategic misrepresentation"), Roosevelt was seeking a resolve that would contain doubt and an indignation that could displace fear. Together, he told his listeners, they would overcome "treachery" with "righteous might," they would escape "grave danger" with "unbounding determination" and gain in time "the inevitable triumph." As in his speeches dealing with economic depression, in the terrible hours following Pearl Harbor FDR embodied the confidence he called for in his countrymen. He offered no consolation, did not linger over tragedy, but presented instead his own unflinching resolution.

He finished as he began, by referring to the date, waving it like a battle flag, a symbol of their just cause. "I ask," he concluded, "that the Congress declare that since the unprovoked and dastardly attack by Japan on Sunday, December 7, 1941, a state of war has existed between the United States and the Japanese Empire."[7]

Undeclared Actions

Since World War II no American president has come before Congress asking for a declaration of the sort FDR requested, but some have done so in an effort to gain legislative and popular support for a series of conflicts and interventions that, no matter the differences in labeling and legal explanation, involved all the same risks and issues. From Truman to Bush they have followed the traditional formula (though without the need to call directly for the expansion of their own powers, as no war was being "declared"), but the war that was definitive for each of them (with the partial exception of Truman, who served in World War I) was Roosevelt's. Continually they have reached back to the clarity of that conflict in justifying their own military engagements. Perhaps that explains why they so persistently began their calls for declarations of war with references to time.

Truman's speech on Korea provides the least dramatic example, with its opening lines, "At noon today, I sent a message to the Congress about the situation in Korea" (PP, Truman, 1950:537).[8] But the echo from Pearl Harbor was more apparent in 1958, when Eisenhower announced the sending of Marines into Beirut (at the request of Lebanon's president). "Yesterday," he began, "was a day of grave developments in the Middle East" (PP, Eisenhower, 1958:553). "Ten days ago" were Richard Nixon's first words in 1970, when he announced the extension of the Vietnam War into Cambodia (PP, Nixon, 1970:405) and in 1983 Ronald Reagan began with "Some two months ago" when discussing both the killing of 269 Marines on a peacekeeping mission

in Beirut (a terrorist drove a truckload of explosives into their com-
pound) and America's invasion of Grenada to overthrow a communist
government (PP, Reagan, 1983:1517). Most dramatic, however, were
George Bush's first words as he announced the Gulf War of 1991. "Just
two hours ago," he reported, "allied air forces began an attack on military targets in Iraq and Kuwait" (PP, Bush, 1991:42).

Since 1941 America's military actions have been justified in terms of
protecting weaker nations and stopping the spread of communism. In no
case did they involve an attack on American territory or a simple and
straightforward threat to national sovereignty. The narrative of causes
Truman offered for intervention in Korea, like those provided by Eisenhower for landing troops in Lebanon and by Johnson and Nixon for
sending American soldiers to Vietnam, was a history of abuses suffered
by another people. Our involvement was principled, its purpose to serve
freedom around the world. After summarizing communist incursions in
Korea, Truman—only five years removed from World War II—told his
audience,

> These actions by the United Nations and its members are of great impor-
> tance. The free nations have now made it clear that lawless aggression will
> be met by force. The free nations have learned the fateful lesson of the
> 1930's. That lesson is that aggression must be met firmly. Appeasement
> leads only to further aggression and ultimately to war.

Making no distinction between national and world security, the president reminded his listeners of the price America had so recently paid,
then asserted without further explanation that the United States was involved "because we know what is at stake here is our own national security and the peace of the world" (PP, Truman, 1950: 53–56).

Eisenhower offered a similar explanation for ordering troops into
Lebanon in 1958. Concluding that the eruption of violence across the
Middle East justified his intervention—the Iraqi royal family (whom
Eisenhower identified only as "the duly constituted government") had
been assassinated and "a highly organized plot against the lawful government of Jordan" had been uncovered—he then "Americanized" Lebanon
to make its cause more acceptable to his audience. He described that nation as "a small country, a little less than the size of Connecticut" and
currently home to about 2,500 Americans. And, he added, it even con-

tained a distinguished institution of higher learning, "the American University of Beirut." But the ultimate justification was to stop aggression there early and to apply the hard-won lessons of both World War II and the Cold War. "[W]hat we now see in the Middle East," he insisted, "is the same pattern of conquest with which we became familiar during the period of 1945 to 1950. This involves taking over a nation by indirect aggression; that is, under the cover of a fomented civil strife." He offered foreign conquests of Greece in 1947, Czechoslovakia in 1948, China in 1948, and Korea and Indochina in 1950 as evidence. And, too, there was the lesson of the last war:

> In the 1930s the members of the League of Nations became indifferent to direct and indirect aggression in Europe, Asia and Africa. The result was to strengthen and stimulate aggressive forces that made World War II inevitable.
>
> The United States is determined that that history shall not now be repeated. (PP, Eisenhower, 1958:556–7)

Lyndon Johnson echoed those sentiments on September 29, 1967 as he addressed the question "Why are we in Vietnam?"

> We cherish freedom—yes. We cherish self-determination for all peoples—yes. We abhor the political murder of any state by another, and the bodily murder of any people by gangsters of whatever ideology. And for twenty-seven years—since the days of lend-lease—we have sought to strengthen free people against domination by aggressive foreign powers. (PP, Johnson, 1967:876)

But idealism was an insufficient justification. He asserted that "the key to all we have done is really our own security." "Is the aggression a threat—not only to the immediate victim—but to the United States of America," he asked, "and to the peace and security of the entire world of which we in America are a very vital part?" Only when the answer is yes, he insisted, is a president justified in putting American troops at risk.

Johnson's argument was the one Truman had employed, though more elaborately developed: that communist aggression, if unchecked, will lead to an inevitable and more dangerous conflict. After describing the threat to the rest of Asia and the Pacific nations, he conceded that he could not say for certain "that a Southeast Asia dominated by communist power would bring a third world war . . . closer to terrible reality," but "all that we have learned in this tragic century strongly suggests to me that it would be so" (*ibid.*:878). The justification for this war was the prevention of a hypothetical worse war somewhere in the future. The primary support for Johnson's suspicion, one still recent when Truman employed it, was by 1967 twenty-two years removed and older than most of the demonstrators protesting American involvement in Vietnam.

When Nixon defended expanding the war into Cambodia in 1970, he, like all his predecessors explaining a military action, narrated the events that made the decision necessary. But, unlike Johnson, Eisenhower, and Truman, he placed emphasis less on stopping the international spread of aggression than on what was required to extricate our troops safely from this war. "A majority of American people," he conceded, "a majority of you listening to me, are for the withdrawal of our forces from Vietnam. The action I have taken tonight is indispensable for the continuing success of that withdrawal program." Only by this act of escalation, he argued, could a recalcitrant enemy be forced to the negotiating table. "The action I have announced tonight," he declared, "puts the leaders of North Vietnam on notice that we will be patient in working for peace; we will be conciliatory at the conference table, but we will not be humiliated" (PP, Nixon, 1970:408).

While presidents continued to employ the containment arguments of Truman and Eisenhower, their rhetoric has shifted in a direction Nixon's speech anticipated. As the opponents grew smaller—and sometimes embarrassingly difficult to dispatch—presidents necessarily distinguished the action they proposed from that which involved the United States in Vietnam, and at the same time they appealed to the wounded pride that was a part of that war's legacy. Ronald Reagan justified America's 1983 presence in Lebanon in the familiar terms of regional stability, but in this instance he presented the issue at stake as economic interest rather than ideology; "the area," he declared, "is key to the economic and political life of the West" (PP, Reagan, 1983:1517).

But the conjoining of two distinct events—the recent tragedy in Beirut and the invasion of a small Caribbean island unknown to most Americans—suggested more complex motives and objectives than simply protecting Suez and Middle Eastern oilfields. Reagan's introduction of a third event even farther removed—the two-month-old Russian attack on a Korean airliner that killed "269 men, women and children"—implied some larger strategy that connected those disparate acts of violence. The impression conveyed by the Beirut bombing and the communist takeover of Grenada was that of a beleaguered America, a great nation being taunted by lesser powers around the world. Linking those with the destruction of the Korean airliner, initially, seemed simply to add one more outrage for which there was no satisfying or appropriate response. But that was not wholly the case; we could act in Grenada. Though the island was small and of little or no strategic importance, Reagan had to make it significant to Americans, not only because a Cuban-sponsored dictatorship had taken over the country, itself an indirect assault upon the Monroe Doctrine, but so that it could meaningfully express America's continued determination—and ability—to protect its interests.

Like Eisenhower introducing his countrymen to Lebanon, Reagan presented Grenada in familiar terms. It is, he told them, "only twice the size of the District of Columbia" and a former British colony. He assured Americans that we had intervened at the request of people in the region. Instead of American University it had St. George's University Medical School, where eight hundred Americans were enrolled. He feared those students would be held as hostages and was determined that "the nightmare . . . of Iran" would never be repeated. "We got there just in time," he announced, taking the island after a "brilliant campaign."

What had been denied to Americans in Vietnam and in the multitude of terrorist insults of more recent years, Grenada provided in the form of a complete victory requiring little time and few casualties. And, Reagan insisted, it was a victory of larger significance than the smallness of the island would suggest. "The events in Lebanon and Grenada, though oceans apart," he explained, "are closely related." The connection— which explained his inclusion of the Korean airliner atrocity—was Soviet. "Not only has Moscow assisted and encouraged the violence in both countries," he continued, "but it provides direct support through a network of surrogates and terrorists" (PP, Reagan, 1983:1521). The real enemy was larger in magnitude and malignity than the small country we had rescued; the victory in Grenada was not the vanquishing of an massively overmatched little island but a blow against the international machinations of a superpower that was in some way responsible for the Marine massacre as well.

The effort to magnify the significance of that brief action turned the subject from security to honor, and Reagan concluded his speech with an anecdote about a tough general visiting wounded Marines in a military hospital. Since all America's military engagements had been lumped into one overarching campaign, the president did not single out the battle in which the young man had been grievously wounded, but told how he caught the attention of his visitor and wrote on a pad of paper "semper fi." "Well," the president said,

> if you've been a marine or if, like myself, you're an admirer of the marines, you know these words are a battle cry, a greeting, and a legend in the Marine Corps. They're marine shorthand for the motto of the Corps— "Semper Fidelis"—"always faithful." (PP, Reagan, 1983:1522)

Finally, Reagan concluded, the issue was one of American faithfulness, the willingness "to stand up for" the country.

Before turning his speech to traditional themes and explanations, Reagan had warned, "The world has changed." In 1991 George Bush both affirmed and denied that assumption when he defended the United States–led Gulf War. Justifying the action with references to the villainy of Iraqi dictator Sadam Hussein, who had not only invaded and "raped" Kuwait, "a small and helpless neighbor," but was developing nuclear weapons and threatening the entire region, Bush's report had more than a hint of World War II in both its tone and its analysis. There was the enthusiasm for the international alliance that had joined this fight, the talk of Allied men and women in uniform with its reassuring associations, the D-Day sound of the announcement ("Just two hours ago, allied air forces began an attack on military targets in Iraq and Kuwait"), and the persistent "Hitlerizing" of Sadam in a 1940s-style newsreel commentary ("While the world waited, Sadam Hussein met every overture of peace with open contempt. While the world prayed for peace, Sadam prepared for war") (PP, Bush, 1991:42–43).

But there was much of Reagan in Bush's presentation as well. The allied goal was limited, "the liberation of Kuwait," and the president promised Americans "this will not be another Vietnam," "the fighting will not go on for long and . . . casualties will be held to an absolute minimum." He, similarly, acknowledged the economic importance of the contested area, emphasizing the threat to the "fragile economies of the third world" and to "the emerging democracies of Eastern Europe," and added at the end, "our own economy." Like Reagan, he concluded with quotations from the field ("If we let him get away with this, who knows what's going to be next").

But Bush noted a great difference, one that returned to a tone reminiscent of the concluding months of the war against fascism:

> This is an historic moment. We have in the past year made great progress in ending the long era of conflict and cold war. We have before us the opportunity to forge for ourselves and for future generations a new world order—a world where the rule of law, and not the law of the jungle, governs the conduct of nations. (*Ibid.*:44)

With the collapse of the Soviet Union and the end of the Cold War, Bush returned to a 1940s vision of a world whose disruptions could be contained by the United Nations, and this time there would be no powerful patron for such conflicts as those in Korea and Vietnam. This war, he implied, was the first stage of a new peace.

For generational reasons, World War II was the exemplary experience behind postwar arguments for limited military interventions, but presidents from Truman to Bush also drew on a "Wilson doctrine" of liberation in justifying America's global policing activities. At the end of the Cold War Bush suggested that at last the world was ready for the new order Wilson had prophesied as he ushered his country into its first global conflict.

TO INSTRUCT AND IMPROVE

As their office became increasingly mobile, presidents joined the orating senators and professional pulpit and platform lecturers who had dominated the speaking circuit in the 1820s and 1830s,[10] finding their place by the end of the century in the nation's traveling word show. President Cleveland, for example, was the featured speaker at the dedication of the Statue of Liberty in 1886, and in 1893 he opened the Columbian exposition in Chicago. As Calvin Coolidge observed, by his time in office (1923–29):

One of the most appalling trials which confront a President is the perpetual clamor for public utterances. Invitations are constant and pressing.
They come by wire, by mail, and by delegations. No event of importance
is celebrated anywhere in the United States without inviting him to come
to deliver an oration.[11]

Increasingly presidents tried to meet the demand. By the middle of the
twentieth century they routinely traveled around the world as well as
around the country representing their office at ceremonial, political,
and diplomatic occasions, speaking in protest at the Berlin Wall and
celebrating at Disneyland the twenty-fifth birthday of an amusement
park. Early in the century politics had already been so transformed by
technologies that brought the president to the people that William
Howard Taft complained, "I have come to the conclusion that the
major part of the President is to increase the gate receipts of expositions
and fairs and bring tourists into the town." Although Taft may sometimes have felt chagrined by this aspect of the job, he more typically
welcomed his time on the road and the access it gave him to his countrymen.[12] In this he shared an enthusiasm with his extroverted predecessor who was, for much of his political career, among America's greatest public attractions.

TEDDY ROOSEVELT'S WESTERN SWING

In 1903 Teddy Roosevelt was away from Washington from the first of
April until the fifth of June, crisscrossing the Western states over more
than 14,000 miles in an effort both to strengthen his claim to the 1904
nomination and to generate support for his progressive brand of Republicanism.[13] The tour centered on Roosevelt's appearance in Saint Louis
on April 29 for the dedication ceremonies of the Louisiana Purchase Exposition, but by then his journey had already taken him through Minnesota and the Dakotas to Yellowstone National Park, including many of
the states carved from the old Louisiana territory. Upon completing his
Saint Louis visit, he went west once more, this time to California and the
Pacific Northwest, states beyond the limits of the Purchase but dependent upon it for their connection to the Union.

Roosevelt made 265 speeches on a wide range of subjects. In Chicago on April 2, he affirmed the Monroe Doctrine and spoke to its twentieth-century application. It was in this speech that he recalled "a homely old adage which runs: 'Speak softly and carry a big stick; you will go far'" (II:266).* The following day he spoke to the same issue in Waukesha, Wisconsin, declaring, "As a nation, if we are to be true to our past, we must steadfastly keep these two positions—to submit to no injury by the strong and to inflict no injury on the weak." On April 3, this time in Milwaukee, he took up "the question of the control and regulation of those great corporations which are popularly, although rather vaguely, known as trusts (I:269)." Farm and labor issues were his subject on April 6 in Sioux Falls, South Dakota. And so he continued, speaking his way across the continent during the fifty-nine days that followed.

There was much to talk about. Internationally the colonial powers had been busily carving up Africa and struggling for advantage in China. America's success in the war with Spain had made it, too, a player in this game (Puerto Rico and the Philippines came under American authority in 1898, and in 1902 Cuba became a protectorate), and there was great disagreement as to what the rules governing its participation should be. Roosevelt had already embarked on a more active role in Latin America and in 1904 would add his own corollary to the Monroe Doctrine to include the policing of our southern neighbors whenever they engaged in "flagrant cases" of "wrong doing."

At home, conflict between workers and corporations had persisted through the 1890s and into Roosevelt's administration. The 1892 Homestead steel strike, work stoppages in the Idaho silver mines, and the 1894 Pullman strike had all brought violence followed by government intervention (in the form of state militias and federal troops) on the side of property and the companies that owned it. In 1894 a ragtag band of unemployed men, dubbed Coxey's Army, had brought its "petition in boots" to Washington, where its leader was summarily jailed and the group dispersed. By contrast Roosevelt had responded to a 1902 strike among coal miners by appointing a commission to consider their grievances and to help negotiate a settlement.

---

*All quotations here from Roosevelt's 1903 Western speeches are taken from *The Works of Theodore Roosevelt in Fourteen Volumes: Presidential Addresses and State Papers, Part Two*, Vols. I and II (New York, 1913).

But one year away from an election and unsure of the support of entrenched party leaders, Roosevelt had politics uppermost in mind. A
dramatic transition was taking place, marked by a weakening of traditional party loyalties and a broad-based and deeply conflicted demand
for reform. In overpopulated, underplanned urban areas the old political machines were besieged by settlement house leaders, social
gospelists, and journalistic muckrakers. Agrarian populism, spurred by
high shipping and mortgage rates combined with crop failures, had
swept across rural America in the 1890s and was especially strong in the
Western states. In the 1892 presidential election the third party Populist
candidate had carried Idaho, Nevada, Kansas, and Colorado and had
done sufficiently well in North Dakota and Oregon to win an electoral
vote in each state. When in 1896 Democrats nominated William Jennings Bryan, who was also the Populist nominee, they carried every
Western state except for California, Oregon, and the Dakotas, where,
four years earlier, the victorious Cleveland had triumphed only in California and Texas. Bryan, on the other hand, lost every Northern state
east of the Mississippi.

In going west Roosevelt sought to build a coalition of Populists and
Progressives, paralleling his own double identity as a New York politician
who had also been a rancher in the Dakota territory.[14] His attempt to
win the support of both Western and Eastern reformers was complicated
by the mutual suspicions and fundamentally different assumptions that
divided the groups. Urban reformers had strong intellectual, even scientific inclinations (as when Roosevelt called in 1805 for a study of the social consequences of women's working outside the home), while agrarian-
ism was, like Bryan, fiercely pietistic and sometimes anti-intellectual.
Urban Progressives wanted efficient and responsible government, while
their rural counterparts wanted righteous government.

Teddy Roosevelt also went west to visit the wilderness areas—Yellowstone, Yosemite, the Sequoia forest, and the Grand Canyon—which he
wanted government to protect. He had published, in 1902, *Outdoor Pas-
times of an American Hunter*, a hymn to wilderness, and he called attention to America's surviving natural treasures whenever possible.

Thus the Roosevelt tour was noteworthy for both the political and the
geographical terrain it covered. Besides foreign relations and the trusts,
he addressed such subjects as roadbuilding, forest preservation, higher

education, tariffs, public service, and public land and water policies. But his overarching subject was national character, that which had brought the country to its present greatness and that which would be required by the future. He was, in fact, telling his audience who they were, recreating them after his own image, and urging them to assume his own sense of mission. At a banquet in San Francisco he declared, "The one indispensable thing for us to keep is a high standard of character for the average American citizen" (II, 414). He frequently recalled past heroes as models, speaking at a San Francisco groundbreaking ceremony for a McKinley memorial, remembering in an Omaha speech that the date was the anniversary of Grant's birth. He spoke in Portland at a monument to Lewis and Clark, dedicated a Lincoln site at Freeport, Illinois, then visited another Lincoln memorial in Springfield. But more even than those great men, he celebrated veterans and pioneers as exemplars of the character he encouraged in his country and his countrymen. "We will never justify the existence of the Republic," Roosevelt told a college audience at Stanford University,

> by merely talking each Fourth of July about what the Republic has done. If our homage is lip loyalty merely, the great deeds of those who went before us, the great deeds of the times of Washington and of the times of Lincoln, the great deeds of the men who won the Revolution and founded the Nation, and of the men who preserved it, who made it a Union and a free Republic, will simply arise to shame us. We can honor our fathers and our fathers' fathers only by ourselves striving to rise level to their standard. (I:380)

Typically the masculine dominated this double lesson in filial and moral obligation, not only before the young men of Stanford but through the entirety of Roosevelt's tour.

That was not a new topic for Roosevelt. In 1900 he had been fond of announcing, "We are a nation of men, not a nation of weaklings," and throughout that campaign he offered his own vigor as an example of the "manliness" he so valued. Mr. Dooley, that astute political observer, invented by Finley Peter Dunne, described twenty-four hours at the Roosevelt estate on Oyster Bay (a day remarkably similar to those George Bush would later schedule at Kennebunkport, Maine as evidence of his vitality):

There, day by day, th' head iv th' nation transacts th' nation's business as follows: four A.M., a plunge into th' salt, salt sea an' a swim iv twenty miles; five A.M., horse-back ride, th' prisidint insthructin' his two sons, aged two and four rayspictively, to jump th' first Methodist church without knockin' off th' shingles; six A.M. rassels with a thrained grizzly bear; sivin A.M., breakfast; eight A.M., Indyan clubs; nine A.M., boxes with Sharkey; tin A.M., bates th' tinnis champeen; iliven A.M., rayceives a band iv rough riders . . .[15]

And so on through a day of exhausting leisure. Pertinent in the agenda mocked by Mr. Dooley, a commentator disinclined toward any exercise more strenuous than lifting a glass or voicing a political witticism, was not only the peculiar dedication with which the president pursued his exercise, but the way energetic activity seemed to represent an end in itself and was, as the sardonic commentator insisted, "the nation's business." The Roosevelt of Rough Rider fame, the man who prided himself on being strong as a bull moose, the man who, running against Taft and Wilson as a third-party candidate in 1912 (after voluntarily leaving office in 1909, he came back to mount a third-party campaign against his successor Taft and the Democratic candidate, Wilson) would insist on delivering a campaign speech even though he had just been shot in the chest by a would-be assassin ("I will give this speech or die") exhorted the nation to find itself in his example.[16] If gaunt, academic Wilson was to lead with the soul, barrel-built Teddy led with the body, on the premise that with the body first engaged, the soul would follow.

The 1903 Western tour was from beginning to end a celebration of masculine values carried out largely in the company of other males. In Pennsylvania the president boarded the engine cab and made his trip across the Alleghenies in the company of what the *New York Times* referred to as "grimy trainmen." The mountains crossed, Roosevelt "climbed down from his lofty seat, and after shaking hands with the engineers and firemen, went back to his car, rather dusty and grimy, but enthusiastic over his novel ride" (*New York Times*, 4/2/03). Throughout the West he was greeted by troops of cavalry and bands of cowboys. In Edgemont, South Dakota, the Society of Black Hills Pioneers provided a bronco-busting exhibition for his amusement; in Hugo, Colorado, he was the guest at a cowboy standup breakfast, after which his train was escorted from the station "amid a chorus of cowboy yells" (*New York Times*, 4/26/03). In Idaho, Indian horseman accompanied him into Pocatello and stayed, mounted, to listen to his speech. And at Yellowstone and Yosemite Roosevelt spent time in the company of guides and other male companions, hiking and taking long trail rides. Whenever possible he spoke to college students, not all male but usually addressed as though they were (*New York Times*, 3/29–6/06/03).

The logic of the venture had been firmly established in advance of his tour and was well understood by his audiences, including the University of Chicago students who offered their own "Dooleyized" lyrics as the Roosevelt carriage rolled onto campus:

> There is a sturdy gent who is known on every hand;
> His smile is like a burst of sun upon a rainy land.
> He'll bluff the Kaiser, shoot a bear, or storm a Spanish fort,
> Then sigh for something else to do and write a book on sport.
> (*New York Times*, 4/3/03)

As vice president Roosevelt had asserted in a 1901 speech celebrating the anniversary of Colorado statehood that "manhood and statehood" were analogous conditions.[17] His use of the word "manhood" implied male and "masculine" in the narrowest sense, not only gender-specific but further limited so that the designation referred to a title that must be earned rather than received as a biological birthright. By analogy the appellation "statehood," according to Roosevelt, was won only when a nation behaved like a "true" man, and the true man in America's experience was almost always a Westerner who proved his manhood through hard work.

The president who brought America into the twentieth century did so with the nineteenth much in mind, extolling the old virtues populists so admired and arguing for their application in the modern context.[18] When he finally arrived in Saint Louis for the exposition, he told his audience of fairgoers:

> We have met here to-day, to commemorate the hundredth anniversary of the event which more than any other, after the foundation of the Government and always excepting its preservation, determine the character of our national life—determined that we should be a great expanding Nation instead of relatively a small and stationary one. (I:342–43)

This work of expansion was by far the greatest work of our people.[19]

But the president needed to distinguish American expansion from what he and his countrymen found repulsive in European colonialism. Until the United States was formed, he argued, history tended to confirm two propositions:

> In the first place, it had always proved exceedingly difficult to secure both freedom and strength in any government; and in the second place, it had always proved well nigh impossible for a nation to expand without either breaking up or becoming a centralized tyranny. (I:345)

It was the genius of the American system that it allowed expansion without threatening self-government and accepted new states on an equal footing with those that preceded them.[20] In short, it worked for equality rather than advantage. Roosevelt offered this as not only a history lesson but also a model for new territorial acquisitions. Later, speaking to a University of California audience, he praised the country's recent record. "When we acquired the Philippines and took possession for the time being of Cuba to train its people in citizenship," he explained, "we assumed heavy responsibilities" (II:408). Those responsibilities were above all to prepare the people of these countries for self-rule. For the United States, "the dominant race that spent its blood and its treasure in making firm and stable the government of those islands," the only "reward" was that which "comes from the consciousness of duty well done" (II:410).

The area in which Roosevelt found the frontier example most immediately applicable was in "the arena" of international affairs.[21] In that context he proposed an America that seemed to be only an expanded version of cowboy character as represented in Owen Wister's *The Virginian*, a book both edited by and dedicated to Roosevelt. The "smile when you say that, mister" school of Western virility the old Rough Rider regarded as equally appropriate for dealing with foreign states. He told his Waukesha, Wisconsin, audience that the United States, as a world power, could not shirk the duty that attended that position, especially in "the furthest Orient, in that furthest West," which is the immemorial East. Then he instructed them:

> We must hold our own. If we show ourselves weaklings we will earn the contempt of mankind, and—what is of far more consequence—our own

contempt; but I would like to impress upon every public man, upon every writer in the press, the fact that strength should go hand in hand with courtesy. . . . I want to see a man able to hold his own. I have no respect for the man who will put up with injustice. If a man will not take his part, the part is not worth taking. That is true. On the other hand, I have a hearty contempt for the man who is always walking about waiting to pick a quarrel, and above all, wanting to say something unpleasant about someone else. (I:268–69)

The man who had chased down rustlers in the Dakota territory and who, in a 1900 essay entitled "The American Boy," wrote "One prime reason for abhorring cowards is because every good boy should have it in him to thrash the objectionable boy as the need arises," intended for America to be the "good boy," unafraid, in world affairs.[22]

But in making international politics the new frontier, the place where men continued to play the old game, Roosevelt conceded that the domestic challenge was different. Even as he called his Saint Louis audience to reaffirm its pioneer legacy, to cultivate in the twentieth century the "virile virtues" of the nineteenth, he acknowledged that the "old pioneer days are gone, with their roughness and their hardship, their incredible toil and their wild half-savage romance" (I:351). The next day, on a less auspicious occasion in Topeka, Kansas—once more heading west—he more directly addressed the difficulty of preserving pioneer virtues in a country where the scarcity of wilderness led to the need for national parks and wildlife preserves. "In our present advanced civilization," he told an audience consisting of the railroad branch of the YMCA, "we have to pay certain penalties for what we have obtained. Among the penalties is the fact that in very many occupations there is so little demand upon nerve, hardihood, and endurance, that there is a tendency to unhealthy softening of fibre" (I:353).

That "softening"—like the disappearance of "the hardy grim, resolute men" he had so lavishly praised in his Colorado speech, those pioneers "who, with incredible toil and risk, laid deep the foundations of the civilization we inherit"—had occurred precisely because those "foundations" were now in place. But while the specific toil of earlier generations had become antiquated, the principle of work had not, and it was work to which, in 1903, Roosevelt attributed character. "The better your training," he told Northwestern University students, "the better the work you can do. We have no room for the idler—the man who wishes to live a comfortable life" (*New York Times*, 4/3/03). He warned Stanford students: "Your education, your training, will not confer on you one privilege in the way of excusing you from effort or from work. All it can do and what it should do, is make you a little better fitted for such effort, for such work" (I:382). And it was the creation of a culture of work that he urged upon adults—teachers and legislators and parents—warning them not to spoil the children of this more comfortable age. In Saint Paul he stated his concern bluntly:

> So often throughout our social structure from the wealthiest down to the poorest you see the queer fatuity of the man or the woman which makes them save their children temporary discomfort, temporary displeasantness, at the cost of future destruction. (I:290)

But Roosevelt did more than espouse the value of work. He also went west to offer a more specific agenda of the work that needed to be done and of the proper way of doing it. Though he continued to encourage mechanics and farmers in their individual efforts to better their lives, he more frequently called individuals to a shared national labor. In Saint Louis he insisted that, while "the peculiar frontier conditions have vanished . . . the manliness and the stalwart hardihood of the frontiersmen can be given even freer scope under the conditions surrounding the complex industrialism of the present day" (I:351). But in Sioux Falls he reminded his audience of how much things had changed, *especially* in industry. "More and more," he observed, "in our great industrial centres men have come to realize that they can not live as independently of one another as in the old days was the case everywhere, and as is now the case in the country districts." The challenge, he argued, applying the same model by which he elsewhere claimed expansion was accomplished without the lessening of freedom and local control, is to create "organizations," "unions," "combinations" that do not require the sacrifice of "individual initiative." Government's role is to provide laws that give all a "square deal" so that none have to resort to such radical action or form such authoritarian organizations that individual rights and interests are lost (I:306).

In large part, Roosevelt's effort to develop and apply frontier virtues in a frontierless age meant recasting the old paradigms so that manhood was displaced by statehood, so that individual interests and actions gave way to cooperative programs. Just as his concept of greatness became less that of the self-contained pioneer (though he kept that image alive on his trip with long solitary hikes in the National Parks) and more that of the bold but restrained nation, so the service to which he called his countrymen was less that of personal conquest and more that of shared achievement.

Whether considering the trusts or land management, he persistently urged his listeners to think of the larger community and future generations and to make the work of a common interest their ennobling labor. When he spoke of better roads or irrigation projects, he reminded his listeners of their growing interdependence and of the ways individual enterprises had increasingly become corporate concerns. At Yellowstone and Yosemite, among the Sequoias and on the rim of the Grand Canyon, he called upon citizens to make their work that of conservation. "I want to ask you to do one thing," he told his Grand Canyon audience, ". . . in your own interest and in the interest of the country—to keep this great wonder as it now is." Then he addressed a pioneer past unmentioned in Colorado Springs and at the Louisiana Exposition:

> We have gotten past the stage, my fellow citizens, when we are to be pardoned if we treat any part of our country as something to be skinned for two or three years for the use of the present generation, whether it is the forest, the water, the scenery. Whatever it is, handle it so that your children's children will get the benefit of it. If you deal with irrigation, apply it under circumstances that will make it of benefit, not to the speculator who hopes to get profit out of it for two or three years, but handle it so that it will be of use to the homemaker, to the man who comes to live here, and to have his children stay after him. Keep the forests in the same way. (I:370–71)

Roosevelt's shift from praising frontier individualism to advocating communal responsibility, his legitimizing of social control as well as self-control, inevitably complicated both the virtues and the obligations he preached to his Western audiences. And, though the fact went unacknowledged, the cultural transformation he described, the growth from frontier adolescence to "civilized" maturity, subtly undermined the gender dichotomizing that came so readily to his mind. In the Minnesota speech in which he warned against spoiling the young, the sexual distinctions that lay at the heart of his calls to "manly" action seemed muddled. "[Y]ou see a great many men," he chided, "and I am sorry to say a great many women, who say, 'I have had to work hard; my boy or my girl shall not do anything.'" He had conventionally identified nurturing as woman's work, of course, but on this occasion he expressed his concern for the future in terms of "the girl" as well as "the boy" without any immediate distinction. "To bring up the boy and the girl so sheltered," he persisted in a rare show of rhetorical inclusion, "that they can not stand hard knocks, that they shrink from toil . . . is wronging the children." Both sexes, if they are to be "worth their salt," must be taught "that the life that is not the life of work and effort is worthless, a curse to the man or woman leading it, a curse to those around him or her." But then the hint of equality vanished as he concluded: "Teach the boys that if they are ever to count in the world they will count not by flinching from difficulties, but by warring with and overcoming them" (I:290–91).

While hardly a rejection of the sexism that dominated Roosevelt's speeches on the tour, such comments hinted of uncertainty as to how neatly the old distinctions could be drawn in the "changed world" of the twentieth century. The work he described as the new American challenge was itself androgynous by the old standards. In urging the cause of social justice—a movement as often as not led by women serving in the slums of New York and Chicago—and in calling for the conservation of natural resources on behalf of future generations, he had been urging young men to build their own sense of vocation around values typically regarded as feminine. And in Topeka, in the same speech in which he warned against any "unhealthy softening of fibre," Roosevelt interrupted his praise of the "manly" to recall a sermon he had recently heard in which the minister had pointed out the mistranslation in the New Testament, as "charity," of the Greek word for "love." That, the president said, he ought to have known but did not. Then he added to his instruction an unusual corrective: "We need the quality of which the preacher spoke when he spoke of love as being the great factor, the ultimate factor, in bringing about the kind of human fellowship which will even approximately enable us to come up toward the standard after which I think all of us with many shortcomings strive" (I:355). The end of work in this context, the end of society, is human fellowship and love.

His fear of "effeminacy" momentarily in abeyance, Roosevelt identi-fied American purpose, masculine and feminine, as union rather than conquest or expansion. In this passage and in the one where he called for boys and girls alike to be prepared for work are signs of the deeply am-biguous attitudes he and his Western audiences had about women. The masculine terrain he chose for his tour—and which he carried entire in the 1904 election—approved women's suffrage well before any Eastern states; the vote was already granted in Wyoming, Colorado, Idaho, and Utah at the time of his visit. During his own brief residence on the fron-tier (a relocation that closely followed the near simultaneous deaths of his mother and his first wife), he had seen the equalizing effect of pioneer life, a life quite different from his own genteel upbringing. While his atti-tudes remained sexist, in acknowledging the differences between the frontier past he so romanticized and the corporate present he hoped to ennoble, he had—perhaps inadvertently but not wholly unnoticed—called into doubt other distinctions.

In Roosevelt's 1905 speech before the National Congress of Mothers, there was no hint of the ambivalence in his 1903 Topeka address. Insist-ing that there was no more important question than that of "how their family life is conducted," he once more dichotomized "duties" according to gender. Men were to work hard and, if need be, fight hard. Women were to be good wives and mothers, "able and willing to perform the first and greatest duty of womanhood," the bearing and rearing of healthy children in sufficient number "so that the race shall increase and not de-crease" (III:283). To be capable of childbearing and yet refuse he equated with "viciousness, coldness, shallow-heartedness, self-indulgence, or mere failure to appreciate a right, the difference between the all-impor-tant and the unimportant" and "merits contempt as hearty as any visited upon the soldier who runs away in battle" (III:288). The unsettling com-bination of sexism and biological patriotism, driven by a social Darwin-ism that depicted "races" engaged in a struggle for dominance and sur-vival, was a curious mixing of old and new thinking, dividing the sexes for productive efficiency as much as to satisfy long-standing stereotypes. But all that was presented in Washington to a group whose members de-fined themselves by their childbearing capacity. In the West, where the equalizing pressures of frontier life had made the appropriate work for women more difficult to pigeonhole, Roosevelt spoke more ambiguously, his praise for masculinity as enthusiastic as ever, but the exact nature of the distinction, finally, less certain.

AN AMERICAN PROBLEM

No president in recent history has more blatantly tried to bend the country to his own will than did Lyndon Johnson. At first glance, however, he did not seem particularly qualified to accomplish that through his rhetoric. Having followed a president much admired for his quickness of wit and the literary polish of his statements, Johnson seemed greatly disadvantaged with his broad Texas drawl and an unsettling inclination for such gestures as lifting his beagle puppy by its ears and showing off his gall bladder scar to reporters and cameramen. His early efforts at sounding presidential presented a jarring contrast with the Kennedy style and suggested little that was encouraging about his ability to represent important causes in compelling ways.

Yet in March 1965, less than a year and a half in office and two months into his own term, he went before the Congress and a national television audience with a special message, one that gained a significant amount of its force and poignancy from precisely the Southern drawl that offended many of Kennedy's most fervent admirers. If Americans had come to associate the late president's wit and charm with the clipped Boston accent, Johnson's voting rights speech was crafted especially for his voice and the cadences of the Southern states in which anti–civil rights feeling was most vitriolic. In fact, this was an address the Texan was uniquely qualified to deliver since its central proof was Johnson himself. Rather than speak across some great ideological gulf or from the lofty distance of high office, Johnson—the grandson of two Confederate veterans—presented himself as a special witness, informed by heritage and experience.

Republican presidential candidates as recently as Hoover had criticized the national Democratic party for its complicity in repressing black Americans in order to keep intact a solid South. But in 1948 Southern Democrats had bolted from the regular party, angered over Harry Truman's efforts to desegregate the armed services and a strong civil rights plank in that year's party platform. By 1960 the South was no longer "solid," and in 1964, despite Lyndon Johnson's landslide victory in the country as a whole, Barry Goldwater carried, besides his native Arizona, six Southern states. Mississippi gave the Republican candidate 87 percent of the popular vote.[23]

In the 1950s and the early 1960s racism was considered a Southern problem, one dividing the nation geographically as well as by color. As the civil rights movement attracted increasing Northern support and protests and demonstrations grew more commonplace, violence against the protestors escalated, played out before television cameras and directed indiscriminately toward children and adults, further separating the South from the rest of the country. The 1963 March on Washington, culminating with Martin Luther King's "I Have a Dream" speech, and the 1965 King-led march from Selma to Birmingham, Alabama, were nationally televised and dramatized the determination of the demonstrators and the brutal intransigence of segregationists. But violence was also erupting outside the South, most dramatically in the Watts neighborhood of Los Angeles, where in the summer of 1965 rioting went on for six days.

Both Eisenhower and Kennedy had addressed civil rights and Southern responses to integration. In 1957 violent reactions to the court-ordered integration of Central High School in Little Rock, Arkansas, prompted Eisenhower to send federal troops to protect the entering black students. Similarly, when African Americans were enrolled in the University of Mississippi in 1962 and the University of Alabama in 1963, the governors of those states (Ross Barnett and George Wallace) personally blocked the doors of those schools and set off riots serious enough to require the presence of National Guard units. In reporting on his action in Little Rock, Eisenhower kept his remarks tightly focused on the issue of defying the law and remained largely silent on matters of race. The problem, he suggested, was limited, the work of a "mob" incited by "demagogic extremists," and he pointedly excluded Little Rock and the South from his complaint. "In that region," he noted—without any apparent sense of punning—"I have many warm friends." He recalled his own military tours of duty "in our Southland" as well as "enjoyable recreational periods." While firm about enforcing the law, he sounded almost sympathetic, if also condescending, to the region, reminding the rest of the country that the Supreme Court's decision "concerning school integration, of course, affects the South more seriously than it does other sections of the country" (PP, Eisenhower, 1957:689–94).

Kennedy was more direct and incensed in his 1963 message. He announced a broad civil rights package that would prohibit discrimination in such areas as public accommodations, schools, and employment even as he described unrest in Alabama. Indignantly he reminded his audience,

> This is one country. It has become one country because all of us and all the people who came here had an equal chance to develop their talents.
>
> We cannot say to 10 percent of the population that you can't have that right; that your children can't have the chance to develop whatever talents they have; that the only way that they are going to get their rights is to go into the streets and demonstrate. I think we owe them and we owe ourselves a better country than that.

But Kennedy's frustration with the South, everywhere evident in the speech, was that of a Northerner who felt, no matter how mistakenly, removed from the problem, and as a consequence his arguments were impersonal, a matter of rights and facts ("The negro baby born in America today . . . has about one half as much chance of completing high school . . . one third as much chance of completing college, one third as much chance of becoming a professional man, twice as much chance of becoming unemployed") (PP, Kennedy, 1963:476).

In 1965 Johnson broadened the issue Eisenhower had tried to narrow. Unlike the two presidents he succeeded, he spoke with an authority that came from firsthand experience of a society openly and willfully built on racial prejudice and discrimination. His own autobiographical connection to the subject he addressed generated a different passion from Eisenhower's pique and Kennedy's frustration. Unlike them—and they both had found the South exotic and bewildering—and unlike any president since Wilson, Johnson's "roots" went "deeply into southern soil." "I speak tonight," the president began, "for the dignity of man and the destiny of democracy."

The problem, Johnson insisted, was not—as Eisenhower had implied—the exception in American life, it was the rule. What was taking place in Selma and Birmingham, he argued, represented a systemic problem for this country, one more blatant in some areas than others, but all-pervasive. The issue was not simply a matter of law or even of desegregation; it was, in Johnson's analysis, racism as a nationwide phenomenon. The sermon-like tone of his opening pronouncement prevailed throughout, and he brought the judgment of scripture to make the point that as much at stake in this crisis as the political fate of an abused minority were the souls of all Americans. "For with a country as with a person," he asked, "'What is a man profited, if he shall gain the whole world, and lose his own soul?' There is no Negro problem. There is no Southern problem. There is no Northern problem. There is only an American problem" (PP, Johnson, 1965:282). By nationalizing the dilemma, making it from the start a matter of more than geography, he justified federal intervention in an area (voting restrictions) that states rights advocates held most dear, but even more he was extending the logic abolitionists had applied to slavery a hundred years earlier, that the entire Union bore responsibility for each of its individual members, both for the security of the individual and the salvation of the whole. Johnson argued that this was the heart of our relation to one another. By presenting himself, a Southerner, as the advocate of that larger Union, the president used his own person to contradict the appearance of inherent polarization. The public perceptions of white against black, North against South, were complicated by the fact that the speaker advocating the rights of black America was white *and* southern. "This is one Nation," he declared, balancing references to Southern racial unrest with Northern examples, "one in which no section has fully honored the promise of equality. In Buffalo as well as Birmingham, in Philadelphia as well as Selma, Americans are struggling for the fruits of freedom" (*Ibid.*, 284).

Johnson advanced his argument along several fronts. The first he engaged directly: The "most basic right of all" is "the right to choose your own leaders." This he asserted as a first principle, but "the harsh fact," he continued, "is that in many places in this country men and women are kept from voting simply because they are Negroes." After enumerating several of the ways local officials interfered with voting rights, Johnson declared: "For the fact is that the only way to pass these barriers is to show a white skin" (p. 282). The conclusion to which this line of argument—this sequence of "facts"—progressed was logically inevitable; if all citizens have an inherent right to participate in choosing their leaders, and if local governments do not honor and enforce that right, then the federal government has a responsibility to "eliminate illegal barriers to the right to vote."

> To those who seek to avoid action by their National Government in their own communities; who want to and who seek to maintain purely local control over elections, the answer is simple:
>   Open your polling places to all your people.
>   Allow men and women to register and vote whatever the color of their skin.
>   Extend the rights of citizenship to every citizen of this land. (p. 283)

That aspect of the matter, Johnson insisted, was clear-cut and unambiguous, and he underlined its certainty in a series of short declarative sentences.

> There is no constitutional issue here. The command of the Constitution is plain.
>   There is no moral issue. It is wrong—deadly wrong—to deny any of your fellow Americans the right to vote in this country.
>   There is no issue of States rights or national rights. There is only the struggle for human rights. (p. 283)

By insisting there were no "issues," only the simple fact of a right denied, any equivocation, whether in Congress or in the country at large, Johnson declared a repudiation of fundamental American values.

Throughout his speech Johnson wove recent events into a portrayal of an America increasingly aware of the extent and perniciousness of its racism, and he used both that national complicity and the "Americanness" of the civil rights movement as the potential basis for an increased sense of oneness, of a shared life. Here he emulated Lincoln's argument from his Second Inaugural as he suggested that even as we were together in the problem we could find ourselves, together, in the struggle to overcome it. Thus Johnson went farther than any previous president to legitimate the civil rights cause, defending even more than its morality its consistency with national values and traditions. "American Negroes," he reminded, were only seeking "to secure for themselves the full blessings of American life," and he depicted the marchers at Selma and elsewhere as patriots, champions of national ideals. By implication the authorities who were harassing them—often justifying their efforts by identifying

protesters as "communist," "un-American," and "outside agitators"—
were enemies of democracy and freedom. "The real hero of this struggle," Johnson declared, "is the American Negro" (p. 285).

By stressing "the effort of American Negroes to secure for themselves
the full blessings of American life," the president moved to counteract
deeply rooted distinctions between the races, the "us" and "them" mentality that divided American society. Having identified the aspirations of
protesting blacks with the society's traditional values, he pleaded: "Their
cause must be our cause too. Because it is not just Negroes, but really it is
all of us, who must overcome the crippling legacy of bigotry and injustice." The word "really" signaled a plea for recognition, flagged an assertion that the speaker declared self-evident but which, in the common
view, remained in doubt. Johnson's "but really" disrupted the tone and
rhythm of his speech, but it underlined the point upon which his case
most depended, the claim for a shared identity that could triumph over
the difference of color. In insisting that the struggle of black Americans
was the quintessential American struggle—the struggle of all Americans—Johnson carried the case for union beyond the Kennedy appeal for
the fuller inclusion of black citizens, suggesting that the nation discover
itself in their protest. By seeing the "American Negro" as the national
hero, the president was calling upon the rest of America to find a missing
part of its own identity in those it had denied and oppressed.

The fact that it came from a Southern white man gave the appeal its
most compelling element. In the dichotomizing relationship of section
and color, the fact that Johnson bore the color and the accent of the "oppressor" gave his argument for the possibility of mutual self-realization a
special poignance since he himself represented the unlikely change he
was pleading for. The ironic legitimacy of his claim to know personally
"how agonizing racial feelings are," and "how difficult it is to reshape the
attitudes and the structure of our society" grew from his awareness of
what it meant to be *white* in a racist society.

The most daring aspect of Johnson's strategy was that claim of special
knowledge, the knowledge that he implied came from guilt (which neither Eisenhower or Kennedy seemed to feel) and repentance. His speech
was about conversion, and when he echoed the words of the movement,
saying "we shall overcome" and "the time of Justice has now come," he
included himself among the believers. In this posture he declared that the

realization of equality by black Americans would be a blessing to all Americans. Johnson subtly offered himself as evidence that change was possible and that what made it possible was the desire of all people to be included.

As Johnson moved back and forth throughout his speech, balancing the image of the black victim with that of black hero, he simultaneously enlarged the category of the oppressed by introducing the suffering of marginalized white Americans. In the process he suggested that a part of the explanation for white poverty was the high cost of discrimination.

> For Negroes are not the only victims. How many white children have gone uneducated, how many white families have lived in stark poverty, how many white lives have been scarred by fear, because we have wasted our energy and our substance to maintain the barriers of hatred and terror? (p. 284)

In this way he linked the goals of the civil rights movement with his "Great Society" agenda. "So," he concluded, "we want to open the gates to opportunity. But we are also going to give all our people, black and white, the help that they need to walk through those gates" (p. 286).

As he neared conclusion Johnson became anecdotal, recalling his first teaching job at a small Mexican-American school, where the students were poor and the victims of prejudice. "Somehow," he suggested, "you never forget what poverty and hatred can do when you see its scars on the hopeful face of a young child" (p. 286). By focusing on children—first African-American children, then poor white children, and finally Hispanic children—the president forced his audience to see prejudice in terms of its most innocent and vulnerable victims. By bringing the faces of the very young to his call for social change, he both added to the moral pressure and tried to make inclusion less difficult. That was not just a sentimental gesture, a tug at the nation's heartstrings. Children were a dramatic presence in the civil rights struggle; they were killed in church bombings, deployed in picket lines, and brutalized with police dogs and fire hoses. Arguably it was in children that segregationists regarded as the greatest threat to their "way of life"; nowhere was the malevolence of race hatred more evident than in the gauntlet run by black pupils as they entered newly integrated schools through mobs of hate-spewing white adults. So Johnson introduced them into his speech as both an appeal to America's humanity and an indictment of its inhumanity.

Ironically and even sadly, the "I" upon which Johnson's case so largely depended, the "I" that was personally connected to the culture of prejudice and that testified to the possibility of change, was displaced in his speech's conclusion. The humble version of himself gave way at last to one far removed from his audience both in office and ambition. In an expansive—and grandiose—finale, Johnson described the legacy he hoped to leave after his presidency: the "richest and most powerful country which ever occupied the globe."

> I want to be the President who educated young children to the wonders of their world. I want to be the President who helped to feed the hungry and to prepare them to be taxpayers instead of tax-eaters.
>
> I want to be the President who helped the poor to find their own way and who protected the right of every citizen to vote in every election.
>
> I want to be the President who helped to end hatred among his fellow men and who promoted love among the people of all races and all regions and all parties.
>
> I want to be the President who helped to end war among the brothers of this earth. (pp. 286–87)

Those were noble aspirations, but Johnson's swollen catalog of achievements for which he wanted to be remembered lessened the force of his previous eloquence. The humility implicit in his earlier remarks—the sense of a country being judged by a righteous complaint, of individuals being called upon to yield long held prejudices, of a Union being summoned from division, and the awareness that great principles compelled the country to be socially reformed—was now undercut by the abrupt and distracting intrusion of his ego. The anecdote of a young schoolteacher doing his best against insurmountable odds was pushed aside by the posturing of "a great man boasting of his service—not to empire but to the goals of love and peace." Having declared the "Negro" the hero early on, he could not finally resist placing his own bust upon that pedestal.

By the time—shortly after his list of presidential goals—Johnson invited "the Congress, Republicans and Democrats alike," to be the legislature that "did all these things for all these people," he had already compromised the invitation by making it clear the agendas and the greatness belonged, above all, to him. That is not to say that Johnson's voting rights speech failed as a work of presidential eloquence, but rather to note how the sudden diversion from the humbling lessons of a history of repression and toward the subject of his own honor and glory diminished his best effort. Having called upon Americans to lessen the distance that separated them, he closed by reminding his audience of the great expanse that, when all was said, lay between himself and them.

Chapter Eight

Mystic Chords

The Rhetoric of Special Occasions II

> Would to God my voice could be heard in every hovel through-
> out the land!
>
> —Andrew Johnson, A Speech in Baltimore, 1866

TO RECALL AND REVERE

The anxiety that dominates war speeches concerns the future. Though the history of past wrongs and of failed deliberations plays a crucial part in those addresses, the audience is most obviously concerned with consequences, the outcome and cost of the approaching conflict. Addresses of the sort Teddy Roosevelt made in 1903 and Lyndon Johnson delivered in 1965, while they speak to past and future as well, are centered in the present, with a condition or attitude they seek to change. By contrast, speeches on commemorative occasions look backward toward some remembered person or event and—since they always recognize heroic achievement—are tempered by the apprehension of comparison, of how well the audience and speaker measure up to that high standard. There is, of course, no end to all the memorials being constructed or the anniversaries being observed by some group or region, and so the choice of what occasions to elevate with a presidential appearance is itself significant, reflecting a particular president's sense of history and of political opportunity. This has been most especially true in the twentieth century.

THE HEIGHTS OF NORMANDY

For members of Ronald Reagan's generation the Allied landing on the beaches of Normandy, the D-Day invasion, epitomized courage and patriotism. It would have been unthinkable for an American president, especially one so nostalgically inclined, not to have addressed the thousands of veterans who, forty years later, returned to the scene of their great heroism. What is somewhat surprising, however, is how wholly—though successfully—elegiac was the address he delivered. Reagan called, at the end of the speech, for Americans to respond to the sacrifices of those who fought in that great cause and "continue to stand for the ideals for which they lived and died," but the body of the president's remarks concentrated on the past, recreating a pageant picture of the invasion and battle (PP, Reagan, 1984: 819).

Reagan did at Normandy what Reagan did best—he narrated a version of that day forty years earlier, a version openly sentimental and reverential. He told it in hushed tones before an audience of veterans, men who, as boys, had captured the beaches and cliffs that served as background to the presidential performance. In the process he made their experience, the one he had not shared, "real" both to them and to their countrymen. At seventy-three, Reagan was older than many of the men who had come back to Normandy, and his age added to the poignance of their shared "remembering." He became the off-screen narrator, unifying a series of particular actions into a larger story, making of disparate moments a whole event. "We stand here on a lonely, windswept point on the northern shore of France," he told them in a gentle fadeback to the violence of 1944.

The air is soft, but forty years ago at this moment, the air was dense with smoke and the cries of men, and the air was filled with the crack of rifle fire and the roar of cannon. At dawn, on the morning of the 6th of June, 1944, 225 Rangers jumped off the British landing craft and ran to the bottom of these cliffs. Their mission was one of the most difficult and daring of the invasion: to climb these sheer and desolate cliffs and take out the enemy guns. (p. 817)

As Reagan continued with his account, a simple story of uncomplicated courage, he relied on cultural clichés, the stuff of mediocre movies and patriotic newsreels. And yet, because it was so simply and sincerely advanced—and because of the very familiarity that comes with cliché—the result was affecting and appropriate. When he surveyed his audience of aging men and said, "These are the boys of Pointe du Hoc. These are the men who took the cliffs. These are the champions who helped free a continent. These are the heroes who helped end a war," his words carried force because his own simplicity and emotional directness gave them credibility. When, in subsequent lines, the artifice grew more complicated ("Gentlemen, I look at you and I think of the words of Stephen Spender's poem. . . ."), as he pretended to be spontaneously recalling poetry stored in a memory that so frequently failed him (a memory more naturally inclined toward anecdotes than poems), the sincerity on which Reagan's most eloquent moments relied was briefly broken, but once again he recovered and returned to his more natural idiom, recounting more portraits of heroic individuals, uplifting accounts that reduced the larger struggle to manageable proportions. "I think I know what you may be thinking right now," he told them, "—thinking 'we were just part of a bigger effort: everyone was brave that day.' Well," he confirmed, "everyone was" (p. 818).

What might appear presumptuous in someone else, this putting of thoughts into other people's heads, seemed appropriate for Reagan, in part because his was the conventional wisdom, and it seemed likely in this inevitably sentimental context that his thoughts and theirs would be the same. What followed was a series of reminiscences, each with a particular name and an accompanying incident of underspoken bravery. He, like most of us, remembered it all as we saw it in movies. In one scene a bagpipe-playing Highlander led reinforcements into battle, "ignoring the smack of the bullets into the ground around him" (p. 818). In another a British officer, a Scottish nobleman, reached a company pinned down by enemy fire, and with Hollywood-style eccentricity apologized for being "a few minutes late . . . when in truth he'd just come from the bloody fighting on Sword Beach" (p. 818).

Because Reagan's "recollections" were couched in popular culture, it was all familiar, a sort of collective memory that moved and amused and reassured in a way that the fragmented experiences of individual veterans could not. In the same manner, when the president turned to motives for the heroics, his questions and answers were equally commonplace:

> Forty summers have passed since the battle that you fought here. You were young the day you took these cliffs; some of you were hardly more than boys, with the deepest joys of life before you. Yet, you risked everything here. Why?

The answer Reagan himself provided was the only answer possible in this scenario, the only acceptable response for such an occasion. "We look at you," he said, "and somehow we know the answer. It was faith and belief; it was loyalty and love." "You were here to liberate, not to conquer," he went on, adding the most wistful and most moving lines of the speech, "and so you and those others did not doubt your cause. And you were right not to doubt" (p. 818).

An old man speaking to old men, Reagan's added assurance—"you were right not to doubt"—spoke not to what these veterans felt on the day they took the heights at Normandy but to subsequent events, their frustration with the world and succeeding generations. Looking back to the last war about which Americans were not "doubtful," back before the Cold War, before Korea and Vietnam, the nostalgia was as much for a simpler, clearer time as for personal confirmation. "You all knew that some things are worth dying for . . . democracy is worth dying for," he reminded those who survived (p. 818).

When Reagan turned to the disappointments of later years—"In spite of our great efforts and successes, not all that followed the end of the war was happy or planned"—he did so in a consoling voice, telling them that they had done their part. After the liberation of Europe, he noted, "some liberated countries were lost," but rather than exploit the occasion as he had in the past by rattling sabres at the "evil empire," he remained subdued. The "great sadness" of communism's postwar conquests "echoes down to our own time in the streets of Warsaw, Prague, and East Berlin. Soviet troops that came to the center of this continent did not leave when peace came. They're still there, uninvited, unwanted, unyielding." Americans were still here, too, he observed, but the "only territories we hold are memorials like this one and graveyards where our heroes rest" (pp. 818–19).

Reagan's nostalgia did not reach much beyond itself, did not introduce the urge to rejoin the fray. He did not, that day, do as other presidents so often have done, issue a rousing call for action. He did not, as Teddy Roosevelt typically did, turn away from the old in order to exhort the young. His was a quiet reminder of previous sacrifice, and while he called on the contemporary world to keep faith with those who fought at Normandy and reminded old allies to recommit themselves to both vigilance and peace, the present never pushed aside the past. Neither did the president of the United States allow his presence and office to displace the heroes of the remembered day. The past seemed to produce in Reagan a quiet humility rather than a personal challenge. Himself comfortable on the sidelines, he legitimated the spectator's role while celebrating the heroic players in a way unthinkable for men like Lyndon Johnson and Teddy Roosevelt (of whom it was said, at the theater he envied the star, at weddings wished to be the bride, and at funerals was jealous of the corpse).[1]

Remarkably, with all the world looking on, Reagan never seemed to be speaking to anyone but the veterans assembled before him. Even when he touched briefly on contemporary events, it was from their perspective. He spoke of Russia sadly, as an old ally from whom we had grown estranged, recalling the terrible sacrifice it had made in that distant war, and wistfully observing that "there is no reconciliation we would welcome more than a reconciliation with the Soviet Union." Even as he concluded ("Here, in this place where the West held together") with "a vow to our dead" that we will "show . . . by our actions that we understand what they died for" (p. 819), the "our" seemed less a national "our" and more the proprietary claim of comrades and contemporaries. This was a reminiscence of old men. All who were too young to remember could only watch respectfully and reverently.

FREEDOM'S VESTAL FIRE

While every bit as worshipful as Reagan at Normandy, Woodrow Wilson could never let the past simply be the past. He was moralist as well as historian; unlike Reagan, he found stories less interesting than the lessons they could teach. He looked back only to return to the present. So when, on September 4, 1916, he chose a far less significant event than the Normandy anniversary (the dedication of a modest memorial in Hogenville, Kentucky, at the supposed site of Abraham Lincoln's birthplace) as an appropriate occasion for a presidential address, it was clearly the teaching opportunity that most attracted him.

At the close of his remarks the president directly stated the reason for his attendance: "I have come here today, not to utter a eulogy on Lincoln; he stands in need of none, but to endeavor to interpret the meaning of this gift to the nation of the place of his birth and origin" (MP, 17:8162). The task of interpretation, of bringing the present into line with the past, lies behind all presidential eloquence. In representing a union that transcends the moment, they seek to demonstrate a consistency of purpose and will in America's history. That is a regular feature of inaugural addresses, but it is also one of the more compelling reasons for speaking at those commemorative events that especially illustrate a president's perception of what holds us together over time. Inevitably there is also a hint of disjunction in such occasions as well, a suggestion of how difficult it is to recover the past and how different things really are. Reagan's remarks at Normandy acknowledged and regretted the difference.

But Wilson's speech at the Lincoln birthplace emphasized connection, not so much in a particular sequence of events but of a more spiritual nature, and in Kentucky the former historian seemed not so much interested in what happened in the past, the object of Reagan's interest, as concerned with the purposes and powers that caused it. The events of the Civil War had been very much on people's minds in previous months as fiftieth anniversaries had been observed with reenactments and celebrations. Just as they would later come to Normandy to honor old comrades and memories, so had aging veterans in Wilson's time flocked to Gettysburg and other fields of battle. Wilson was younger than they, and his memories of the war were the fragmented recollections of a small child. Besides, his personal ties were to the losing side. His father, then pastor of a Presbyterian church in Augusta, Georgia, had supported the Confederacy, and Wilson said his earliest memory was of hearing "that Mr. Lincoln was elected and there was to be a war," an anecdote that suggests how strong a presence Lincoln was in his life and how profoundly his sense of identity was linked to that olympian figure.[2] Though Wilson went to Kentucky to honor Lincoln, he went as well to place himself in the same lineage. He approached this delicate business obliquely in an awe-filled declamation on the mysterious workings of American history, and he began by calling his audience to a kind of worship.[3] "Is not this," he asked,

> an altar upon which we may forever keep alive the vestal fire of democracy as upon a shrine at which some of the deepest and most sacred hopes of mankind may from age to age be rekindled? For these hopes must constantly be rekindled, and only those who live can rekindle them. The only stuff that can retain the life-giving heat is the stuff of the living heart. (MP, 17:8162)

With images and sentiments borrowed from the Gettysburg Address (which also focused on altars and called upon the "living" to carry on "the unfinished work"), the president used his martyred predecessor's birthplace to attempt a "rekindling" of the democratic flame and the spirit of Gettysburg. "Its compulsion is upon us," he concluded:

> It will be great and lift a great light for the guidance of the nations only if we are great and carry that light high for the guidance of our own feet. We are not worthy to stand here unless we ourselves be in deed and in truth real democrats and servants of mankind, ready to give our very lives for the freedom and justice and spiritual exaltation of the great nation which shelters and nourishes us. (17:8163)

His subject was literally "inspiration," the vital force that connects the past with the present, and Wilson used the traditional image of fire to symbolize this "breath" that passes between generations. In calling Americans to this shrine, he was asking them to take up its flame in their own time and to cast its illumination beyond national boundaries. It was to be, in their hands, "a great light for the guidance of the nations"—this in a year in which he, having proclaimed America's neutrality, offered to negotiate peace in warring Europe. By asking his countrymen to be servants of "mankind," even to give up "their lives"—not for the safety of the nation "which shelters and nourishes" them but for its "exultation"—he urged them to be faithful to democracy without qualification.

Wilson was no more explicit than that; he only issued the charge and did not identify its particular application. Instead he turned back to the birthplace, hailing it as a place for national "re-creation," and devoted his remarks to this process, making his subject the ways by which purpose and identity are conveyed over time. The process begins, he suggested, with national altars that serve as physical connections to the past, spiritual transmitters that bring us into a greater union. As the presiding "priest" at the Kentucky shrine, he did not attempt to make Lincoln "real" but rather treated him as a sign, a proof in a larger matter. "How eloquent this little house within this shrine is of the vigor of democracy!" he said, then moved immediately from the particular structure to what it represented. "There is nowhere in the land any home so remote, so humble, that it may not contain the power of mind and heart and conscience to which nations yield and history submits its processes." That is the first lesson the house teaches, and its corollary immediately followed:

> Nature pays no tribute to aristocracy, subscribes to no creed of caste, tenders fealty to no monarch or master of any name or kind. Genius is no snob. It does not run after titles or seek by preference the high circles of society. It affects humble company as well as great. It pays no special tribute to universities or learned societies or conventional standards of greatness, but serenely chooses its own comrades, its own haunts, its own cradle even, and its own life of adventure and of training. (17:8160)

That may sound a little like the "every child can aspire to the presidency" school of democracy, but it contains too much awe to fit that model, and Wilson clearly was suggesting that it is "nature" rather than the electorate that is in charge.

The pivotal term was "genius," but the particular referent was odd. Rather than saying simply that "genius" (rather than a common man who would be uncommonly elevated) was born in this cabin, Wilson's grammar placed "genius" in "nature," the "it" that controls democracy's destiny, the guiding spirit at work in American history. "Here is proof . . .," he exclaimed.

> This little hut was the cradle of one of the great sons of men, a man of singular, delightful, vital genius who presently emerged upon the great stage of the nation's history, gaunt, shy, ungainly, but dominant and majestic, a natural ruler of men, himself inevitably the central figure of the great plot. (17:8160)

The lesson above all others was that there is a "plot," a plan at work in the past and the present. Ours is an authored story, Wilson argued, and service to that supreme narrative was what he asked of Americans. In his plea, Lincoln was not a model for emulation but evidence that there is a purpose beyond reason *and* beyond us, and it can be trusted. "No man can explain this," he said,

> but every man can see how it demonstrates the vigor of democracy, where every door is open, in every hamlet and countryside, in city and wilderness alike, for the ruler to emerge when he will and claim his leadership in free life. Such are the authentic proofs of the validity and vitality of democracy. (17:8160–61)

There was much Presbyterianism in the predestination the president described, a view of life (sometimes near-blasphemous in its implications) in which the outcome is determined and the faithful are called upon to play their preordained part in joy and exultation. In that context the presidency, or at least the line of greatness that Wilson sees running through it, becomes a mystic succession, called forth and ordained by Providence or history or a special supernatural democratic spirit, to provide the inspired leadership, the "genius," required by the nation in hours of moral need and extremity. The legacy suggests, in Wilson's interpretation, that we do not bear alone the historical burden handed to us, that it is tended by some enduring presence that can raise up Lincoln from humble anonymity to ultimate greatness. On the basis of such evidence we can act boldly and confidently regardless of our time or the challenges we face.

The wonder of democracy's survival, that it has endured in such clumsy and, often, unlikely hands, all the incredible twists and turns through which the Union has made its way—these were the miracles that validated Wilson's democratic gospel. And above all there was Lincoln, that inexplicable creation of "nature and providence and a free polity." "This," Wilson proclaimed, "is the sacred mystery of democracy, that its richest fruits spring up out of soils which no man has prepared and in circumstances amidst which they are least expected. This is a place of mystery and reassurance" (17:8161). Like Lincoln's own conviction of "mystic chords of Union," Wilson affirmed a cosmic purpose at work in America and called upon his countrymen to take courage in that fact and to serve its purposes no matter how daunting they might seem in their new century. That he himself had risen from a more likely cradle of "genius"—a minister's son, extensively educated and titled—might suggest that as Lincoln's opposite Wilson was not one of democracy's "richest fruits," springing as he had from the most cultivated of American soils. But in dedicating a humble cabin as a national shrine he was declaring his own connection, asserting his personal kinship with Lincoln both in his reverence before democracy's mystery and in his compatible "mind and heart and conscience."

In the unique civil religion that persists in this nation's life (as the opening lines of annual messages unfailingly indicate), the work of democracy is often transformed from a political and social consideration into a matter of transcendent importance: history's work, Nature's work, God's work. Persistent in presidential politics through history is the conviction that democracy is divinely favored and providentially guided, that its survival is both miraculous and destined. Lincoln repeatedly emphasized this view, and Wilson saw in Lincoln its finest proof. And so the double message: The challenge of democracy lies with its people, and it succeeds or fails according to their faithfulness; but those people, in their faithfulness, will be served in times of greatest danger by the same mysterious power that raised up Lincoln from "soil which no man has prepared," the same deity who in Melville's *Moby-Dick* is the "great democratic God" who "didst pick up Andrew Jackson from the pebbles," "who didst hurl him on a war-horse," and "who didst thunder him higher than a throne."[4]

In the "theologies" that emerge from that civil religion, like those elaborated by more conventional faiths, the two competing (sometimes in the same person) explanations of "salvation" coexist. The first builds on grace, the mystic theme that runs from Washington's appeal to the deity "who rules over the universe, who presides in the councils of nations, and whose providential aids can supply every human defect," on down through the intervening God whose hand Lincoln discerned in the Battle of Gettysburg and in the supernatural power that Wilson insisted reared up a Lincoln in the hour of national need. In this view we are called to do our best as citizens and persons, but America's survival and well-being, ultimately, can be explained only by divine favor and support. "The Almighty," Lincoln insisted, "has His own purposes," and those purposes are so intertwined with the fate of this country that its existence and survival are always dependent upon grace.

The counter-explanation, of course, is work, a view in which America's achievements are the consequence of human effort and can be rationally explained. The emphasis upon Enlightenment reason and more mundane common sense demystifies history and politics and places our fate in our own hands, a matter of right conduct rather than of awe. That is the great Jeffersonian theme, picked up by even more confident Jacksonians and their New Deal descendants. It stresses self-assurance more than reverence, and its spokesmen typically insist that what is called for is plain speaking (sometimes to the point of irreverence) and the action that an informed—but still conventional—wisdom dictates. From Wilson's perspective his inspired leadership saves democracy and America. For Jackson or Truman it is "the people." For Calvin Coolidge, Wilson's earnest repudiator, genius itself was suspect. "It is a great advantage to a President," he wrote in his autobiography, "and a major source of safety to the country, for him to know that he is not a great man."[5]

TO DEDICATE AND CONSECRATE

Lincoln and Jefferson at Gettysburg

Lincoln's address at Gettysburg was both a war speech, an attempt to shape the national character, *and* a commemorative message. Consequently, the past, present, and future are equally its subject. Garry Wills has argued that the words presented at the battlefield-turned-cemetery provided a powerful and radical corrective to the country's view of itself and its legitimacy and "remade America."[6] Midway between Lincoln's two inaugurals, this Gettysburg speech marks the transition from the assumptions of the first to those of the second, the movement from a view held in common with presidents who had preceded him to one newly conceived out of civil war.

When Martin Van Buren spoke of union and when Franklin Pierce referred to the model of the founding fathers, their object was the same: to make faithfulness to the vision of Washington and his contemporaries the test of stewardship for subsequent generations. Before 1863, all presidential utterance presented itself as an extension of the views of the founders and described the first generation as sitting in spectral judgment on Americans who came after. That was the significance of Washington's grave in Pierce's Inaugural and of all the other evocations of Washington that were expounded generation after generation: to remind Americans that they were being watched and held responsible by a heroic past. But at Gettysburg Lincoln questioned that past and dared to judge the founders themselves.

Despite charges to the contrary by his opponents, Lincoln, more perhaps than any of his predecessors, revered both the founding documents and the men who shaped them, most especially the Declaration of Independence and Thomas Jefferson. In a letter written in 1859 he declared, "The principles of Jefferson are the definitions and axioms of free society"; and a little later:

> All honor to Jefferson—to the man who, in the concrete pressure of a struggle for national independence by a single people, had the coolness, forecast, and capacity to introduce into a merely revolutionary document, an abstract truth, applicable to all men and all times, and so to embalm it there, that today, and in all coming days, it shall be a rebuke and a stumbling-block to the very harbingers of re-appearing tyranny and oppression.*

Lincoln repeated those sentiments when, on his way to Washington, D.C. and the presidency, he stopped in Philadelphia and spoke on successive days at Independence Hall. Emphasizing the connection of that place with both the Constitution and the Declaration—elevating the latter to a loftier status than a "merely" revolutionary document—he said on the first day,

> I have never asked anything that does not breathe from those walls [of Independence Hall]. All my political warfare has been in favor of the teachings coming forth from that sacred hall. May my right hand forget its cunning and my tongue cleave to the roof of my mouth, if ever I prove false to those teachings. (4:239)

The evocation of verses five and six of the Psalm 137 ("If I forget you, O Jerusalem, let my right hand whither! Let my tongue cleave to the roof of

---

*Roy Basler, ed., *The Collected Works of Abraham Lincoln*, 3:375–76. Subsequent Lincoln quotes in this chapter are from this edition.

my mouth, if I do not remember you . . . !") gains special pertinence and emphasis from the biblical context of Israel's lament during the Babylonian exile (the Psalm begins, "By the waters of Babylon, there we sat down and wept when we remembered Zion") and its ironic prefiguring both of slaves held captive in America and America held captive by slavery. The sacred, the "Jerusalem" of Lincoln's lament, are the Constitution and the Declaration, and in his second Philadelphia speech he reiterated the depth of his commitment to them: "I have never had a feeling politically that did not spring from the sentiments embodied in the Declaration of Independence." Dramatically he concluded, "if this country cannot be saved without giving up that principle [all men are created equal]—I was about to say I would rather be assassinated on this spot than to surrender it" (4:240).

In the days following the Union victories at Gettysburg, Lincoln's thoughts turned to that great principle on which he had repeatedly based his opposition to slavery and which, increasingly after the Emancipation Proclamation, was the war's justification—the one that conceived of the restored Union as one of free persons more than of states. Responding to serenaders on July 7, 1863, he revealed not only how much Jefferson's words were on his mind but the way in which the great themes of the Gettysburg Address already were taking shape.

Fellow-citizens: I am very glad indeed to see you to-night, and yet I will not say I thank you for this call, but I do most sincerely thank Almighty God for the occasion on which you have called. How long ago is it?— eighty odd years—since on the Fourth of July for the first time in the history of the world a nation by its representatives, assembled and declared as a self-evident truth that "all men are created equal." That was the birthday of the United States of America . . . and now, on this last Fourth of July just passed, when we have a gigantic Rebellion, at the bottom of which is an effort to overthrow the principle that all men were [are] created equal, we have the surrender of a most powerful position and army on that very day, and not only so, but in a succession of battles . . . on the 1st, 2d and 3d of the month of July; and on the 4th the cohorts of those who opposed the declaration that all men are created equal, "turned tail" and run. Gentlemen, this is a glorious theme, and the occasion for a speech, but I am not prepared to make one worthy of the occasion. I would like to speak in terms of praise due to the many brave officers and soldiers who have fought in the cause of the Union and liberties of the country from the beginning of the war. (6:319–20)

The appropriate "occasion" presented itself four months later on November 19 at the dedication of a cemetery on the Gettysburg battlefield, and the speech that Lincoln gave was a formal reworking of his comments to the serenaders in July. "How long ago is it?—eighty odd years" became "Four score and seven years ago." "All men are created equal" remained the same. "[A]nd now . . . when we have a gigantic Rebellion" gave way to "Now we are engaged in a great civil war." The two speeches—the first informal, spontaneous, colloquial, and the second formal, composed, literary—are congruent at nearly every point, differing primarily in the more extended emphasis given in July to the Declaration of Independence.

It is the Declaration, however, Jefferson's revolutionary document and its abstract truth, that loomed over Lincoln at Gettysburg even though direct references—mention of the Declaration by name—all came earlier in Washington, D.C. To declare July 4, 1776, the national birthdate and to identify this country's conception with the signing of the Declaration of Independence (a document lacking legal weight and constitutional authority), while not particularly surprising, is not so obvious a thing to do. Even as his inaugural arguments stressed the Constitution and portrayed the defense of the Union as an imperative of that document, so at Gettysburg could Lincoln have turned to its constituting work for legitimacy. But from the time he counted back "eighty odd" years to the moment when he reworded the gap to "fourscore and seven," Lincoln looked to Jefferson and Jefferson's words, which stood for the sixteenth president "as a test for all other things (even the Constitution) since it is outside American history while being inside it."[7]

In his remarks to the serenaders Lincoln provided a brief chronology of significant Independence Days, starting with the signing of the Declaration and ending with the surrender at Gettysburg; in between he recalled the deaths of Jefferson and John Adams—who, he pointed out, were the only signers to be elected president—on that same date in 1826. Following Daniel Webster's lead, he identified Jefferson as the writer and Adams as the ablest defender of the Declaration, and their near simultaneous deaths on the fiftieth anniversary of the signing he declared a sort of divine italicizing of that document's significance.

For all the years between himself and the founding event, American presidents had looked back to the national fathers with awe and trepidation and had accepted as their foremost obligation the preservation of the Union. Lincoln accepted that charge but, in the midst of secession, treated it as one of principle rather than organization, insisting that union involved more than simply holding states together. Equality gave union its meaning, and the sacrifice of that "self-evident truth" he came to see as the profoundest national failure. The Civil War was more than an attempt to maintain the nation's geographical integrity; it became—*after secession*—an opportunity to realize Union more fully on the basis of its single legitimizing condition. That is what the inspired founders had declared but not accomplished, not wholly. In the distance between their words and their creation lay the crux of Lincoln's Gettysburg message, and it required a subtle shift in how the founders were regarded; they had "brought forth" a nation dedicated to a proposition which they could "conceive" and "dedicate" but could not themselves enact, and from that conjunction of principle with compromise came the terrible anguish of those who had to resolve their conflicted legacy.

Lincoln's brief message at Gettysburg recalled Jefferson's eighty-seven-year-old text through more than its reiteration of their shared first principle. The Declaration's influence on Lincoln's remarks was so subtle and thorough that reading the nineteenth-century speech requires that the eighteenth-century document also be kept in mind. The interplay was apparent with the ironic echo that came in Lincoln's first line as he placed the battlefield and its commemoration in time, defined in radically different terms from those offered in 1776. The Declaration's opening, "When in the course of human events," is an abstraction, not a reference to the "reality" of time but rather to an idea of time, a sort of "whenever" introducing a universal proposition. It is, logically, the indifference of the premise—the fact that it is uncompromised by the specific and particular—that recommends it and gives it the stature of an axiom. But Lincoln began his own speech by asserting and specifying both his own moment and Jefferson's. "Four score and seven years ago our fathers brought forth on this continent a new nation, conceived in Liberty, and dedicated to the proposition that all men are created equal." Thus are two specific "human events" identified and then connected, the principle abstractly declared in the first and physically enacted in the second. Lincoln retained the cadence and balance of Jefferson's opening but changed its syntax and logic. The deductive reasoning of the Declaration gave way to induction at Gettysburg. There the particular—as is always the case with the inductive—stands in judgment of the general; the pain and frustration of the specific confront the imperious and impersonal abstraction. When at Philadelphia Lincoln praised Jefferson for placing his "abstract proof" into a "merely revolutionary"—a particular—document, he recognized the importance of founding principles. And as the "founder," standing at the beginning, Jefferson necessarily enunciated universals.

Having established the larger terms, Jefferson acknowledged the particular offenses of the English king and declared the just cause of a specific collection of colonists, but his general tendency was to stand on the side of the universal, to see the particular as it fits into the larger abstraction. So the inherent tension appeared at Gettysburg when the particular carnage on a particular battlefield was placed beside Jefferson's grand view.

What is most striking about the Declaration, what Lincoln was alluding to in his tribute to Jefferson, who "in the concrete pressure of a struggle for independence . . . had the coolness, forecast, and capacity" to present its principled case, is its incredible control, its deliberate, methodical composition, something we do not expect in revolutionary rhetoric. The long periodic sentence with which it opens delays, first, the declaration of a grammatical subject and then, when that turns out to be "respect," the subject of the document as a whole. There is no wrath, no obvious passion in the opening lines. There is, instead, the careful and irresistible movement of an argument and, correspondingly, a process rooted in a necessity and an inevitability derived from "natural law." Rhetorically, however, the inevitability is generated by the syllogistic structure of the argument. The Declaration in its entirety is the presentation and elaboration of a single syllogism, a strategy announced in the opening lines of the second paragraph and kept before the reader throughout the document. The conclusion to which it progresses is unavoidable once the premises are in place. Jefferson's argument is powered by the necessity of logic, and once it has begun, no matter how refined and literary that beginning might be, there can be no stopping, no digressing.

Having identified "life, liberty, and the pursuit of happiness" as among those rights endowed equally to all men by their creator, and having declared the purpose of government to be the securing of those rights, Jefferson presented his major premise, "That whenever any form becomes destructive of these ends, it is the right of the people to alter or abolish it, and to institute new government." The minor premise—"The history of the present King of Great Britain is a history of repeated injuries and usurpations, all having in direct object the establishment of an absolute tyranny over these states"—is then substantiated through a long list of indictments that make up the middle portion of the document. The conclusion—"We must, therefore, acquiesce in the necessity which denounces our separation and hold them, as we hold the rest of mankind, enemies in war, in peace friends"—necessarily follows.

The genius of the Declaration lies in its general coolness. The speaker is characterized by the document not as a destroyer of tradition, not as a hot-headed radical intent on undermining the social foundations, but as prudent, representing order rather than disorder, deliberate both in action and in language. Above all, the speaker serves the necessity at work in nature and in nations. In linking those two worlds—a connection asserted by the twin billing given in the opening sentence to "Nature" and to "Nature's God"—he makes the political process an extension of natural process. Thus the first reference to the rebellion of colony from parent country is described as a peaceful, even a natural act, dictated as such acts are by the nature of things and not by the arrogance of rebels: "When in the course of human events it becomes necessary for one people to *dissolve* the political bands which have connected them with another . . ." Whether implying divorce and the legal "dissolving" of matrimonial bands or the chemical action by which material substances disintegrate, the process is one made necessary by "law."[8] Ironically the same image appears later in the text—with wholly negative connotations—among the indictments of the English king: "He has *dissolved* representative houses repeatedly for opposing with manly firmness his invasions on the rights of the people. He has refused for a long time after such *dissolutions* to cause others to be elected." In the opening reference to "dissolve" the suggestion is one either of eroding or of judicial resolution, a separation that occurs without violence. But the dissolving of "representative houses" is a different matter from the dissolving of "bands," albeit political ones, and the word assumes a meaning that, rather than neutral, is wholly negative. Dissolution in this context is both unnatural and immoral.

Thus is established the pattern of Jefferson's rhetoric: The speaker in the Declaration serves natural as well as civil law. He is governed by a deep respect for order, is a scientist and philosopher rather than a politician, and so he serves the truest nature of things rather than personal or partisan ambitions. He is a lawyer whose canon is not the English constitution or the law of any particular nation, but the law of creation itself. Remarkably, the Declaration assumes a conservative stance, speaking less, finally, of liberty than of law and order. The case argued is that of all peoples, not that of the colonists alone; its context is the course of human, not American, events. This "one people," dissolving the political bands connecting them to another (or rather announcing that nature has dissolved those bands), does so in obedience to universal rights and obligations.

In contrast to the actions of the "one people" are those of an English king who is not only the first particularized element of the argument but also the one whose actions pursue narrow and idiosyncratic ends. If the American argument is governed by universals and is dictated by a respect for law, the King of Great Britain is a lawless agent of disorder and destruction. The indictments against the crown present a chain of abuses and the first among these is a consistent disregard for legal processes and institutions. "He has," the list begins, "refused his assent to laws, the most wholesome and necessary [he opposes necessity as well as virtue] for the public good." And it continues: "He has forbidden his governors to pass laws of immediate and pressing importance. . . . He has refused to pass other laws. . . . He has called together legislative bodies at places unusual, uncomfortable and distant from the depository of their public records. . . . He has dissolved representative houses [and] obstructed the laws for naturalization of foreigners. . . . He has obstructed the administration of judgment. . . . He has made judges dependent on his will alone." The emphasis throughout is less on personal wrongs done to Americans and more upon the king's opposition to the great principles that all legitimate governments serve. If the argument prior to the introduction of the British king and his "tyrannical" actions was based on the nature of things in the abstract, the actions of the crown are offensive precisely because they deny any authority greater than the person of the king. They are acts of caprice and whim in which "his will alone" stands above all else, the particular defying the universal.

It is, in Jefferson's formulation, the king who is the radical, the rebel against natural laws and natural rights. It is he who exposes the state "to all the dangers of invasions from without and convulsions within." In contrast to the positive functions of government stressed in the opening paragraphs, his actions have been negative: *refusing* "his assent to laws," *forbidding* "his governors to pass laws," endeavoring "to *prevent* the population of these states." Jefferson's present participles grow more damning as the clauses they control fall like hammer blows: "cutting off," "imposing," "depriving," "transporting," "abolishing," "taking away," "suspending,"—until they shift to past participles, powerful in their finality: "He has plundered . . . ravaged . . . burned . . . and destroyed." In those lines emotional fervor—so notably absent from the opening presentation of principles—is at last unleashed, culminating in the image of the king allied with merciless savages murdering women and children.

The tension central in Jefferson's argument is not that between colonist and crown, but that between universal and particular, law and whim. The persuasiveness of the opening two paragraphs results from the tone of heightened rationality and the tightness of the composition. Emotional power, on the other hand, is always derived from the particular—not suffering generally but specific suffering—and this the Declaration generates when it finally identifies the wrongs Americans have suffered, building to claims of impressment at sea and massacres at home. But it is crucial to the argument as a whole that emotional appeals are kept closely under control, so that it is not personal retribution to which the audience ultimately acquiesces, but necessity, the very "necessity" the British king has consistently ignored.

Necessity, in Jefferson's argument, follows two lines: First is the line of sweet reason—sweet because it is complete and unquestionable—the necessity of universal truth. The second is necessity as judgment, the judgments against the crown delivered in a relentless chain of indictments, which in its repetitions of clauses and sentence constructions creates its own irresistible expectancy.

Jefferson's was a brilliant strategy, turning the tables so that those declaring their independence are the calm and rational parties while the king is the erratic one. Even the text's measured, considered words are juxtaposed to the irrational and capricious actions of the monarch, and in that juxtaposition the need for this declaration is demonstrated. Prudent men, as Jefferson argues early in the document, do not change governments for whimsical or even transient reasons. They do so only when driven to a point where the risk of dissolving the political bands is less than that of enduring the dissolute behavior of a tyrannical government.

If the end of Jefferson's Declaration is to assert the former colonies' rights as "free and independent states . . . to levy war, conclude peace, contract alliances, establish commerce and do all other acts and things which independent states may of right do," then his audience, the candid world to which he addresses his case, must be other states; those states alone have the ultimate power to validate the American declaration. The lofty road that he takes both in argument and in language was in many ways dictated by that removed, disinterested, international audience, the kind of audience (a philosopher's fiction) with which Jefferson, by temperament, was most comfortable.

On the nineteenth day of November 1863, Abraham Lincoln stood on a terrible battlefield about to become an enormous cemetery. There was, in that place and that time, no way to escape the particular, no way to soar on logical wings above the grief and devastation of so earthbound an occasion. Jefferson and his colleagues declared the rights of the living, but Lincoln came to bury the dead, men dead in the service of Jefferson's great principle and Lincoln's awful command. Nor on that fall day had the command been rescinded; the war went on and its casualties grew in numbers nearly equal to those lost before Gettysburg. Lincoln spoke not at the end of his nation's great anguish, but in the midst of ongoing carnage, carnage that stood in judgment of both himself and Jefferson.

For all his emphasis upon the Declaration, Lincoln did not imitate its enumeration of the enemy's offenses, did not assign guilt and innocence or divide the dead on the basis of blame; he offered no catalog of Southern indictments comparable to the charges Jefferson had leveled at the British king. Even more significant is the absence of a syllogism and the logician's certainty. Having begun his remarks by grounding himself and his countrymen in the Declaration and its great principle, he immediately emphasized the distance separating the dead of this place from the pronouncement of that previous time.

Dedicating the Gettysburg cemetery, Lincoln recalled the nation's cre-

ation with the imagery of conception and birth. He concluded his opening sentence with the phrase "and dedicated to the proposition that all
men are created equal." The word "dedicate" recurs four more times,
making the dedication at Gettysburg—that of the soldiers who died
there as well as the official act of creating the cemetery—inseparable
from the founding fathers' dedication to the liberal principles of the Declaration.

Never in his remarks did Lincoln refer to the Revolution, to the price
paid in their own time, on their own battlefields, by the fathers, a sacrifice the Declaration anticipates in its own conclusion. His sole point of
reference was the intellectual and rhetorical beginnings of the nation. In
juxtaposing the violence of Gettysburg with Jefferson's calm composition, Lincoln dramatized the limits of reason. What in the logic of 1776
was to come with the fullness of time to a world governed by natural law
had led in this generation to the unnatural carnage of civil conflict. The
"new birth" was required because the original conception had been
flawed. Enlightened philosophes believed in the triumph of reason, believed the irrational world would wither away, and Jefferson, who had
condemned slavery in his first version of the Declaration and laid its
blame at the English monarch's feet, thought that institution doomed by
its own absurdity, its violation of logic as well as morality. It would disappear in time simply because it did not make sense, a premise Buchanan
reiterated in his despairing final annual message. But the Enlightenment
language of Jefferson, eighty-seven years into the national experience,
gave way to Lincoln's biblical tones. The philosopher's rationalism yielded to the religious consecration of those who had seen their liberal assumptions torn asunder and had come to bury their sons. Jefferson's arguments grew from a belief in progress and a profound faith in reason;
Lincoln's were rooted in an ancient notion of sacrifice, the hallowing that
comes from anguish and death. The former dedicated propositions, the
latter cemeteries.

Where Jefferson started with an abstract principle, Lincoln began with
a fact, that of the founding. Where Jefferson continued by introducing a
chain of propositions constructing a syllogism, Lincoln went on to a second fact: that of the war and the present purpose. Lincoln offered no
counterpart to the logician's certainty (if this is true and that is true, then
this must follow); the wisdom of Gettysburg was that nothing *must* fol-

low, there is only the matter of possibility. The body of the Declaration focuses upon rights, upon what a people can do; the body of the Gettysburg Address is rooted in limitation ("we cannot dedicate—we cannot consecrate—we cannot hallow;" "The world will little note, nor long remember what we say here") and as a consequence leads not to an inevitable conclusion but to an appeal for resolve, for the will necessary to create what in the Declaration seemed to be itself necessity and thereby to sustain the old conclusion. The Declaration and the Gettysburg Address are committed to the same great principle, but one the war had proved to be neither irresistible nor irreversible. What had been declared in 1776 could be sustained in 1863 only by specific acts of sacrifice. The God who presided at Gettysburg was older and less "reasonable" than the God of enlightened philosophes, the representative of ancient assumptions rather than progressive thinking.

In the argument of 1776 the concept of equality vindicates the right to dissolve "the political bands" connecting "one people" with another. Lincoln argued against dissolving such bands, in part because Americans were *only* one people, insisting that those who pursued such a course did so because they were unwilling to endorse the principle of equality. "It is for us the living rather," he concluded, making the issue both specific and personal,

> to be dedicated here to the unfinished work which they who fought here so nobly advanced. It is rather for us to be here dedicated to the great task remaining before us—that from these honored dead we take increased devotion to that cause for which they gave the last full measure of devotion—that we here highly resolve that these dead shall not have died in vain—that this nation, under God, shall have a new birth of freedom—and that government of the people, by the people, for the people, shall not perish from the earth.

From birth, through death, to rebirth, Lincoln led his audience through the particulars of loss and suffering to a different national foundation from that offered by the Declaration. Only in that way could he and the other survivors give meaning to the otherwise senseless evidence of Gettysburg. He repudiated the old implications of natural progress and logically enlightened advancement but affirmed, in the grandeur only tragedy can bring, the founders' great principle. He extended it with the abolition of slavery even to that logical conclusion they could not reach and grounded it, literally, with every repeated "here," in the specific soil of Gettysburg.

The measurement of score was most consistently applied—then as now—to the span of a human life, the biblical norm of three score and ten, and Lincoln's manner of dating—four score and seven—emphasized the fact that the years of this nation's existence were not many more than the typical human allotment. Its near perishing after so short a period suggested how fundamentally human it is, how bound to human caprice and folly, how much its longevity depends upon human dedication and will. That of course was how Lincoln remade Jefferson's mythy country, and in so doing converted it from a union of logic and convenience, one in which self-interest and idiosyncrasy promoted secession, into a single nation, united through the anguish of civil war, reborn on fields of death.

The United States of the Gettysburg Address was not a creation drawn up on a scholar's desk or the work of reasonable men convening in a constituting assembly. This re-United States drew its vitality from the altar of Gettysburg and was sanctified by the sacrificial blood of those who died there; this was the nation Lincoln described in the Second Inaugural. The old story about fathers and sons and judgment, the redundant pattern of time and peoples that Jefferson had conveniently ignored, must have weighed unbearably on that modern Abraham who not only endured the death of his favorite child during the war but also took responsibility for the deaths of all the other sons claimed by the conflict. In this telling of the story, this rewriting of the old account, Isaac (who in the original version is spared because of his father's righteousness) dies not once, but over and over again.

In a reversal of the biblical narrative, Lincoln came to one of the places of death and built an altar of rededication and consecration. Gettysburg, as he reconceived it, provided the basis for a new covenant, one bound by the "mystic chords" of anguished memory. But Lincoln's story linked both biblical testaments and gave this new covenant a resurrecting power for both the country and the martyred sons. Sacrificed to the presumption of the fathers and the judgment of a righteous God, the young "shall not have died in vain," and their spirits will live in the nation they redeemed.

In the terrible context of civil war the scriptural implications of the name Abraham resonated throughout the North. Patriotic songwriters and Unionist ministers saw the possibilities and elaborated the theme for troubled congregations.[9] But the beleaguered president drove the connection far beyond the poetics of coincidence; he took the conflict itself as biblical in scope and implication. He knew the Abraham story went beyond the drama of the righteous father who put his son Isaac at risk on a wilderness altar. In his letter to the Galatians, Paul of the New Testament wrote

> . . . it is written that Abraham had two sons, one by a slave and one by a free woman. But the son of the slave was born according to the flesh, the son of the free woman through promise. Now this is an allegory: these women are two covenants. One is from Mount Sinai, bearing children for slavery; she is Hagar. Now Hagar is Mount Sinai in Arabia; she corresponds to the present Jerusalem, for she is in slavery with her children. But the Jerusalem above is free, and she is our mother. (Gal., 4:22–26)

In Paul's application of the Old Testament account, the Christian message extends the promise of Abraham to the gentiles. They too were called to freedom and made heirs to the old covenant through Christ's sacrifice, a sacrifice that carries to completion the one begun by Abraham. This extension of promise, this expansion of the old covenant into a more inclusive blessing, becomes in Galatians another dimension of Abraham's work, one too that Lincoln—called father by this time by both soldiers and freed slaves—assumed at Gettysburg as he rewrote both the biblical text and Jefferson's declaration to focus them on "freedom." Thus Isaac's story becomes an "allegory" about the extension of promise, and that promise is where America—the America that survives—must seek its solace; this is the cause for hope in the midst of judgment, and is all that can redeem America from its own presumption. "For freedom," Paul declared, "Christ has set us free; stand fast therefore, and do not submit again to a yoke of slavery" (Gal., 5:1). That was what Lincoln was learning in the years separating his two inaugurals, and Gettysburg provided the hinge upon which his wisdom and his rhetoric turned, the pivot on which he was moving America's understanding of the war and its own purpose.

TAKING TO THE AIR

While listening to the great eighteenth-century evangelist George White-field, Benjamin Franklin attempted to estimate the carrying range of the preacher's voice and calculate the number of hearers. Franklin was testing the traditional limits of audience, limits as old as human speech.[10] If the boundaries of the old storyteller's labors were established by the parameters of a hearth's light or the campfire's illuminated circle, those of the orator were defined by the range of his voice. Like opera, platform oratory conveys its message through expansion, an enlargement of gesture and sound that can carry to the back rows, and the intimacy of the old-fashioned stump is in fact an intimacy of theater, the creation of an art we have come to think of as simple, but that is as complex as anything television requires.

The electronic revolution allowed the orators to approach their audience more closely even as it dramatically increased the size of that listening body and allowed a greater range of inflection and intonation. Simply the fact of amplification, while it did not eliminate oratorical theatrics, introduced a wider array of options, even to platform speakers. But broadcasting complicated as well as facilitated presidential communication, primarily in the way it simultaneously expanded and narrowed the audience. "FDR's fireside chats suggested a new model of communication," Kathleen Hall Jamieson suggests: "one person in the private space of his living room chatting with millions of other individuals in theirs." But then she asks,

> Could such discourse properly be labeled public address? Some argued that the mass media's small families and solitary viewers were not a public in any traditional sense. Moreover, conversing privately with families through publicly accessible channels did not seem to approximate address. It's "public" turned private and it's "address" turned conversation; "public address" joined bustles in the linguistic attic.[11]

What Ms. Jamieson notes as this century's rejection of the "orator" for the "speaker" is inseparable from the movement of political discourse from the forum to the home and the intimacy that allows. In previous times democratic politics has been spectacle, with candidates entering and exiting in torchlight parades, their messages grand in duration and enthusiasms. Theirs was rhetoric meant to be heard in a crowd, the shared experience as essential to the effect as the message being delivered.

Broadcast discourse cannot replicate the effects of citizens standing shoulder to shoulder in a common space, cannot create the exhilarating sense—no matter how fleeting—of a common life. It no more satisfies the political and psychological needs of a democracy than television serves as theater. What it does, however, in narrowing the audience down to the individual or family, is to acknowledge our own importance and sometimes calm the fear of being left out that a system of mass politics and majority rule can arouse. No matter how many other homes the president enters at that same moment, he addresses us and implies that we are the appropriate test of what he says. Not all politics is personal, but nearly all electronic politics, of necessity *is*. That is, at once, the great strength of broadcast eloquence and its great weakness.

The President in the Parlor

Herbert Hoover, in his enthusiasm for all technology, embraced radio and understood its political potential, but he seemed never able to relax in its presence. "Of the untold values of the radio," he told a broadcast audience in 1929, "one is the great intimacy it has brought among our people. Through its mysterious channels we come to wider acquaintance with surroundings and men" (PP, Hoover, 1929:294). His words were prophetic, as they described the use not he but Franklin Roosevelt would make of a new medium, one that enabled a president to address in a single evening an audience larger than the first Roosevelt had reached on his entire Western tour.

While others made the mistake of simply performing old-style bombastic oratory in front of a microphone or of developing smarmy tones of exaggerated friendliness, Franklin Roosevelt realized the potential of broadcast intimacy without seeming to presume upon it.[12] He managed to enter the home but never forgot that such an act did not make him family. Opening with "my friends" or "my fellow Americans," he kept a degree of reserve but managed to be both familiar and formal in a manner that reduced the presumption of intruding into the private realm. With businesslike economy he explained in the first few minutes the subject of his broadcast ("I want to talk . . . about banking . . . I want to tell you what has been done in the last few days, and why it was done, and what the next steps are going to be."),* implying a respect for his listeners' time and intelligence. The workmanlike pace fitted particularly well with the pervasive tone—in the midst of high unemployment—that he and his audience were doing their respective jobs, his in the government and theirs in feeding their families as best they could.

In fact, the "Fireside Chats" were not "chatty," at least not in the sense of being casual or conversational. FDR spoke as *the* president without denying the distance his office placed between himself and listeners. And his speaking style, with its exaggerated enunciations, elongated syllables, and dramatic pauses, hardly sounded everyday or commonplace to most Americans. He said in his 1935 explanation of his work relief program, "I shall recognize six fundamental principles, (p. 67)" slowing for emphasis *"six–funda–mental–principles,"* rippling the words with his voice, making them rich and full in a manner that was later adopted by highbrow announcers of opera and classical music broadcasts. He emphasized rather than obscured some aspects of his patrician New York accent, overriding his "r"s ("fuhst" for "first", "fewcha" for future), softening and elongating some sounds, hardening others like the second "a" in "again," making the word rhyme with "rain" and ringing the last syllable so that, to the more conventional ear, it carried an exotic lyricism. At the same time FDR's language could be relatively colloquial—"Americans as a whole are feeling a lot better—a lot more cheerful than for a number of years" (p. 65), and "There are chiselers ("chiselers" was an FDR favorite as "idlers" had been for TR) in every walk of life" (p. 69)—relaxed, but enunciated carefully enough to retain its decorum.

Somehow in all his addresses FDR managed to maintain a magisterial quality while at the same time giving the impression of speaking to peers. "It has been wonderful to me to catch the note of confidence from all over the country," he said in his first "chat" broadcast. "I can never be sufficiently grateful to the people for the loyal support they have given me" (p. 16). Just as the phrasing betrayed the upper-class upbringing, so too was there the slightest hint of superiority in the remark, setting him

*All "Fireside Chat" quotations are taken from Russell D. Buhite and David W. Levy, eds., *FDR's Fireside Chats* (Norman, OK, 1992). This one, about banking, is from p. 12.

apart from the audience he was embracing. Far from undercutting Roosevelt's mass appeal, however, such gestures seemed to enhanced it by satisfying a need to be affirmed and accepted by one's "better."

Although FDR was a great admirer of his cousin Theodore and a careful observer of Teddy's skill at generating popular confidence, his radio persona seemed to have been most profoundly influenced by Wilson. Adopting a more genial version of the professorial voice, he instructed with each "fireside chat," a mini-lecture, often outlined with enumerated sections and illustrated with analogies (government is compared to shipbuilding in a 1935 "chat" (p. 64), and in a 1937 talk on the Supreme Court he likened the present government to a troika being pulled by only two horses (p. 86).) Sometimes he gave homework, sending his audience to their maps in February 1942 so they could follow his references "to the world-encircling battle lines of this war (p. 207)" and asking them to read and reread the Constitution of the United States in March 1937 so they could better understand his comments about the Supreme Court (p. 87).

His emphasis was always on clarity ("I want to leave in your minds one clear fact, [p. 64]" "I want to talk with you very simply tonight about the need for present action in this crisis" (p. 86). Words like "simple," "clear," and "honest" recurred regularly and were treated as virtual synonyms. Teacher-like, he emphasized the process of shared reasoning, a mutual capacity to understand an issue and evaluate a response once information had been provided. In every speech he laid out his argument step by step ("First of all let me state the simple fact . . . the second step . . . the third stage . . . one more point before I close" (pp. 13–16). None of it was condescending but instead came across as an attempt to recover practical issues from the technical jargon of experts. In his first "chat" he explained, "I recognize that the many proclamations from the state capitals and from Washington, the legislation, the treasury regulations, and so forth, couched for the most part in banking and legal terms, ought to be explained for the benefit of the average citizen" (p. 12). In that way he used his radio classroom to fulfill his campaign promise to make government intellectually accessible and consistent with the common sense that "average" citizens exercised in their daily lives.

Coming to office during a Depression, a time when people felt fearful and isolated—emotions Huey Long and Father Coughlin exploited—Roosevelt used radio to demystify government and to encourage his hearers to believe their officials not only knew they were out there but were acting as a positive force on their behalf. "Your government," as he persistently identified it, he described as an instrument of their collective interests, an activist servant of their welfare. With its creative involvement, he insisted, the suffering nation could generate its own recovery, and his radio talks were an occasion to explain the logic and progress of federal actions. The test of government, he insisted, was not its size but rather its ability to explain itself clearly and convincingly. "Another question that you will ask is this," he told his first fireside audience after explaining the bank holiday. "Why are all the banks not to be reopened at the same time? The answer is simple, and I know you will understand it" (p. 14). At the close of that evening's chat, he concluded, "I hope you can see, my friends, from this essential recital of what your government is doing, that there is nothing complex, nothing radical, in the process" (p. 16). Complexity as a negative proof was simply the other side of his clarity argument. "I believe," he reported in a 1934 "chat," "in practical explanations and in practical policies" (p. 51).

Confusion and uncertainty among the public, Roosevelt insisted, was a failure of leadership, so he made understanding the primary test of rhetorical legitimacy. Accordingly, reason rather than passion was the primary faculty appropriate to persuasion. Even on the political attack, he tended to contain his indignation, to make his refutation of opponents teacherly, and to restrain sarcasm with humor and a posture of good will.[13] Because he served in times of crisis, that emotional control, along with the emphasis on reason and deliberation, was central not only to gaining support for his policies but also for instilling public confidence.

Always Roosevelt called his countrymen, regardless of the crisis, away from extremes, from self-deception as well as panic and, without directly saying so, presented himself as a model. Before America's entry into World War II, responding to the doomsayers on one side and the pollyannas on the other, he declared his own credo: "I did not share those illusions. I do not share those fears. Today we are more realistic" (p. 154). Following the liberation of Rome in July 1943, he addressed published predictions as to when the war would finally end; one writer had suggested that the end would come that same year, and another predicted 1949. "Of course," Roosevelt counseled, "both extremes—of optimism and pessimism—are wrong" (p. 265). His emphasis on moderation and realism were designed to reassure emotionally as well as logically; his cause depended as much upon calming people as on persuading them. To deal with crises effectively the country had to get control of itself psychologically as well as politically.

In a radio talk on September 11, 1941, FDR addressed the subject of a German submarine attack on the USS *Greer*. He began with an account of the situation, offered in considerable detail but concisely and clearly, explaining the cargo (mail) and destination (Iceland) of the *Greer* and the sequence of events. Throughout his remarks the president emphasized that the attack was "deliberate" and unprovoked—"I tell you the blunt fact that the German submarine fired first." He then outlined previous aggressions German submarines had committed against American vessels, showing a chain of flagrant hostilities that amounted to "piracy, legally and morally." Despite such incitement, he insisted, "we Americans are keeping our feet on the ground," "we are not becoming hysterical," "we are taking a long-range point of view." His tone throughout was forceful, laced with righteous indignation, and yet deliberate, evidence of both the resolve and the calm that he had insisted, throughout previous crises, was the way a sensible and confident America reacts to peril (pp. 189–91). "Your government," he would tell his audience in 1942, "has unmistakable confidence in your ability to hear the worst, without flinching or losing heart" (p. 213).

Even stirring his countrymen to preparedness three months prior to the attack on Pearl Harbor, the president built his case on common sense rather than fear, arguing a design in Nazi aggression, a design "it would be inexcusable folly" not to see (p. 191). He had begun remarks in a similar vein in December 1940 by saying, "My friends, this is not a Fireside Chat on war. It is a talk on national security" (p. 164). At that time he suggested the crisis with Germany was comparable to that of the national economy which they had previously faced together, and in subsequent remarks he equated the contemporary challenge to ones faced by John Adams and Thomas Jefferson, reassuring by analogy, pointing to moments of similar danger when the nation had persevered and prevailed. In arousing his countrymen, he crafted his argument and his tone so as not to overly excite or push them either into panic or dangerous and premature reaction.

His indignation had a theatrical quality. When he delivered rebukes or ultimata, as in 1941, when he told the German government "You shall go no further" (p. 194), he slowed his speaking pace, elongated the vowels, and enunciated every syllable clearly and strongly. On other occasions he expressed contempt with sustained analogies that were themselves little stories. Explaining how the Nazi government should be dealt with, his voice climbed to a higher pitch, sharp and mocking: "When you see a rattlesnake poised to strike, you do not wait until he has struck before you crush him" (p. 194). Again there is both an indulgence and containment of emotion in a comparison that admits danger but does not inflate it and in the commonsensical remedy it presents. The sardonic edge of condescension is shared with the audience and directed against the arrogance of their common enemy, balancing anger with camaraderie.

In calling an uncertain nation toward resolve, in depression and in war, FDR insisted that deliberation prevail over passion and attributed America's advantage over its enemies to that tendency. In closing his remarks on the *Greer*, he addressed both his hesitant country and the aggressive Nazis, tried to steel one and discourage the other as he warned German and Italian vessels that attacks in neutral waters would be resisted, declaring this policy his duty and America's right. Combining his familiar appeal for careful consideration with a passion sufficient to indicate and encourage resolve, he declared, "I have no illusions about the gravity of this step. I have not taken it hurriedly or lightly. The times call for clear heads and strong hearts" (p. 194). The linking of crisis with clarity, of gravity with deliberation, testified to the triumph of reason and the achievement of maturity. "Our type of democratic civilization has outgrown the thought of feeling compelled to fight some other nation by reason of any single piratical attack on one of our ships" (p. 191). Here he showed himself more the successor of Wilson than of his cousin Teddy, as he asserted that the American democracy had achieved a political maturity and civilization—both indicative of reason's elevation—in contrast to the barbarous new governments of Europe. Instead of the Rough Rider's depiction of a youthful and excitable America among older world powers, FDR stressed a ripened wisdom, the United States as the adult responding to a particularly perverse European child.[14]

The wartime "chats" all followed the same basic formula Roosevelt had developed in the 1930s, with the president-teacher catching up the student-nation on what was taking place, correcting the false impressions offered by his critics, and rallying his listeners. Less than three months after Pearl Harbor he paired realism with hope as he addressed his countrymen on the subject of "things as they are today, and things as we know they shall be in the future." He served the latter by recalling the overwhelming odds George Washington faced in the Revolution; he served the former by reporting that "this war's a new kind of war" (p. 207).

To explain the terms of this "new kind of war," he asked his listeners to take out a map of the world and, after admitting that he could not "cover everything in one short report to the people" (p. 207), offered a capsule explanation of where and how the global conflict was being conducted. In so doing he repudiated those who called for retreat to a fortress America, insisting that, despite devastating losses, the defense strategy developed over the previous forty years precisely for resisting Japan in the Pacific, a strategy of delay and regroup that MacArthur furthered simply by impeding the Philippine invasion, was working. Even with the devastation of Pearl Harbor, FDR declared, America's plan of defense had not been discredited, and in a rare outburst he excoriated the "rumor-monger and poison peddlers in our midst" together with their "damnable misstatements" (p. 213). His chief concern had to do with what he insisted were exaggerated figures for the losses at Pearl Harbor, which, while terrible, were not so devastating as was being rumored.

FDR's strategy even in the worst of situations, even when the threat under discussion was no longer that of domestic depression but of foreign aggression on a scale completely unfamiliar to Americans, was to reassure his audience by seeming to tell them everything and suggesting that, knowing the truth, they had looked the worst in the face and discovered that, bad as it was, they could deal with it. His commentary suggested an unembroidered realism, calmly presented and coolly assessed. The psychological genius of Roosevelt's leadership began with the assumption that people are more afraid of what they don't know than of what they do. FDR always explained his own refusal to despair in terms of a belief in democratic government and a faith in his countrymen. He justified his positive view in terms of their strength. And in that way he encouraged them to grow stronger.

What Roosevelt offered his frightened nation with all his radio chats was a sense of perspective and balance and even more, perhaps, of order.

After Pearl Harbor he denied that the Japanese had taken the initiative away from America, insisting that we had our own plans and strategies, and that those depended on keeping our heads and doing our work. "Uninterrupted production," rather than confusion, was to be the American response to the Japanese attack. "I stress," he emphasized, "that word uninterrupted" (p. 214). He offered his countrymen something to do, a way to regain, first, the psychological advantage the enemy had taken and, second, the military/political edge America appeared to lose in the Pearl Harbor devastation. All that depended upon a perception that the president *did* speak straightforwardly, that his clarity represented reality in the face of political and psychological distortion. But it depended as well on radio, on the voice that spoke in people's homes addressing fears that were deeply private and personal as well as public. It depended upon his ability to keep in touch.

Even as he exploited the one-on-one relation radio offered speaker and audience, the intimacy his audience, in its times of apprehension, so desired, FDR compensated for one of the medium's principal deficiencies, the isolation of listeners from one another. The president continued to emphasize union, reminding his countrymen of their deep and abiding connections to one another. He did so in a variety of ways, beginning with repeated references to their shared values and their common past. Whether alluding to the trials of the Revolutionary army or of Lincoln during the Civil War, he regularly pointed to what had preceded their own time of crisis, and since great numbers of them were the products of more recent migrations to America, he was recreating United States history to include them, allying them with the ongoing mission of their country whatever the date of their own arrival.

In crisis, regardless of the cause, FDR argued that individual security was inseparable from that of the country as a whole. "Singleness of national purpose," he argued, would be necessary if America was to prevail over the dangers it confronted, and he warned against the forces of internal division: "Men can lose confidence in each other, and therefore lose confidence in the efficacy of their own united action. Faith and courage can yield to doubt and fear. The unity of the state can be so sapped that its strength is destroyed" (p 161). FDR recognized preserving that "unity" as his central presidential obligation, and in all of his "chats" he prevailed upon the various members of his audience to consider the others, not visible to them, who were hearing his words at that same moment. On one occasion he began his remarks by noting, "Tonight my single duty is to speak to the whole of America"; on another, broadcasting on a Sunday, he reminded his listeners of the larger context in which they were assembled, saying, "On this Sabbath evening, in our homes and in the midst of our American family . . ." (p 154), changing in a spontaneous act of revision the original version that was printed "in the midst of our American famil*ies*."

As Roosevelt struggled to create a core of common opinion, so too did he try to lessen the divisions of class. He did so in part by arguing America's commitment to equality. On Labor Day eve, 1936, he declared:

> In other countries the relationship of employer and employee has been more or less accepted as a class relationship not readily to be broken through. In this country we insist, as an essential of the American way of life, that the employer–employee relationship should be one between free men and equals. We refuse to regard those who work with hand or brain as different from or inferior to those who live from their own property. We insist that labor is as entitled to as much respect as property. (p. 81)

He reminded his radio audience during the 1937–38 recession that as president he was "constantly thinking of all our people—unemployed and employed alike"—thinking of them in terms of their common needs, "their human problems of food and clothing and homes and education and health and old age," of their universal need for "security" (p. 115). He used radio messages as a means of connecting his audience, drawing together people who—given all the barriers that stood between them—were unlikely, under normal circumstances, to stand in company with one another. By linking them with his voice, separated as they were in their various homes, he helped realize the larger Union, invisible, but through him nonetheless present, applying the newest technology to the preeminent obligation of his office.

Whenever possible he made those connections personal, introducing his countrymen to one another, first by vocation and eventually by name and personal details. During the war he concluded a call for national sacrifice by telling about a sixty-year-old missionary doctor, Dr. Corydon Wassell, who saved six wounded soldiers during their escape from Java,

and about Captain Hewitt Wheless, who successfully completed a
bombing mission and saved wounded crew members despite massive
damage to his plane. (pp. 227–29). In September 1936, addressing the
division between farmers and urban labor that some politicians (William
Jennings Bryan in particular) had dramatically exploited, the president
told of what he had seen on a recent tour of the drought-stricken central
agricultural states. "My friends," he began, "I have been on a journey of
husbandry." Then he described what he had seen and the Americans he
had met, elaborating their various kinds of "husbandry"—care of a
household, conservation of resources, agricultural cultivation—and asserting concern for each as part of his presidential obligation, but also offering each as a metaphor for the office he filled.

> I talked with families who had lost their wheat crop, lost their corn crop,
> lost their livestock, lost the water in their well, lost their garden and come
> through to the end of the summer without one dollar of cash resources,
> facing the winter without feed or food—facing a planting season without
> seed to put in the ground. (p. 74)

After several such examples of human suffering and natural devastation,
Roosevelt praised the tenacity and courage of America's struggling farmers. "It was their fathers' task to make homes; it is their task to keep those
homes; and it is our task to help them win their fight" (p. 75). Then,
proposing federal assistance to the drought victims, he reminded the rest
of his audience of their own interest in saving both farms and the people
who tended them: "it is worth our while as a nation to spend money in
order to save money" (p. 76).

> Every state in the drought area is now doing and always will do business
> with every state outside it. The very existence of the men and women
> working in the clothing industry of New York, making clothes worn by
> farmers and their families; of the workers in the steel mills in Pittsburgh
> and Gary, in the automobile factories of Detroit, and in the harvester fac-
> tories of Illinois, depend upon the farmers' ability to purchase the com-
> modities that they produce. In the same way it is the purchasing power of
> the workers in these factories in the cities that enables them and their
> wives and children to eat more beef, more pork, more wheat, more corn,
> more fruit and more dairy products, and to buy more clothing made

from cotton and wool and leather. In a physical and in a property sense, as well as in a spiritual sense, we are members one of another. (p. 77)

FDR's lessons in economic interdependence echo an argument for Union that extends back to George Washington, but so, as well, does his plea for a profounder sense of community, one familial and spiritual. "Members one of another" is the New Testament description of a community of faith, its members linked like the parts of a body, a single being, bonded in a common purpose even as each is distinguished by his or her own special gifts and abilities. That is Lincoln's Union, in which neither the parts nor the whole can survive in a diminished state.

The only president to master radio—virtually the only one to have the opportunity—Roosevelt exploited the personal connection the new medium brought to his office, without sacrificing eloquence. There was always, even in the midst of "plain speaking and "directness," a sense of composure, a capacity to find language that could be at once clear and lyrical. Memorable phrases—"we do not forget the silenced people" (reference to the German occupation)—occurred regularly enough to keep things interesting and inspiring but without lifting the occasion to high formality. Addressing the disappointment and hardships of the 1937–38 recession, FDR concluded his remarks by requesting "a personal word to you" and went on to describe the reciprocal relationship between people and president and the nature of the talk between the two. One of the most eloquent moments in any of Roosevelt's "chats," it required the intimacy of the medium combined with a great orator's sense of the poetic. "I never forget," he said, "that I live in a house owned by all the American people and that I have been given their trust." Having identified what he "never forgets," to check his presumption, he turned to what he always remembers:

> I try always to remember that their deepest problems are human. I constantly talk to those who come to tell me their own points of view; with those who manage the great industries and financial institutions of the country; with those who represent the farmer and the worker; and often, very often, with average citizens without high position who come to this house. (p. 122)

Then he explained the presidential challenge of bringing the two together, the people and the office, and of how he prepared for his executive work.

In this part of the process the usual roles were reversed, with him as the student and the people he served giving the instruction.

> And constantly I seek to look beyond the doors of the White House, beyond the officialdom of the national capital, into the hopes and fears of men and women in their homes. I have traveled the country over many times. My friends, my enemies, my daily mail, bring to me reports of what you are thinking and hoping. I want to be sure that neither battles nor burdens of office shall ever blind me to an intimate knowledge of the way the American people want to live and the simple purposes for which they put me here. (p. 122)

On the basis of that knowledge—delivered by a catalog of professions and classes, including farmers and merchants, factory workers and manufacturers—he did the presidential work of making and explaining policies. Amid the anxiety of "this troubled world" he described the president's job as trying to reconcile the different interests of these groups. But, he admitted,

> I cannot expect all of the people to understand all of the people's problems; but it is my job to try to understand all of the problems.
>
> I always try to remember that reconciling differences cannot satisfy everyone completely. Because I do not expect too much, I am not disappointed. But I know that I must never give up—that I must never let the greater interest of all the people down, merely because that might be for the moment the easiest personal way out.
>
> I believe that we have been right in the course we have charted. To abandon our purpose of building a greater, a more stable, and a more tolerant America, would be to miss the tide and perhaps to miss the port. I propose to sail ahead. I feel sure that your hopes, I feel sure that your help is with me. For to reach a port, we must sail—sail, not lie at anchor—sail, not drift. (pp. 122–23).

Here are all the great themes, not just of FDR's speeches but of the presidency itself; the democratic notion of an executive elevated in order to serve, the great individual made servant to the masses, living in their "house," and trying to fathom their needs; the reconciler, joining together all the disparate elements of a pluralistic society; the unionist seeking a more inclusive society. It is a message that gains from the intimacy of the living room—that is, when delivered in this way, personal. The image of the family gathered around a radio is one of the more compelling representations of the New Deal era, but it is not our only image of 1930s broadcast politics. A contrary image—available both in photographs and on film—was an alternative use of radio's capacity to serve a leader's interest, the scenes from Fascist Italy of people gathered not in living rooms but in the town square, looking up to elevated speakers broadcasting Il Duce's voice, projecting a leader far above them and calling them from their own lives and families to serve his superior purpose.

Only Roosevelt took full advantage of radio and, though his successors have continued to make radio addresses, America ceased to be a radio culture shortly after FDR's death. When television displaced radio at midcentury, one might have assumed that it would merely carry the personalization of the presidency a step farther than audio. Its effect, however, was quite different. Radio listeners are drawn toward the sound of a president's voice, unhampered by visual distractions, but television presents a whole panoply of competing details as it "frames" an event in a smaller-than-life box. This new broadcasting technology excelled at presenting spectacle, at bringing the viewer into the presence of big events—conventions, inaugurals, congressional hearings—but it interfered with the intimacy that FDR's "chats" fostered. Television delivers the office—both literally and figuratively—and all of its trappings, as well as the man. The audience sees the surroundings as well as the speaker, and the context becomes as important as the voice, often distracting from the latter's immediate impact. The visual stimuli, however, are mostly commonplace (dress, furnishings, and the like), and they detract from the larger issues—the world the speaker is addressing. Radio-age citizens had to invent their own pictures while listening to FDR. They had to use their imaginations to supply the details. In so doing, they became accessories to and participants in the "chat," literally making the president a presence in their midst. Television changed all that. It made the viewers more passive, intimidated them with the actual setting, and no matter how hard the person seated before them worked to put them at ease, the result was not the same as when the encounter had occurred in their own homes. The television camera reverses the radio relationship; it is not the president who enters America's homes, but America that enters his. He becomes the host and we the intruding visitors.

AN ADAPTABLE OFFICE

One of the remarkable aspects of the American presidency is its adaptability to such different personalities, such contrasting moral visions. In accommodating the energetic first Roosevelt as well as his wheelchair-bound cousin; the professorial Wilson; the laid-back, good-natured Reagan; and the tragically inclined Lincoln, the office has allowed America to keep defining itself and to grow, sometimes in spite of itself. In a sense, each of the speeches considered here have been concerned with encouraging Americans to do something they were reluctant to undertake, calling them to be more than they had yet aspired to be. All have been efforts in some way to keep faith with our oldest and most demanding commitments.

Chapter Nine

Executive Farewells

In the sweep of things, a President has only so much time—a very allotted time—to do the things that he really believes in and he thinks must be done. Within those limits, he can only give it the best he has . . . we leave the plow in the furrow, and actually the field is only half tilled.

—Lyndon Johnson, 1969 Farewell Address

The Constitution stipulates the precise manner in which every elected presidency begins, and to the legal requirement of taking the oath of office custom has added the inaugural address. But there is no precise formula for how an administration should end. In part that is because of the variety of ways in which presidents leave office—they can depart through death, defeat, and resignation as well as by personal choice—and how they mark the occasion—when it is in their power to do so—depends very much on their personality and the circumstances of their passing.

Since administrations are inevitably recounted as stories, their plots are inseparable from a general perception of how things turn out. The ending, as with all stories, greatly influences the popular interpretation of everything that went before. Presidencies that have attained the "triple crown" of executive politics—election, reelection, and the retirement of a revered statesman—provide our ultimate success stories. Presidencies that end in death, especially death by assassination, become accounts of promise cut short, of how the mighty are fallen, and are dominated by the powerful closing images of the funeral cortege and a mourning nation. The worst-case scenario, more troubling even than death, is that of impeachment, of being dishonored in office. The vast majority of the accounts in our political anthology, however, tell of careers compromised by either mediocrity or electoral defeat, in which incumbents depart without any sense that their leaving matters much one way or the other.

While imminent departure gives a certain weight to a president's last words in office, relatively few have chosen to exploit that opportunity. Most have simply let attention shift to their successors with little more than a nod toward Congress in their final annual message. For a long time the only exceptions were heroes of the success story, Washington and Jackson, who used the authority of their good fortune to instruct the nation. But increasingly those favored few have been joined by presidents (following the lead of Andrew Johnson) who, having fared less well, have tried at the end to explain themselves, to represent the best in their service, and to contemplate the meaning of their fate. Whatever the form or the message, farewell remarks provide the last official opportunity for presidential eloquence.

MOVING TO THE MANSIONS OF REST

Both George Washington and Andrew Jackson seemed to be saying in their farewells a more ultimate goodbye, each suggesting that the close of his career and the end of his life were very nearly coincidental. "My own race is nearly run," Jackson said; "advanced age and failing health warn me that before long I must pass beyond the reach of human events and cease to feel the vicissitudes of human affairs" (MP, 4:1527). Washington's mortality also lay heavily on his final message, and he ended with the request that his country forgive the errors of his administration, "that, after forty-five years of my life dedicated to its service with an upright zeal, the faults of incompetent abilities will be consigned to oblivion, as myself must soon be to the mansions of rest" (MP, 1:216).

More typically, outgoing presidents have spoken as less dramatic retirees, anticipating a quiet period in their lives, with long-awaited time for home and family. Responding to a testimonial sent from Congress, John Adams—himself not far removed in age from either Washington or Jackson at the time of their farewells—accepted the legislature's applause "after the close of the last scene of the last act of my political drama," then continued, "There is now no greater felicity remaining for me to hope or desire, than to pass the remainder of my days in repose, in an undisturbed participation of the common privileges of our fellow-citizens under your protection."[1] Those remaining days added up to more than a quarter of a century.

Ulysses Grant was more abrupt. In his eighth Annual Message he concluded: "With the present term of Congress my official life terminates. It is not probable that public affairs will ever again receive attention from me further than as a citizen of the Republic" (MP, 9:4367). Only in his mid-fifties at the close of his second term, those words spoke of neither death nor retirement—even if his use of "terminates" sounded a bit ominous. Mostly he seemed intent on denying sentimental attachment to either Congress or the presidency.

Except for Andrew Jackson, who fancied himself a second Washington, and the much-maligned Andrew Johnson, no nineteenth-century president followed George Washington's example of issuing a formal farewell message to the nation. Thomas Jefferson saw the need only for a polite paragraph at the close of his final State of the Union message, a word of "sincere gratitude" to the legislators for their "many indulgences" in the past and a request for one more in the future. "In the transaction of . . . business I cannot have escaped error. It is incident to our imperfect nature. But I may say with truth my errors have been of the understanding, not of intention, and that the advancement of their [the people's] rights and interests has been the constant motive for every measure." For an imperfect "understanding" and for being human he "solicited" their final "indulgence" (MP, 1:444).

Jefferson's immediate successors continued his example of a few lines added to the final annual message. Madison departed with words of appreciation and affection for his countrymen, indulging "the proud reflection that the American people have reached in safety and success their fortieth year as an independent nation" (MP, 2:564) and praising the Constitution he had so greatly influenced. Monroe offered similar sentiments: "Having commenced my service in early youth and continued it since with few and short intervals, I have witnessed the great difficulties to which our Union has been exposed, and admired the virtue and intelligence with which they have been surmounted" (MP, 2:832–33).

The Virginians who occupied the White House from 1801 through 1824 all typified the successful presidency and closed their electoral careers without any apparent need to justify themselves, offering only a polite goodbye to the legislature. A few of their less distinguished successors followed their example. John Tyler, who had succeeded Harrison, was not the Whig candidate in 1844, but he left office congratulating Congress on the country's present "state of prosperity" and suggesting that the continuation of this happy condition would be "closely connected with the honor, glory, and still more enlarged prosperity" that would come with Congress's "sanction" of measures recently placed before it (MP, 5:2205). The last seems to have been a curiously oblique endorsement of Texas's annexation, an action that the Whig nominee, Henry Clay, opposed.

James K. Polk, who—though popular—had not sought reelection, left his reputation to history but with a parting statement that suggested some slight anxiety as to what that judgment might be. "The impartial arbitrament of enlightened public opinion present and future, will determine how far the public policy I have maintained and the measures I have . . . recommended may have tended to advance or retard the public prosperity at home or to elevate or depress the estimate of our national character abroad" (MP, 6:2520).

Millard Fillmore, elected with the Mexican War hero Zachary Taylor, whose term he completed, was displaced from the 1852 Whig ticket by another hero of that war, Winfield Scott. Fillmore left office humbly but unchastened, reminding Congress at the close of his last annual message that the country owed its blessings "to the happy Constitution and Government which were bequeathed to us by our fathers, and which it is our sacred duty to transmit in all their integrity to our children." Accepting his modest role in that process, he recalled that his coming to office was "unexpected" and that he "entered upon its arduous duties with extreme diffidence." Now, at the end of his stewardship, he said, "I claim only to have discharged them to the best of an humble ability, with a single eye to the public good, and it is with devout gratitude in retiring from office that I leave the country in a state of peace and prosperity" (MP, 6:2718).

Chester Arthur offered a similarly constrained estimate of his service when he left office in 1885. He too (following the assassination of James Garfield) had moved into the White House through vice presidential succession. When Republicans turned to James Blaine in 1884 and were then defeated by the Cleveland ticket, Arthur left quietly, pausing only to thank legislators for "their unfailing courtesy and . . . harmonious cooperation" and to acknowledge the support of his "fellow citizens" (MP, 10:4841).

FOR THE SAKE OF MY SUCCESSOR

In 1953 Harry Truman offered a formal farewell address—following the example of Washington, Jackson, and Andrew Johnson, but a tradition ignored since 1869—a gesture repeated by nearly all retiring presidents since.[2] Truman was characteristically direct in his final address, saying of his personal plans only, "A short time after the new President takes his oath of office, I will be on the train going back home to Independence, Missouri." Though hardly leaving office on a wave of national affection, he marked his departure with a simple but generous effort at closure, delivering to his countrymen "a good object lesson in democracy," the very thing he told them they would observe in Eisenhower's swearing in. Truman avoided personal sentiment and partisanship and celebrated instead the peaceful transfer of power—even though that meant turning the executive office over to the opposing party. "Inauguration Day," he declared, "will be a great demonstration of our democratic process. I am glad to be a part of it—glad to wish General Eisenhower all possible success as he begins his term—glad the whole world will have a chance to see how simply and how peacefully our American system transfers the vast power of the Presidency from my hands to his" (PP, Truman, 1952–53:1197).

Every bit as colloquial as Reagan would be in his farewell, Truman nevertheless was at his most presidential as he brought his own time in office to a close. He set aside "political statement" and "policy announcements" in order to serve the office he was about to relinquish. He gave his listeners a brief lesson on the presidency and told them what had taken place during his tenure and "at his desk" in a manner that eased the way for his successor.

The greater part of the President's job is to make decisions—big ones and small ones, dozens of them almost every day. The papers may circulate around the Government for awhile but they finally reach this desk. And then there's no place else for them to go. The President—whoever he is— has to decide. He can't pass the buck to anybody. No one else can do the deciding for him. That's his job.

Truman then summarized his eight-year administration, starting with FDR's death and continuing through the Korean conflict, which remained unsettled even as he spoke. "I want you to realize," he said,

> how big a job, how hard a job, it is—not for my sake, because I am stepping out of it—but for the sake of my successor. He needs the understanding and the help of every citizen. It is not enough for you to come out once every four years and vote for a candidate, and then go back home and say, "Well, I've done my part, now let the new President do the worrying." He can't do the job alone.
>
> Regardless of your politics, whether you are Republican or Democrat, your fate is tied up with what is done here in this room. The President is President of the whole country. We must give him our support as citizens of the United States. He will have mine, and I want you to give him yours. (PP, Truman, 1953:1198–99)

An element of self-justification is discernible in all this, but Truman nevertheless insisted that he was surveying his own tenure with an eye to ongoing concerns and dangers, describing his own hard decisions—to drop atomic bombs on Japan, to take up arms in Korea—less to defend his own work than to build sympathetic support for Eisenhower as the new president shouldered the burden. He described a hopeful future, not as evidence of personal accomplishment but in support of "a deep and abiding faith in the destiny of free men."

Enlarging upon the modest goodbyes of Fillmore and Arthur, Truman made it clear that he was neither humbled by his unpopularity nor overly proud of personal accomplishment. "When Franklin Roosevelt died," he remembered, "I felt there must be a million men better qualified than I to take up the Presidential task. But the work was mine to do, and I had to do it. And I have tried to give it everything that was in me."

Though Truman had served nearly two full terms, his ratings in the polls were low and his party had been rejected in the recent election. As a result he did not speak with the authority of a revered Washington, as Eisenhower would eight years later. He offered only the relatively simple lessons he had learned. Among his successors, Lyndon Johnson, Gerald Ford, and Jimmy Carter spoke after more direct and personal public rejections. Both Johnson and Ford left office with personal messages of closure that placed their presidencies in the context of larger Washington careers, messages that suggested an acceptance of their fate.

A LACK OF RESOLUTION

Appearing before the legislature in 1969 to give his final *State of the Union,* Johnson treated the occasion as a homecoming. "Now my friends in Congress," he said,

> I want to conclude with a few very personal words to you.
>
> I rejected and rejected and then finally accepted the congressional leadership's invitation to come here to speak this farewell to you in person tonight.
>
> I did that for two reasons. One was philosophical. I wanted to give you my judgment, as I saw it, on some of the issues before our Nation, as I view them, before I leave.
>
> The other was just pure sentimental. Most all of my life as a public official has been spent here in this building. For 38 years—since I worked in that gallery as a doorkeeper in the House of Representatives—I have known these halls, and I have known most of the men pretty well who walked them.
>
> I know the questions you face. I know the conflicts that you endure. I know the ideals that you seek to serve. (PP, Johnson, 1968–69:1269)

In relating his subsequent career in the executive branch, where Johnson never seemed fully at home, he suggested that it was the legislature that had given him solace during times of "turbulence and doubt, and fear and hate." During the difficult recent months, he said, he had "been sustained by my faith in representative democracy—a faith that I had learned here in this Capitol Building as an employee and as a Congressman and as a Senator."

Johnson's Washington farewell, understandably, was more concerned with the legislature than the presidency. But in a separate goodbye in New York City he discussed his impending retirement from another perspective. "Perhaps," he told that gathering,

> the time will come for Mrs. Johnson and myself, perhaps some long reflective moment when we are walking along the banks of the Pedernales ... we can look back upon the majesty and the splendor of the Presidency, and I guess we will find it very hard to believe that I ever occupied that office.
>
> But tonight I want to say this to my good and lasting friends who have come here—I want to say beyond any peradventure of a doubt; I know that I have been here. (p. 1260)

That "doubt" should be so oddly emphasized—"peradventure of a doubt"—suggested the bittersweet nature of Johnson's parting and the profound ambivalence it involved.

Gerald Ford, though he left Washington after a political defeat, remained the object of much good feeling. Like Johnson's, his own affection for government was centered in the Congress. "It is not easy to end these remarks," he told the legislature at the close of his final State of the Union address.

> In this Chamber, along with some of you, I have experienced many, many of the highlights of my life. It was here that I stood 28 years ago with my freshman colleagues, as Speaker Sam Rayburn administered the oath. I see some of you now—Charlie Bennett, Dick Bolling, Carl Perkins, Pete Rodino, Harley Staggers, Tom Steed, Sid Yates, Clem Zablocki—and I remember those who have gone to their rest. It was here we waged many, many a lively battle—won some, lost some, but always remaining friends. It was here, surrounded by such friends, that the distinguished Chief Justice swore me in as Vice President on December 6, 1973. It was here I returned 8 months later as your President to ask not for a honeymoon, but for a good marriage.
>
> I will always treasure those memories and your many, many kindnesses. I thank you for them all. (PP, Ford, 1976–77:1057)

Recalling both his distinguished career in the legislature and the years that followed, Ford reminded his congressional audience that, unique among America's presidents, he had never been elected to any position in national government other than his seat in the House, that he had been appointed vice president to fill Spiro Agnew's unexpired term and then had succeeded Nixon when Nixon resigned. In fact, under the terms of the Twenty-fifth Amendment, Ford had been voted into the vice presidency by the Congress following nomination by then President Nixon. Thus, more even than Lyndon Johnson, Gerald Ford found his career inseparable from the legislature. Even when he had moved to the executive branch, it had been the confidence of Congress and not the electorate that promoted him.

Having spent the last year of his term enmeshed in the Iranian hostage crisis, Jimmy Carter could not leave office with any pretense of resolution so long as the captives remained in Iran. This he admitted in his closing remarks:

> During the next few days I will work hard to make sure that the transition from myself to the next President is a good one, that the American people are served well. And I will continue, as I have for the past 14 months, to work and pray for the well-being of the American hostages held in Iran. I can't predict yet what will happen, but I hope you will join me in my constant prayer for their freedom. (PP, Carter, 1980–81:2893)

Closure, Carter suggested, could come only with word of the Americans' release. So personal had he allowed that crisis to become, with so much of his presidency and his identity invested in the fate of the captives, he could not pretend to any satisfying conclusion. Nor could he escape the judgment that he, in daily White House reports, had called down upon his own head. More than the political defeat (to which the hostage crisis had greatly contributed), Carter made the release of the captives the true close of his presidency. That resolution—the one he clearly hoped would come even in the last minutes of his term—he was denied.

Although the Iranian crisis did not compare to Lyndon Johnson's Vietnam humiliation ("I regret more than any of you know that it has not been possible to restore peace to South Vietnam," he had admitted to Congress), the presidency was the whole of Carter's Washington experience, and at its conclusion he could not stand before friends on the hill and recall better times, allowing nostalgia to be his final word. Instead of turning to the past for consolation, he looked to the possibility of future service. "As I return home to the South," he concluded, where I was born and raised, I look forward to the opportunity to reflect and further to assess, I hope with accuracy, the circumstances of our times. I intend to give our new President my support, and I intend to work as a citizen, as I've worked here in this office as President, for the values this Nation was founded to secure.

Carter had opened his remarks by declaring that he was laying down this office "to take up once more the only title in our democracy superior to that of President, the title of citizen."[3] In concluding he suggested that in that role he would continue to serve the principal concerns of his presidency: human rights and international reconciliation. The closure denied him by defeat at home and irresolution in Iran he promised to pursue in a postpresidential career.

NOT BAD AT ALL

Ronald Reagan, concluding one of the few presidencies that has met the criteria for an executive "success" story, deviated from the pattern followed by the other members of that exclusive club. He spoke neither solemnly nor to the ages, but familiarly and colloquially. Lamenting that in office "you're always somewhat apart," speeding by "in a car someone else is driving and seeing the people through tinted glass," he remarked on how he had "wanted to stop, and reach out from behind the glass, and connect." Then he added, "maybe I can do a little of that tonight."

In some respects his speech resembled Truman's, but while Truman outlined the work of the presidency, Reagan focused on its emotions. Rather than catalog the contents of his "desk," Reagan listed the things to be seen from the White House windows, a postcard survey of Washington with a few more "prosaic things" thrown in—"the grass on the banks [of the Potomac], the morning traffic as people make their way to work, now and then a sailboat on the river" (PP, Reagan, 1989:1719). Where Truman emphasized the burden of the office, Reagan emphasized its mundane pleasures.

But more than any previous farewell, this was one of celebration and personal triumph. Typically sentimental, his message began with a hint of lovers parting—"we have been together eight years now, and soon it will be time for me to go"—and continued through a series of anecdotes ("life has a way of reminding you of big things through small incidents") interspersed with a kind of self-congratulation in which Reagan did not usually indulge. Besides the listing of political and military triumphs, "from Grenada to the Washington and Moscow summits, from the recession of '81–'82 to the expansion that began in late '82 and continues to this day," there were more idiosyncratic assertions of self. Recalling his first economic summit, he said, "I sat there like the new kid in school and listened, and it was all François this and Helmut that. They dropped titles and spoke to one another on a first-name basis. At one point I sort of leaned in and said, 'My name's Ron.'" Two years later, "another economic summit," and the same exclusive crowd realized who was in their midst: "All of a sudden just for a moment I saw that everyone was looking at me." Silent, he implied, with admiration and awe, they finally asked the "kid" they had once ignored to tell them about the "American miracle" he had performed.

The self-referential nature of Reagan's remarks continued as he mentioned, first, the "nickname" he had won, that of "The Great Communicator," and then what "they call . . . the Reagan Revolution." And though each time he offered a demurrer ("I wasn't a great communicator, but I communicated great things"; "the Reagan Revolution for me . . . always seemed more like The Great Rediscovery"), it was a thin veil designed to enhance rather than conceal his importance. "We meant to change a nation, and instead we changed the world," he announced, implying a victory over his liberal critics at home, the international forces of communism, and even the Françoises and Helmuts of Europe.

Late in his speech Reagan acknowledged previous messages of this genre. "Finally, he said, "there is a great tradition of warnings in Presidential farewells, and I've got one that's been on my mind for some time." Having already reiterated the political themes of his administration—tax cuts, free market capitalism, a strong military—he turned to "an informed patriotism." "Those of us who are over 35 or so years of age," he reported, "grew up in a different America," one in which "we absorbed, almost in the air, a love of country and an appreciation of its institutions." This, he insisted, "we" gained at school, from neighbors "who lost someone at Anzio," from popular culture, and parents who had not yet sunk into doubt as to whether "an unambivalent appreciation of America is the right thing to teach modern children." To recover the old certainty he called for the teaching of an American history "based not on what's in fashion, but what's important: Why the pilgrims came here, who Jimmy Doolittle was, and what those 30 seconds over Tokyo meant." Asserting that in America "all great change . . . begins at the dinner table," he instructed "children, if your parents haven't been teaching you what it means to be an American—let 'em know and nail 'em on it." And in an odd aside he added, "That would be a very American thing to do" (p. 1722).

In his eagerness to assert a solidarity with his audience, not to stand "apart," Reagan rejected the role of statesman, of the paternal figure for whom self-justification is no longer necessary. His tone was combative, and his "we" and "they" seemed a more partisan distinction than any Truman drew, implying an American "them" still to be "nailed." Thus he recruited "Reagan's Regiments" for the "Bush Brigades."

The wisdom he offered was conventional, just as the history he praised was that of cultural cliché, the work of screenwriters, not scholars. The great achievement of the speech was the way in which it made Reagan seem no different from the ordinary people to whom he was speaking; its weakness, in contrast to that of the equally ordinary Truman, was its suggestion that even with the unique opportunities given to him, when he came to the end of his term he had nothing to tell them that they didn't already know.

He ended, "My friends," clearly identifying his audience throughout, "We did it"—and a movie-style fadeout: "all in all, not bad. Not bad at all. And so goodbye."[4] Three days later, in his last radio address, he seemed more the familiar Reagan, modest and conciliatory, playing out his cowboy role with the simple declaration, "Nancy and I will head back to the ranch" (pp. 1735–36).

SURRENDERING OFFICE

The presidential stories that most grip the public imagination and that most inspire and frighten White House occupants are not the modest muddling through of an Arthur or a Ford but the extremes of success and failure. On one hand there is the tragic account in which Union fails, in which things do not at last hold together, and alternatively there is the "comedy" of wholeness, the story of Union and coherence affirmed. Truman in his simple homily argued the latter no matter how the polls read or how contemporaries characterized his presidency. And so in their own troubled fashion did Ford, Carter, and LBJ. All suggested, ironically, that defeat was only personal and not systemic or even, finally, all that important. But the temptation to dichotomize, combined with a taste for political melodrama, generates a popular polarity with Mount Rushmore at one end and impeachment at the other. This last scenario we have only approached, and then only twice—when Andrew Johnson and Richard Nixon moved out of the White House embarrassed by congressional efforts to evict them.

Andrew Johnson had been chosen as Lincoln's 1864 running mate because he was a pro-war Democrat from Tennessee who had served as military governor of that state from 1862 through 1864. That balancing of the ticket was designed to encourage a coalition that could defeat the Democrats and their nominee, General George McClellan, who called for an immediate end to military action and a negotiated peace. At the other extreme radicals in the Republican party suspected that Lincoln was insufficiently anti-Southern and overly inclined toward leniency. With his assassination and Johnson's succession, they found an easy target for their indignation and their ambition.

Eager to reincorporate the rebel states as quickly as possible, Johnson resisted both Congress's punitive actions and its efforts to grant suffrage to all freed slaves regardless of qualification. He vetoed legislation like the Freedman's Bureau bill (giving the military authority over persons accused of depriving former slaves of their civil rights), the Reconstruction Acts (dividing the Southern states into military districts with army commanders overseeing the electoral process), and the Tenure of Office Act (prohibiting the president from removing any officials without the consent of the Senate). Of his twenty-nine vetoes, Congress succeeded in overriding fifteen. When, in 1868, in violation of the Tenure of Office Act, Johnson fired Secretary of War Edwin M. Stanton, the House of Representatives voted to impeach him for "high crimes and misdemeanors." After his trial before the Senate he was acquitted when the vote fell one short of the two-thirds necessary for conviction.[5] The narrowness of his escape and his constant vilification by the Northern press had, not surprisingly, wounded Johnson deeply, and just as he had taken his case to the people in an ill-conceived 1866 speaking tour, so he used his departure from office as an opportunity to deliver his complaint once more to the public.

Johnson's speech, while offered as public instruction, was a personal and frequently angry defense of his own service and character. "In surrendering the high office to which I was called four years ago, at a memorable and terrible crisis," he began,

> it is my privilege, I trust, to say to the people of the United States a few parting words in vindication of an official course so ceaselessly assailed and aspersed by political leaders, to whose plans and wishes my policy to restore the Union has been obnoxious.[6]

The sardonic "I trust," especially when it so closely followed "surrendering," struck at the presumption of a Congress that, he argued, had done all it could to undermine executive authority, and mimicked the beggarly role to which the presidency had been reduced. Thus in opening he suggested an office circumscribed, a chief executive who must seek permission for the most basic "privileges." What followed was a lengthy indictment of the congressional radicals and their contemptuous treatment of both the executive office and the Union.

> In a period of difficulty and turmoil almost without precedent in the history of any people, consequent upon the closing scenes of a great rebellion and the assassination of the then President, it was perhaps too much on my part to expect of devoted partisans who rode on the waves of excitement, which at that time swept all before them, the degree of toleration and magnanimity which I sought to recommend and enforce and which I believe in good time would have advanced us infinitely farther on the road to permanent peace and prosperity than we have thus far attained.

Johnson simultaneously condemned his opponents as "partisans" who obstructed the cause of peace and union and defended his own administration as having erred only in thinking too highly of other political leaders.

Speaking with an indignation that presumed to be both righteous and provoked—by wrongs not to him alone but to the Constitution that he had sworn to uphold and the people whom that Constitution protects ("It has been clearly demonstrated by recent occurrences that encroachments upon the Constitution cannot be prevented by the President, however devoted or determined.")—the departing president presented his case to future generations, most especially to the young who had grown to adulthood "amid the cannon and the din of arms" and those even younger who were "just beginning to use the ballot box." The latter, he trusted, would exercise their new vote to demand that "their representatives . . . observe all the restraints which the people, in adopting the Constitution, intended to impose on party excess." The former, "who [after the war] quietly returned to the farms, the factories and the schools of the land," he offered as alternative examples to those currently in political power who refused to allow the restoration of peacetime conditions and continued to agitate passions that had carried the young off to war in the first place. He called upon retiring veterans to prevent further violence, telling them they must be, as citizens, "jealous lest the civil be made subordinate to the military."

The overridden vetoes were especially galling to him—no wonder, since one of the bills passed over his objection provided the basis for his impeachment—and he briefly interrupted his praise of the beleaguered Constitution to admit that one defect "which under the aggressive tendency of the Legislative Department of the Government, may readily work its overthrow." His proposed remedy, since the "veto power is generally exercised upon constitutional grounds," was that all vetoed bills be reviewed by the Supreme Court and when ruled constitutional immediately become law and when ruled otherwise be discarded without congressional recourse.

Apart from recommending a veto amendment, Johnson proposed little and opposed much. Above all and in everything he said, he was—despite his protests to the contrary—attempting to redeem himself from the calumny of the past three years, and he could do so only by discrediting Congress. He defended his stewardship in the classic presidential language of oneness besieged by special interest. Like Washington before and Eisenhower after, though under a duress unique to him, he addressed the difficult matter of returning to "normalcy" in the aftermath of war. As Commander-in-Chief at the war's end of nearly a million men in arms, Johnson implied he could have used that extraordinary authority to strengthen his executive hand, but he reminded that he had willingly relinquished that advantage: "One of my first acts was to disband and restore to the vocations of civil life this immense host and to divest myself so far as I could of the unparalleled powers then incident to the office and the times."

There had been those who advised him to keep the army intact, to send it south to drive the French out of Mexico, thereby uniting Americans against a foreign enemy. He had chosen instead to reduce the army and to yield his own war powers. "Let the people whom I am addressing from the Presidential chair during the closing hours of a laborious term," he urged, "consider how different would have been their present condition had I yielded to the dazzling temptation of foreign conquest, of personal aggrandizement, and the desire to wield additional power." Then, defending his own conduct, which the legislature had declared criminal, he added, "Let them with justice consider that if I have not unduly magnified mine office, the public burdens have not been increased by my acts, and perhaps thousands or tens of thousands of lives sacrificed to visions of false glory." His "ambition" had not proved to be of "the criminal kind." But of course there were those who served such ambitions, and who sought "to grasp more and unwarranted powers" and pandered "to popular prejudice and party aims." It was Congress, he asserted, that had proved itself criminal, while he desired only "to restore the Union of the States, faithfully to execute the office of President, and to . . . preserve, protect, and defend the Constitution." With the recent impeachment proceedings in mind, he declared his innocence. "I cannot be censured," he argued, "if my efforts have been impeded in the interests of party faction."

An opportunistic legislature had seized the power he yielded in an effort to expand its own influence. Congress had, he argued, become the despot the president refused to be, and the main body of Johnson's remarks asserted a "catalogue of crimes" the legislature had committed. "After all dangers had passed," he charged, implying cowardice as well as abuse of power,

> when no armed foe remained—when a penitent people bowed their heads to the flag and renewed their allegiance to the Government of the United States, then it was that pretended patriots appeared before the nation and began to prate about the thousands of lives and millions of treasure sacrificed in the suppression of the rebellion. They have since persistently sought to inflame the prejudice engendered between the sections, to retard the restoration of peace and harmony, and by every means to

keep open and exposed to the poisonous breath of party passion the terrible wounds of a four years war.

The heavy alliteration—"a penitent people" juxtaposed to "pretending patriots" and their "prating"—the recurring "r"s as well as "p"s, both indulged and indicted the excesses he was attacking, and the heavy meter echoed the Declaration of Independence's iambic measure in identifying the crimes of the king. All those effects emphasized the extreme gravity of Johnson's accusation; the Republican Congress and its allies were betraying the war. "They have," he asserted in his most devastating indictment,

> prevented the return of peace and the restoration of the Union; in every way rendered delusive the purposes, promises and pledges by which the army was marshaled, treason rebuked and rebellion crushed: and made the liberties of the people, and the rights and powers of the President, objects of constant attack.

The refusal to allow the restoration of a full peace, along with the continued abuse of the defeated states for their already "expiated sins," Johnson argued, was accompanied by a growing congressional encroachment upon executive powers and a careful circumvention of the Supreme Court. Thus Johnson presented his own humiliation in the impeachment proceedings as but one part of a larger pattern in which a political party conspired for absolute control of the government.

Concluding a term in which his reputation and honor had been under continual attack, Andrew Johnson retired with as much show of statesmanship as he could muster, but still sounding the alarm and insisting that America's constitutional government had been challenged, first by war and then by victory.[7] Through it all he defended his faithfulness. "Calmly," he told his countrymen—contrasting that "calmness" with the inflammatory passions of partisan zealots—"Calmly reviewing my administration of the Government, I feel that (with a sense of accountability to God, having conscientiously endeavored to discharge my whole duty), I have nothing to regret."

Judged harshly by the dominant political forces of his time, he turned at last to the higher authorities of God and history. But Johnson offered little reassurance about the future of the Union and even hinted that the dissolution Congress represented would eventually provide the negative proof of his own good service. In the end the calm he praised eluded him, and the peace for which he hungered was nowhere apparent in his final remarks. A gifted if wholly self-educated orator (he never attended any school), Johnson was a stump speaker who knew how to handle the rough-and-tumble of Western politics, but in the presidency, with powerful and subtle enemies, he became a victim of his own style as well as his opinions. His opponents targeted not only his mild approach to reconstruction but also his vigorous and combative rhetoric, portraying him as emotionally unstable and out of control. In his farewell remarks he did little to dispel that image. The excessiveness of his alliteration was typical, and an extended comparison of the legislature's conduct with that of the Roman tyrant Sulla went on for more than thirty lines. The passion of his self-defense, as well as the frequency with which it was repeated, carried a desperate tone, and at the last, defending his record through a series of rhetorical questions, he seemed reduced to pleading. "I can," he asserted, "in all sincerity inquire, whom have I defrauded? Whom have I oppressed? or at whose hand have I received any bribe to blind my eyes therewith?" Rather than gain attention for the matter of his speech—his warning against an overreaching Congress, the appeal for a more conciliatory approach to reconstruction, and his defense of the constitutional limits placed on each branch of government—he called it to himself and the manner of his speaking. In the end the man who asked to be buried wrapped in the American flag and with a copy of the Constitution for a pillow could no more restrain himself than could his intemperate opponents.

LOSING ONESELF

The only other president to face the real possibility of impeachment, Richard Nixon, avoided such a confrontation by stepping down, and in doing so he combined his farewell with a resignation announcement. Then on the following day, in his final moments in the White House, he said goodbye to his personal staff in a speech that was, like his earlier official statement, broadcast on national television, and was so widely seen that it effectively merged with, if not superseded, his formal resignation address.

The resignation, on August 8, 1974, was unprecedented in American history, and even though the public in previous months had heard Nixon's desperate defense of his presidency and had watched a congressional probe into his involvement with the Watergate burglary and cover-up, it required some clearer explanation of why this had happened and what it meant. Vietnam had left a distrust of national leaders, further exacerbated when Nixon's vice president, Spiro Agnew, left office in October, 1973 to avoid prosecution for accepting bribes.[8] While Nixon's farewell messages provided a degree of closure, his prolonged and contradictory exit neither consoled nor reassured.

The resigning president, in the main body of his official remarks, recounted his successes, especially in foreign affairs. He had ended the war that destroyed Lyndon Johnson, had opened diplomatic contact with China, had improved relations with the Arab states, and had eased tensions with the Soviet Union. He offered those accomplishments both as personal vindication and as evidence that, despite its present demoralization, America's prospects had been brightened by his diplomatic accomplishments. "This is the 37th time I have spoken to you from this office where so many decisions have been made that shaped the history of this Nation," he began, reminding his audience just who he was and how long he had exercised the power of the executive office. "In all the decisions I have made in public life," he went on, "I have always tried to do what was best for the Nation" (PP, Nixon, 1974:626–27).

Nixon continued that theme of duty, of putting the country's interest before his personal desire, and three times in his opening paragraphs he asserted that his resignation was another instance of his self-denial: "I would have preferred to carry through to the finish, whatever the personal agony it would have involved, and my family unanimously urged me to do so. But the interests of the Nation must always come before any personal consideration." And a little farther on: "I might not have the support of the Congress that I would consider necessary to back the very difficult decisions and carry out the duties of this office in the way the interests of the Nation will require." Then once more, even more emphatically and personally: "I have never been a quitter. To leave office before my term is completed is abhorrent to every instinct in my body. But as President I must put the interests of America first." Unspoken was the very real threat of impeachment, but the repeated reference to his lack of support—euphemistically described as his not having "a strong enough political base in the Congress"—diverted the issue from abuse of presidential power to a matter of practical politics, of clout and influence. When he declared in opening his remarks that "[t]hroughout the long and difficult period of Watergate, I have felt it was my duty to persevere," he converted the catchword for his scandal into a segment of time; Watergate became merely a label, not a criminal act or a presidential cover-up.

Nixon's strategy in his resignation/farewell address was consistent with the general psychodrama he had made of his entire political life, one revolving around the notion of crisis, which he elaborated in his 1962 book, *Six Crises*. In the late 1940s and early 1950s the crisis was external, and he began his career as a kind of alarm bell, awakening the populace to the threat of domestic communism. But as his career continued, his concept of crisis became internal, personal. In his watchdog role he was aggressive and abrasive, doing what needed to be done in the face of national peril. In the second context—and the two were never wholly distinguishable—it was always Nixon who was the target, Nixon who was imperiled, and in that role he could often become obsequious. The famous "Checkers" speech, in which as the nominee for vice president he responded to charges of making personal use of a slush fund, presented a very different persona from the brash young Red hunter doing battle against powerful and insidious forces. Exchanging bravado for pathos, it introduced instead a vulnerable family man who was himself recklessly accused.

Six Crises examined a series of dramatic moments in Nixon's career ("The Hiss Case," "The Fund," "The Heart Attack," "Caracas," "Khrushchev," "The Campaign of 1960"). In his recollections he blurred not only the distinction between public and private, between Nixon and America, but also the very meaning of "crisis." Of the six events on which Nixon focused, only two represented a conventional personal crisis. His reputation threatened by scandal and his political career at risk, what he oddly entitled "The Fund" (making it somehow parallel to "The Hiss Case" and "The Heart Attack"—the latter belonging not to him but to Eisenhower) clearly marked a trauma deserving of the title. Perhaps, too, we would accept that the 1960 presidential "defeat" might also qualify, but the other four sections concern events that might more appropriately be labeled "challenges" or "opportunities."[9]

The concept of "crisis," no matter how fuzzy his definition, provided the leitmotif of Nixon's career and his sense of identity. The wariness inherent in his political personality, his tendency to be ingratiating on one hand and contemptuous on the other, presumed the constant presence of danger. Sometimes his suspicions seemed evidence merely of an acute insecurity, at other moments paranoia, an apprehension of dark intentions directed toward his person from some mysterious source.

Quite remarkably Nixon elaborated his sense of always being at risk into a theory of personality that explained his peculiar emphasis on crisis. "We often hear it said," he wrote, "that truly 'big' men are at their best in handling big affairs, and that they falter and fail when confronted with petty irritations—with crises which are, in other words, essentially personal" (*Six Crises*, p. xiv). No one who watched Nixon's political career could doubt his deep and abiding fear of being merely a small man; the point of his *Six Crises* was to prove that, under the test of fire, he *was* a "big" man and, by implication, when he "failed" in his life it was in matters that were "petty," "essentially personal."

Nixon pushed his thesis further, insisting not only that men prove their "bigness" in confronting crises but also that they develop an addiction to these experiences and seek them out. Asking ". . . does a 'man' enjoy crisis?" he continued,

> I certainly did not enjoy the ones described in this book in the sense that they were "fun." And yet, life is surely more than simply the search for enjoyment in the popular sense. We are all tempted to stay on the sidelines, to live like vegetables, to concentrate all our efforts on living at greater leisure, living longer, and leaving behind a bigger estate. But meeting crisis involves creativity. It engages all a man's talents. When he looks back on life, he has to answer the question: did he live up to his capabilities as fully as he could? Or were only part of his abilities called into action? (p. xvi)

But then the language shifts away from "enjoyment" and "creativity" and toward morality, with Nixon implying that true crisis comes from losing oneself in a just cause:

> A man who has never lost himself in a cause bigger than himself has missed one of life's mountaintop experiences. Only in losing himself does

he find himself. Only then does he discover all the latent strengths he never knew he had and which otherwise would have remained dormant.

Crisis can indeed be agony. But it is the exquisite agony which a man might not want to experience again—and yet would not for the world have missed. (p. xvi)

Here, mixed with an enthusiasm for conventional "manliness," the stuff of military heroism and athletic accomplishment, is inserted the antithetical paradigm of the New Testament, one that rejects conventional notions of honor for humility, substitutes self-sacrifice for conquest, and sides with the lowly rather than the mighty.

Nixon's ideal of the "big man" asserted a concept of personal justification based on works. In this context crisis tests mettle and establishes worth, and those who pass the test are properly rewarded with the admiration of others. That was Teddy Roosevelt's view too, a Horatio Alger formula in which greatness is a matter of character proved through accomplishment, in which "big" men can be justifiably proud of honors they both win *and* deserve. But to lose is to be proved small, diminished in value as well as significance, and while Teddy Roosevelt seemed always to take his "greatness" for granted, Nixon's obsession with the issue suggested a deep fear that he was, despite his protests, a small man.

His reference to a contrary version of personal justification based on grace, the ultimate meaning of finding oneself by losing oneself, suggested an alternative drawn from his Quaker background, one in which individuals do not save themselves but are redeemed through God's unqualified love. But that was not the direction Nixon turned. Rather he made losing oneself another kind of work, a challenge that further demonstrates individual accomplishment and deserving. He, like Theodore Roosevelt, seemed to regard grace as a feminine quality, associated in his farewell remarks with his saintly mother. He refused to accept for himself even the "how you play the game" compromise, insisting that while "[h]ow you play the game does count . . . one must put top consideration on the will, the desire, and the determination to win" (*Six Crises*, p. 402).

In April and again in August 1973 he had addressed the nation concerning the Watergate burglary. On both occasions he blamed any illegal activities on "overzealous" individuals exercising bad judgment in the heat of a campaign. He minimized the significance of the misconduct and suggested that the scandal involved precisely the sort of petty issue that, as he had noted in *Six Crises*, "big" men are inclined to mishandle. Far from being himself involved, he had, he insisted, been unaware of the break-in, so busy was he with the responsibilities of his high office.

In August 1974 Nixon arrived at his ultimate crisis. In his effort to avoid being finally proved small, he argued his greatness and insisted he was "losing" himself in a transcendent cause. He was, he claimed, resigning to save the nation from its own torment and to allow it to heal. He was resigning so that Americans could "put the bitterness and divisions of the recent past behind us and . . . rediscover those shared ideals that lie at the heart of our strength and unity as a great and as a free people" (PP, Nixon, 1974:627). His was, he insisted, an act of self-sacrifice. Were self-interest his guide, he would remain in the fight until he had prevailed, until his vindication. But he was choosing the other path, was—in short—a man losing "himself in a cause bigger than himself." "There is one cause above all," he told his television audience, "to which I have been devoted and to which I shall always be devoted for as long as I live." That cause was "peace among nations." "This, more than anything, is what I hoped to achieve when I sought the Presidency" (p. 629). And this, he suggested, his resignation, in some oblique way, could serve.

In his last tormented hours in office Nixon perversely turned to Teddy Roosevelt for emotional support, calling upon him not once but twice. The first mention came in the official resignation speech:

> Sometimes I have succeeded and sometimes I have failed, but always I have taken heart from what Theodore Roosevelt once said about the man in the arena, "whose face is marred by dust and sweat and blood, who strives valiantly, who errs and comes [up] short again and again because there is no effort without error and shortcoming, but who does actually strive to do the deed, who knows the great enthusiasms, the great devotions, who spends himself in a worthy cause, who at the best knows in the end the triumphs of high achievements and who at the worst, if he fails, at least fails while daring greatly" (p. 629).

In this revisionist explanation of his fall, the resigning president offered himself as a "bloody but unbowed" romantic hero. It was not Watergate but the *Man of La Mancha*, where "shortcoming" testifies—ironically—

to greatness (of both "enthusiasm" and "devotion"). That was the stuff of gladiators in the arena of noble cause, not the amateurish cover-up of a bungled burglary that aspired to nothing more than insider information on a campaign whose outcome was already assured. Here, too, was the effort to blur the biblical business of finding oneself through losing oneself, of the last being made first and the defeated named the victor: quixotic to the end, both Christ and a parody of Christ, both the chivalric hero and that hero's caricature.

But more striking was Nixon's second reference to Teddy Roosevelt, this one in the personal farewell to staff and Cabinet. In those remarks, disjointed and maudlin, the outgoing president tried to reassure the people who had shared in the work of his administration, telling them they could be proud of their service, defending them against the charges that had destroyed him:

> I am proud of our White House Staff. As I pointed out last night [in the resignation speech], sure, we have done some things wrong in this Administration, and the top man always takes the responsibility, and I have never ducked it. But I want to say one thing: We can be proud of it—5½ years. No man or no woman came into this Administration and left it with more of this world's goods than when he came in. No man or no woman ever profited at the public expense or the public till. That tells something about you.
>
> Mistakes, yes. But for personal gain, never. You did what you believed in. Sometimes right, sometimes wrong. And I only wish I were a wealthy man—at the present time, I have got to find a way to pay my taxes—and if I were, I would like to recompense you for the sacrifices that all of you have made to serve in government. (pp. 630–31)

Typically ambiguous, Nixon's farewell to those who served him posed as praise but was, in fact, an effort to implicate them. The "I" became "we" and then "you." "I" took the blame, "we" can be proud," "you" made mistakes. Then, as a sort of surrogate taking on the nation's debt, the president expressed the longing to pay them, financially, out of his own substance, all the while suggesting that, morally and politically, he had made precisely this sacrifice for them: He had resigned over the failures of subordinates. They had served him in his presidency, but in the end he became—on their behalf—the suffering servant. Here once more was the perennial Nixon, troubled by his smallness (yet emphasizing it in his pursuit of pathos)—"I only wish that I were a wealthy man," "I have got to find a way to pay my taxes"—and asserting his largeness, "the top man" who lays down his career for his country and his staff.

The poignant fact of the matter was that the Nixon who addressed his loyalists on that last day in the White House could not distinguish between large and small, first and last, humility and pride. Upstairs, earlier—or so he reported to his executive aides—he had said goodbye to the personal staff, the housekeepers of the executive mansion, "you know, those who serve here in the White house day in and day out." Then, in an odd digression, Nixon began talking about the mansion itself, diminishing it—"This isn't the biggest house. . . . This isn't the finest house"—through comparison to the "great houses of the world," older ones, housing priceless art treasures. "But," he concluded, "this is the best house," best because of the people who serve in it, the little people who are its "great heart."

> We said goodbye to them upstairs. But they are really great. And I recall after so many times I have made speeches, and some of them pretty tough, yet, I always come back, or after a hard day—and my days usually have run rather long—I would always get a lift from them, because I might be a little down but they always smiled. (p. 631)

To those house servants, those who were there when Nixon arrived and would serve his successor, he was Mr. President, doing important work, making "tough" speeches. And always the praise returned to him; "they are really great" because they serve the "big man" who, "after a hard day" "always comes back."

Strangely, when the departing president introduced the subject of his parents, he portrayed them as just such people as the personal staff, and in that context he seemed to distance himself from the "big" people. "I remember my old man," he told his audience. "I think that they would have called him sort of a little man, common man." The first "they" of his remarks had been the upstairs help; this second "they" referred to the powerful forces that Nixon had always sensed shadowing him, people scornful of his intellectual skills ("I am not educated, but I do read books"), those forever intent on exposing his smallness. This "they" would regard his father with contempt for being only a streetcar motorman and a lemon farmer, and—the implication followed—for being poor: "It was the poorest lemon ranch in California, I can assure you. He sold it before *they* found oil on it" (emphasis added). But like the White House help, he too "was a great man, because he did his job, and every job counts up to the hilt, regardless of what happens."

Nixon then presented his mother as—far from common—"a saint" who nursed dying boys, two of her sons among them, but saint or not, "nobody will ever write a book, probably" about her. Implicit here, of course, was that the "nobody" belonged to the "they" that call his father "little" and that found the oil after the Nixons sold the farm. But his mother's greatness came from criteria other than worldly success, came rather from self-sacrifice, from being "last."

And here again, he turned to Teddy Roosevelt, but in a far different mood from the "Invictus" atmosphere of the previous day. This time Nixon adopted a storytelling tone and told a sentimental fairy tale that began with the hero as "a young man. He was a young lawyer in New York. He had married a beautiful girl, and they had a lovely daughter, and then suddenly she died, and this is what he wrote. This was in his diary." What followed was a long quotation from the young Teddy Roosevelt, a description of his despair after the death of his first wife, a passage that concludes, "And when my heart's dearest died, the light went out of my life forever." That she died "when she had just become a mother," and she too was called saintly, pointed back to the eulogized Nixon mother. Indirect and maudlin as the anecdote was, the loss behind all those other losses, the one that inspired the stream of illogical and inappropriate recollections, was that of Nixon's presidency. At least a part of him wanted his situation to be viewed as the sort of fairy tale he had projected onto Teddy Roosevelt's story, suggesting that the presidency had been some fair maid, pure and joyous, and he the loving suitor, deserving if a bit besmirched.

He told his White House audience, "That was T.R. in his twenties," and then Nixon abruptly shifted the moral of the story:

He thought the light had gone from his life forever—but he went on. And he not only became President but as an ex-President, he served his country, always in the arena, tempestuous, strong, sometimes wrong, sometimes right, but he was a man. (p. 632)

There is life, even redemption, the message runs, after the loss of the beloved, and not only in the grand prize of the presidency but also, oddly, as an ex-president (a role the Rough Rider, in fact, found difficult to play), where out of office the hero can continue in "the arena" alongside the other "big" men, and though too old to be the youthful suitor, he can remain "tempestuous" and "strong," a revised incarnation of the romantic, grieving groom. The bottom line for Nixon, however, was not merely that "the light" need not go out "forever," but rather that being a "man" is what matters most. The telling statement, "But he was a man," suggested Nixon's own self-justification, that he himself had been "man" enough to take responsibility for what underlings did at Watergate, and that this willing sacrifice argued his own claim, even in relinquishing the executive position, to some high "office"—if not his mother's sainthood then Teddy Roosevelt's manhood.

The shame of the aspirant who has been found out, the smallness revealed when the majesty of high office is stripped away—these were the terrible subjects that haunted Nixon's last presidential moments, and like the description of his father, all his remarks reflected a deep ambivalence as he strained simultaneously to affirm and negate. All the self-deprecation—offered as a disguise that the audience was meant to penetrate—rang as hollow as his own forced humor, because what he offered as the mask was so obviously his own face. "We think sometimes," he told his audience,

> that when things happen that don't go the right way; we think that when you don't pass the bar exam the first time—I happened to, but I was just lucky; I mean my writing was so poor the bar examiner said, 'We have just got to let the guy through.' We think that when someone dear to us dies, we think that when we lose an election, we think that when we suffer a defeat that all is ended. We think, as T.R. said, that all the light had left his life forever.

In this bizarrely inappropriate listing of losses (the death of a loved one, failure of a bar exam, defeat in an election, and the great unspoken one, the loss of honor and the presidency), the incomparable are not only compared but equated. The defeated president was preparing for the resurrection of the old Nixon, the man strengthened by accusation and defeat, the resilient warrior. To the temptation to think all the light has gone, Nixon declared, "Not true."

It is only a beginning, always. The young must know it; the old must know it. It must always sustain us, because the greatness comes and you are really tested, when you take some knocks, some disappointments, when sadness comes, because only if you have been in the deepest valley can you ever know how magnificent it is to be on the highest mountain.

Thus Nixon concluded his presidency, not by admitting defeat or personal failure, but by declaring his suffering the work of outside forces, a sort of cosmic testing of his will.

One of the most telling aspects of this informal farewell was that the resigning president, unlike his predecessors in their parting words, did not portray himself as either returning home or rejoining the fellowship of ordinary citizens. From the first Nixon spoke of a "them," but there was no comparable "us." "They" were, alternately, the little people he so desperately wanted to rise above and a powerful elite (defined sometimes by intellectual pretensions and other times by wealth) who throughout his life denied him what he deserved; but he stood alone, a sort of imperial "we," or more properly, the petulant "me."

Concluding his first farewell, Nixon implied that failure was not a bad thing if it came while "daring greatly." But his fall had nothing to do with daring; it came as the consequence of smallness, of trying—absurdly—to lessen the risk and cut the odds. As he himself had prophesied all those years ago, he tripped over the very pettiness he so feared. In an oddly elliptical approach he recalled that earlier concern in the more personal remarks of his second goodbye, warning his staff and friends, "never get discouraged, never be petty," and told them instead, "always remember, others may hate you, but those who hate you don't win unless you hate them, and then you destroy yourself." The irony was overwhelming: the voice of the sainted mother, after all those years, warning the son about his own nature, and the clichéd advice, so unsophisticated in its Sunday school tone, its simplistic assurance, had yet again proved true.

In the end, his presidential work aborted, Nixon did not turn to the Quaker's grace even though he rediscovered his mother's commonplaces. It was still, as with all his earlier defeats, work that would redeem him. Amazingly, he made this ultimate humiliation merely another crisis, another opportunity to prove his manhood by coming back once more. To achieve the stature for which he so profoundly longed, he would stand in the arena, unbroken, until his very fortitude silenced critics.[10] "You are here to say goodbye to us," he told his White House audience, "and we don't have a good word for it in English—the best is *au revoir*. We will see you again."

In that parting promise lay the most telling aspect of the entire episode. If the lesson of this latest crisis was not, as so many of the Watergate underlings (Charles Colson, Jeb Magruder, and John Ehrlichman among them) discovered, the need to be born again through grace, then it required some act of self-resurrection, some work sufficient to undo Nixon's disgrace. Facing this dilemma, the resigning president drew on a lifetime's experience in overcoming lesser defeats and made the peculiar response, circular in its logic, that on previous occasions had enabled him to declare triumph in the midst of humiliation. His "theology" called for rehabilitation, not through repentance and forgiveness, but through some significant act that could "prove" a redeeming greatness. Ironically, in Nixon's case that act was simply "coming back." The secret of all Nixon's political resurrections was the conviction that, to prove himself the great man, meant not going away, meant surviving no matter the embarrassment.

THE WEIGHT OF YEARS AND THE LESSONS OF COMMAND

Inevitably, George Washington provided the best of all possible presidential endings in his 1796 farewell, exemplary both for the political advice it offered and for the aesthetic wholeness it completed. Faced with the challenge of closing his own chapter without threatening the ongoing national story, he drew on two similar experiences from his past. At the close of the Revolution Washington had resigned his commission, bidding farewell first to his officers (November 2, 1783) and then to Congress (December 3, 1783). Each occasion was so highly charged that both Washington and his audience broke into tears. "Mr. President," he declared before Congress:

> The great events, on which my resignation depended, having at length taken place, I have now the honor of offering my sincere congratulations to Congress, and of presenting myself before them, to surrender into

their hands the trust committed to me, and to claim the indulgence of retiring from the Service of my Country.

Happy in the confirmation of our Independence and Sovereignty, and
pleased with the opportunity afforded the United States of becoming a
respectable nation, I resign with satisfaction the appointment I accepted
with diffidence; a diffidence in my abilities to accomplish so arduous a
task, which, however, was superseded by a confidence in the rectitude of
our cause, the support of the supreme Power of the Union, and the patronage of Heaven . . .[11]

The courtly tone of his remarks conveyed a sense of high ceremony, as
he, the victorious general, "surrendered" his "trust" and his army to the
civil body. The gesture was grand and theatrical as he delivered to the
legislature his superior authority. In that way he used his resignation as
an opportunity to validate not only his new country but this group of
representatives as its government. Concluding his address to Congress,
Washington declared, "Having now finished the work assigned to me I
retire from the great theater of action; and bidding an affectionate
farewell to this august body under whose orders I have so long acted, I
here offer my commission and take my leave of all the employments of
public life." The "great theater of action," the stage of history as well as
of combat, lowered its curtain as the general made his exit and revolutionary work gave way to the more mundane pursuit of peace and normalcy.

But it was in his November "Farewell Orders to the Armies of the
United States" that Washington provided the clearest preview of both his
presidential service and his executive leave-taking. "It is not," Washington explained to the men he had led in war, men about to enter the
world their service had transformed,

the meaning nor within the compass of this address, to detail the hardships peculiarly incident to our service, or to describe the distresses,
which in several instances have resulted from the extremes of hunger and
nakedness, combined with the rigors of an inclement season. Nor is it
necessary to dwell on the dark side of our past affairs. Every American officer and soldier must now console himself for any unpleasant circumstances, which may have occurred, by a recollection of the uncommon
scenes in which he has been called to act no inglorious part, and the as-

tonishing events of which he has been a witness, events which have seldom, if ever before, taken place on the stage of human action; nor can they probably ever happen again.[12]

Having acknowledged, in addition to their sufferings in war, their frustration with the states for not paying them, Washington pointed to a greater compensation in the "astonishing events" they had witnessed. "For who has before seen," he asked,

> a disciplined army formed at once from such raw materials? Who, that was not a witness, could imagine, that the most violent local prejudices would cease so soon; and that men, who came from the different parts of the continent, strongly disposed by the habits of education to despise and quarrel with each other, would instantly become but one patriotic band of brothers? Or who, that was not on the spot, can trace the steps by which such a wonderful revolution has been effected, and such a glorious period put to all our warlike toils?

They were, he told them, the greatest wonder of the Revolution, and their most marvelous achievement, more than any military victory, was their unique community. Taking leave of "those he holds most dear," this civic father bidding farewell to his enlisted sons, insisted that they themselves embodied the country they had fought to create, that in coming together as an army they had anticipated the maturation from local prejudice to "one patriotic band of brothers" that could make union possible in peace as well as war. He offered them as the enduring example, the rhetorical paradigm of American oneness.

Washington did not ignore the tension that alienated many in his retiring army from their civilian government—most notably the failure of the government to pay them back wages—but directed his remarks away from the "dark side" of those past affairs and toward the future's promise. To those soldiers reentering the economic and political life of the country, Washington offered a double reward: the privilege of having participated in a unique historic event and the opportunity to secure a prosperous life in this new nation. Insisting they would be paid for their service despite the slowness of some states to acknowledge their obligations, he nevertheless argued that this incompetence exemplified the folly of antifederalism—all the more reason they should make the cause of union their own. Thus the retiring Commander-in-Chief, "as his last injunction to every officer and every soldier," urged the men he no longer commanded to become unionists, building a federal government sufficiently strong to allow, among other things, payment of its legitimate debts. In serving a national government, he told them, they served themselves.

The retiring general's address to his troops, short as it was, provided a complicated mix of messages. Coupled with the exhortation to become loyal and productive citizens was the reminder of their power; they were the army that had accomplished the miracle of revolution, and they could be, in peace, the civilians who directed a nation. A victorious army, as Andrew Johnson acknowledged, represents a powerful interest group, one that can prove especially unsettling to a republic whose government is never so efficient as the military that serves it. But Washington called his troops away from temptation—despite the wrongs they had suffered—called them instead to civic virtue, to recreate in political and commercial life the solidarity they had embodied in their service. "And shall not the brave men, who have contributed so essentially to these inestimable acquisitions [independence and sovereignty]," he asked, ". . . participate in all the blessings which have been obtained? In such a Republic, who will exclude them from the rights of citizens and the fruits of their labors?"

Washington's words and demeanor emphasized the paternal, a father's pride and instruction, fondness and advice. In bidding his armies an "affectionate" farewell, he began his remarks "the Commander-in-Chief . . . wishes to indulge himself a few moments in calling to mind a slight review of the past. He will then take the liberty of exploring with his military friends their future prospects, of advising the general line of conduct, which, in his opinion, ought to be pursued." Like a parent addressing the child who is about to enter an impersonal world, Washington delivered a message that was both a commencement address and a benediction, and he would depart from the presidency in a similar manner.

Thirteen years later, Washington's presidential farewell enlarged upon the same issues and sentiments. Once more he spoke for the communal bonds uniting his audience and for a corresponding connection in the nation they served. Each time he exploited the emotionally charged moment of his own departure to affirm the most doubtful element in the new country's character: its capacity to be one. On both occasions an unspoken but powerful proof for his case was the common affection Americans felt for him, and Washington did implicitly what succeeding generations would explicitly do; he made his countrymen's devotion to one another a test of their love for him.

His 1796 speech offered instruction to the citizenry he had served, lessons about government and the conduct of its business and about national identity and the common bonds that define a union of persons as well as states. But the dramatic tension throughout lay in the contrasting themes of his own mortality and the nation's permanence. Time and the significance of its passage provided the great motif of his address, and he applied that perspective to the differing but equally dramatic contexts of his physical decline and the enduring life of the union. He began and ended with the personal: "begging" his countrymen not to misunderstand his leaving the executive office as an abandonment of them, reassuring them that he was motivated "by no diminution of zeal for [their] future interest, no deficiency of grateful respect for [their] past kindness," and that his decision was, by contrast, "compatible with both." He had hoped to retire earlier, had even prepared—prior to the previous election—"an address to declare it to you," but then had accepted a second term because of the "perplexed and critical posture of our affairs."[13] But now, he argued, conditions were such that he might step down:

> I rejoice that the state of your concerns, external as well as internal, no longer renders the pursuit of inclination incompatible with the sentiment of duty or propriety; and am persuaded, whatever partiality may be retained for my services, that in the present circumstances of our country you will not disapprove my determination to retire. (MP, I:205)

Washington, alone among departing presidents, had to argue his dispensability, had to persuade his countrymen that they could get along without him and that the Union would persist in his absence. Referring to doubts he had expressed in his first inaugural, reservations concerning his qualifications for the office, in retiring he reminded his audience both of what had been accomplished and the limitations of the president who had helped achieve it:

> In the discharge of this trust, I will only say, that I have, with good intentions, contributed towards the organization and administration of the

Government the best exertions of which a very fallible judgment was capable.—Not unconscious in the outset of the inferiority of my qualifications, experience in my own eyes, perhaps still more in the eyes of others,
has strengthened the motives to diffidence of myself; and every day the
increasing weight of years admonishes me more and more that the shade
of retirement is as necessary to me as it will be welcome.

Whether or not his country recognized the "fallible judgment" and the
"inferior" qualifications, it could not deny "the increasing weight of
years" and thus had to accept his decision to step down. But Washington
gave positive value to those same years when he spoke of the government.
For the nation, the passage of time brought increased vitality rather than
decay. Those contradictory implications of time provided the frame
upon which Washington hung both his emotional and his logical appeals; what indicated mortality in the man indicated increasing strength
and longevity in the nation. "Satisfied," he argued, "that if any circumstances have given peculiar value to my services they were temporary, I
have the consolation to believe that, while choice and prudence invite me
to quit the political scene, patriotism does not forbid it" (pp. 205–6).

Thus Washington, simultaneously patriot and pater, duty and love,
reconciled the citizenry to his loss, by referring, even as he spoke of himself in terms of "termination," to the country's "preservation" and "per-
manency." Having attributed his own success to the loyalty of his countrymen, to their "constancy" in overcoming "vicissitudes of fortune" and
the agitation of "passions," he declared that resistance to the transitory
and the divisive was the key to national longevity. That belief, he insisted, he would carry "to my grave, as a strong incitement to unceasing
vows that Heaven may continue to you the choicest tokens of its beneficence; that your union and brotherly affection may be perpetual." With
possessive pronouns throughout, "my" and "your," rarely "our," Washington stressed his own identification with the past and theirs with the
future.

Utilizing a rhetorical authority based both on the esteem he commanded and on his imminent departure ("These will be offered to you
with the more freedom as you can only see in them the disinterested
warnings of a parting friend"), Washington asserted that his countrymen
were now a "People" in fact and that the "Unity of government which

constitutes you one people, is . . . now dear to you." While warning that, "from different causes and different quarters much pains will be taken, many artifices employed, to weaken in your minds the conviction of this truth," Washington insisted that "Unity of government" is "the edifice of your real independence, the support of your tranquility at home, your peace abroad, of your safety, of your prosperity, of that very liberty, which you so highly prize" (pp. 206–7). Thus it was to the Union that they

> should cherish a cordial, habitual, and immovable attachment . . . accustoming yourselves to think and speak of it as the palladium of your political safety and prosperity; watching for its preservation with jealous anxiety; discountenancing whatever may suggest even a suspicion that it can in any event be abandoned, and indignantly frowning upon the first dawning of every attempt to alienate any portion of our country from the rest, or to enfeeble the sacred ties which now link the various parts.

In his parting effort to represent their natural unity and to counter the competing claims of state and region, Washington insisted that a shared past and a common purpose must generate a loyalty stronger than those of local attachment. This, he argued, had already been accomplished in the Revolution and the first years of nationhood. Union, he declared, was not simply a goal worth pursuing but a present and undeniable reality.

> For this you have every inducement of sympathy and interest.—Citizens by birth or choice of a common country, that country has a right to concentrate your affections.—The name of American, which belongs to you in your national capacity, must always exalt the just pride of patriotism, more than any appellation derived from local discriminations.—With slight shades of difference, you have the same religion, manners, habits, and political principles.—You have in common cause fought and triumphed together.—The independence and liberty you possess are the work of joint councils, and joint efforts—of common dangers, sufferings and successes.

Insisting that the Union had the "right" to their primary affection, he argued the same geopolitical case Lincoln would offer in his First Inaugural. The economic advantages of Union (the issues of "interest" rather than of principle), Washington explained, grew from a natural interdependence. Each section's prosperity depended upon "unrestrained intercourse . . . protected by the equal laws of a common government," upon the commercial and maritime resources of Northern states and the agricultural industry of the South, combined in a single economic community. Similarly, with "the progressive improvement of interior communications, "the *East*" and "the *West*" were tied in a common market, each essential to the other's well being, the entire country "directed by an indissoluble community of interest, as *one nation*."

> While, then, every part of our Country thus feels an immediate and particular interest in union, all the parts combined cannot fail to find in the united mass of means and efforts greater strength, greater resource, proportionably greater security. (p. 208)

But, though Washington insisted that "these considerations speak a persuasive language to every reflecting and virtuous mind," he could not deny that many in America believed otherwise. Those contrary voices, he implied, must be either unreflecting or motivated by something other than virtue. "Is there a doubt, whether a common government can embrace so large a sphere?" he asked, then gave a quintessential Enlightenment response to the question: "Let experience solve it.—To listen to mere speculation in such a case were criminal."

The president's scientific appeals, his call for empirical evidence rather than theoretical or ideological proclamations, added a practical dimension to his earlier emphasis upon sentiment and obligation. On such a basis he warned against innovations that undercut the authority of the national government:

> In all the changes to which you may be invited, remember that time and habit are at least as necessary to fix the true character of governments as of other human institutions; that experience is the surest standard, by which to test the real tendency of the existing constitution of a country; that facility in changes upon the credit of mere hypothesis and opinion exposes to perpetual change, from the endless variety of hypothesis and opinion. (p. 210)

While conceding that the viability of a unified government had not been wholly confirmed or universally accepted, he told his countrymen, "We are authorized to hope that a proper organization of the whole, with the auxiliary agency of governments for the respective subdivisions, will afford a happy issue to the experiment."

"Experiment" and "experience" are to be found on nearly every page of the message, providing both the method and the authority for an enlightened people. When arguing for separation of powers, he called as evidence "experiments ancient and modern"; similarly, it was "reason and experience" that should prevent us from believing national "morality can be maintained without religion." Warning against alliances with other nations, he argued, "history and experience prove that foreign influence is one of the most baneful foes of Republican government."[14]

Behind this language lay the pervasive eighteenth-century conviction that in dispassionate science could be found an alternative to the passions of partisanship—and Washington rarely missed an opportunity to link "party" to "passion." But there was another reason for urging an uncertain nation to trust fledgling experience, which he identified near the end of his message. Explaining his conduct of foreign affairs, he said, "With me a predominant motive has been to endeavor to gain time for our country to settle and mature in its yet recent institutions, and to progress without interruption to that degree of strength and consistency which is necessary to give it, humanly speaking, the command of its own fortunes" (p. 216). In gaining time, that which strengthens common affection, he allowed the experiment of union to continue and prove itself. His tenure in office had, he believed, so proved the value of the national connection that present doubts must be directed at those who still challenged its worth:

"Tis well worth a fair and full experiment. With such powerful and obvious motives to Union, affecting all parts of our country, while experience shall not have demonstrated its impracticability, there will always be reason to distrust the patriotism of those, who in any quarter may work to weaken its bands.

The focus of the word "patriotism" was critical, not just to the argument at hand but to the issue of primary loyalty that would endure into secession. The general inclination among Washington's listeners was toward a narrow application of that commitment, but he called them to invest their greatest love and loyalty in a Union only slightly older than his two terms. He redefined American paternity and declared Americans children of the recent Revolution rather than of the political structures that preceded it; he urged his countrymen to see themselves as "fathered" not by the colonial past that gave their states claim to patriotic preference but by the authors ("the joint councils") of independence and the revolutionary army (those who endured "common dangers" and "sufferings")—in short, themselves. That shared paternity, embodied in the Constitution and in Washington himself, provided a common identity large enough to contain the varying resources, interests, and institutions of states and yet small enough to allow a "fraternal" connection and mutual commitment. The founding fathers had made a family of them all.

The opposition between passion and experience provided the basis for this part of Washington's instruction. Whereas experience serves union, passion is the servant of faction. Experience unfolds in time, while passion is the work of the moment. It follows, then, that reason, which relies on experience and the calm consideration of evidence, must be the primary instrument of a republican government. Thus it is not surprising that Washington attacked the ideas of foreign alliance and domestic partisanship as both the creation and creators of passion, "a fire not to be quenched," demanding a "uniform vigilance to prevent its bursting into a flame, lest instead of warming, it should consume." But, of course, Washington's message began and ended with a passion positively endorsed: the affections between citizens and the love of country that have been vindicated by both reason and experience.

So he closed his public career recognizing that, while "unconscious of intentional error—I am nevertheless too sensible of my defects not to think it probable that I may have committed many errors." Those failings he asked God to mitigate and Americans to view with indulgence, weighing against "the faults of incompetent abilities" the forty-five years he had dedicated to the service of his country. He also asked his countrymen to indulge his longing to retire to the particular place that held his deepest affection, "the native soil of himself and his progenitors for several generations." If that seemed inconsistent both in the depth of "passion" the sentiment expressed and in the fact that the object of the passion was a region hallowed by old associations, he reassured Americans that the pleasure afforded by the ancestral home was possible because of his confidence in the nation as a whole and was now inseparable from his love of the Union.

I anticipate with pleasing expectation that retreat, in which I promise myself to realize without alloy, the sweet enjoyment of partaking, in the midst of my fellow-citizens the benign influence of good laws under a free government,—the ever favorite object of my heart, and the happy reward, as I trust, of our mutual cares, labors, and dangers.

Thus at the end Washington reconciled his retirement—even his death—and his country's well-being, the love of a particular region or place and a deeper loyalty to the whole ("the ever favorite object"). Such was the larger ambition of his message: to reconcile his countrymen to the consequences of time that weakens men but strengthens union, to reconcile them to a change in administration even as he urged them not to change their government, and—above all—to reconcile them to one another as fellow countrymen and dearest allies. If they did not yield to political seducers and transitory passions, he assured them, they would discover in the fullness of time the deepest joys of a more perfect union. While he had concluded his remarks to that earlier "miracle" of union, the Revolutionary army, by declaring the "curtain drawn," the "scene closed," upon leaving the presidency he reassured his fellow citizens that their national drama was only beginning.

His final official words before retiring to "the mansions of rest," both the one at Mount Vernon and the heavenly version, asserted union as a spiritual state even more than a political arrangement, promised that the soul, broken by its own factions and divided by its own conflicted alliances, could find wholeness and peace. At the heart of Washington's farewell was a desire to arrive at last at home, and ultimately that was not Mount Vernon but the Union.

DANGERS MORE EVIDENT

The hero of America's second war, Andrew Jackson, was the first of Washington's successors formally to bid his countrymen goodbye. The five intervening presidents felt either that such a message was, in their particular cases, unnecessary or that Washington's much-admired effort was the only such address the nation required. But in 1837 Jackson, never constrained by modesty, felt called upon to offer his own version, one that regularly alluded to the first president's farewell, echoing some passages, quoting others, and generally repeating its same thematic and formal characteristics.

"The necessity," he reminded his fellow Americans, "of watching with jealous anxiety for the preservation of the Union was earnestly pressed upon his fellow-citizens by the Father of his Country in his Farewell Address." He noted that the time Washington had sought for his country had been granted—"We have now lived almost fifty years under the Constitution framed by the sages and patriots of the Revolution ... Our Constitution is no longer a doubtful experiment." From that fifty years' view, he reaffirmed both Washington's logic and his conviction. Borrowing many of the earlier president's words, he declared:

> It is no longer a question whether this great country can remain happily united and flourish under our present form of government. Experience, the unerring test of all human undertakings, has shown the wisdom and foresight of those who formed it, and has proved that in the union of these States there is a sure foundation for the brightest hopes of freedom and for the happiness of the people. At every hazard and by every sacrifice the Union must be preserved. (MP, 3:294)

Above all, he reminded them—once more employing Washington's vocabulary—Union must be rooted "in the affections of the people."

Insisting that the president must not be a captive of sectional interest, Jackson urged his countrymen to remember "that the citizens of other States are their political brethren," "that their own interest requires them to be just to others, as they hope to receive justice at their hands," and when he asked, "What have you to gain by division and dissension?" he gave his own prophetic answer:

> Delude not yourself with the belief that a breach once made may be afterwards repaired. If the Union is once severed, the lines of separation will grow wider and wider, and the controversies which are now debated and settled in the halls of legislation will then be tried in fields of battle and determined by the sword. (p. 296)

Like the first president, America's seventh Commander-in-Chief had previously delivered a farewell to officers (those of the Division of the

South whose command he relinquished in 1821), and just as his last presidential address would attempt to imitate Washington's, so was his final military message deeply influenced by the one delivered to the Revolutionary army. Jackson, too, briefly reviewed the past ("Together we have seen the termination of one British and two Indian wars.") and the sufferings his soldiers had endured; he, too, praised their unity, the "attachments and friendships" formed during the hardships of their service, and he, too, called them to the continued "cultivation of that harmony and friendship towards each other which will render you a band of brothers." Like Washington, he noted a wrong perpetrated against the military by its civilian government, in this case a reduction of the army that caused "valuable officers" to be "suddenly deprived of the profession which they had embraced, and thrown upon the world." And like Washington he consoled them with the knowledge that "your country still cherishes you as her defenders and deliverers," and the satisfaction of "that which cannot be taken from you—the consciousness of having done your duty . . . of having defended the American eagle wherever it was endangered."[15]

Jackson also presumed a paternal role in relation to his audience, but in explicitly declaring that commanding officers are necessarily parents to their men, he concerned himself with the issue of authority rather than republican citizenship, a telling shift—in light of the rest of his message—from the emphasis of his revolutionary predecessor. "It ought to be borne in mind," he admonished those who would remain in uniform, "that every captain should be to his company as a father, and should treat it as his family—as his children. . . . Treat them like children, admonish them, and if, unhappily, admonition will not have the desired effect—coercion must." Whereas Washington devoted his instruction to an army about to return to civilian life and adult concerns, Jackson emphasized a childlike need for discipline among those who would remain in military service.

That concern took on special significance when the general received, on the day following the first draft of his original message (May 31, 1821), an order from President Monroe decrying the excessive number of desertions from the Army of the South and attributing it to "the conduct of officers toward their men" and, more specifically, to discipline of "undue severity." The reprimand from the Commander-in-Chief itself stressed the paternal obligation of officers but emphasized the role of "protector" rather than punisher. That Jackson, given his recently penned statement about a parent's coercive duties, should find the charge offensive is not surprising, and so he appended a reply to his original farewell, defending his officers and himself, and declaring the real cause of desertion to be, ironically, "the want of adequate punishment."

Apparent in this early farewell is both Jackson's reliance on Washington as a model and a personal prickliness (to put it mildly) that violated the paradigm, a contrast again apparent in the vehemence of his appended complaint. While Washington had not ignored his soldiers' grievances, neither did he allow this frustration to overshadow the positive conduct he urged upon them. And while Jackson in his original draft called for a similar civilian behavior, his subsequent remarks (a rebuttal of Monroe's charge that ran twice as long as the original message), placed the greater emphasis on complaint. Where Washington moved persistently toward union and harmony, Jackson was, characteristically, diverted into dissension and agitation.

And so, too, did an air of grievance break into his 1837 presidential farewell. He dwelt at great length on the "mischiefs and dangers" of a paper currency, arguing on the basis of "experience" (a word he used nearly as often as Washington had), and devoted even more energy to repeating his old attacks on a National Bank. Where the first president had sustained a positive tone and praised his countrymen even as he instructed them, Jackson's voice was edged with suspicion and admonition. "Knowing," he explained, "the path of freedom is continually beset by enemies who often assume the disguise of friends, I have devoted the last hours of my public life to warn you of the dangers" (MP, 3:307). Though Washington had also offered "warnings," his were carefully contained, and his prevailing emphasis remained hopeful, even celebratory, rather than darkened by the foreboding to which Jackson regularly returned.[16]

While Jackson wanted to emulate Washington both as a paternal figure and as the champion of union, his own nature and attitude continually intervened. Where the first president emphasized trust, suspicion dominated the views of the seventh. Hope yielded to frustration, and personal contentment to anger. In part that was natural; the influence of special interests had grown rather than lessened in the intervening years, and despite "general prosperity and splendid success," Jackson reported,

> the dangers of which [Washington] warned us are becoming every day more evident, and the signs of evil are sufficiently apparent to awaken the deepest anxiety in the bosom of the patriot. We behold systematic efforts publicly made to sow the seeds of discord between different parts of the United States and to place party divisions directly upon geographical distinctions: to excite the *South* against the *North* and the *North* against the *South* . . . and the possible dissolution of the Union has at length become an ordinary and familiar subject of discussion. Has the warning voice of Washington been forgotten, or have designs already been formed to sever the Union? (p. 295)

Careful to refine the evil of partisanship so that the culprit was not parties of the sort he himself so vigorously championed but only parties with no national base—parties determined solely by geography—Jackson foresaw the threat to union increasing with time, not diminishing.

In 1861 Lincoln would warn secessionists that separation is habit-forming and that, once begun, it would continue, an argument Jackson anticipated when he asserted, "The first line of separation would not last for a single generation; new fragments would be torn off, new leaders would spring up, and this great and glorious Republic would soon be broken into a multitude of petty States" (p. 296). In that process liberty would inevitably be lost, along with security and prosperity. Jackson argued for the Union, but paradoxically for one that had grown less, rather than more, perfect, one in which fundamental divisions—declared the prerogatives of states—were sanctioned and defended while those based on moral disagreement were deemed pernicious and unpatriotic.

When the first president addressed the issue of faction, his concern lay almost entirely with the political and ideological distinctions of the kind dividing Alexander Hamilton and Thomas Jefferson, the split between Federalists and Anti-Federalists, Republicans and Tories. He recognized the strong tendency to emphasize state and regional loyalties but did not regard these as alliances primarily instigated by slavery. When Jackson spoke, although tariffs and the National Bank were highly controversial issues, often dividing the country along regional lines, they lacked—as

Jackson well understood—the ultimate power to separate that was inherent in the institution of slavery. When he warned that division, once begun, could not be stopped, he repressed the fact that slavery was in itself the most blatant exercise of distinction and exclusion, that it had already set in motion the very machinery of separation against which he spoke. Where Washington's term of choice for his audience was "the people," Jackson, to be more technically accurate, referred to "citizens" and "freemen," and in so doing compromised his own message of oneness and unity. He underlined that fact with the terrible irony of his carefully worded observation, "Under our free institutions the citizens of every quarter of our country are capable of attaining a high degree of prosperity and happiness without seeking to profit themselves at the expense of others" (p. 298).

Jackson's tone reflected the immoderate age in which he served. While he affirmed as best he could Washington's vision of union, he felt compelled to voice his own deep frustrations and, in so doing, revealed the ideological distance that separated him from his hero. Although he never referred directly to the institution of slavery, it haunted his message as it did his country. Abolitionists were among his most obvious agents of "discord" (persons who "cast odium" upon the institutions of other states), and his attack upon them focused on "justice—full and ample justice," but justice applied to regions, to "every portion of the United States," rather than to persons. The terrible irony of pursuing unity in a nation divided between slave and free, of being "just" to geography even though it meant tolerating injustice to those human beings who were neither citizens nor freemen, had strained the nation to a point where the breaking could be foreseen even if it was not yet at hand.

Even with those concerns, in the end Jackson's issue of choice was money. It was the root of all republican ills, he asserted—"we find nothing that has produced such deep-seated evil as the course of legislation in relation to the currency" (p. 301). The enemy looming behind the threats to union, he insisted, was the "moneyed interest"—"with its boundless means of corruption and its numerous dependents"—to which had been given, through paper currency and bank monopoly, "the power to regulate the value of property and the fruits of labor in every quarter of the Union, and to bestow prosperity or bring ruin upon any city or section of the country as well as might best comport with its own interest or policy"

(p. 303). This enemy was common to the vast majority of citizens and was not exclusive to any region. By focusing on it as the great cause of division (and using it in his own dividing effort to define an "us" and "them"), Jackson suggested an economic community that could transcend other forces for separation. "The agricultural, the mechanical, and the laboring classes have little or no share in the direction of the great moneyed corporations," and, he suggested, those classes could constitute a nationwide alliance, one that united workers against those who "amass wealth without labor" and control the public currency. Ingeniously, Jackson sought to prevent the dissolution Washington feared and to serve the cause of union precisely through the influence of party and special interest. Since his coalition would represent all sections of the country and all productive professions, it satisfied his own nationalist criteria for political legitimacy.

Though it violated much of the spirit of Washington's injunction, Jackson's farewell outlined a political strategy noteworthy both for what it evaded and for what it addressed, one that provided a model his Democratic party would continue to exploit for the next century and beyond. It was a message constructed around both suspicion and faith, the former apparently focused on the few—the moneyed interest—and the latter on the many, the vast laboring majority. But in the end we are all both, no matter how convenient to speak otherwise; we are the speculators who long to get more than our labor deserves, and at the same time we are the underappreciated laborers. This, in his closing paragraphs, Jackson partly acknowledged, and he warned his countrymen against their own worst natures. "[F]rom the earliest ages of history to the present," he told Americans, "there have never been thirteen millions of people associated in one political body who enjoyed so much freedom and happiness as the people of these United States" (p. 307). Those blessings were no longer at risk from abroad, he continued:

> It is from within, among yourselves—from cupidity, from corruption, from disappointed ambition and inordinate thirst for power—that factions will be formed and liberty endangered. It is against such designs, whatever disguise the actors may assume, that you have especially to guard yourselves.

Closing his tenure as president, the great democrat grown old in office warned, even as he advocated alliances that would give more of his fellow citizens access to power, that the great weakness of a democracy is an internal faction rather than an external enemy—those impulses, corrupt and corrupting, that are within each of us. This old man, full of warnings, warned us at last against ourselves, and, ironically, his most compelling proof was his own divided soul.[17]

TO MAINTAIN A BALANCE

Dwight D. Eisenhower was well aware of the analogies between his own popular image and that of George Washington, and in 1961 he offered a farewell similar in temper and spirit. Where the first president waited until closing to remind his audience of his forty-five years of national service, Eisenhower began his farewell address by pointing out that when, "three days from now," he yielded his office to another, it would mark the conclusion of "half a century in the service of our country." On the basis of that claim and the special authority it lent to his words, he came before his countrymen "with a message of leave-taking and farewell, and to share a few final thoughts with you." Those final thoughts, more than one hundred seventy years after the presidency began, echoed Washington's concept of the office without Jackson's frustration and inconsistency (PP, Eisenhower, 1960–61:1035–36).

Like the first president, Eisenhower was a man rhetorically devoted to moderation, and as he addressed a people who had emerged at mid-twentieth century as "the strongest, the most influential and most productive nation in the world," he began by emphasizing the obligations that accompany international preeminence. If Washington stressed his countrymen's allegiance to their nation as opposed to their states, Eisenhower directed them to consider their responsibility to the international arena. That expansion of loyalty, that enlargement of identity, in sharp contrast to Washington's suspicion of foreign alliance and Jackson's anti-European sentiments, Eisenhower treated as an extension of traditional American values and a matter of keeping faith with the armies who had fought the Nazi powers.[18] He called his countrymen to world citizenship in the exercise of their newly achieved but unrivaled "material progress, riches, and military strength," called them to use "our power in the interests of world peace and human betterment." After two terms in office he reiterated the internationalist message of his inaugural address, but, strengthened in his resolve by eight years of Cold War experience, he called more emphatically for America to globalize its democratic mission. Once more Eisenhower reaffirmed this country's duty "to foster progress in human achievement, and to enhance liberty, dignity and integrity among people and among nations." "To strive for less," he insisted, "would be unworthy of a free and religious people."

Like Washington, the thirty-fourth president urged his audience toward an enlarged sense of community. In a world torn between freedom and communism, a return to American provincialism would be neither practical nor moral. When Washington had spoken gratefully of "our detached and distant situation," he spoke to a world view since made archaic by two world wars, jet planes, and national boundaries that, at the end of Eisenhower's presidency, stretched not only from coast to coast but all the way from the Arctic to Hawaii. Nevertheless, Eisenhower brought to this changed world lessons and values similar to those Washington had proclaimed at the first stage of "America's adventure in free government."

This former general also had bid farewell to troops, addressing in 1948 a two-paragraph message "To The American Soldier." The sentiments were familiar as he spoke of the affection that bound him to the men whose command he was about to surrender. Their shared "fellowship" Eisenhower declared his "most prized possession," and, he insisted, his "fondest boast" would ever be, "I was their fellow soldier." In that early message he foreshadowed the internationalism he would press on his civilian countrymen in 1961, a challenge that in 1948 he praised his veteran audience for having successfully met. Those soldiers, whose "[p]ride of service," "loyalty to the flag," and "love of country" "strengthened them beyond the common strength given to men," had, he told them, both preserved "their country from its enemies" and freed "their world from evil tyrannies." In their service they had exemplified America's postwar obligation, to serve itself and the world simultaneously, to see "evil tyranny" as mankind's common enemy. And like Washington, he recognized in his army and its wartime service a model for the nation's peacetime responsibility.[19]

In words that echoed Washington's measured and dispassionate appeal—in an age equally beset by passionate opinions—Eisenhower's prevailing image in his 1961 farewell was that of an old-fashioned scale and a seeking after balance. In making political decisions, Eisenhower insisted, each proposal must be weighed in the light of a broader consideration: the need to maintain balance in and among national programs—balance between the private and public economy, balance between cost and hoped for advantage—balance between the clearly necessary and the comfortably desirable; balance between our essential requirements as a nation and the duties imposed by the nation upon the individual; balance between actions of the moment and the national welfare of the future. Good judgment seeks balance and progress; lack of it eventually finds imbalance and frustration. (p. 1037)

Nothing was to be done in haste; nothing was to be carried to extremes. The call was for reason and temperance.

Defending moderation, Eisenhower offered a carefully considered response to the inflammatory issue of how best to confront the "hostile ideology" challenging America, a matter much on the national mind, especially since the presidential canvass of the previous fall had focused on military preparedness. John Kennedy, in his campaign, had portrayed the country as under-armed and indecisive. He had pointed to communist aggression throughout the world and had insisted that the Republican administration had conceded too much and challenged too little.[20] Three days before Kennedy's inauguration Eisenhower, without bitterness or enmity, addressed that matter. He advocated a restrained approach to defense and called America away from its infatuation with arms. This country's preeminent twentieth-century general made his final message a thoughtful analysis of the dangers of an unchecked "military-industrial complex" and issued a modern-day counterpart to Washington's warning against a large standing army. "This conjunction of an immense military establishment and a large arms industry," he reminded his listeners,

is new in the American experience. The total influence—economic, political, even spiritual—is felt in every city, every State house, every office of the Federal government. We recognize the imperative need for this development. Yet we must not fail to comprehend its grave implications. Our toil, resources and livelihood are all involved; so is the very structure of our society. (p. 1038)

By asserting his authority in military as well as political matters, the outgoing president called upon his fellow citizens to see the subtle and pervasive influence of America's unprecedented postwar military machine, to see its implications not only for defense and the economy but for the nation's moral and spiritual condition. After elaborating on the complex nature of modern technological research and the vast sums of government money it required, he warned of the danger of directing scientific investigation away from free inquiry and toward a system in which "government contract becomes virtually a substitute for intellectual curiosity."[21] And, as he would indicate in his meeting with the press the following day, Eisenhower noted with chagrin the American romanticization of weapons (a tendency he surely recognized in the militant Kennedy). He took it as evidence of spiritual deterioration, a threat to "the very structure of society."[22]

Returning to another theme of the 1796 farewell, the 1961 address raised the issue of time. "Another factor in maintaining balance," Eisenhower suggested,

> involves the element of time. As we peer into society's future, we—you and I, and our government—must avoid the impulse to live only for today, plundering for our own ease and convenience, the precious resources of tomorrow. We cannot mortgage the material assets of our grandchildren without risking the loss also of their political and spiritual heritage. We want democracy to survive for all generations to come, not to become the insolvent phantom of tomorrow. (p. 1039)

As the allied commander and head of NATO, Eisenhower had been an international leader before he became a chief of state. In his farewell he spoke to a world community, inviting other peoples to join in common cause with Americans as part of an allied "union."

> To all the peoples of the world, I once more give expression to America's prayerful and continuing aspiration:
> We pray that peoples of all faiths, all races, all nations, may have their great human needs satisfied; that those now denied opportunity shall come to enjoy it to the full; that all who yearn for freedom may experience its spiritual blessings; that those who have freedom will understand, also, its heavy responsibilities; that all who are insensitive to the needs of others will learn charity; that the scourges of poverty, disease and ignorance will be made to disappear from the earth, and that, in the goodness

of time, all peoples will come together in a peace guaranteed by the binding force of mutual respect and love. (p. 1040)

To this vision of peace, this belief in the "goodness of time," the old warrior gave his final word. A man who had led armies and planned bold invasions cautioned a new generation against rashness, called it to moderation and—with the conviction of an old soldier—to love.

WHAT IT COMES TO

The aspirations that fuel the larger American story are completeness and union. Washington and Eisenhower more than any other concluding presidents were able to provide in their benedictory speeches an air of personal and historical completion, a sense of symmetry. While there was melancholy in their parting, it was mixed with a certain pleasure: the country's reluctance to yield the object of so much affection and yet a satisfaction that things had turned out so well, the small gift of reassurance that comes from seeing a leader who has aged into contentment and who seems at peace with himself and his country.

But apart from those favored two (and to a more limited extent, Reagan), no other presidents have come to such comforting conclusions. There have been those who left office under relatively happy circumstances, starting with the three Virginians who presided over the first quarter of the nineteenth century. But Jefferson was not the sort to see the literary point of closure; he was a scientist and an ally of a reality that is ongoing. Madison, who did understand such gestures, had already collaborated on the consummate farewell when he helped compose Washington's words and can be forgiven for not trying to compete at the end of his own presidency not only with the father of his country but his younger self. Monroe is harder to assess, but it seems unlikely that he would deviate on such matters from the example of his two predecessors, who were his mentors as well as his friends. Teddy Roosevelt, despite serving nearly two full terms, departed at such an early age (fifty) that either assuming the patriarchal mantle or speaking of retirement would have seemed inappropriate. Wilson, on the other hand, left office already retired in all but title following a stroke nearly two years earlier. Reagan came to the end much loved, but his address was narrow in its focus, more concerned with declaring victory and, like Jackson's, warning against any deviation from his specific policies. His departure was neighborly rather than fatherly and offered a moment of pleasant reminiscence and satisfaction, without any attempt at wisdom.

Jackson could not leave on so happy a note. He tried to deliver Washington's message of affection but was more inclined to see enmity. His message, while professing hope, was full of fears and uncertainties. "Knowing," he told his countrymen, "that the path of freedom is continually beset by enemies who often assume the disguise of friends, I have devoted the last hours of my public life to warn you of the dangers." No small part of that fear was the absence of either a Washington or a Jackson to defend that freedom, and he seemed less sure than the first president that the country could survive his passing.

Harry Truman, though he served nearly eight years, was elected president only once. Unlike Teddy Roosevelt, he was at the time of his retirement much maligned, dwarfed by the public enthusiasm for his predecessor *and* his successor. Nevertheless, he seized the opportunity and told a story larger than his own, speaking on behalf of the office and all who would hold it. His great contribution was to identify the presidency with the people, not in the protective pose of Washington and Eisenhower but in a far more populist interpretation. It was, he insisted, their office, and it needed their strength and wisdom.

Lyndon Johnson finally just went home, leaving Vietnam to others and trusting that future historians would find his "true" story in the domestic legislation he had crafted over a political lifetime. Jimmy Carter, however, could not let go and hungered for a more satisfying closure than history had offered him. When, in defeat, he was denied the return of the hostages, he began a long struggle to rewrite his final line. Despite his often stated belief in grace, he sought to build his new conclusion on good works. His first modest contributions as a volunteer carpenter gave way to grander efforts as a global peacemaker, both in Korea and in Haiti, and the attention he commanded on those occasions suggested an eagerness to close his story with a Nobel Prize or some end other than the humiliation in Iran or the defeat by Reagan.

But the counter-story to Washington's and Eisenhower's is not that of personal disappointment and defeat. It is rather one in which the center will not hold, and failure lies in the very nature of things. Andrew Johnson's message achieved its poignancy less from his frustrated relation to the Congress, his impeachment and near conviction, than from the cogent fear that, having won the war, America had somehow still lost the Union. Though his own position, politically and morally, was deeply compromised, and his authority virtually nonexistent, this Johnson in his leave-taking tried to represent the cause of the whole, but his effort only emphasized how terribly imperfect the Union was even after its apparent victory over secession.

More disconcerting, however, is Richard Nixon, who in his final discontinuity of mind and statement revealed what most imperils our hope of being one. The breakdown of a president's personality, the growing disjunction between the nature of the office (as defined by Washington) and the man who held it, the rambling, fragmented utterances, the unseemly protestations of his last days in office ("I am not a crook"), suggested more than the pathology of one individual; in the context of the times they hinted as well at a national affliction. The aftermath of Vietnam, the fall from that pinnacle of power on which Eisenhower had stood, racial strife, and the growing uncertainty of national purpose and values all hinted that perhaps more than betraying his country Nixon embodied it. In the anguish of his collapse, harking back to an idealized mother (whom his political humiliation would surely have shamed), he recalled his long journey to this final failure, seemingly salting the very wound he was pretending did not exist or, existing, would not prove fatal.[23] Beyond the pathos of Nixon's personal disintegration, the schizophrenia of his two farewells was terrifying because all too familiar, a mirroring of America's own inner doubts about the possibility of wholeness, the terrible fear that it could all come down to this, not just for the man but for the nation.

George Washington at the beginning spoke to what we could be, what politically we had committed ourselves to achieving; he spoke of personal as well as corporate longing, the hope of the self, and the reconciliation of the disparate elements of a pluralistic society. Nixon, on the other hand, came to represent what we fear might be our own sad truth, one in which union is a delusion, a terrible and trivial tragedy where dissolution proves inevitable. At the end we were embarrassed not by Nixon's desperate effort at personal redemption, but by how much, in his weakness, he exposed the presumption of our grand purposes and the inevitable fall toward which all presumption tends.

In the end things either come together or they fall apart—or so in our simplifying view we tend to assume. It is not clear at the beginning which will prevail, and without the conclusion we cannot really know the point of the story that precedes it. Thus the suspense, the thrilling urgency of all political life.

NOTES

CHAPTER ONE

1. Greenough's *George Washington*, 1832, is now on exhibit at the National Museum of American History in Washington. For a brief but thorough account of the Washington Monument's evolution see Pamela Scott's "Robert Mills and American Monuments," in *Robert Mills*, edited by John M. Bryan (Washington, DC, 1989), pp. 157–72.

2. The eagle is mentioned in several reports on the monument. See Rhodri Windsor Liscombe's discussion in *Altogether American: Robert Mills, Architect and Engineer, 1781–1855* (New York, 1994), p. 264. Also present at the festivities were a distinguished group of women including Dolley Madison and Mrs. Alexander Hamilton. Donald W. Riddle, *Congressman Abraham Lincoln* (Champaign, IL, 1957), p. 79.

3. Greenough's discussion of the Washington Monument can be read in the collection of his writings entitled *Form and Function: Remarks on Art, Design, and Architecture*, edited by Harold A. Small (Berkeley, CA, 1966), pp. 23–30.

4. Speaker of the House Robert C. Winthrop made this point in his oration at the cornerstone ceremony when he called upon his audience to "let the column which we are about to construct be at once a pledge and an emblem of perpetual union." Robert C. Winthrop, *Addresses and Speeches on Various Occasions* (Boston, 1852–1886), Vol. 1, p. 88. Winthrop was also invited to speak in 1885 at the dedication ceremonies. Too ill to attend, the old man wrote a moving message that was read by a congressional substitute. In it he noted the ironic history of the monument, recalling that in the Civil War era, one could almost read on the unfinished shaft "in letters of blood, 'Divided! Weighed in the balance! Found wanting!'" But in an America redeemed from secession, the obelisk confirmed for all time the

national motto, "That compact, consolidated structure with its countless blocks . . . held firmly in place by their own weight and pressure, will ever be an instructive type of the National strength and grandeur which can only be secured by the union of 'many in one.' " Vol. 4, p. 533.

5.   The language of "one people" in the opening sentence ("when in the course of human events it becomes necessary for one people to dissolve the political bands"), however, implies shared identity and not just a shared complaint among the colonies and their citizens.

6.   As has already been implied, the word *union* in the eighteenth century was most commonly associated with marriage.

7.   Henry Adams, "The Session," in *The Great Secession Winter and Other Essays* (New York, 1958), pp. 63–64.

8.   Max Farrand ed., *The Records of the Federal Convention of 1787*, rev. ed. (New Haven, 1987), 1: 113.

9.   In his book *This Country of Ours* (New York, 1897), former president Benjamin Harrison reflected on the viability of multiple presidents and came to Wilson's conclusion. "Two presidents or three, with equal powers, would as surely bring disaster as three generals of equal rank and command in a single army. I do not doubt that this sense of single and personal responsibility to the people has strongly held our Presidents to a good conscience and to a high discharge of their duties" (p. 72).

10.   Such are the references to the first president in Henry Adams's two novels, *Democracy* and *Esther*, as well as in *The Education of Henry Adams*.

11.   Former field commanders from Washington to Eisenhower have, on the basis of military experience, provided our best commentary on the role affection plays in social organization. Inclined to speak of their relation to those who have served under them and to the mutual feeling within their armies as love, they have also emphasized that sentiment's importance in national life.

12.   This is the central emphasis of Wilson's discussion of the presidency in his treatise *Constitutional Government in the United States* (New York, 1908), based on lectures he delivered as a member of Princeton University's faculty. "The nation as a whole," he explained, "has chosen him, and is conscious that it has no other political spokesman. His is the only national voice in affairs. Let him once win the admiration and confidence of the country, and no other single force can withstand him, no combination of forces will easily overpower him. His position takes the imagination of the country. He is the representative of no constituency, but of the whole people. When he speaks in his true character, he speaks for no special interest." *The Papers of Woodrow Wilson*, edited by Arthur Link (Princeton, NJ, 1974), 18: 114.

13.   *Ibid.*

14.   In *Democratic Eloquence* (New York: W. Morrow, 1990), Kenneth Cmiel notes two quite different acts of personification occurring in the eighteenth century. The first was the conception of "public opinion" and the second a modern notion of rhetorical persona. He observes that despite the assertions of rhetoric textbooks of the period that a "unified self" prevented bad men from convincingly creating

"good" versions or themselves, a general fear was emerging that "the self was breaking apart" and "character was disappearing for role playing" (p. 27). Both the singularizing of public opinion and acknowledging the multiple masks a "self" can don have complicating implications for the emerging shape of American politics.

15. Few things about presidential politics excite more suspicion than the use of speechwriters. We tend to think that the words, if they come directly from the executive mind and hand, will reveal true character and talent, and we are inclined—when we are reminded that other authors do much of the work—to feel deceived, cheated. But as much as we would like to believe that the words are the invention of the president, it is at least as true that the president is the creation of the words. The choice of those who assist in this venture, as well as the responsibility for what finally gets said, however, belongs to the president as surely as does the personality that must hold it all together and give it whatever credibility it can achieve. St. Augustine (in *On Christian Doctrine*) wrote in the fifth century that "there are men who can speak well but cannot think of anything wise to say. If they take something eloquently and wisely written by others . . . and offer it to the people in the person of the author, they do not do wickedly." While we might wish for more personal literary talent in our presidents, we judge them on the merit of the words and not on the purity of their authorship.

16. Link, ed., *Papers of Woodrow Wilson*, 29: 363–64.

17. Plato's *Gorgias* presents Socrates at his most devastating in his humiliation of rhetoric, but that subject takes its lumps in many of Plato's writings, including *The Republic*.

18. Thomas Jefferson, *The Writings of Thomas Jefferson*, 20 vols. (Washington, DC: Thomas Jefferson Memorial Association, 1905), 16: 30.

19. Quoted in Thomas Reeves, *Gentleman Boss: The Life of Chester A. Arthur* (New York, 1975), p. 275.

20. Two years later the comment was repeated in one of the "obituary addresses" delivered in Congress for the recently deceased Webster on December 14 and 15, 1852.

21. "Now, Mister Speaker, my scholarship is about from a . . . to crucifix [referring to the headings of dictionary pages], which I take ain't no small circumstance of learning; but, sir, I give you a speech as isn't got a might of grammar or geography, or choncology in it, and perhaps their mought be a considerable sprinkle of sense in it for all." *Crockett's Yaller Flower Almanac for '36* (New York, 1836), p. 6.

22. Charles F. Browne, *The Complete Works of Artemus Ward* (New York, 1898), p. 177. Artemus Ward was Browne's stage persona.

23. George H. Derby, *The Squibob Papers* (New York, 1865), pp. 19–20.

24. Quoted in Edmund Pearson, *Queer Books* (Garden City, NY, 1928), p. 25. Pearson provides other examples of oratorical extravagance in a chapter entitled "Making the Eagle Scream."

25. Cicero, *De Inventione*, translated by H. M. Hubbell, (Cambridge, MA, 1949), I.ii.3. Cicero continues, "Certainly, only a speech at the same time powerful and entrancing could have induced one who had great physical strength to submit to justice without violence, so that he suffered himself to be put on a par with those

among whom he could excel, and abandoned voluntarily a most agreeable custom, expecially since this custom already acquired through lapse of time the force of a natural right."

26. Farrand, ed., *Records of the Federal Convention*, 2: 642–43.

27. Letter to James Madison, November 5, 1786, in *The Writings of George Washington from the Original Manuscript Sources, 1745–1799*, edited by John C. Fitzpatrick, (Washington, DC, 1939), Vol. 29, p. 51.

28. This concept is the basis of Jeffrey Tulis's important study, *The Rhetorical Presidency* (Princeton, NJ, 1987).

29. John Quincy Adams, after a particularly difficult election, asked Americans in his Inaugural Address to move beyond the "jealousies of partial . . . interests" and, the election over, to embrace "as countrymen and friends." "The collisions of party spirits," he argued, ". . . are in their nature transitory." Presidential success depends upon a person's ability to participate in those "collisions" without remaining captive to them, to contain them in their proper season and then persuade the public to leave them behind so "that the rights of the whole might also endure." *Inaugural Addresses of the Presidents of the United States from George Washington 1789 to George Bush 1989* (Washington, DC, 1989), p. 55.

30. At the Constitutional Convention, when tempers were strained and delegates began to indulge in antagonistic hyperbole, they were asked to speak more as brothers than advocates, an admonition to which many of them responded positively. Farrand, ed., *Records of the Federal Convention*, 1: 467.

31. Perhaps the two most important words in America's nineteenth-century vocabulary were "self" and "union," terms that seem inherently to move in opposite directions. The word "union," the touchstone of every political vocabulary, and the word "self," exalted by the country's most revered philosophers and poets, are not, in fact, placed in opposition by their users.

32. Daniel Webster, *The Writings and Speeches of Daniel Webster* (Boston, 1903), Vol. 1, pp. 307–8.

CHAPTER TWO

Announcement speeches, to my knowledge, have never been collected in a single volume, nor, except for those of sitting presidents, are any included in the presidential papers. The best sources are newspapers. Usually we turn to the *New York Times* as the paper "of record," but the *Times* does not publish every announcement speech (in the days of the brief note allowing a candidate's name to be put forward, it was a more consistent source), usually only those it deems particularly important and newsworthy. When the full text is not provided the *Times* carries a report on both the event and the speech with selected quotations.

For recent campaigns I have found, perhaps because of the Iowa Caucus, the *Des Moines Register* to be a more reliable source. To make it easier for readers to investigate other sources, I include here a chronology of announcements and the location where the speech was made.

1948

Harold E. Stassen	Dec. 17, 1946	Washington, D.C.
Sen. Robert A. Taft	Oct. 24, 1947	(a letter to the Ohio Republican Committee)
Gov. Earl Warren	Nov. 13, 1947	Sacramento, California
Henry A. Wallace	Dec. 29, 1947	Chicago, Illinois
Gov. Thomas E. Dewey	Jan. 16, 1948	(delivered by an aide in Albany, New York)
Pres. Harry S. Truman	Mar. 8, 1948	(delivered by Chairman of Democratic National Committee at White House)

Gen. Douglas MacArthur (message arrived in the United States on Mar. 9, 1948, but statement was issued in Tokyo the previous day)

1968

Gov. George Romney	Nov. 18, 1967	Detroit, Michigan
Sen. Eugene McCarthy	Nov. 30, 1967	Washington, D.C.
Richard M. Nixon	Feb. 1, 1968	(letter to New Hampshire voters)
George Wallace	Feb. 8, 1968	Washington, D.C.
Sen. Robert Kennedy	Mar. 16, 1968	Washington, D.C. (in same Senate Office Bldg. room in which JFK announced in 1960)
Vice Pres. Hubert Humphrey	Apr. 27, 1968	Washington, D.C.
Gov. Nelson Rockefeller	Apr. 30, 1968	Albany, New York

(Sen. George McGovern entered the race on Aug. 10, 1968, in a last-minute effort to hold together the supporters of the assassinated Robert Kennedy.)

1988

Gov. Pierre DuPont IV	Sept. 16, 1986	Wilmington, Delaware
Rep. Richard Gephardt	Feb. 23, 1987	St. Louis, Missouri
Bruce Babbitt	Mar. 10, 1987	Manchester, New Hampshire
Rep. Jack Kemp	Apr. 6, 1987	Washington, D.C.
Sen. Gary Hart	Apr. 13, 1987	Red Rocks Park, Colorado
Gov. Michael Dukakis	Apr. 29, 1987	Manchester, New Hampshire and, a few hours later, Boston, Massachusetts
Sen. Paul Simon	May 18, 1987	Carbondale, Illinois
Sen. Albert Gore, Jr.	June 29, 1987	Carthage, Tennessee
Rev. Jesse Jackson	Oct. 1, 1987	Raleigh, North Carolina
Rev. Pat Robertson	Oct. 1, 1987	Brooklyn, New York

Vice Pres. George Bush	Oct. 12, 1987	Houston, Texas
Sen. Robert Dole	Nov. 9, 1987	Russell, Kansas

1992

Paul Tsongas	Apr. 30, 1991	Lowell, Massachusetts
Gov. Douglas Wilder	Sept. 13, 1991	Richmond, Virginia
Sen. Tom Harkin	Sept. 15, 1991	Winterset, Iowa
Sen. Robert Kerry	Sept. 30, 1991	Lincoln, Nebraska
Gov. Bill Clinton	Oct. 3, 1991	Little Rock, Arkansas
Edmund G. Brown, Jr.	Oct. 21, 1991	Philadelphia, Pennsylvania (Independence Hall)
Patrick J. Buchanan	Dec. 10, 1991	Concord, New Hampshire
David Duke	Nov. 18, 1991	Washington D.C.
Pres. George Bush	Feb. 12, 1992	Washington D.C.

Both Eugene McCarthy and Harold Stassen made token appearances in the race, as did an actor named Tom Laughlin.

1.   At the east entry to the Senate Chambers *Patriotism* is presented in relief as a citizen, sword in hand, reclining against that same agricultural implement. On the west wall, in a scene two thousand years removed, the Massachusetts patriot Israel Putnam is portrayed receiving his own call to duty from a uniformed rider urging him to join in the defense of Cambridge and the battle of Breed's Hill. Putnam plows with horses, but the essential ingredients are the same: the lover of country called from his private activities to public service.

2.   So he was portrayed in the Italian republics, and so, too, in America, where his name was borrowed by officers of the Revolutionary army who after the war was won pledged themselves as Sons of Cincinnatus to vigilance and service. They named George Washington as head of their order. In turn, America's first great Western city took the name, honoring both the modern fraternity and its ancient namesake.

3.   Party labels are confusing—or at least that is the case with "Republican"— because of changes over time in their application. Jefferson and other opponents of federalism identified themselves as Republicans in the late eighteenth and early nineteenth centuries. By 1824 all the candidates identified themselves as Republicans of one variety or another. In the 1828 election, John Quincy Adams ran as the candidate of National Republicans while Jackson's followers called themselves Democrats. The distinction in 1836 was between Whigs and Democrats. In the 1850s the label "Republican" returned to identify a new party opposed to slavery. For a brief history of nominating conventions see chapter 2 of Gerald Pomper's *Nominating the President: The Politics of Convention Choice* (Evanston, IL, 1966).

4.   See James W. Davis, *The Presidential Primaries: Road to the White House* (New York, 1967).

5.   Damon Wells, *Stephen Douglas: The Last Years, 1857–1861* (Austin, TX, 1971), pp. 239–58.

6. Arthur M. Schlesinger, Jr., ed, *History of American Presidential Elections, 1789–1968* (New York, 1971), 2:1814.

7. Calvin Coolidge, *The Autobiography of Calvin Coolidge* (New York, 1929), p. 219.

8. *Let The Word Go Forth: The Speeches, Statements and Writings of John F. Kennedy, 1947 to 1963*, edited by Theodore C. Sorensen (New York, 1988), p. 90.

9. Davis, *Presidential Primaries*, pp. 45 ff. Woodrow Wilson also championed selection of national candidates through primary elections. Both the letter from the governors and Roosevelt's reply were published in the *New York Times*, February 26, 1912.

10. Few of Harding's acquaintances would have regarded his reservation as mere coyness (he was often described as genuinely humble), nor was he wrong to wish for a more qualified candidate. He had few political qualifications apart from a skillful manager who was a powerful force in Ohio Republicanism. No one regarded Harding as a major presence in the Senate in 1920. Convention delegates turned to him only after General Leonard Wood, California Senator Hiram Johnson, and Governor Frank Lowden of Illinois were deadlocked after the first day's balloting. Then Harding's campaign manager and future Attorney General, Frank Daugherty, pushed his man to the fore. In the end it *was* Ohio and its power brokers and not Harding's stature that won the nomination. See Eugene H. Roseboom and Alfred E. Eckes, Jr.'s *A History of Presidential Elections* (New York, 1979), p. 148.

11. *The Public Papers and Addresses of Franklin D. Roosevelt* (New York, 1941), 9:293.

12. More than any other, Andrew Jackson's campaign stressed this analogy, referring to his service in the Revolution (he enlisted at the age of thirteen and was a British prisoner of war) and his heroics in the War of 1812. Now, Democrats insisted, he was being called to deliver the nation once again. As a young congressman, Abraham Lincoln recognized his country's infatuation with generals and, mocking the Democratic presidential nominee, General Lewis Cass, he declared himself a military hero. "Yes, sir," he declared, "in the days of the Black Hawk War I fought, bled, and came away." . . . If Gen. Cass went in advance picking huckleberries, I guess I surpassed him in charges upon the wild onions. If he saw any live fighting with Indians, it was more than I did; but I had a good many bloody struggles with the mosquitoes; and although I never fainted from loss of blood, I can truly say I was often very hungry." Roy P. Basler, ed., *The Collected Works of Abraham Lincoln*, vol. 1 (New Brunswick, NJ, 1953), pp. 509–10.

13. Chester Arthur, who had served as quartermaster general, also held the rank of brigadier general. He became president after Garfield's assassination but was never a candidate for the office himself.

14. The contempt for politics and politicians typical of general-candidates can reveal itself, as with Sherman, in an indignant rejection of office. In Grant's case it led to an oversimplification of presidential leadership and his refusal to assume full responsibility for the political work that had been placed in his hands. But most frequently this contempt, born from the prerogatives of military command combined with an awareness of the sacrificial service of the soldiers commanded, expresses itself in the appealing attitude that politicians needlessly complicate and confuse, from either corrupt self-interest or incompetence, and that a general who has been

tested under fire must rescue the troubled state. Thus did General McClellan challenge Lincoln in 1864, insisting that political ends (emancipation) were being inappropriately pursued with soldiers' lives. Eisenhower found a most effective strategy when he used his lack of conventional political experience and his wartime service to present himself as a purer candidate than those whom he opposed as well as one who could straighten out the mess lesser men had created in Korea. Generals, when they can control their ambition and not seem napoleonic, are best able to appear both practical and virtuous.

15. Eisenhower's request, after leaving office, that President Kennedy restore his title as general suggests the depth of this sentiment.

16. To some extent the general asserted a "right" about which there *was* some confusion, namely the appropriateness of a working five-star general pursing an elective office that he could, according to the legislation that created this rank, hold only in retirement. Hence the crucial distinction in his remarks between being an active candidate and being the beneficiary of other people's efforts. To continue in his NATO command he had to deny official candidacy, and yet in order for his name to appear on primary ballots—or otherwise be considered by states choosing convention delegates—he was forced both to declare his party affiliation and to affirm a willingness to run.

17. In the absence of disinterested generals, governors have dominated recent elections (e.g., Carter, Reagan, and Clinton), running as reformers of both party and the presidency. They both sound the alarm and answer it, are both Cincinnatus and the citizen calling him from his agriculture.

18. Schlesinger, *History of American Presidential Elections*, 4:3114.

19. This, of course, had been Teddy Roosevelt's reason for running in 1912, but it was left unstated in his letter of announcement.

20. "Certainly, I never suffered any delusion that lightning would suddenly strike and I would be nominated," he acknowledged in 1990. "1948 gave me my one real chance; but each time, when I announced that I would run for President, I got a temporary forum to expound my views." Harold Stassen, *Eisenhower: Turning the World Toward Peace* (St. Paul, 1990), p. viii.

21. In both imagery and evangelical style, Wallace seemed much influenced by William Jennings Bryan, who also portrayed his campaigns as religious crusades.

22. In 1948 the Dixiecrats had walked out of the Democratic convention in protest over its civil rights plank. They subsequently founded the States' Rights party and nominated Senator Strom Thurmond for the presidency. In the general election he carried four Southern states.

23. Nelson W. Polsby and Aaron Wildavsky, *Presidential Elections* (New York, 1984), p. 93.

24. In the wake of the assassinations of Martin Luther King and Robert Kennedy, unrest and political suspicion ran high by August. What was later described as a "police riot" raged outside the convention hall as war protesters and "Yippies" fought with Chicago policemen, while inside the anger was nearly as great if not quite so violently expressed.

25. Early announcements had become so accepted and expected by 1988 that New York's Governor Mario Cuomo would be chided by the press and fellow De-

mocrats for not having decided whether to run by an earlier date than the entry of any candidate in 1968.

26. Theodore H. White, *The Making of the President 1972* (New York, 1973), p. 53. McGovern had made a late and largely symbolic entry into the 1968 race. He offered himself on August 10 as a stand-in for the fallen Kennedy.

27. *Ibid.*

28. In December 1973 he stumped the game show panel on *What's My Line?* Even without their usual "mystery guest" blindfolds, the panel couldn't identify the Georgia governor. Betty Glad, *Jimmy Carter: In Search of the Great White House* (New York, 1980), p. 216.

29. Both Senator Paul Simon and Governor Dukakis delivered preannounce-ment announcements of this sort.

30. Echoing Kennedy was common among Democratic hopefuls. Senator Joseph Biden was often so inclined, as in the line, "We must rekindle the fire of ide-alism in our society, for nothing suffocates the promise of America more than un-bounded cynicism and indifference." Representative Gephardt also struggled to cap-ture the Kennedy mantle: "Instead of asking something of us," he declared, "they have given us a call to selfishness. They have not summoned us to think about the future, but only to think about ourselves."

31. Thus Dole did what Coriolanus refused to do, exposed his wounds to influ-ence his audience. Lyndon Johnson had given the country a bizarre version of the gesture when he lifted his shirt after gall bladder surgery, exposing both his scar and an ample belly.

32. Compare this with George Bush's claim in a Garrison, Ohio, campaign speech (12/5/87) that, when he was shot down in the Pacific, what came to mind, after his parents, was the great constitutional principle of the separation of church and state.

33. During Jackson's remarks in Raleigh, the Old South made an appearance in the form of a demonstration by supporters of a former Klan leader and aspiring politician, David Duke.

34. Peggy Noonan, *What I Saw at the Revolution: a Political Life in the Reagan Era* (New York, 1990), p. 296.

35. When contemporary politicians, especially conservatives, challenge courage they nearly always have in mind verbalized principles. Only Dole, in fact, had a combat record equal to Bush's, while Pat Buchanan, who was fond of terms like "wimp," had none whatsoever. In the 1980s and 1990s participation in the Vietnam War counted less among Clinton critics than what one had *said* about that conflict.

36. Such self-promotion was more direct in the 1988 campaign than in any other. Senator Dole had told his Kansas enthusiasts, "I *can* make a difference. I *have* made a difference. I *will* make a difference."

37. The "new South" Democrats all embrace the civil rights revolution and pro-claim Martin Luther King a hero. The Republicans who won control of Congress in 1994, by contrast, rarely comment on that historic era and, for the most part, sound like *old* South Democrats. This is literally true of Strom Thurmond, Republican Chair of The Senate Armed Services Committee and the 1948 Dixiecrat nominee, and for 1996 presidential aspirant Sen. Phil Gramm.

CHAPTER THREE

As with announcements of candidacy, messages accepting the nomination are included in presidential papers only in the case of sitting presidents. But with the exception of the very first letters of acceptance, some of which predate the *New York Times*, they are reliably published. Available in a great variety of publications, including *Vital Speeches of the Day* as well as all major newspapers, readers have any number of options. Many can be found in Schlesinger's *History of American Presidential Elections.*

1.   Barry Goldwater, the 1964 Republican nominee, offered little in the way of conciliatory gestures after being nominated by a rancorous and divided convention. "Anyone who joins us in all sincerity," he declared, "we welcome. Those, those who do not care for our cause, we don't expect to enter our ranks in any case." The "us" was not the Republican party but only its most conservative elements, and in his most quoted phrase, Goldwater taunted the moderates he thought had depicted him as "a crazy." "Extremism in the defense of liberty is no vice. . . . Moderation in the pursuit of justice is no virtue." The passage was italicized in the candidate's text. Johnson won the election in a landslide. Schlesinger, ed., *History of American Presidential Elections,* 4:3669. Subsequent page references in this chapter are from this source unless otherwise noted.

2.   Earlier acceptances were widely circulated and Coolidge and Hoover broadcast theirs, but it was the delivery on the convention floor that gave it its present importance and drama.

3.   William M. Holland, *The Life and Political Opinions of Martin Van Buren, Vice President of the United States* (Hartford, CT, 1835), p. 351.

4.   Wayne Cutler, ed., *Correspondence of James K. Polk* (Nashville, TN, 1989), 7:241.

5.   R. G. Horton, ed., *The Life and Public Service of James Buchanan* (New York, 1856), pp. 414–15.

6.   Elbert B. Smith, *The Presidencies of Zachary Taylor and Millard Fillmore* (Lawrence, KS: University Press of Kansas, 1988), p. 41.

7.   H. Montgomery, ed., *The Life of Major Zachary Taylor* (New York, 1860), p. 393.

8.   Lincoln had made a similar promise at the close of his spoken remarks in 1860. Shortly thereafter he sent a very brief note formally accepting the nomination and endorsing the convention's platform.

9.   In 1896 William McKinley formally accepted the nomination several weeks after the convention, already well into the "front porch" campaign in which he regularly addressed visitors at his Ohio home. His letter to the convention responded point by point to the platform, focusing on sound money and antisilver arguments. It affirmed his agreement with the party leadership. Treated as a campaign speech for a stay-at-home candidate, it was widely circulated with more than 250,000 copies published. But throughout, McKinley deferred to the party and represented himself as its dutiful servant. (*New York Times,* 8/27/1896). For Theodore Roosevelt see *The Works of Theodore Roosevelt, Presidential Addresses and State Papers* (New York, n.d.), 3:47–94.

10.   Even Woodrow Wilson, however, before leading his country into the war

that would make the world safe for democracy, took the "exemplary" stance. "The example of America," he declared in 1915, "must be the example not merely of peace because it will not fight, but of peace because peace is the healing and elevating influence of the world, and strife is not. There is such a thing as a man being too proud to fight. There is such a thing as a nation being so right that it does not need to convince others by force that it is right." Link, ed., *The Papers of Woodrow Wilson*, 33:149.

11. Slightly more than a decade after Frederick Jackson Turner told Americans that the frontier, which had provided the great safety valve for the nation's enormous energy and restless spirit, no longer existed, Teddy Roosevelt—whose own writings expressed agreement with Turner's thesis—directed his countrymen toward newly identified "frontiers."

12. The word "example" appears repeatedly in Harding's speech, as though to reassure his listeners that the age of presidential activism had ended both abroad and at home.

13. The communist threat shadows much of Harding's thinking though he seems uncertain of where exactly to locate the danger, whether in domestic labor movements or in the world at large. In considering international affairs, communism is both a reason for staying away from world organizations and for a lesser degree of global involvement. "It is folly," he argued, "to close our eyes to outstanding facts. Humanity is restive, much of the world is in revolution, the agents of discord have wrought their tragedy in pathetic Russia, have lighted their torches among other peoples, and hope to see America as a part of the great Red conflagration."

14. William G. McAdoo, Wilson's Secretary of the Treasury, said of Harding's oratory, "His speeches leave the impression of an army of pompous phrases moving over the landscape in search of an idea." Quoted in Samuel Hopkins Adams, *Incredible Era: The Life and Times of Warren Gamaliel Harding* (Boston, 1939), p. 115.

15. Kenneth Cmiel describes the mixture of the "refined" and the raw in such nineteenth-century leaders as Jackson and Lincoln as "middling style," but those extremes of speaking, while practiced by the same persons, were usually not intermixed. In the twentieth century, by contrast, FDR created a "middling style" that combined eloquence and idiomatic speech. It was not one moment a "high" style and another a "low," but remained somewhere between while retaining its eloquence.

16. Coolidge had actually thought more on rhetorical matters than any other twentieth-century president. His education at Amherst had, by his choice, a strong classical emphasis, and in his writings about the presidency he emphasized the importance of speechmaking and of the careful thought that activity required. He noted as well that "greatness" was not a quality to be desired in an American executive, and his own rhetorical commitment was not to the sort of eloquence to which Senator Harding aspired but to clear and direct expression.

17. The Nineteenth Amendment required only one more state's endorsement to go into effect when Harding made his acceptance speech.

18. Lou Henry Hoover was a graduate of Stanford, where she had been one of that university's first female geology majors. She was an important and active participant in all of her husband's professional endeavors, both his mining work and his public service. She also served as national president of the Girl Scouts.

19. *The Public Papers and Addresses of Franklin D. Roosevelt* (New York, 1938), vol. 1, pp. 647–59.

20. The chain of "deals" in presidential sloganeering runs from Teddy Roosevelt's "Square Deal" to FDR's "New Deal," to Truman's "Fair Deal." The connection to Twain's Yankee, himself a common man defined by popular culture, is obvious in this card game metaphor.

21. "Bush Takes the Lead and Defines His Mission," *Congressional Quarterly Almanac* (Washington, 1988), pp. 41–44-A.

22. Wilson similarly spoke of a genius of the common, but in his formulations the common always seemed rarified and ethereal.

23. *Public Papers of FDR*, 5:230–36.

24. Of course, Roosevelt has not been the only model available to nominees. In 1952 Adlai Stevenson turned to Lincoln's example for his address to the Democratic convention. He began by stating his preference for a "stronger, wiser" candidate than himself and repeated the old disclaimer about not seeking the honor. But it was the biblical Lincoln that most dramatically influenced Stevenson and made his address one of the most memorable—and strange—examples of the acceptance genre. "I have asked the merciful Father of us all to let this cup pass from me," he intoned. "But from such dread responsibility one does not shrink in fear, in self-interest, or in false humility. So if this cup may not pass away from me, except I drink it, thy will be done." The self-comparison with Christ at Gethsemane seemed a wildly contradictory expression of humility in the reluctance it portrayed, and a show of pride in the wholly inappropriate implied analogy (*New York Times* 7/26/52).

25. "Texts of Acceptance Speeches: Carter Speech." *Congressional Quarterly Almanac* (1976), pp. 851–53. Carter's speech was delivered on July 15, 1976.

26. "Reagan Chooses Bush as Vice President," *Congressional Quarterly Almanac* (1980), p. 36B.

27. "Acceptance Speeches: Reagan: Time To Recapture Our Destiny," *Congressional Quarterly Almanac* (1980), pp. 36–39-B. Reagan's speech was delivered on July 17, 1980.

28. Reagan repeated this emphasis in his brief survey of America's history, beginning with the "group of families" who formed the Mayflower Compact.

29. Neither history (other than the very recent) nor quotation made much of an appearance in Roosevelt's speeches.

30. *Public Papers of FDR*, 1:651.

31. *Ibid.*, p. 658.

32. "Acceptance Speeches: Reagan," p. 38.

33. *Ibid.*, p. 37.

34. *Ibid.*, p. 39.

35. The Reverend Pat Robertson would so pronounce it in his speech to the 1988 Republican delegates.

36. The one who came closest to violating conventional propriety (to the point of making some in his audience uncomfortable) was the liberal Democrat who Reagan claimed had driven him into the Republican party, Adlai Stevenson.

37. Having omitted in 1988 any reference to the privileged childhood and ado-

lescence that stood between him and typical American experience, Bush asserted his commonness four years later in his second acceptance speech with a language as colloquial as anything Truman ever uttered. Using words like "heck," "lingo," "cahoots," and "fishy," and phrases like "you bet," and "now, O.K.," he attempted to lighten the general tone and suggest an unpretentious and intellectually unremarkable speaker. Similarly, Bush represented himself as an enthusiast for popular culture and working-class views when he told not one but two Elvis Presley jokes, laughed at his yuppie opponent's appearance in running shorts, and mocked congressmen who used blow-dryers. The jocularity suggested his own ease and good humor, despite a disappointing economy and slumping polls (*New York Times*, 8/21/92).

CHAPTER FOUR

All quotations from inaugural addresses, except for Clinton's, are taken from *Inaugural Addresses of the Presidents of the United States from George Washington 1789 to George Bush 1989* (Washington, DC: U.S. Government Printing Office, 1989).

1.   See *Life*'s photo spread on the inauguration in the February 1, 1937 issue.

2.   "The trip through the Tennessee Valley was a great success," FDR wrote to John Nance Garner in November 1934, "especially the visit to the Hermitage. The more I learn about old Andy Jackson the more I love him." Elliott Roosevelt, ed., *F.D.R. His Personal Letters, 1928–1945* (New York, 1950), 1:433.

3.   Adams carried the Northern states and Jefferson the South plus Pennsylvania.

4.   At his second inauguration Jefferson reflected on these issues from a slightly different perspective, employing a tone uncharacteristically ironic in his instructions to his countrymen. After defending the Louisiana Purchase, explaining why the country could afford the expenditure and elaborating on the advantage of rescuing that territory from European hands, he took up what seems to be the issue of the nation's "aboriginal inhabitants"—a population greatly enlarged by his recent acquisition—declaring them "endowed with the faculties and the rights of men." The government, he continued, had tried to assist them in learning "agriculture and the domestic arts . . . and to prepare them in time for that state of society which to bodily comforts adds the improvement of the mind and morals." Here is the "knowledge and virtue" which in Adams's inaugural were the twin pillars of liberal government, but Jefferson suggested that those efforts confronted "powerful obstacles":

[T]hey are combatted by the habits of their bodies, prejudices of their minds, ignorance, pride, and the influence of interested and crafty individuals among them who feel themselves something in the present order of things and fear to become nothing in any other. These persons inculcate a sanctimonious reverence for the customs of their ancestors; that whatsoever they did must be done through all time; that reason is a false guide, and to advance under its counsel in their physical, moral, or political condition is perilous innovation; that their duty is to remain as their creator made them, ignorance being safety and knowledge full of danger; in short, my friends, among them also is seen the action and counteraction of good sense and of bigotry; they too have their antiphilosophists who find an interest in keeping things in their present state, who dread reformation, and exert all their faculties to maintain the ascendancy of habit over the duty of improving our reason and obeying its mandates. (pp. 20–21)

Jefferson's "among them also" and "they too" made clear that his real complaint was not with "aboriginals" but with fellow citizens. He was pointing to the antiliberal, anti-enlightenment forces that resist progressive change, the "antiphilosophists" of his own race who impede the "advance of this great experiment."

5.   In 1877, speaking only days after the results of his own controversial election had been determined, Rutherford B. Hayes—defeated in the popular vote and victorious in the Electoral College only though the most devious of party maneuvering—spent his speech reassuring Southern Democrats. In an atmosphere of political recrimination, electric with the loose talk of armed confrontation, he tried to put the best face on things by suggesting that the settlement of the electoral dispute could provide an important lesson to a world of less enlightened nations:

It has been reserved for a government of the people, where the right of suffrage is universal, to give to the world the first example in history of a great nation, in the midst of the struggle of opposing parties for power, hushing its party tumults to yield the issue of the contest to adjustment according to the forms of law. (p. 159)

Twelve years later, when Benjamin Harrison won an unquestioned victory in the Electoral College, but with fewer popular votes than his opponent Grover Cleveland, he responded more eloquently and persuasively to the implications of the contest, and without understating the potential danger:

Let us exalt patriotism and moderate our party contentions. Let those who would die for the flag on the field of battle give a better proof of their patriotism and a higher glory to their country by promoting fraternity and justice. A party success that is achieved by unfair methods or by practices that partake of revolution is hurtful and evanescent even from a party standpoint. We should hold our differing opinions in mutual respect, and, having submitted them to the arbitrament of the ballot, should accept an adverse judgment with the same respect that we would have demanded of our opponents if the decision had been in our favor. (p. 184)

6.   Quoted in Walker Lewis, *Speak for Yourself, Daniel: A Life of Webster in His Own Words* (Washington, DC, 1969), p. 300.

7.   The latter claim played loose with biographical fact, as Harrison was actually born on a Virginia estate, but it fit well with the Whig desire to both imitate and renounce their nemesis.

8.   Grover Cleveland in his 1884 acceptance letter made a similar case on the grounds that it would liberate the presidency from the corrupting temptations that the desire for reelection can arouse.

9.   The *New York Times* reporter thought this a reference to the high responsibility of the office. "President Pierce is evidently very deeply impressed by the magnitude of the trust committed to his hands. . . . The touching sentiment of his

opening sentence evidently rests at the bottom of his heart, and gives character and tone to his comments upon public affairs" (*New York Times*, 3/5/1853).

10. Both the child's injury and the mother's grief were sensationalized in the press. The *New York Daily Times* reprinted an eyewitness account:

> Go with me, Mr. Editor, to that house [where the injured had been taken], and look with me awhile on that scene of suffering and sorrow. In one room were Gen. PIERCE and his lady, in the opposite apartment lay the remains of their little boy—and oh! so sad a sight! The blow, by which he was instantly killed, struck his forehead, and was so violent as to remove the upper portion of the head, leaving a part of the brain exposed. The face, with the exception of a bruise about the right eye, still remained uninjured, but bathed in blood. (*New York Daily Times*, January 7, 1853, p. 1)

11. See the discussion of Reagan's 1980 acceptance speech in Chapter Three.

12. Speaking in 1858 to a convention of Illinois Republicans that had just pledged him their support for the Senate, Lincoln had declared: "A house divided against itself cannot stand." Democrats attacked Lincoln for promoting war between the states and for opposing the Union in the form the fathers had given it.

13. At least this is the logic of the Second Inaugural. In an August 14, 1862 address on colonization to a "committee of colored men," Lincoln insisted that the races were irreconcilably divided and that it "is better for . . . both, therefore, to be separated." So he urged relocation to Liberia or the creation of a Central American colony. His tone was a mixture of beseeching and condescension, and his remarks suggest frustration with a black presence in America almost as much as with slavery. See Roy P. Basler, ed., *The Collected Works of Abraham Lincoln* (New Brunswick, NJ, 1953), Vol. 5, pp. 570–75.

CHAPTER FIVE

1. Hayes had been elected in the most controversial presidential election since that of John Quincy Adams. His victory came only after large numbers of Democratic votes in Florida and Louisiana were disqualified. The issue was decided by a bipartisan panel that voted eight to seven in Hayes's favor and determined the election outcome only a few days before the Inauguration. The Compromise of 1877 provided for the withdrawal of Federal troops and helped calm Southern feelings. See Schlesinger, ed., *History of American Presidential Elections*, 2:1349–1435.

2. This "war," broadly interpreted, would dominate American thinking until the 1980s, understood, as Dwight Eisenhower described it at midcentury, as a conflict in which "freedom is pitted against slavery; lightness against the dark," with communism identified in the Cold War era as the enslaving power (p. 296).

3. Hoover came the closest, because of both his private employment in places like China and Australia and his public service in European relief. Eisenhower, however, as head of NATO, was leader of the free world *before* he became president.

4. Roosevelt's own refusal to be "paralyzed," despite his inability to use his legs, provided a personal confirmation of his public messages. "Paralysis" was a word and a concept he frequently invoked.

5.   The line echoed a sentiment often expressed by Teddy Roosevelt, who in 1905 had told his inaugural audience, "There is no good reason why we should fear the future, but there is every reason why we should face it seriously" (p. 211).

6.   Johnson used the word "union" more readily than any other twentieth-century president. "Underneath the clamor of building and the rush of our day's pursuits, we are believers in justice and liberty and union, and in our own Union" (p. 512).

7.   Nixon's admiration for Woodrow Wilson was deep and enduring, and he sought to emulate him above any other president. References to Wilson are found throughout Nixon's writings.

8.   Reagan's "well" is more evident in transcriptions of his speeches than in official, edited versions.

9.   Bush's distinguished service as a combat pilot in the Pacific, like Kennedy's naval experience, deeply influenced his sense of America's international obligation. He served as ambassador to the United Nations in 1971–73 and as U.S. Liaison in China in 1974–75. Of the postwar presidents preceding Clinton, Johnson and Reagan had the least military experience. Johnson's was limited in duration (he served in the Navy from December 1941 to July 1942 while retaining his House seat), but he was awarded the Silver Star by General MacArthur. Reagan was kept from combat because of visual problems and spent most of his time in a motion picture unit. Carter spent seven years in the Navy, beginning in 1946.

10.   Clinton's message formally parallels Kennedy's as much as Jackson's did Washington's and Reagan's FDR's. Kennedy began, for instance, "we observe today not a victory of party, but a celebration of freedom—symbolizing an end as well as a beginning—signifying renewal, as well as change." Clinton opened, "Today we celebrate the mystery of American renewal."

It is striking that each of the three imitative speeches makes a claim on a particular presidential and rhetorical model while contradicting the message of the earlier address. Jackson spoke against Washington's federalism; Reagan repudiated New Deal principles; and Clinton rejected the Cold Warrior mentality that dominated Kennedy's inaugural.

11.   Though the Kennedy echoes dominated the speech, it was a reminder of Martin Luther King that could be heard in the concluding injunction, "From this joyful mountain top of celebration, we hear a call to the valley."

CHAPTER SIX

1.   Arthur M. Schlesinger, Jr., "Annual Messages of the Presidents: Major Themes of American History," in Fred Israel. ed., *The State of the Union Messages 1790–1966* (New York, 1966), I:xvii.

2.   In 1798 yellow fever killed more than two thousand people in New York City alone.

3.   Washington, by contrast, spent little time on the subject of foreign relations, telling Congress in 1793 simply, "The connection of the United States with Europe has become extremely interesting."

4.   Only during the second Harrison's administration (1889–93) were more states, six, admitted.

5.   The Panic of 1819 is generally thought the consequence of rampant land speculation and domestic banking problems as well as trade problems.

6.   Monroe made this point more dramatically when he reported that "[p]ossession of East and West Florida has been given to the United States," and in 1822 he offered the next episode in this ongoing and somewhat redundant story, reporting that Florida had been successfully organized under a territorial government and, with "Europe still unsettled," restrictions on American trade with British colonies were revoked. (I:186)

7.   Because America's argument against further colonization was based in part on the antagonism of political systems—democratic America against authoritarian Spain—Monroe was telling Europe that his country would not involve itself in liberal revolutions on that continent despite a sentiment favoring "the liberty . . . of their fellow men on that side of the Atlantic."

8.   In as much as Tyler's term "foreign" is applied to immigrants from other countries—a continuing concern for state of the union messages—America's attitude has been variable and mixed. Polk, Tyler's successor, celebrated the fact "that immigrants of every lineage and language . . . transfer their heart, not less than their allegiance, to the country whose dominions belong alone to the people." Teddy Roosevelt stated the most persistent American attitude when he declared, "We cannot have too much immigration of the right kind, and we should have none at all of the wrong kind." Arthur Schlesinger, Jr., points out in his introduction to *The State of the Union Messages* that Roosevelt meant the distinction to be one of merit rather than national origin (he disagreed with Chinese exclusion laws), but without such qualification the quotation more aptly describes the American attitude.

9.   This was the question raised by Hector St. John de Crèvecoeur in his 1782 tract, *Letters from an American Farmer*, and repeated by generations of commentators since.

10.   The analogy is, of course, very loose. The American Colonization Society purchased land in Africa as a place to relocate free African Americans, as a means both of removal and of African "improvement." The capital of the settlement was named "Monrovia."

11.   Native Americans remained a presidential subject, of course, long after Fillmore's administration. Lincoln was concerned in 1861 with the possible recruitment of Southwestern tribes by the Confederate states, and conflicts between white settlers and native peoples continued through much of the century. President Hayes, echoing sentiments previously expressed by Grant, took up the issue of Indian victimization in 1877, declaring, "Many, if not most, of our Indian wars have had their origins in broken promises and acts of injustice upon our part." And he exhorted his countrymen to help Native Americans "at least" attain "that degree of civilization that they may be able to reach" (II:1350–51).

12.   The states differed greatly in their own provisions for "citizenship," with some, notably in New England, enfranchising black male residents well before the Civil War, but constitutional guarantees did not come until passage of the Fifteenth Amendment.

13. The Dred Scott decision raised several legal issues, but most specifically that of whether a slave (Scott) transported from a slave state to a free state or a free territory was made free by that move. The Supreme Court not only ruled in the negative but went on to declare the Missouri Compromise unconstitutional on the grounds that it deprived persons of their property without due process. Thus slavery could not be excluded from the territories.

14. Wilson made this observation in his 1892 study, *Division and Reunion: 1829–1889.*

15. "All right we are two nations/America our nation has been beaten by strangers who have bought the laws and fenced off the meadows and cut down the woods for pulp and turned our pleasant cities into slums and sweated the wealth out of our people." (John Dos Passos, *The Big Money* [New York, 1969], p. 469. Originally published in 1936.)

CHAPTER SEVEN

1. This in itself was not unusual; Jefferson delighted in composing such messages and had made a special point of instructing his Western representatives—especially Meriwether Lewis and William Clark—to run a virtual travel agency for tribal ambassadors interested in making his acquaintance. His messages, while using the language of father and children to describe the relationship between president and native populations, consistently address his Indian audience as "brothers." Typical in emphasis are his words to "the Wolf and people of the Mandan Nation" encouraging them to travel to the cities of the United States to "see how many friends and brothers you have here." More than a hundred pages of Volume 16 of *The Writings of Thomas Jefferson* (Washington, DC, 1905) are devoted to "Indian Addresses."

2. Saul K. Padover, ed., *The Complete Madison: His Basic Writings* (New York, 1953), pp. 327–30.

3. This is a fundamental point about rhetoric and about so rhetorical an office as the American presidency; the interplay of speaker and audience, the continual effort by each to reshape the other after its own image, generates a dynamic relationship in which both participants are recreated in response to one another and the rhetorical moment. The hubristic temptation of speakers to believe, as did the Sophists of Plato's Dialogues, that they, because of their eloquent superiority, are in command is self-deluding, ignoring the ways in which in order to persuade their listeners they are themselves changed.

See Plato's *Gorgias* and the exchange between Socrates and Callicles regarding exactly this point.

4. Karlyn Kohrs Campbell and Kathleen Hall Jamieson, *Words into Deeds: Presidential Rhetoric and the Genres of Governance* (Chicago: University of Chicago Press, 1990), p. 105.

5. The matter of a Mexican "invasion" and the shedding of "American blood upon American soil" was less than certain (the one-term Congressman Abraham Lincoln, for one, would express doubts), which exemplifies Campbell and Jamieson's fifth characteristic of "strategic misrepresentation."

6.   Bryan had found his president biased toward the British and resigned after Wilson condemned Germany for the sinking of the *Lusitania*.

7.   America's official involvement in the European conflict began three days later, when Japan's allies, Italy and Germany, declared war on the United States.

8.   See also "Communist Attack on Korea a Violation of U.N. Charter," *Vital Speeches of the Day*, 16 (August 1, 1950), pp. 610–12.

9.   See "War with Iraq," *Vital Speeches of the Day*, 62 (February 1, 1991), pp. 226–27.

10.   Daniel Webster presided over notable anniversaries at—among other historically significant sites—Plymouth Rock and Bunker Hill as well as commemorating the great heroes of his father's generation as they passed into immortality with his rhetorical assistance. So, too, did Edward Everett, the featured speaker at Gettysburg, and a host of other public orators of the time.

11.   Coolidge, *Autobiography*, p. 219.

12.   Taft traveled so often and for such lengths of time that newspapers captioned caricatures with "Travels on the slightest provocation." Taft himself admitted, "I want to get in as much traveling as I can during these four years for after they are over I do not know when I will get another opportunity." For more on his wanderings see Judith Icke Anderson, *William Howard Taft: An Intimate History* (New York, 1981), esp. pp. 33–36, 177–78.

13.   This was not the first time a president had gone on tour to win the support of the general public. Andrew Johnson had taken his fight with the radical Republicans in Congress on the road in 1866, but the overall result was negative, and he was condemned for being unpresidential.

14.   Roosevelt served in the New York State Assembly from 1882 until 1884, the year in which his first wife died. He then went to Dakota, where he ranched until late 1886, then returned to New York and ran, unsuccessfully, in the 1886 New York City mayoral election.

15.   Peter Finley Dunne, *Mr. Dooley at His Best* (New York, 1938), p. 97.

16.   He returned during his 1903 tour to greet his old neighbors in Medora, reminding them that twenty years earlier he had "stopped at your houses and shared your hospitality. With some of the men I have ridden guard around the cattle at night, worked with them in the round-up, and hunted with them, so that I know them pretty well" (I:321).

17.   Theodore Roosevelt, "Manhood and Statehood," *The Strenuous Life* (New York, 1901), pp. 201–14.

18.   This was a point made by the president of Northwestern University during Roosevelt's 1903 stop in Chicago. "You, sir, are the first President of the twentieth century," President James declared, "not merely in time, but in temper. Your predecessors for more than fifty years looked forward to, grappled with, or looked back upon problems of the nineteenth century—problems which seem to us now more than a century old. They belong to history. You are the first to face resolutely and fully the problems of a new generation and a new age" (*New York Times*, 4/3/03, p. 2).

19.   What he called in Saint Louis "the *work* of expansion" he had identified in Colorado Springs as "the winning of the West." The mixed language of labor and

play, of "work" and "winning," runs through all of Roosevelt's writing, suggesting how fully the two activities had intermingled in his and in the popular mind. America's "play" was to work, and its "work" was to "win."

20. The exclusion of Native Americans in this political and moral "test," given the issues raised in the Philippines, was a notable omission and logical inconsistency in Roosevelt's argument. He tended to regard indigenous populations in this country's past merely as challenges to a Euro-American pioneering spirit.

21. "No nation," he told the Minnesota legislature,

> which has bound itself only to do easy things ever yet amounted to anything, ever yet came to anything throughout the ages. We have become a great people. At the threshold of this twentieth century we stand with the future looming large before us. We face great problems within and great problems without. We cannot if we would refuse to face those problems. All we can decide is whether we will do them well or ill; for the refusal to face them would itself mean that we were doing them ill. We are in the arena into which great nations must come. We must play our part. (I:291–92)

22. "The American Boy" is included in Roosevelt's *The Strenuous Life*. The quoted passage appears on p. 136.

23. Theodore H. White, *The Making of the President, 1964* (New York, 1965), Appendix A, p. 405.

CHAPTER EIGHT

1. Reagan's greatest gift in dealing with audiences was his capacity to appear convincingly as one of them. He looked out over the veterans of D-Day and conveyed the sense that he was genuinely there to honor and not to compete with them. That was typical of Reagan. When "stars"—athletes, entertainment figures, or ordinary citizens thrust by fate into the spotlight—came to visit the White House, he was able to stand by appreciatively, warmly, apparently secure enough in himself that he could be comfortable in a lesser light, a fan who felt compelled neither to outdo his heroes nor even, despite his apparent activist political agenda, to push his audience much beyond an observing role. This was in part because for him the contest had lost, at the level of manhood, its Darwinian teeth. The "iron qualities" Teddy Roosevelt thought requirements for both man and state, for Reagan were required solely by the latter. In his view of things the state fights the old battle for survival in order that its citizens, individually, can be less hardy, less devoted to work, less self-sacrificing. Reagan's West culminated in the deserved leisure of Palm Springs, not in Badlands heroics.

2. Link, ed., *Papers of Wilson*, 2:67.

3. On February 12, 1914, ground had been broken for the Lincoln Memorial in Washington, D.C. The reverential mood of the building and the statue it houses are consistent with Wilson's tone and message in 1916.

4. Herman Melville, *Moby-Dick*, ch. 26, "Knights and Squires."

5. Coolidge, *Autobiography*, p. 173.

6. Garry Wills, *Lincoln at Gettysburg: The Words That Remade America* (New York: Simon & Schuster, 1992).

7. Wills, *Lincoln at Gettysburg*, p. 110.

8. The Oxford English Dictionary indicates that both usages were common.

9. One of the more popular recruiting hymns was "We Are Coming Father Abra'am 300,000 Strong," whose lyrics describe a Northern horizon lined with young men who have left their farms to answer Lincoln's call. In the fourth and final verse the singers declare their readiness "to lay us down for Freedom's sake,/ Our brothers' bones beside" and then close, "Six hundred thousand loyal men/ And true have gone before./ We are coming, Father Abra'am,/ Three hundred thousand more." The president of the Confederate States, Jefferson Davis, was more fortuitously named.

See Michael Paul Rogin's provocative discussion in "The King's Two Bodies," in *Reagan the Movie, and Other Episodes in Political Demonology* (Berkeley, CA, 1987). I have been much influenced by this essay in my understanding of Wilson and Nixon as well as Lincoln.

10. Benjamin Franklin, *The Autobiography of Benjamin Franklin*, edited by Leonard W. Laharee (New Haven, 1964), p. 179.

11. Katheen Hall Jamieson, *Eloquence in an Electronic Age: The Transformation of Political Speechmaking* (New York, 1988), p. 55.

12. Roosevelt was not the first president to be heard on radio, but he was the first fully to understand its possibilities. For Coolidge and, to a considerable extent, Hoover, it was primarily a means of amplification, of bringing a larger audience to the traditional presidential address, and even in the studio they had difficulty adjusting to the changed dimensions of their speaking space.

13. In contrast to the bathos of Nixon's "Checkers" speech (a response to improprieties of accepting inappropriate and perhaps illegal campaign gifts and contributions), when, voice trembling, he declared that he would not return his children's pet dog even though it had been a gift, FDR dealt with criticism that his dog Fala had traveled with him at government expense by saying, "These Republican leaders have not been content with attacks on me, or my wife, or on my sons. No, not content with that, they now included my little dog, Fala. Well, of course, I don't resent attacks, and my family doesn't resent attacks, but Fala *does* resent them." See *The Public Papers and Addresses of Franklin D. Roosevelt* (New York, 1950, 13:290).

14. Ironically FDR's 1941 remarks echo some of the sentiments of Wilson's 1915 speech, after the sinking of the *Lusitania* by a German submarine. That was when Wilson, taking the superior path, had said, "There is such a thing as a nation being so right that it does not need to convince others by force that it is right." *The Papers of Woodrow Wilson*, 33:49. These comments appeared in a speech to a group of newly naturalized citizens, an address that powerfully asserts Wilson's distinction between his country and the rest of the world.

CHAPTER NINE

1. *The Works of John Adams, Second President of the United States* (Boston, 1854), 9:236.

2. George Bush did not give a major farewell address upon leaving office in 1993.

3.   In this he echoed Truman, who had told his countrymen in 1953, "I will once again be a plain, private citizen of this great Republic." Eisenhower, by contrast, after he had stepped down from the presidency asked to have his old title of general restored.

4.   In her discussion of how the speech was composed, the speechwriter Peggy Noonan surrounded the event with talk of co-workers who fell in love, and her own infatuation with the president ("so because you're so dazzling and the President of the United States and you're Ronald Reagan . . ."). She remembered that the Head of the National Security Council, after reading an advance copy, had called it "flighty." "Flighty," she mocked, "my, my what an interesting word for a big man in epaulets to use about a speech written by a woman." What seemed more the case was that the speech Reagan read seemed less his own words than those of someone who wanted him to recognize her admiration and respect. Peggy Noonan, *What I Saw at the Revolution: A Political Life in the Reagan Era* (New York, 1990), pp. 332, 334.

5.   For a well documented overview of Johnson's career, see Hans Trefousse, *Andrew Johnson: A Biography* (New York, 1989).

6.   *New York Times*, 3/4/1869. All subsequent references to Andrew Johnson's farewell are from this source.

7.   As the Military Governor of his home state of Tennessee in the first years of the war, Johnson came to the White House well aware of how it felt to be vilified as a traitor. But having paid that price for his loyalty to the Union, he must have found the Republican attacks even more humiliating, since they suggested contempt for the very "sacrifice" he had made in joining their 1864 ticket.

8.   Agnew, facing charges of bribery and extortion dating from his term as Governor of Maryland, resigned on October 10, 1973. His half-page letter to the President foreshadowed the lines of Nixon's self-defense. He was, he said, stepping down "in the best interests of the nation" and because he foresaw "a long, divisive and debilitating struggle in the Congress." Subsequently Agnew wrote his own account of events, *Go Quietly . . . or Else* (New York, 1980), in which he insisted that he had been betrayed by Nixon and, he suspected, marked for assassination by the White House Chief of Staff (pp. 189–90).

9.   Of course, they can all be seen as turning points, moments of decision that might be called "crises," but Nixon's use of the term is not so etymologically driven. Crisis for him was personal and psychological and always implied danger. Richard Nixon, *Six Crises* (New York, 1962). His theory of crisis is elaborated in the introduction to the first edition.

10.   He entitled his account of the presidential years *In the Arena* (New York, 1990).

11.   Worthington Chauncey Ford, ed., *The Writings of George Washington* (New York, 1891):10:338–39.

12.   *Ibid.*, p. 331.

13.   That earlier address was, with some revision the one he was delivering here. Jefferson, in a letter to Justice William Johnson, described the manner in which it was composed:

With respect to [Washington's] farewell address, to the authorship of which, it seems, there are conflicting claims, I can state to you some facts. He had determined to decline re-election at the end of his first term, and so far determined, that he had requested Mr. Madison to prepare for him something valedictory, to be addressed to his constituents on his retirement. This was done, but he was finally persuaded to acquiesce in a second election, to which no one more strenuously pressed him than myself, from a conviction of the importance of strengthening, by longer habit, the respect necessary for that office, which the weight of his character only could effect. When at the end of his second term, his Valedictory came out, Mr. Madison recognized in it several passages of his draught, several others, we were both satisfied, were from the pen of Hamilton, and others from that of the President himself. These he probably put into the hands of Hamilton to form into a whole, and hence it may all appear in Hamilton's hand-writing, as if it were all of his composition. (June 12, 1823)

The Writings of Thomas Jefferson (Washington, DC, 1905), p. 443.

14. Subsequent national leaders have often recalled Washington's warnings against foreign entanglements, political parties, and an "overgrown military," but in context even these are inseparable from his primary concern for Union. Foreign alliances—a reaching outside the Union for support and protection—weaken connections with those closer at hand, and if pursued by the states independently would allow a dangerous alternative to their loyalties to one another. Likewise political parties (a shrinking of the scope of loyalty) "organize faction" and "put in the place of the delegated will of the Nation, the will of a party." And large militias incite suspicions and fears when one's neighboring states are fellow countrymen rather than foreigners.

15. James Parton, *The Life of Andrew Jackson* (New York, 1860), 2:590–91.

16. It is telling that while, in his farewell, Washington warned against a strong military—thinking of the suspicions militias could generate between the states—Jackson in his parting message urged a major expansion of the navy in order to react against "any nation [that] will wantonly insult us or needlessly provoke hostilities." The old duelist was quick to suspect insult from many quarters and was determined to have the weapons at hand to defend national or personal honor.

17. The next "savior" general and two-term president was Ulysses S. Grant, but his farewell consisted of only those few lines attached to his last annual report. Given the failures of his administration, perhaps the presumption of a last fatherly lecture was deemed inappropriate. Besides, since he had never shown an inclination for such paternalism and was that rarity among generals, a small "d" democrat, he was probably disinclined by nature to assume such a role.

18. Eisenhower regarded his post as Supreme Allied Commander much as Washington had his command of the unified colonial troops, and at the end of the war he treated them with a similar loyalty and with a similar emphasis on the model they provided the postwar world.

19. Louis Galambos, *The Papers of Dwight D. Eisenhower* (Baltimore, 1978), 9:2241.

20. Kennedy's hawkish campaign often focused on such communist insults as the Berlin Wall and the shelling of Quemoy and Matsu, small islands off the Chinese coast claimed by the Taiwanese government.

21. Eisenhower had a different perspective on research from most presidents. As president of Columbia University from 1948 to 1950, he had at least glimpsed the complicated financial considerations that drive scientific research.

22. The day after his farewell address (on January 18, 1961), still preoccupied with the warning he had delivered, he added extemporaneous commentary to those earlier remarks, commentary that gains credibility for being rough-edged:

> But just by the very nature of the thing, when you see almost every one of your magazines, no matter what they are advertising, has a picture of the Titan missile or the Atlas. . . . There is becoming a great influence, almost an insidious penetration of our own minds, that the only thing this country is engaged in is weaponry and missiles. And I'll tell you we just can't afford to do that.

Here is the reasoning behind the composed and formally articulated warning of his farewell, and in this unpolished utterance Eisenhower laid personal claim to his earlier words. He elbowed aside his speechwriter to tell America the basis of his own concern (PP, Eisenhower, 1960–61:1045).

23. His summoning of the parental ghost sounded bizarrely similar to America's desperate efforts in times of need to raise up the memories of its founders—the ancestors whose examples it cannot live up to.

A GUIDE TO RELATED
MATERIALS

PRESIDENTIAL ELOQUENCE

Presidential messages, those delivered while in office, can be found in a variety of publications ranging from newspapers to the collected papers of individual executives. Depending upon one's interest, the most appropriate source may be determined by genre (collected speeches of a particular type) or by president, or by the historical moment. The choice is largely a matter of convenience, but different textual juxtapositions provide different intellectual opportunities. Seeing a particular inaugural address in the context of other inaugurals is not the sane as seeing it in the context of a president's other papers or surrounded by the news of the day. Each presentation provides the same literal text but in surroundings that force us to view the words differently. As a result there is for the material examined in this book rarely a single, definitive published source but rather a variety of sources reflecting the many lives a public text leads.

PRESIDENTIAL PAPERS

The Manuscript Division of the Library of Congress is the primary repository for the papers of presidents preceding Herbert Hoover. The papers of subsequent presidents (including Hoover) are housed in individual presidential libraries across the country. In 1897 *A Compilation of the Messages and Papers of the Presidents* was published under the editorship of James D. Richardson. That effort was later extended through Warren G. Harding. (The abbreviation MP used in the text refers to this compilation.) In 1958 Congress authorized publication of the *Public Papers of the Presidents of the United States* (abbreviated PP in the text), a series that includes

Hoover and all subsequent presidents except for Franklin Roosevelt, whose speeches can be found in *The Public Papers of Franklin Roosevelt* (New York, 1938–50). Presidential papers may be found in a number of different sources. I have attempted in each chapter to use the most common and readily accessible. Although many presidents have had their papers collected in individual editions, sometimes including their nonpresidential writings, all have been corporately collected, first in MP and since Herbert Hoover in PP. (Coolidge's papers are available on microfilm from the Library of Congress.) These collections contain only the presidential papers and not the larger body of material written by those who have held the office. For some presidents, mostly obvious ones like Washington and Lincoln, the larger body of their writings, including their presidential messages, are available in collected works. For an overview see Frank Leopold Schick's *Records of the Presidency: Presidential Papers and Libraries from Washington to Reagan* (Phoenix, 1989).

Vital Speeches of the Day, a monthly publication, provides the text of many presidential speeches as well as convention acceptance speeches (not often included in presidential papers). Since September 1851 the *New York Times* has published the major presidential messages and is the newspaper source most frequently available (on microfilm) at libraries.

In addition to those sources, a wide array of publications devoted to the speeches of presidents, reflecting the tastes and enthusiasms of particular editors, can be found on most library shelves. They generally provide reliable texts but sometimes abridge without clearly indicating the change.

Twentieth-century presidential speechmaking has also been captured on recordings, film, and videotape. These are available at a number of archives around the country. I did most of my listening and watching at the Library of Congress's Motion Picture, Broadcasting, and Recorded Sound Division; the Television News Archives at Vanderbilt University in Nashville; the Museum of Television and Radio Library in New York; and The Museum of Broadcast History in Chicago.

Since my own method has been to read the presidency, as much as possible, through the messages delivered by those who have held that office, I have provided little in the way of biography or psychology that is not introduced by the speeches themselves. In that sense mine has been a literary approach. Historians and biographers, qualified in ways I am not, have given us an incredible range of commentary on individual presidents and presidencies, much of it noteworthy both for its scholarship and for its readability. The list is far to long to include in this bibliographical note. I single out the work of Garry Wills for the consistency with which it has addressed rhetorical issues in the context of America's public life. *Lincoln at Gettysburg: The Words That Remade America* (New York, 1992) and *Inventing America* (Garden City, NY, 1978) deal most obviously with political rhetoric, but rhetoric lies close to the heart of all Wills's treatment of the presidency, providing an invaluable resource.

For those of us who require constant assistance in locating events and persons, I recommend William A. DeGregorio's helpful *The Complete Books of the Presidents* (New York, 1991). It is an unpretentious, amusing, and rich guide through the American Presidency.

RHETORIC AND RHETORICAL ANALYSIS

The place to begin any investigation of things rhetorical is with the criticism of that discipline delivered in the Dialogues of Plato, especially the *Gorgias* and the *Phaedrus*, and *The Republic*. Aristotle's *Rhetoric*, translated by W. Rhys Roberts (Oxford, 1954), provides the best defense as well as the most commonsensical approach to rhetorical analysis. The Roman teacher Quintilian (in *The Institutio Oratorio*, translated by H. E. Butler in the Loeb Classical Library [Cambridge, MA, 1920]) and the Roman Orator Cicero (in *De Inventione*, translated by A. M. Hubbell in the Loeb Classical Library [Cambridge, MA, 1949] and *DeOratore*, translated by E. W. Sutton and H. Rackham, also in the Loeb [Cambridge, MA, 1942]) provide a rich supply of anecdotes and practical instruction on the subject.

One president, John Quincy Adams, was a former professor of rhetoric. His *Lectures on Rhetoric and Oratory Delivered to the Class of Senior and Junior Sophisters in Harvard University* (Cambridge, MA, 1810) allows an interesting comparison of theory and practice. Appropriately it recognizes the need for a national "orator," arguing that such was the appointment God gave to Aaron when he designated him spokesman for the less articulate Moses.

The text most read by nineteenth-century American students, including future presidents, was that of the Scottish academic Hugh Blair, whose often reprinted *Lectures on Rhetoric and Belles Lettres* (Harold F. Harding, ed. [Carbondale, IL, 1965]) was a staple of American education for the century following its 1783 publication. It was adopted, for instance, at Yale in 1785 and continued in use there until 1860.

By the twentieth century what remained of rhetorical education had been divided between the elocutionary concerns of speech departments and the composition programs typically administered by departments of English. As a consequence it is difficult to identify a common, or even a coherent, notion of the subject in contemporary education. Most helpful among more recent efforts to formulate a systematic treatment of rhetoric is Chaim Perelman's *The New Rhetoric: a Treatise on Argumentation*, John Wilkinson and Purcell Weaver, translators (Notre Dame, IN, 1969), but there is no common text that either presidents or the electorate has read.

Kathleen Hall Jamieson's rhetorical studies have defined the field for recent scholarship. Her *Packaging the Presidency: A History and Criticism of Presidential Campaign Advertising* (New York, 1984) and *Eloquence in an Electronic Age: The Transformation of Political Speechmaking* (New York, 1988) are invaluable to anyone interested in either rhetoric or the presidency. *Deeds Done in Words: Presidential Rhetoric and the Genres of Governance* (Chicago, 1990), written with Karlyn Kohrs Campbell, establishes the generic foundations scholars have long needed in order to distinguish more meaningfully the kinds of speeches presidents deliver.

Similarly, Jeffrey K. Tulis's *The Rhetorical Presidency* (Princeton, NJ, 1987) reestablished among political scientists the connection between the office and the words that represent it. I am grateful not only for the considerable wisdom of the book but also because the response it provoked reinvigorated a subject area nearly moribund among American scholars. I am one of many who benefited from that reawakening.

I also want to call attention to Kenneth Cmiel's *Democratic Eloquence: The Fight over Popular Speech in Nineteenth-Century America* (New York, 1990), an invaluable study of how Americans, presidents included, struggled to find their voice.

Finally, I cannot leave this category without recommending Richard Weaver's *Ethics of Rhetoric* (Chicago, 1953), the little book with which my own reading on this subject began many years ago.

This list is no more than a sampling, a place for an interested public to begin to reacquaint itself with the methods and issues that lie behind this survey of the eloquence of America's presidents.

ACKNOWLEDGMENTS

My interest in what presidents say began a long time ago and has been informed by a great many people. Politics and politicians were a constant source of discussion among the farmers and blue-collar workers who peopled my childhood, and it was their talk, always animated and often heated, that first made me take rhetoric seriously. In that context I learned that such matters were of life-and-death importance and yet also a source of play and amusement. I learned that the adults around me saw our future at stake in the political debates of the day and learned, too, how much pleasure they found by joining in those disputes.

In the 1960s, while I was a graduate student at the University of Chicago, Stuart Tave provided my first serious lessons in rhetorical analysis and introduced me to Aristotle. Robert Streeter taught me—and many other graduate students—how broad and deep is American literature and especially to appreciate the richness of its rhetoric. It was he who guided me through my first fumbling efforts to "read" American politics as well as my subsequent work in this area.

Hours—now years—of conversation with Kurt Olsson and Harry Marten have given me an opportunity to think through the application of "literary" techniques to political materials. Their gentle criticism and wise counsel has influenced all my writing in more ways than even I realize. Among my colleagues in Washington University's English Department I am especially grateful for the continuous support of Steven Zwicker, Robert Wiltenburg, and Naomi Lebowitz. Their work in connecting literature and politics, though in quite different fields, has added much to my own. The opportunity to share an office with Gerald Early has been a special gift from the University and has added immeasurably to my education as an Americanist.

But not all my instruction has come from the English Department. I owe much to a host of other friends and colleagues from across the University and especially to those with whom I have co-taught courses on subjects pertinent to this book: George Pepe from Classics; Glen Holt, Henry Berger, Michael Weinberg, and Iver Bernstein from History; Charles McManis from the School of Law; and Robert Salisbury from Political Science. George Graham of Vanderbilt University's Political Science Department has, over the years, also contributed greatly to my understanding of American politics, and it was he who introduced me to the ongoing discussions of the Political Theory group of the American Political Science Association.

Karen Johnson Fields, who as far back as graduate school heard many of these ideas and typed and edited them through their early written expressions, contributed much to whatever clarity they have ultimately achieved. Our children also tolerated their father's peculiar academic preoccupations and eventually contributed in various ways to the publications those preoccupations provoked; in the present instance Sarah helped with typing and advice on legal interpretations, Aaron checked over quotations and critiqued the "interest" quotient, and Elizabeth spent an entire summer gathering and assembling the documents that finally made this book possible.

In 1988, in an effort to grapple with contemporary political discourse (after a career spent largely in the past century), I received permission from political aides and speechwriters involved with the primary campaigns of Paul Simon and Robert Dole to observe the rhetorical efforts of those two camps. In the early primaries Paul Furiga with the Simon for President Committee and Stan Wellborn and Dale Tate with the Dole campaign gave me an opportunity to see how the speeches of presidential hopefuls get written. Then, after their candidates had prevailed, Bill Woodward in the Dukakis campaign and Josh Gilder with Bush gave me a glimpse of the same composing work after nominations were secured. That exposure both updated and renewed my interest in presidential rhetoric.

This final manuscript owes much to several readers and critics. Robert Streeter, Robert Salisbury, Rowland Berthoff, Iver Bernstein, and Joni Kinsey all read early drafts, and their thoughtful warnings saved me from uncounted embarrassments. They, along with the other participants in Washington University's American Culture program, have been, and continue to be, my most important teachers. Albert and Naomi Lebowitz and Robert Wiltenburg also read, advised, and encouraged throughout the project. I am obligated as well to a vast array of under-graduates and graduate students (especially Barbara Dineen and Kylie Hansen) who have, for more years now than I care to count, done their best to educate me.

It happens that the writing of this book almost precisely overlaps with my tenure as dean of University College. I thank my colleagues in January Hall for their tolerance and help.

A project of this scope also involves the support of a great many libraries and librarians. I am much indebted to the Washington University Library and its staff, most especially to William Olbrich, the Government Publications librarian. Scarlett Graham and her colleagues guided me through the Television News Archives at Vanderbilt University. I also benefited greatly from libraries and librarians at the University of Chicago, the University of Iowa, the University of Wisconsin, the University of Illinois, and the Museum of Broadcast Communications in Chicago, as well as the National Archives, the Library of Congress, and the presidential libraries for Presidents Eisenhower, Kennedy, Johnson, Nixon, and Reagan. I am grateful for the kind assistance of all those institutions and the people who make them run. Thanks as well are due to Jay Semel and the Center for Advanced Studies at the University of Iowa for providing a congenial atmosphere in which to complete this manuscript.

Much of the credit for *Union of Words* belongs to Adam Bellow of The Free Press, who helped conceive and shape it. It was in many ways as much his idea as mine. I thank him, too, for assigning me to Joyce Hackett, whose careful editing led me to rethink and reshape some of the final copy's most important sections.

That I have any books at all, I suspect, is the doing of Elaine Pfefferblit, who first guided me into print and continues to encourage and support my work. I am similarly indebted to my agent, Gail Hochman.

Finally we are all the products of the institutions and teachers who open the world of our discourse to us. I am grateful to Augustana College and the University of Chicago for the encouragement to take an inclusive view, and to Washington University for allowing me to follow my own peculiar academic path, mixing literature and politics with what must have seemed at times a promiscuous abandon.

Whatever is of value in this work is largely to the credit of those I have just acknowledged. For all that is folly or error, I required no outside help.

INDEX

farewell address of, 328–39, 362–63; inaugural addresses of, 165–66; inauguration of, 225; on international responsibilities, 160; "Kitchen Debate" with Khrushchev, 222; parents of, 335–36; resignation of, 166, 319, 328–30; Six Crises by, 330–33; special address of, on Vietnam War, 243, 244, 246; and Vietnam War, 165–66, 329; Wilson's influence on, 380n7
Nominating conventions, 73
Nomination acceptance. *See* Acceptance speeches
Noonan, Peggy, 61, 386n4
Nuclear weapons, 160–62

Pacific Northwest, 185
Paine, Thomas, 99–100
Panic of 1819, 381n5
Peace Corps, 163
Peale, Norman Vincent, 101
Pearl Harbor, 241–43, 302–303
Perelman, Chaim, 391
Perot, Ross, 39, 45
Philippines, the, 251
Phoenix, John, 15
Pierce, Franklin: annual messages of, 204–206, 211, 212; compared with Kennedy, 164; inaugural address of, 130–32, 281, 282, 378–79n10; presidential nomination of, 36; and son's death, 379n11
Plato, 5, 16, 367n17, 382n3, 391
Polk, James K.: acceptance speech by, 73–74; annual messages of, 198, 204, 228; on expansion, 204; farewell address of, 314; inaugural address of, 129–30, 131; and Native Americans, 198; special address of, on Mexican War, 236–37, 238; and Washington National Monument, 2
Polsby, Nelson W., 55
Populist party, 252
Presidency: adaptability of, 309; contradictory behavior between election and, 20–21; eloquence of presidents, 11–13, 16; Harrison on multiple presidents, 366n9; Mason on trinitarian presidency, 6; persona of, 9; rhetorical presidency, 19, 20–21; themes of, 307–308; unifying presidency of Washington, 3, 7, 8, 19, 37, 117–19, 228, 306; Wilson on, 8, 9, 366n12. *See also* specific presidents
Presidential candidates, selection process for, 28–29. *See also* Candidacy declaration; and specific candidates
Presidential papers, 389–90
Primaries, 29–32, 44–45, 371n9
Progressive party, 252
Puerto Rico, 251

Pullman strike, 251
Putnam, Israel, 370n1

Quintilian, 391

Race relations. *See* Blacks; Civil rights movement
Radio, 8, 295–309, 385n12
Reagan, Nancy, 168, 322
Reagan, Ronald: acceptance speeches of, 71, 98–104, 112, 166–67, 376n28; assassination attempt on, 62; Bush as vice president with, 61–62; candidacy declaration in 1984, 34; candidacy of, in 1980, 60; and decision to run for reelection, 34; farewell address of, 320–22, 360, 361, 386n4; and Grenada invasion, 181; hearing problem of, 168; inaugural addresses of, 167–68; on international responsibilities, 160; Lincoln alluded to by, 134; military experience of, 380n9; on New Deal, 159; Noonan as speechwriter for, 61; personality of, 64; rhetorical style of, 12, 54, 102, 109, 167–68, 380n8; and F. Roosevelt, 98–104, 157, 166–68; special address of, on Beirut, 243–44, 246–47; special address of, on D-Day invasion, 272–75, 384n1; special address of, on Grenada, 244, 246–47; and Stevenson, 376n36; and visitors to White House, 384n1
Reconstruction, 144, 207–10, 323
Reed, Ralph, 66
Republican National Convention of 1964, 40
Republican party, changes in over time, 370n3, 373n37
Revolutionary War, 115, 130, 155, 302, 303, 339, 341, 370n2, 371n12
Rhetoric: Aristotle on, 9–10, 11, 16, 24, 391; campaign versus presidential rhetoric, 20–21; congressional rhetoric, 13, 14–15; definitions of, 9–10; interplay of speaker and audience in, 382n3; Plato on, 5, 16, 367n17, 382n3, 391; of presidents, 11–13; suspicion of, 16–19; Webster on, 23–24. *See also* specific presidents
Riots, 263, 372n24
Robertson, Pat, 59–60, 61, 66, 369, 376n35
Rockefeller, Nelson, 51–52, 369
Roman orators, 13, 16, 28, 127–28, 391
Romney, George, 50–51, 53–54, 369
Roosevelt, Franklin: acceptance speech in 1932, 71–72, 89–94, 96, 98–104, 112; candidacy declaration in 1944, 35; on Cincinnatus paradigm, 73; communication with party by, 78; compared with Carter, 96–97; compared with Kennedy, 109;

DATE DUE

HIGHSMITH #45115